Reprints of Economic Classics

POLITICAL ECONOMY

AND THE

PHILOSOPHY OF GOVERNMENT

Also published in

Reprints of Economic Classics

by J. C. L. Simonde de Sismondi

POLITICAL ECONOMY [1815]

POLITICAL ECONOMY

AND THE

PHILOSOPHY OF GOVERNMENT

Selections from the Writings of

J. C. L. SIMONDE de SISMONDI

[1847]

REPRINTS OF ECONOMIC CLASSICS

AUGUSTUS M. KELLEY · PUBLISHERS
NEW YORK · 1966

LIBRARY OF CONGRESS CATALOGUE CARD NUMBER
65-19654

PRINTED IN THE UNITED STATES OF AMERICA
by SENTRY PRESS, NEW YORK, N. Y. 10019

POLITICAL ECONOMY,

AND THE

PHILOSOPHY OF GOVERNMENT;

A SERIES OF ESSAYS SELECTED FROM THE WORKS OF

M. DE SISMONDI.

WITH AN

HISTORICAL NOTICE OF HIS LIFE AND WRITINGS

BY M. MIGNET.

TRANSLATED FROM THE FRENCH,

AND ILLUSTRATED BY EXTRACTS FROM AN UNPUBLISHED MEMOIR, AND FROM

M. DE SISMONDI'S PRIVATE JOURNALS AND LETTERS,

WITH A PRELIMINARY ESSAY,

BY THE TRANSLATOR.

LONDON:
JOHN CHAPMAN, 121, NEWGATE STREET.
MDCCCXLVII.

LONDON:
GEORGE WOODFALL AND SON,
ANGEL COURT SKINNER STREET.

TO

MADAME DE SISMONDI,

THIS ATTEMPT TO MAKE

THE CHARACTER AND OPINIONS

OF HER JUSTLY REVERED HUSBAND BETTER KNOWN TO

THE ENGLISH READER,

IS AFFECTIONATELY INSCRIBED BY

THE TRANSLATOR.

PREFATORY NOTICE.

Most of the following Essays were originally published in a French periodical. Enlarged, and in some respects differently arranged, but with no alterations that materially affect the general views, they form, with several other essays written at different times on similar subjects, part of one of M. de Sismondi's latest works, "*Études sur les Sciences Sociales.*"

The form in which these Essays first appeared, it was thought would be more popular and more likely to attract the attention of the English reader than the three large volumes of which that work consists, and would give, at the same time, a correct view of M. de Sismondi's opinions on the subjects of Political Economy and the theory of Government. The translator hopes, however, that these selections may lead to a more extensive acquaintance with that valuable and interesting work.

The Introduction to the Essays on the first of these subjects, and the Essay on Constitutional Monarchy, which seemed necessary to complete the series of those on the last, have been added from the "*Études sur les Sciences Sociales.*"

The translator has been so fortunate as to obtain some extracts from the private letters and journals of M. de Sismondi, which are added at the end of the work.

CONTENTS.

HISTORICAL NOTICE

OF THE

LIFE AND WORKS OF M. DE SISMONDI.

BY M. MIGNET[a].

GENTLEMEN,

THE sciences are of no country: they belong to the whole world. Those who cultivate them are but separated by the frontiers of states, and they understand one another, notwithstanding the difference of languages. Fellow citizens by thought, they form a vast intellectual society, obeying the same laws, those of the human mind; pursuing the same end, the discovery of universal truths; and animated by a common feeling, which is, so to speak, the patriotism of civilization. Learned bodies, established to be, as it were, the representative assemblies of this great society, receive into their bosom men of all nations, noted for the eminence of their works and the celebrity of their names. Thus the old academy of physical and mathematical science elected as associates Newton and Leibnitz, Linnæus and Euler.

The Academy of Moral and Political Sciences has followed this excellent custom. It has associated to itself five foreign members, and has chosen them among the most remark-

[a] Read to the Academy of Moral and Political Sciences, (at the public sitting of the 17th of May, 1845,) of which M. de Sismondi was Foreign Associate, and of which M. Mignet is Permanent Secretary.

able philosophers, jurisconsults, economists and historians in Europe. M. de Sismondi, whose life I have to relate to you to-day, was of this number. This rare distinction was due to the eminent man who has consecrated more than forty years to the study and the progress of the social sciences; to the generous economist who wished to introduce human feelings into a science till his time as inexorable as calculation; to the learned writer who has traced with so skilful a hand the picture of the Literature of the South of Europe; to the eloquent historian who, after having made the Italian republics live over again in the excellent work of his youth, passed the last quarter of his life in powerfully unfolding the long annals of our country;—in short, to the true-hearted philosopher who has constantly aimed at benefiting humanity with the ideas and in the language of France.

John Charles Leonard Simonde de Sismondi was born at Geneva the 9th of May, 1773. He traced his origin to the illustrious family of the Sismondi. Fallen from their ancient splendour, the Sismondis of Pisa had taken refuge in France with the army of Frederico Buzzolo, in 1524, after the definitive subjection of their country. They established themselves in Dauphiny, where in the oblivion of a long exile they had almost lost their name, which a foreign pronunciation had perverted by contracting it, and transformed into Simonde. Lastly, after having embraced Protestantism, they were obliged to expatriate themselves a second time, at the period of the revocation of the edict of Nantes. They went to seek an asylum in that city of Geneva, to which those banished from France for religion had, in the sixteenth century, given its constitution and its greatness, and which became a refuge for all the persecuted in Europe. There had been received, and there had lived honoured, under the name of Simonde, the great-grandfather, grandfather, and father of Sismondi, who, at a later time, guided by the resemblance of the two names and by the preservation of the same arms in his family, reassumed the old Pisan name of the Sismondis, and gave it new distinction.

The first years of his childhood were passed in a charming country house, called *Châtelaine*, which his family possessed at the gates of Geneva, at that very point where the troubled waters of the Arve mingle with the limpid Rhone, just issuing from the lake, by which, smoothed and pacified, it loses its impetuosity. Opposite the majestic chain of the Alps and the smiling brow of the Jura, in the middle of the magnificent basin formed by these mountains, young Sismondi early looked with interest on the grand spectacles of nature. But what he first discovered was a precocious taste for political science. He was of the same country which had produced Rousseau, and he came into the world at the moment of revolutions. Thus, when scarcely ten years old, the natural disposition for imitation in children had for its object the gravest subjects, and he amused himself in founding a little ideal republic with his young friends, among whom was the brother of Benjamin Constant. This was in 1783, and the amusements and sports of children already announced the future labours of men and fathers. Assembled in a little grove, where they had raised a monument to Rousseau, the little republicans had decreed, as was fit, that in their republic everybody should be virtuous and happy. Sismondi, without any ceremony, was ordained its Solon, and established this doctrine, at the end of a discourse of fourteen pages.

But this legislator of ten years old, after having made a constitution, must go to school. Hitherto brought up under the paternal roof, he must learn Latin and Greek at the school, and attend lectures at Geneva (A)[a]. When he had finished his studies, he was sent to Lyons to acquire a knowledge of commercial business in the house of the Egnards, one of the greatest Genevese firms in that city. The father of Sismondi had some fortune, but he had endangered it by placing it in the French funds, through his confidence in the financial plans of his countryman, M. Necker. His losses determined him to

[a] The letters between parentheses refer to the Appendix of Notes at the end of the Historical Notice.

place his son in a business which was not agreeable to him, but which might make him rich, wealth being then considered of as great importance at Geneva as it is now in every country. Young Sismondi submitted to the paternal will. He became an excellent clerk, and by his acquaintance with commercial business prepared himself to be an able economist. Every thing is useful to men of superior merit, even what is opposed to their wishes. Their minds are formed wherever they may be, and the strength of their vocation, with the assistance of some favourable circumstance which never fails to present itself, relieves them sooner or later from the false positions in which they have been placed, and affords them an opportunity of entering on their true path (B). This is what happened to Sismondi. The troubles of Lyons obliged him, after 1792, to return to Geneva. This republic soon received the impression of French opinions. The popular party overthrew the aristocratic families who directed the government. The father of Sismondi was imprisoned, and he was not spared himself. The remains of their fortune was put under contribution, their house was stripped of every thing of value, and when they came out of prison they decided upon a new emigration. Revolutions seemed to pursue from asylum to asylum a family so little favoured by fortune. After having quitted Italy for France, and France for Switzerland, it then left Switzerland for England (C).

Sismondi profited by his residence in that great country to study its language, its literature, its institutions, its industry, its agriculture, and its manners. Thus were developed those qualities which we recognise in all his writings: the spirit of an observer and the feelings of a cosmopolite. But at the end of eighteen months he was obliged once more to resume his wanderings. His mother, to whom he was devotedly attached through his life, though strong minded, was of a melancholy temperament. Her steady good sense and religious resignation were not proof against the sorrows of exile, and she could no longer support a continued residence in England.

She wanted to see again the lake and the mountains of her native country, to hear its language spoken, to find herself once more, even at the risk of meeting again the dangers from which she had fled, under the roof-tree of her family abode. The family, therefore, set out for Geneva, and re-established themselves at their favourite Châtelaine.

It was not for long: a cruel catastrophe marked their return. One of the poor ancient syndics, proscribed by the popular party, M. Caila, closely connected with the family of the Sismondis, came to ask an asylum from them, and was hidden in a shed at the bottom of the garden, whence he could, at the least appearance of danger, pass into the neighbouring territory of France. Young Sismondi being placed as sentinel to watch over his safety during the night, heard, about two o'clock in the morning, the pacing of horses, and the sound of voices. He knocked at the door of the shed, which he found fastened, and vainly called with redoubled cries; the old syndic, who was deaf and sound asleep, did not answer. Soon the gendarmes came up, and he was himself struck down by blows with the butt end of a carbine, in attempting to defend the friend of his family, the guest of their house. The door was forced open and the unfortunate Caila was awakened from his sleep only to fall into the hands of his enemies (D). Madame de Sismondi, who had run to the place at the moment when they were dragging him away, bade him a mournful farewell, then throwing herself on her knees, continued in prayer till, towards morning, the distant sound of fire-arms informed her, that there was no more to hope from men, or to ask from God.

After this fatal event the Sismondi family again quitted Geneva. They seemed intent upon leaving it for ever, for they sold, though not without regret, Châtelaine, which might have induced them some time to return. This time they set out for Tuscany. There, with the price of that country house, which they called with poetic sorrow, their *Paradise lost*, they thought of buying a farm to which they might retire and on which they could live. Sismondi was commissioned to look for one: he traversed on foot those charming valleys which are formed on this side by the bends of the Apennines.

The rich territory of Pescia in the *Val di Nievole* between Lucca, Pistoia and Florence, attracted his attention by the beauty and variety of its cultivation. Its verdant plain, watered with astonishing art, cut into almost equal sized fields, covered with corn or cultivated as meadow land, gardens, orchards, all bordered with poplars intertwined with the branches of the vines; its hills formed in stages where the ground, kept up by walls of trees and grass, displayed, according to the exposure of their slopes, cheerful alleys of vines, pale olive woods, groves of orange and citron trees; lastly, even the summits of the mountains crowned with forests of chestnuts, and ornamented with villages, filled him with admiration. He did not hesitate fixing his family in this beautiful industrious abode. He found, in a little valley called *Val Chiusa*, a country house in an enchanting situation, standing half way down the southern slope of the hill, from whence the eye wanders over the plain of Pescia, whose towers and steeples are outlined on the verdure of the opposite hill. It was in this agreeable abode, settled with his family, that Sismondi gave himself up to the care of its cultivation, and to the pleasure of deep study. It was there that, with the exception of some short imprisonments inflicted on him by the parties who alternately conquered Italy (E), he lived happily for five years. It was there that he composed his first and charming work on the agriculture of Tuscany, that he prosecuted his vast labour on the constitution of free nations, and that he prepared himself for writing the beautiful history of the Italian republics (F).

The work on the Agriculture of Tuscany appeared in 1801. It is purely descriptive. In it M. de Sismondi presents us with as soft and animated a picture of the labours and manners of the Tuscan agriculturists, as the one which, at a later period, he drew of the unpeopled but imposing *campagna* of Rome was vigorous and gloomy. He was at this time a fervent disciple of Smith. The two volumes which he published in 1803 on commercial wealth, show that he was so without any reservation. In his admiration of the celebrated Scotch economist, he wished to apply the whole of his theories to France, of which the canton of Geneva was become a department. He avowed himself the advocate of complete freedom of trade, and raised his voice against monopolies, custom-houses, colonial privileges, and all those restrictive measures by which, yielding to the wish of protection, according to him ill understood, the laws of a country shackle its prosperity, with the view of increasing it. Latterly he had little value for this work, when, led by the study of history from theoretic abstractions to social realities, he began to think that the sciences relating to man have not the same rigidness as those relating to matter; that the laws of the latter are unvarying, because the actions which they regulate are simple and constant, whilst the complex and changing acts of the former will only admit of varying laws; that consequently, if those where every thing is fixed act on absolute principles, the others, where all is succession and rotation, where the present state proceeds from a state that is past and differs from it, where interests make slower steps than ideas, where manners and customs long resist innovation, are founded on more qualified principles, and whose true merit consists in an opportune and cautious application of them. However that may be, this work on *commercial wealth* began and advanced very much the reputation of M. de Sismondi (G). Shortly after he had published it, the chair of political economy, which was vacant in the University of Wilna, was offered to him with a considerable salary. He was then at Geneva, whither he had been brought back in 1800 by the wisdom of the Consular government, and where he had been named secretary of the Chamber of Commerce of the *Léman*. So advantageous an offer might have seduced him, and been a temptation especially to his poverty. He refused it, that he might not lose any of his liberty, and that he might remain near his mother (H). Become a French citizen, he was for a moment disposed to seek employment for his talents in the career of administration and of business; but the prudence of Madame de Sismondi turned him from this design. She knew her son better than he knew himself. His bold convictions, which he would never have been able to bend to the varying exigencies of politics; his generous sentiments, which it would have been as difficult for him to sacrifice as to satisfy; an absolute love of right which would not easily admit of temporizing or delay; that deep pride which causes embarrassment in the presence of others when it does not give the power to govern them; the enthusiasm of a thinker, the awkwardness of a recluse, the candour of an upright man, little flexibility, no address, but a strong intellect, high talent, constant meditation on right and useful things, rendered M. de Sismondi less suited for public affairs than intellectual labour. His mother persuaded him to become an historian He followed this advice, which was also in accordance with his own taste, and also because he had not found it possible to publish his manuscript on the Constitutions of free nations, of which he had brought the first part to Pescia. Theories did not meet with the same favourable reception which they had formerly done. Their time seemed to be gone by—that of history was come.

Among all nations, history shows itself latest of all the productions of mind. It is the work of their intelligence arrived at maturity, as the epic is the triumph of their imagination in the first spring of their youth. To excel in it, it is requisite to be in a position to know well, in a state fully to comprehend, having a right to pass judgment on every thing. Thus history has never truly existed except in enlightened ages, and in free countries. It is at Athens, at Rome, at Florence, in England, in France, enlightened by the most vivid intelligence, by the teaching of the grandest scenes, under the protection of the liberty of the state, or of independence of thought, that the masters in the art of writing history have been formed. The favourable conditions amidst which these have appeared have been renewed in our times, and are still extending. A philosophical revolution which has made the reasoning of the historian more sound; a political revolution which has made it more free; the progress of certain sciences which have given him a more complete knowledge of facts, of times, of places, of men, of institutions, so many fruitful experiments, so many instructive events, accumulated for him in half a century, beliefs abandoned and resumed, communities destroyed and formed afresh, the excesses of the people, the errors of great men, the fall of governments, the prodigies of conquest, and the calamities of invasions; after the most extended wars, the longest peace, and the worship of interest succeeding to enthusiasm for ideas, have shown him the different aspects of human affairs, and must have made him penetrate more deeply than any of his forerunners have been able to do, into the secrets of history. Thus his responsibilities are increased with his resources. To make use of the spirit of his own times, in order to become acquainted with those of former ages; to unite firmness in judging and fidelity in describing; to unfold the consequences of events by ascending to their causes; to show every fault followed by punishment, every aggression provoking reprisals; to assign, in the performance of actions, what share is owing to individual will, attesting the moral liberty of man, and what to the operation of the general laws of human nature, tending to great ends under the hidden direction of Providence: such is this day his mission. Hence, history becomes a spectacle full of emotion, and a science fertile in instruction, the drama and lesson of human life.

M. de Sismondi was one of the first who entered on this new path. His inquiries into the constitutions of free countries had made him acquainted with the varied and stormy existence of the Italian republics of the middle ages. He then undertook to retrace their history, so original, so little known, so difficult; the history of that country which has outstripped every other in prosperity and in misfortune; which has twice conquered and organized the world, under the Romans, and under the Popes; of that Italy, which in a manner expiating her victories and her dominion, has fallen from the height of greatness and of unity into the excess of weakness and division; has been by turns invaded by barbarous nations and by the chiefs of the military monarchies of the continent; yet has been strong enough during six centuries to triumph over all conquerors, has been able to re-establish herself in disunion; has produced and made republics, some of which have become considerable states; and thanks to the natural genius of the admirable race of her inhabitants, has preserved the moral government of Europe in spite of her weakness, has continued during the middle ages to be the country of wealth, the principal seat of thought, the school of art, the stage on which have been performed the most important events, and where the greatest men have appeared.

M. de Sismondi has treated this subject in a manner at once learned and brilliant. He has gone back to the origin of those numerous cities, proudly erected into republics on the ruins of the imperial power, or of feudal establishments: he has described their constitutions, shown their interior existence, related their struggles, exhibited their end. Turbulent Genoa, heroic Milan, mournful Pisa, prudent and powerful Venice, democratic Florence, and all those republics which, confined in a small space, had during a short period more animated life, more intoxicating passions, more varying vicissitudes than the kingdoms of the continent; and which have all fallen sooner or later under an ambitious usurper, because they were too free, or under the attacks of foreigners, because they were too weak; this is the long and grand history which has been retraced by M. de Sismondi. He has drawn it with vast knowledge, in a noble spirit, with vigorous talent, considerable art, and much eloquence. The interest which he gives to it, comes, as it always does, from the interest he takes in it. He does not merely relate the events; he passes judgment on them, he is moved by them; we feel the heart of the man beat in the pages of the historian. He carries us on with animation, his colouring is free, his thoughts are judicious. In spite of the defect—

want of unity—which his subject presents, and over which M. de Sismondi has not been able in his work entirely to triumph, we pass without effort from one of his recitals to another, feeling, as in the cantos of Ariosto, regret for what we leave, till we are again carried away by what we take up (I).

The sixteen volumes of the Italian republics, begun in 1803, were not finished till 1818. It was not till 1807, and then with some difficulty, that M. de Sismondi succeeded in getting the two first volumes printed at Zurich. Their success facilitated the publication of the rest of the work, and gave it value.

During these fifteen years, the life of M. de Sismondi was spent in labour; his works and his affections were its principal events. M. Necker having conceived a friendship for him, he became from 1803 one of the accustomed guests at the chateau of Coppet, which was enlivened by the talents of Madame de Staël, where he met the clever Benjamin Constant; the celebrated historian of Switzerland, Jean de Müller; the learned critic, Schlegel; where he became acquainted with Cuvier, and was introduced to De Candolle, and which was visited by the most remarkable men of Paris and of Europe. He there found himself in the society of his equals. Superior minds were mutually enriched and improved by a useful interchange of ideas, by happy and involuntary emulation. M. de Sismondi received excellent advice, and gained much in this illustrious and intellectual society. His thoughts embraced a greater number of subjects, and he learned to be more difficult in pleasing himself with what he wrote (J).

A tender and unchanging friendship bound him to Madame de Staël as long as she lived. He accompanied her in her travels in Italy (K) and Germany, when she visited those countries to compose her eloquent work "Corinne," and to trace the brilliant picture of a foreign literature which, at a later period, was destined to open to ours, new and bold views (L).

Nearly at the time when Madame de Staël was prepared to

make known the great productions and the celebrated men of contemporary Germany, M. de Sismondi devoted himself to an analogous labour on the literature of the South of Europe. In 1811 he gave at Geneva a course of public lectures on this subject, which had the most eminent success, and which, at a later period, afforded matter for an excellent book. The Provençale, Italian, Spanish, and Portuguese literatures, produced in countries near one another, having a sort of relationship, from their languages being all sprung from the same Latin stock, developed at different times and under different conditions, denoting in their works the successive phases of society in the middle ages, have been learnedly distinguished by M. de Sismondi as to what they possess that is original, and how much has been borrowed, in the resemblances of their forms, and the peculiarities of their genius.

We see that M. de Sismondi finds as great a charm in giving them again to the world, as he did in studying them. He quotes ample fragments, and submits them to a skilful analysis: especially he considers each in its relations with the political and religious history of the nation which has produced it. His object is to show how the works of the intellect, and most particularly those of the imagination, a faculty which seems to depend only on itself, are however subject to austere laws of progress and decline, of fertile production or of sterile imitation, according to the social state of nations, and the general condition of their intelligence. He established the fact that letters acquire their greatest brilliancy at the moment when the nationality of a country arrives at its greatest strength, and that their decline begins with the abasement of the state. In this very attractive work it may be seen that great poets, those representatives of the imagination of nations, have no fertile inspirations but what have struck every imagination at the same time, as there are no great thoughts but what are in the minds of every one.

At the beginning of 1813, M. de Sismondi came to Paris to publish the four volumes of his lectures. It was the first time that he had visited this great city, where he became intimately acquainted with many persons of distinguished merit, and formed some lasting friendships. The public mind at that moment was very little directed to literary subjects. Agitated by a recent and immense disaster, the future was regarded with anxiety. Soon, in fact, the empire came to an end, and Geneva, which had been annexed to its territory, recovered her ancient independence. Elected member of the sovereign council of the republic, M. de Sismondi assisted in the work of its reorganization. The joy caused by the reestablishment of his country and the return of peace, was not of long duration. He was afflicted at the manner in which the allied kings abused their victory. In Europe, the arbitrary distribution of territories and of souls, without regard to the indications of justice, or the wishes of the people; in France, the threatening spirit of intolerance and reaction, filled him with grief and distrust (M).

Thus when Napoleon returned in 1815 from the Isle of Elba to the Tuileries without any obstacle, and without any fighting, M. de Sismondi, who was in Paris, saw in him the triumphant chosen of the people, the defender of those principles and results of the revolution which had been compromised, the legitimate representative of a great nation, whose choice and independence ought to be respected by the sovereigns of Europe, and after the publication of *l'Acte Additionnel* of the *Champ de Mai*, the framer of the best constitution which had yet been given to France. M. de Sismondi, who not long before blamed the excess of his ambition and of his power, declared himself openly in his favour, without being afraid of appearing inconsistent (N). In a series of remarkable articles inserted in the "Moniteur," he ably defended his cause and his acts. The Emperor was very much struck with them. He wished to give M. de Sismondi a token of his satisfaction, and offered him the cross of the Legion of Honour, which M. de Sismondi refused, that by preserving his approbation disinterested it might have more power. But Napoleon invited him to *l'Elysée Bour-*

bon; and in a long conversation spoke to him of his return, of his position, of his projects, of the character of the different nations of Europe, on the principles of the revolution, on forms of government, with a frankness, a clear-sightedness, an equity, which charmed and won upon his free and respectful interlocutor. Already he was rising to that superiority of judgment, he was showing that serenity of mind which afterwards, at St. Helena, added the calm greatness of thought to the old and dazzling greatness of power and glory.

The sentiments which influenced M. de Sismondi in this meeting continued to animate him after the second triumph of the European coalition, and during the period of the Restoration (O). He wrote with power, and not without effect, against the slave trade in 1817; in 1823 he was enthusiastic for the emancipation of Greece; he applauded the attempts of those countries which endeavoured to make themselves free, and suffered much at their reverses. The love of the human race was in him so sincere, so lively, so universal, that it had the power of giving him the greatest delight and the deepest affliction. It governed him to such a degree that it affected the theories of his mind, as well as the dispositions of his soul.

He had assisted the great economical revolution which has been effected in our time. He had followed and admired the brilliant effects of those doctrines which had set labour free, overthrown the barriers which companies, corporations, customs levied in the interior of countries, and the multitude of monopolies, opposed to its productions and exchanges; which had excited the abundant production and free circulation of commodities; encouraged the emulation of competition; made even the elements of nature serve to accomplish the work of man with a skilful exactness, a productive promptitude; and which, aided by the disciplined forces of matter, the expeditious processes of science, the accumulated action of capital, the vast eagerness for wealth, brought forth those miracles of industry, which have raised so high, and carried so far, the power and prosperity of states.

But soon he penetrated farther, and spectacles less suited to make him proud of the progress of man, and to reassure him as to human happiness, were presented to him in that very country where the new theories had been most quickly and most completely developed, in England, where they reigned with power and authority. What had he seen there?—all the grandeur, but also all the abuse, of unlimited production, every progress of industry causing a revolution in the means of living; every closed market reducing whole populations to die of hunger; the irregularities of competition; that state naturally produced by contending interests, often more destructive than the ravages of war; he had seen man reduced to be the spring of a machine more intelligent than himself, human beings heaped together in unhealthy places, where life does not attain half its length; where family ties are broken, where moral ideas are lost; he had seen the weakest infancy condemned to labours which brutalize its mind, and prematurely waste its strength; he had seen the country, as well as the towns, transformed into manufactories; small properties and trades disappearing before great factories; the peasant and the artisan become day-labourers, the day-labourers falling into the lowest and most indigent class, and thus becoming paupers; in a word, he had seen extreme wretchedness and frightful degradation mournfully counterbalance and secretly threaten the prosperity and the splendour of a great nation.

Surprised and troubled, he asked himself if a science which sacrifices the happiness of man to the production of wealth, which oppresses thousands of creatures with labour without securing them bread, was the true science, the science which, according to the primitive sense of its name, ought to be the rule of a city and of a household? He answered no; and he uttered a cry of alarm to warn governments and nations of the danger which threatened them. From that moment he contended that political economy ought to have for its object much less the abstract production of wealth, than its equitable distribution. He maintained that all the members of society had a right to work and to happiness, as it had been proclaimed in the preceding century that they had a right to justice and to liberty. He set forth his views in the work which he published in 1819, under the title of *Nouveaux principes d'économie politique*, (New Principles of Political Economy,) and to which he gave its latest form in 1836. In this work, consisting of two volumes, of which one relates to *landed property and the condition of the cultiivators*, (*richesse territoriale et a la condition des cultivateurs*,) and the other to *commercial wealth, and the condition of the inhabitants of towns*, (*à la richesse commercielle et à la condition des habitans des villes*,) he raised his voice against the effects of letting land in large farms, and of applying the manufacturing system to land, declaring that the consequence of it would be to transform fields of corn into pasturage, to replace men by machines, or to drive them off the land to be succeeded by sheep. He attacked the abuses of competition, the disturbances and gluts of production, and deplored in a style of eloquence the sudden ruin caused by the too frequent crises of ill regulated industry.

M. de Sismondi excels in showing the evil, but he does not point out the remedy. He nowhere dares to invest the community with the power of moderating the movement, and regulating the distribution of public wealth; for in that case it must preside at the production of all commodities, dispose of all property, divert the freest faculties of man, restrain his sudden advance, limit his enterprises, circumscribe his knowledge. Thus M. de Sismondi has laid down the problem without resolving it.

At all events his warnings have been opportune and salutary. They have powerfully contributed to awaken the attention of the economists and the solicitude of governments. If they have led some generous but rash minds, to imagine impracticable systems in the organization of labour, if they have not been free from dreams, hardly dangerous in an age so little chimerical, they have inspired producers with more circumspection in their undertakings, masters with more humanity towards their workmen, the workmen themselves with a greater spirit of order and economy. Thanks to this useful impulse, the state has laboured, proportionably to its powers, at the amelioration and well-being of the labouring classes; it has moderated the labour of children, opened houses of refuge, multiplied primary schools, established saving banks, founded *conseils de prud'-hommes*[a], and facilitated to these classes, so deserving of interest, the means to obtain instruction, property, justice.

Without doubt the inconveniences of the system which M. de Sismondi attacked have not all disappeared. Some of them are inherent in its nature, for here below there is good and evil in every thing. Restrained by too strict rules, human nature vegetates; set at liberty, it develops itself with exuberance. Too happy if it could advance towards liberty with moderation, towards wealth with safety, use the intellect without self-deception, follow the passions without doing wrong, wisely satisfy its wants, without being carried away by the warm pursuit of its interests. But God has not made life so easy, man so moderate, the world so regular. He has ordained that the well-being of life, the wisdom of man, the equilibrium of the world, shall be purchased by great and long efforts. It is, however, towards this magnificent end that He has directed

[a] The conseils de prud'hommes were instituted by divers laws and imperial decrees in 1806, 7.

They are formed by an election of manufacturers, foremen, and *ouvriers patentés*, that is, workmen who purchase what is called a *patente* licence to open a shop on their own account.

There are conseils de prud'hommes for each arrondissement, and one general one.

They are commissioned to reconcile and to decide on the differences which arise among the manufacturers, or between them and their workmen, on questions of wages, the performance of work, contracts of apprenticeship, and the right of each manufacturer to put a mark on his fabrics.

In 1840, 59 conseils de prud'hommes had to decide 15,578 contested cases; but 13,664 only came before the court of conciliation, (*bureau de conciliation,*) 1914 having been amicably arranged between the parties; 12,672 cases were made up by private courts, 972 were sent up to the general court to be tried, 468 only were brought before it; of these 468, 297 were finally decided, 172 admitted of appeals, but of these 12 only were referred to the higher courts.

humanity, by giving to men intelligence to regulate better and better their relations to one another: the idea of justice to correct their deviations from right, the feeling of beneficence to repair misfortune. (P)

The limits of this notice do not allow me to expatiate either on the numerous and important articles inserted by M. de Sismondi in periodical collections, or on a crowd of works, political, historical, and even belonging to the imagination, which, with an indefatigable activity of mind, he did not cease to produce and publish. I will only just mention the instructive novel of *Julia Severa*, in which, following, at a distance no doubt, the steps of the celebrated novelist who, by the help of dramatic pictures, has so deeply penetrated into history, he has made us acquainted, in a manner more exact than interesting, with the state of Gaul in 492, at the moment of the invasion of the barbarians. I shall also only name in passing the *Précis des Républiques Italiennes*, (Summary of the Italian Republics,) and the *Tableau de la chûte de l'Empire Romain*, (Picture of the fall of the Roman Empire,) which appeared in 1832 and 1835 in one of the most esteemed English Cyclopædias. Neither shall I examine with detail his *Etudes sur les Conditions des Peuples* (Studies on the Condition of Nations); a book which, after having been the idea of his youth, became the work of his experience, and in which he sets forth the different forms of political societies, appreciates the nature and bearing of each principle of government, and advises states to advance towards liberty by the natural developments of their internal constitution, and not by the sudden application of theories foreign to their history. (Q)

But there is a work of M. de Sismondi, the fruit of the labour of twenty-four years, the greatest of his historical compositions, one of the principal foundations of his fame, on which I must detain your attention for a longer time. After having finished the history of the Italian republics, M. de Sismondi undertook that of a country equally dear to his recollections. He wrote the history of that people whose territory having been the field of so many passing conquests, was formed of the wrecks of so many invasions, who preserving the impetuosity of the Gauls, Roman traditions, Germanic independence, intelligent, warlike, stirring, reasoning, with a character turned towards high enterprises, with a mind inclined to prompt conclusions, disciplined in action, unruly in repose, has for seven centuries prosecuted the great work of its national formation, beginning from the most extreme disunion to become most strongly united; which has been brought to equality through monarchy; and which, externally, placed by its central position in contact with the different nations of Europe, adding their ideas to its own, interfering continually in their destinies, having thence acquired a genius more extended, a more noble character, a more philanthropic patriotism, has been in times past, as in our own days, the promoter of general ideas, the support of universal interests, and has more than any other served the great cause of human kind. (R)

At the moment when M. de Sismondi began *L'Histoire des Français,* (the History of the French,) his mind was in its fullest power. The profound study of original documents, a labour as rigorous as intellectual, allowed of his presenting this history in a more complete and truthful manner than had ever been done before. Far better than any of those who preceded him, he has apprehended and treated most of those great problems which belong to the invasions and co-existence of many nations on the same soil, to feudalism, and to the formation of different classes in the same state; ultimately, to the progressive triumph of monarchical power; through that, to the slow consolidation of the territory, to the mixed composition of the nation, to the gradual concentration of the government. Many of these problems have suggested to him satisfactory solutions, since admitted wholly or in part; and it may be said, that among the modern insights into historical science, many belong to him.

He was the first to trace with exactness the dark picture of the Roman empire in its decline, the disorganizing action of the central power on the provinces, the misery of the towns, the depopulation of the country, the ruin of the free and military class, the exhausted state of public wealth; he has been the first to assign to the Germanic invasions their true character; he has shown their feeble beginnings; he has shown the operation of the mixture of barbarism and organization in the two first races; he has assigned the complex causes of the fall of the Carlovingian empire. With not less knowledge and sagacity has he related the local history of each portion of the territory decomposed under the feudal *régime*, traced back the origin of the municipalities, (*communes*,) pointed out the first associations of burghers and of peasants, and made known the state of property, the relations of commerce, the regeneration of industry in the middle ages. It is on these subjects that M. de Sismondi excels. No one has so well shown the influence which economical changes, taking place in the interior condition of a nation, have exercised on the form of its government, and the crises of its existence. He has equally well pointed out the share which the provinces have had in the history of the kingdom, and followed out the relations of the kingdom with the rest of Europe.

It is to be regretted that to these eminent merits M. de Sismondi has not added others which would have given something more exact, and particulars more finished, to his work. We wish for more art in the composition, more life in the recitals, more colouring in the descriptions, more elegance in the language. It is to be wished also that he had gone beyond the judicious explanations of detail, to present us with the grand laws of the whole, that he had passed judgment on the manners of the time, and the actions of men, not according to a moral rule, absolute and inflexible, but by estimating ideas which are no longer ours, wants which we have ceased to feel. We should like, in short, not to perceive sometimes the spirit of the Protestant and of the citizen of the republic of Geneva, in the severity of the historian, towards Catholicism and royalty. In spite of these imperfections, the History of France is a vast monument raised to the honour, and for the instruction of our country, by a man who loved it, though he was sometimes severe towards it: a man of immense knowledge, of sound and steady judgment, of great ability, of scrupulous honesty; who, belonging to two distinct eras, has marked the transition between the school of the eighteenth century, whose generous principles he has followed up without its scoffing levity, and that of our own time, whose knowledge he possessed without having all its freedom of mind.

The History of the French, of which at a later time M. de Sismondi made an abstract in two volumes, was the assiduous employment of the remainder of his life. He was able to devote himself to it more completely, because he had refused, in 1819, a chair of political economy which had been offered to him in France, and in 1835, the title of special professor of history, which had been awarded to him by the Council of State at Geneva. To the first of these refusals he had been prompted by the wish to pass, as he had till then always done, part of the year in Tuscany with his mother.

But of this happiness he was soon deprived. He had lost his father suddenly in 1810, without being present to close his eyes. A similar misfortune struck him still more grievously in 1821: he was at Geneva, when he learned, at the end of the month of September, that his mother was dying at Pescia. He set out immediately, travelled day and night, and arrived too late. On the 30th of September, in the evening, Madame de Sismondi, feeling the approach of death, and preserving to the last her strong and pensive imagination, caused herself to be carried to the window of her room, where, in sight of the beautiful landscape lighted by the setting sun, she expired in a transport of pious ecstasy, with no regret but that of not having her son by her side. The grief of M. de Sismondi was extreme at losing one who had been the guide and the joy of his life.

He soon quitted Pescia, where he left a married sister to whom he was much attached, and whose children were to him a constant object of solicitude, as beneficial as it was affectionate.

He returned to Geneva to the dear companion whom he had made his own two years before. He had married, in 1819, Miss Jessy Allen, whose elder sister was the wife of his friend, the intellectual and celebrated Sir James Macintosh, and he found in her an elevation of mind, a beauty of character, a sweetness of disposition, an agreeableness, a tenderness and devotion of heart, which spread a charm over the rest of his life.

After his marriage he had established himself in a country house which he had bought, near the village of Chêne, at a league and a half from Geneva. With the exception of occasional journeys into France, England, and Italy, he there passed more than twenty years, occupied by his learned and useful labours, exercising a cordial hospitality, especially towards those who were expatriated by the misfortunes of liberty, and encompassed by that great and pure fame which made the Genevese proud of his talents, and which procured him visits from the most illustrious foreigners. There his days rolled on with little variety; eight hours at least were set apart for history; the remainder of his time was given to propagating some generous idea, or to the defence of some noble interest, to the recreation of walking, to the effusions of correspondences full of mind, of tenderness, and of grace, which he kept up with persons who were dear to him in the different countries of Europe; and his evenings to the animated repose of conversation, which he could keep up in the language of each of his guests.

It was there that, in 1838, he heard with allowable satisfaction the choice which the Academy of Moral and Political Sciences had made of him as one of its five foreign associates. It was there also that he received, in 1841, as a precious remembrance of France, the distinction which had been offered to him in 1815 by the emperor, and which he had then so nobly refused.

In an unpublished journal, the depository of his sentiments and of his thoughts, he prayed Providence to grant him life to finish the great history which he had undertaken. But this wish of a noble mind, which, before quitting this world desires to finish its task, was not wholly granted. Almost uninterrupted labour for forty-seven years, long and warm friendships broken by death, generous hopes in great measure destroyed by events, had produced the most cruel of diseases. During a long time he suffered from a cancer in the stomach, and he continued during two years writing the History of France amidst the anguish of this terrible complaint, which was accelerated in its progress by the troubles which overthrew the constitution of Geneva in 1841.

M. de Sismondi had always rigidly and zealously fulfilled his duties to his country. In the councils of the republic he had wisely contributed, concurring particularly with Etienne Dumont, to the amelioration of the constitution of 1814. Geneva wàs governed by four annual syndics, a council of state, removable, and a representative council which was chosen by the whole of the citizens; when the radical party, finding this government not sufficiently democratic, violently overthrew it, and demanded the convocation of a constituent assembly. M. de Sismondi was elected a member of it, and notwithstanding his state of suffering and weakness, he caused himself to be carried there to defend to the last the old and salutary institutions of his country. Alone he dared to resist the popular torrent, and alone he combated the changes proposed by the victorious party, with the energy of a soul which pain had not the power to subdue, with all the brilliancy of talent which seemed to rise higher before it disappeared for ever. On the 30th of March, 1842, in a pathetic speech, interrupted by feelings of suffocation and almost by faintings, he made his countrymen hear, but in vain, the advice of experienced reason, and of stern patriotism. This trial exhausted all his remaining strength: he returned to Chêne, never again to leave it; he did not think himself so near his end, and he hoped still to be able to go into Tuscany. "I shall have nothing to regret," wrote he, "in going away from hence: almost all my Genevese friends are dead, and I shall feel myself relieved in losing sight of so much ruin, and so many tombs." Alas, he was not long in discovering, by signs every day more certain, that he must abandon that last hope, and give up the conclusion of his great work which he had so much wished to terminate before his death. He could only continue it to the twenty-ninth volume, of which the last proofs were corrected with a hand growing weaker and weaker. His strength of mind did not fail him for a moment; he bore with unalterable serenity the slow approaches of a cruel death. Extended on his bed of pain, he shed consolation around him, and when his voice failed, casting on his agonized companion a look of tender resignation, he expired on the 25th of June, 1842, aged sixty-nine.

M. de Sismondi is one of those men who have done most honour to literature by the greatness of their labours, and the dignity of their lives. No one has more earnestly considered the duties of intellect. Amiable in his private relations, devoted in friendships, indulgent towards others, severe to himself, endowed with an activity which never at any time relaxed, with a sincerity which never on any occasion belied itself, he possessed in the highest degree the love of justice, and a passion for good. With these noble sentiments he has imbued politics, history, social economy; to make these contribute to the cautious progress of the institutions of states, to the instruction and well-being of nations. For half a century he has thought nothing that was not honourable, written nothing that was not moral, wished nothing that was not useful; thus has he left a glorious memory, which will be ever respected. In him the Academy has lost one of its most eminent associates, Geneva one of her most illustrious citizens, humanity one of its most devoted defenders. (S)

NOTES

CONSISTING OF EXTRACTS FROM AN UNPUBLISHED ARTICLE

ENTITLED

"VIE ET TRAVAUX DE CHARLES DE SISMONDI."

A

At school he was remarked for his uprightness, his candour, the entire and conscientious employment of his time, and his uncommon docility. Independently of his classes, he had private masters, and though he was not born for the arts, and was not very fond of them, he cultivated music and drawing with the same assiduity which he carried into all his studies. Greek, by which he had gained prizes at school was, at a later time, almost useless to him, and he had almost ceased to attend to it, at the period when, for his historical labours, he had to learn so many different idioms.

B

He repressed his high faculties to employ them in making himself an able arithmetician, an excellent book-keeper. More than once when, become a man, he had to weigh with deep thought the interests of the masses, to calculate the results of labour, to compare wages, to throw light on the entangled questions of capital and income, to hold the balance of exchange between nations; more than once must he have congratulated himself on the energy with which he applied to studies which were at first distasteful to him. All those who had any money transactions with him (he was soon at the head of the house) had reason, on their side, to bless that exactness, that punctuality, that spirit of order, so often unknown to artists and men of letters, and which Sismondi owed to the conscientious labours of his youth.

C

In the month of February, 1793, the family Simonde sought an asylum in England, and boarded with the rector of the small parish of Bearmarsh, in Sussex. They staid all the summer in the vicarage, where solitude becoming too melancholy for their social habits, they went to spend the winter at Tenterden, in Kent.

This time of exile was not lost to Charles; he employed it in familiarizing himself with the language of the country. But the study of idioms and literature was not sufficient employment for the activity of the young man. He reflected on the constitution of the country, on her laws, on her usages. He familiarized himself with the trial by jury, with the customs of courts of justice, and took full notes on every thing. A short stay in London allowed of his seeing the best actors of the time, and made him acquainted with the state of dramatic literature. He visited the prisons, the public edifices, celebrated institutions, in short, he made every possible advantage of a journey which was shortened, to his great regret, by his mother's sad state of health.

D

Unable to make himself heard, or to break open the door, the young man decided on defending it; his last hope was that the noise and tumult at the door might awaken Monsieur Caila, and that he might still escape; he listened with a beating heart to hear the door open which led to France. The shriek of Madame de Sismondi, on seeing her son struck to the ground by a blow from the butt-end of a musket, did indeed awake M. de Caila, and he might still have fled, but disdaining a life to be purchased only by endangering those of his hosts, he generously presented himself to his executioners. Charles, still anxiously listening, had the anguish to hear the wrong door unlocked, and to see his revered friend led off to certain death. The day had scarcely broken on that painful night, when the family, still on their knees in prayer, heard the discharge of fire-arms, which finished the sufferings and the lives of the four virtuous magistrates.

E

Tuscany passed alternately from the hands of the Austrians into those of the French. Charles, suspected by the first, was seized with sixteen other inhabitants of Pescia, and thrown into prison, where he passed the summer of 1796.

It was a hard trial for one who enjoyed rural pleasures so much, and who had taken his share in the feasts, as well as in the labours of the peasantry. How often, with his mother, whose aristocratic tendencies did not lessen her familiar goodness, he had taken his place in the harvest feasts, those of the *Battitura*, and of the vintage! Now it was, behind bars, that he thought of those enjoyments of the people, of which he has drawn such winning pictures, and for whom to the last, he alone, among all economists, has pleaded, repeating that " Man does not live by bread alone."

From the terrace of Madame Forti (his sister) they could see the prison; soon the mother and the son spoke by signs, and the songs of the prisoner reached his family. A less vague correspondence was opened by means of their bailiff, Gian Antonio Spiccioni, whose business it was to take Charles his food. The Austrian habitually refuses to his captives pen, ink, and paper; he pretends to famish the soul as well as the body. Bits of paper, ends of pencil, were hidden in the candlestick, in the bread, in the meat, even in the bottles of wine; and the letters of Madame de Sismondi, safely received, were every day answered. The necessity of cheering and consoling his mother, and a lively attachment to those principles from which he never deviated are apparent in all these little notes, in which Sismondi continually repeats—" Love me; do not afflict yourself; when I converse with you, and when I read, I feel myself really out of prison."

During the days of suffocating heat, so difficult to bear when air and space are meted out, a simple mark of the attachment and goodness of his bailiff cheered the solitude of Charles. Every evening ices were brought, as from Madame de Sismondi. The thanks of the prisoner, and the astonishment of the mother, discovered the affectionate fraud of Antonio to lighten, in his way, the captivity of his young master: in his simplicity he did not suspect that the notes he carried might betray his generous imposition.

A second time the suspicions of the Austrian government snatched Sismondi from his peaceful labours. He was confined in an airy convent at Pescia, and the means of writing were not denied him; he had permission to search the library of the monks, and with this condition, imprisonment would not have appeared hard, if the health of his mother had not failed from vexations and anxiety. Examinations had not been able to produce a single charge against him, but still his promised enlargement was deferred from day to day, from month to month; this feverish expectation wore out the strength of Madame de Sismondi. With gay and gentle chat her son endeavoured to divert her grief.

"You do not know the history," wrote he, "of one of your English notes, found when they took away my pens and ink, and carried to the commandant, then to the vicar, who each did their utmost to find some learned philologist who could explain it. At last an abbé presented himself; but in vain had he recourse to the dictionary; understanding nothing of this conjuring book, he ended by declaring himself too orthodox to decipher the writing of a woman. Then they sent to Pistoia; the gentlemen translators could not understand how writing in English could only be about my dinner and my supper; in short, they understood nothing about it, because they wished to understand too much."

Sismondi also endeavoured to take advantage of the measures of an absolute government to destroy the aristocratic prejudices of his mother. She could not forget that it was the inroad of new ideas which had exiled her from her country, that a republican soldier had nearly killed her son before her eyes, that it was in the name of liberty that her guest, her friend, had been shot, almost in her presence. It will be always difficult to teach women to distinguish principles from their effects.

"If you could say—these are tyrants, monsters, Frenchmen,—they only do what it is their business to do; injustice triumphs, it is the lot of human kind; virtue will have its turn,—you would console yourself," wrote Charles to his mother. "But no, these are the favourites of your heart, those whom you so ardently wished for, those from whom you expected so many benefits, who deceive you with so much cruelty. You do not know how to reconcile your opinions, your feelings, and your sufferings; and till you are convinced that there is neither honour, justice, virtue, or happiness for a country except in freedom, and that a counter-revolution is a hundred times worse than a revolution, you will doubly suffer.

"Do not blaspheme philosophy," he again writes, "for she is gentle and consoling, and religion still more so. The sermon I read to-day enchanted me; the text was, 'The works of the wicked are deceitful.' I read it in Italian to my priest, and I do not think the words have lost any thing of their eloquence, it is become so easy to me to translate as I read."

"I forget men," says he in another note; "I hate only parties. These moral bodies are alone guilty; before every thing the motives of those who compose them have a right to be examined. And then the hatred with which a party inspires you, is not nearly so painful as that which is nourished against an individual."

EXTRACTS FROM SOME NOTES WRITTEN TO HIS MOTHER FROM HIS PRISON, IN JANUARY, 1796, MOSTLY WRITTEN IN ENGLISH, WITH A PENCIL, AND SENT SECRETLY.

"Do you still blaspheme the noble English liberty, the habeas corpus, the trial by jury, and fixed laws? Even the poor copy which the French have preserved of them would shelter us from the injustice under which I am suffering, if we were in France."

"I am not a Frenchman, I do not approve their actions nor their government, (at this time he had been arrested by the French party,) but I adhere more firmly than ever to the opinion, that without liberty there is neither honour, nor justice, nor virtue, nor happiness, and that a counter-revolution is still worse than the revolution which preceded it. I am not a friend to democracy, but I should be ashamed to call myself an aristocrat, and to bear this name in common with the lower nobility of Pescia."

"I will endeavour to obtain permission to draw, for it would be a great resource. Adieu, beloved mother, love me, but do not grieve for me; my gloomiest moments are those in which I am thinking, consequently when I am writing; but when I am reading, or talking with my friends, I feel as if I were out of prison."

"How impatient I am! I have no feeling but impatience! I languish to get out, I languish for all I anticipate; nevertheless I am well, and as we had obliging guards, I had company, and I am gay to-day; be gay also, dear mother, it is impossible but that I should be soon liberated. I am accused of no fact, the witnesses have only their opinions to allege."

" As to politics, I would say little. My opinions on liberty are too steady ever to change: as to the French, what they make me suffer will not make me think worse of them, nor will it ever make me think better of kings and their satellites."

F

The father of Sismondi, returning to Geneva, gave up to his son the care of directing the little farm of Valchiusa. It had been held on lease during thirty years, by an honest family of peasants, and its produce in kind, divided into two parts, according to the custom of the little farms among the hills, was to provide subsistence for the masters, farmers, and servants. Devoted to this cultivation with all the ardour of his age, he increased the activity of his mind by the numerous labours of rural life, and imbued his vast intellect with the study of agriculture, that fruitful source of ever varied, ever attaching, ever new observations.

His free and generous mind reproached the tyrants of Italy with the progressive increase of the barren moors, uncultivated plains, and bogs; nature, as he said, taking again the gifts which man did not know how to manage. Struck with admiration at sight of the dikes, which forced the devastating torrent, an immense river of mud, to restore the slime which it was carrying to the sea, and to transform into fertile fields what would have changed its mouth into infectious marshes, Sismondi thanked for these admirable metamorphoses the zeal of the religious orders, which have so often in Italy, as lately in France, renewed the face of the earth.

G

At this time Sismondi employed his mind on those questions of political economy which were later resolved by his heart, when he boldly declared himself the adversary of the English school, of the Ricardos, of the Maccullochs, of the Says, of all those who see in the mass of men only a machine to create the wealth which will afterwards crush them. He weighed in his judgment, full of sagacity, the advantages of small and large properties, of short and long leases. He studied the great farms let in *livello* (corn-rents) on leases for lives, and the modest *podere*, which is cultivated on a rent of half the produce by a *mezzaiuolo* (partner) who enjoys without possessing, and does not feel that he is poor. The young man, almost alarmed at the complex ideas which arose in his mind, asked himself, "If an active, numerous, and poor population was not worth more than a small number of idle and rich inhabitants? Whether the extinction of laborious and active families is not a loss to states? Whether they ought to protect a material advantage, founded on the annihilation of the poorer classes?"—*Agricolture Toscane.*

H

The news of this negociation, by turns broken off and renewed, arrived at last at Valchiusa, and raised a tempest in the heart of Madame de Sismondi. Her letters, bathed in tears, begged her son to listen only to the interests of his fortune, of his long future life; she repeats, "that foreigners, learned men, men of letters, are better received in the north than in the other parts of Europe; that they find more roads to fortune open; that they often make rich marriages." Then, after having enumerated all the advantages it offered, she cries, "Do not ask me how I *feel* this affair of Wilna: I have too much pain in driving off this *feeling.* But have you not guessed it? You, who are alarmed at spending ten years far from the country you prefer; do you not know that these ten years are all of life that remains to me? From the day that they begin, all will be over for me. I do not say that I shall die of it; it is in the vigour of one's age that one imagines one shall die of grief that seems insupportable, and that one thinks the measure of moral strength must be that of life. Those who have grown old amidst storms, learn that they wither us, bow us down, but do not carry us off. Sorrow eats up life, but a stroke of nature must give death." Then, frightened at having allowed this cry of anguish to escape her, the poor mother accuses herself of weakness, and begs her son and her husband to forget her unworthy terrors, to reckon them as nothing, to weigh with *sang froid* the advantages and inconveniences, assisted by the information of those who knew the country, and afterwards to decide, putting her interest quite out of the question.

I

Sismondi wrote and re-wrote with inconceivable rapidity the beginning of his History of the Italian Republics, "of that labyrinth of equal and independent states, where he saw displayed more great characters, more ardent passions, more rare talents, more virtue, courage, and true greatness, than in a number of indolent monarchies." It seemed as if many lives were not enough to study the obscure annals of each of these states in particular. No one had dared to penetrate this intricacy, and he undertook to make these divers histories proceed together, and to unite them in one point of view.

His introduction had satisfied both Madame de Staël, who heard it read with lively interest, and Madame de Sismondi, who mixed with her praises the counsels of the most delicate taste. "Take care," she wrote to her son, "to avoid every thing which approaches at ever so great a distance the manner of the philosophical haranguers of 1789, who thunder as soon as they open their mouths; warmth must come from development. It is agreeable to perceive the fire under the ashes before the explosion, and the reader more willingly shares the opinions of the author when they come to him by degrees."

On the contrary, as he went deeper into these dark chronicles, Sismondi felt himself frozen. His father and grandmother had listened coldly to the first chapters of his history; Madame de Staël, so delighted with the Introduction, treated what followed as dry, and wanting life. The author began and began again with his indefatigable perseverance, but the impossibility of finding a publisher added painful disappointment to a fatiguing progress; a thousand apprehensions arose in the mind of the young man. He experienced at the entrance of this career all the agonies of that struggle in which a poor author, doubtful of his ability, can only be supported by the love of fame and the necessity of writing for his bread.

"I have never before attempted history, have I the necessary talent?" he asked himself. Then came that depressing discouragement, in which he complains, "Detached from the present and the future," added he in his journal, "my life is only a series of moments not connected together; I perceive existence only by the continuity of suffering." At last, attacked by fever, he wished to sink under it, forgetting the inexhaustible love of her whose letters were full of the most energetic exhortations, the most tender encouragement.

"I am afraid of every thing," Madame de Sismondi wrote to him. "I am afflicted at the way in which your imagination is excited, is depressed. I should rather say why does it not gather something from the future, with such a fertile field before it. Come, my child, rouse yourself; electrify yourself by every means; all those, of course, that are sure and honourable. Dear child, I exhort you, I conjure you, do not let your heart be oppressed by the obstacles you experience; they are the natural and necessary consequence of the profession of an author; all begin by that. I will not suffer you to speak ill of the lot of a man of letters. Come, let me teach you to see things on their favourable side; when I say *favourable side*, it is a flower of rhetoric, for I only ask you to be just and consistent. No doubt the man of letters has his own little particular load, as every vocation has; but generally he carries a less heavy share than others of the common burden. Great shocks rarely touch him, except indirectly; trouble, that is to say labour, is one of his pleasures; its reward is double and often very attractive.—Indeed, if I had to live over again and to choose, I should adopt a literary life as the happiest."

J

These exhortations were seconded by less sedentary habits, by excursions to Coppet, where Sismondi often staid several days; by journeys to the glaciers; lastly by the lively and animating conversation of Madame de Staël, and by the chosen society that she attracted around her.

His frequent visits to Coppet did not prevent Charles from working assiduously at his history, of which the progress may be followed in the letters of his mother, and the advice inspired by the different aspects of the work. With what admirable justness of mind does she resist that disposition in her son to absolute opinions, to proselytism, even of doubts, the inherent malady of youth and inexperience.

"You must not thus throw about fire and flame," she wrote to him; "reflect on it, you who require love so much. It is not merely enemies of a day that are made by this decided tone; they are exasperated, and for life. It is not, indeed, very surprising that those who uselessly attack opinions on which men have founded all their happiness, should be hated by them. They may be erroneous, but long received errors are more respectable than those we would substitute for them: for it is not truth which is found, when the system of religion generally received has been pulled down, since this truth, if it is not repeated, is hidden beneath the impenetrable darkness of the human mind. Leave the Trinity, the Virgin, and the Saints in peace; to the greater part of those who are attached to these doctrines, they are the columns which support all the edifice: if you shake them it will crumble away. And what will become of the souls that you will have deprived of all consolation, and of all hope? Piety is one of the sweetest affections of the soul, and the most necessary to its repose; it must exist in every religion, except in that which, by lopping off the branches to which our senses cling, by too much spiritualizing, makes us fall into abstract ideas, into a desolating vague state of mind. Promise me, at least, before you publish, to consult some clever person, not of the court of Madame de Staël. She can bear hatred, she has so many adorers; but you, you would be irritated, would suffer, would become dry, and I cannot bear the thoughts of it."

K

Soon afterwards, that journey which was the origin of *Corinne*, took place, and put M. de Sismondi into communication with all the most distinguished minds in Italy. Though congratulating herself on a companionship which promised her son so many advantages, Madame de Sismondi, uneasy, redoubled her injunctions, and forewarned her son not only against his own imperfections, but those of his illustrious friend.

"Ah!" writes she, "you are going then to travel with Madame de Staël! You are only too happy to have such a companion. But take care, travelling is like a short marriage: always, always together, people see too much of one another; defects have no corner in which they can hide themselves; the spoiled child of nature and the world, as she is, must have in the mornings moments of fatigue and *ennui;* and I know who is revolted by a defect in those he loves. He should therefore be doubly attentive to open his eyes to his own defects, and to keep them steadily shut to those of his companion. How curious I am to know how she will get on in society in that country. No doubt she will form particular intimacies only with those who know French; for how can she express her thoughts in Italian? she! it is impossible. However well she may understand it, know it, read Dante better than three-quarters of his countrymen, she will never find the means, in that language, of making conversation flow as it ought. How can words be found in the language, when opinions and ideas are yet unborn? You will see that she will not like the Italian prosody either. However, she will be admired, and she will excite fanaticism (*fera fanatisma*), as we say."

The prediction was literally accomplished. Charles wrote from Rome: "Madame de Stael pleases everywhere, but she finds nothing which pleases her; she is angry at this fine sounding language, which says nothing. In the poetry which they boast of to her, she finds no ideas, and in conversation no sentiment."

L

At the end of a year entirely devoted to work, and which was passed in the middle of his family, Sismondi again found himself thrown into the vortex of the world.

Madame de Staël travelled in Germany, where she was charmed to present "to every one," as she said, "the new historian, preceded by his fame." Received with all imaginable kindness, living at Vienna at the house of Madame de Staël, admitted into the bosom of that choice society, distinguished by its exquisitely polished manners, by its sparkling conversation; acting plays with princesses, dukes, counts, with the courts of Germany and Russia; surrounded at the Monday suppers of his illustrious hostess, by all those whom the city contained, most distinguished by talents and by rank, Sismondi saw pass before him the old ministry of Maria Theresa, worn out, grey-headed, broken in the service of Joseph, of Leopold, and of Francis. These ministers, acute men, not devoid of talent, having an inclination to be liberal, attached to their master by habit, he saw them, inactive, without the capacity of foresight, without judgment, without will, discouraged about the government. He saw the complete ruin of the finances, the relaxation of all the machinery of government; in short this monarchy, the defence of old opinions against the new, and which, endeavouring to rally around it noble sympathies, placed itself as an adversary to the military despotism of Napoleon, he saw falling into dissolution because all power was in one hand, that of the emperor, and that hand was paralytic.

For a moment Sismondi hoped, by his Memoir on Paper Money, (*Mémoire sur le Papier Monnaie,*) to apply a remedy to the greatest of the evils which he witnessed, to that which reached every class, by the disorganization of public wealth and private fortunes. In this writing, which could not have been published at a more opportune moment, Sismondi proves that "currency, of which stability ought to be the principal characteristic, can never be the production of credit, essentially variable in its nature, and the object of which being to borrow and transmit value, cannot create it; a power belonging to labour alone." After having demonstrated that "the most false of all money is paper, that this value, fictitious and deceptive, destroys all real value in the state, which disappears that it may not be estimated by this false measure," the writer points out the incalculable evils which flow from this disorder: "Commerce struck to death by stock-jobbing; the legitimate rewards of labour and industry subjected to the chances of gaming; activity become a cause of ruin; whilst easy circumstances appear to be the fruit only of idleness and inactivity; public charity annihilated by universal indigence; prodigality and dissipation permitted to call themselves wisdom; lastly, the laws concurring with vice in the destruction of the community."

The enumeration of these evils is followed by an indication of the remedy. "There is only one, the suppression of paper, the revocation of every order by which confidence is imposed, is commanded. From the moment that it is demonstrated that the circulation of forced notes is a continual bankruptcy, it is to the degradation, not to the annihilation of paper, that the sufferings of the people must be attributed: it must therefore be cut to the quick." Sismondi does not the less find numerous hidden causes which soften a shock, which he calls an *extraordinary tax* pretty equally divided, thanks to the number of hands through which paper money passes: for the rapidity of the circulation, by multiplying losses, has at least this advantage, that when the notes will no longer circulate, it equalizes them, and blunts the shock by dividing it among all.

Strongly supported by the Prince de Ligne, considered, discussed, praised by the ministers of Austria and Russia, presented to the Archdukes John and Charles, approved by the Archduke Renier, attentively read in manuscript by the emperor, printed at Weimar, the paper of Sismondi, which for a moment raised the hopes of commerce, had no other result than to give its author the satisfaction of throwing light on an important subject, and having conscientiously laboured for the interests of the community. Trembling, and as it were fascinated, Austria dared not hazard the least movement, and seemed breathlessly to await the sword of Napoleon.

M

When in the month of January, 1815, Sismondi came to Paris to publish the 9th, 10th, and 11th volumes of his Republics, they were celebrating, at Paris, the funeral obsequies of Louis the Sixteenth. Though the nation had, with justice, cast off all responsibility of the death of the unfortunate monarch, it saw an insult in this appeal to ancient animosity, and severed itself more and more from a family which, far from endeavouring to fill up the bloody abyss hollowed out between it and France, made efforts to enlarge its wide-opening mouth. "The old courtiers disturbed those who had acquired national properties, and covered with lace, played at greatness, as if they had been young upstarts." The king is sitting for his portraits; he is now at the eleventh; and the people cannot accustom themselves to contemplate the abuse of weakness, in those same places where, a few months before, reigned the abuse of strength.

N

The landing of the 20th of March, and the rapid progress of Napoleon, gave a new aspect to every thing. After having seen the Bourbons "commit every fault of presumption for ten months, and every fault of weakness for ten days," Sismondi read the proclamations of the emperor, fixed by the side of the royal ordinances which put a price on his head. It seemed to him that after such a return, the man of the Revolution could not disown his mother; "that he had too well proved the weakness of monarchical alliances to court them afresh;" and two decrees issued from l'Elysée Bourbon, to abolish the slave trade, and to establish the liberty of the press, seemed to confirm all these generous hopes. Persuaded that once entered on the route of concession, power endeavours in vain to go back; that it is better to ameliorate than to begin again; that the most formidable danger at this period was from foreign bayonets, and a second reaction, Sismondi, without stopping to discuss questions of detail, and of interior administration, thought only of rallying round the national colours all the patriotism there was in France. His *Examen de la Constitution Française*, (Examination of the French Constitution,) published in the *Moniteur* and in some other journals, demonstrates without enthusiasm, but with great power of reasoning, that the *Acte additionnel* secures the liberties of the citizens, by giving them for guarantees, the responsibility of the ministers; the independence of an irremovable magistracy, and of a jury chosen among the people; lastly, the liberty of the press, the confirmation of every other liberty. On the other hand, by increasing the number of deputies, and acknowledging that every Frenchman may be elected a deputy of the nation, this act promises to all the enjoyment of political rights, the noblest education that man can receive.

Surprised, without doubt, that lips perfectly pure, a mind as liberal as it was enlightened, should have undertaken his defence, Napoleon wished to see Sismondi [a].

O

When he returned to Coppet, in 1815, he was received with the same affection by Madame de Staël, but at Geneva it was otherwise. His friends looked upon him as a deserter, because in his eyes the end did not justify the means, because he had a horror of foreign intervention, because the union between the Jacobins and the Royalists, which he had long refused to believe, inspired him with profound disgust, because his heart bled at this war of hatred; and seeing our fields stripped, our town swept down, he cried, "I could console myself for the sufferings of the rich, of those who

[a] See note at the end.

have brought this scourge upon us; but the state of ruin, but the misery, but the despair of the unhappy peasants rend my heart."

The death of his friends Labedoyère and Ney, the persecutions of the south, the violence of the royalist Chamber, "a counterpart to the Convention," all contributed to make his thoughts gloomy, and "finding more melancholy than pleasure in his recollections," he took refuge in his work. "I have always endeavoured to forget myself," said he, "and thanks to my studies, I can live in other ages than my own."

In July, 1817, as he was going to Paris to print the four last volumes of his history, he was detained at Coppet. There had just been brought the lifeless body of her who had made that abode so agreeable, of her who had so long been his friend, his second sister. "There is something confusing," wrote Sismondi to his mother, "in a misfortune which has taken place at a distance; at first one sees nothing changed around one, and it is only slowly and by degrees that one learns to know one's own grief. It is over, then, for me; this abode where I have lived so much, where I always felt myself so much and so happily at home! It is over—that animating society, that magic lanthorn of the world, which I there saw lighted up for the first time, and where I have learned so much! My life is grievously changed; there was no one, perhaps, to whom I owed more than to *her*. How I suffered on the day of her funeral! A discourse by the minister of Coppet at the bier, in presence of Madame de Broglie and Miss Randall kneeling before the coffin, had begun to soften my heart, to make me feel the full extent of my loss, and I could not restrain my tears."

When, on publishing the conclusion of his great and admirable work, Sismondi cast a glance backwards on the twenty-two years devoted to his history, he might have felicitated himself with just pride, on finding at the last page of his sixteenth volume, the same moral tendency, the same political principles, which had inspired him at the beginning. "During this long period, tormented by the eager strife between nations thirsting for liberty, and princes obstinate in refusing it, Europe had seen over and over again her institutions destroyed, and different political doctrines by turns proscribed and proclaimed;" but the historian of the old times remained the same, becoming more enlightened without being changed, enlarging his ideas without abandoning them. His style acquired, however, as he proceeded, more firmness, more dignity, less endeavour after effect; and yet with what fervent candour he replies to his critics.

"It was never voluntarily, never knowingly, that I have employed unusual terms and expressions. But to fulfil the task which I had imposed on myself, to attain the truth which I had engaged to present to the public, I have been obliged to live in some sort out of my maternal tongue. I have been obliged habitually to write and think in Italian or in Latin, and occasionally in German, Spanish, Greek, English, Portuguese, Provençal. I have been obliged to pass from one of these languages to another, without reflecting on the form in which thought was clothed, almost without perceiving the substitution of one dialect for another. Then a form of speech which I had met with a thousand times, I thought French, because I had been accustomed to it, in another idiom."

P

The new views, indicated by the article "Political Economy," in the Edinburgh Encyclopædia, published in 1818, and written in English by Sismondi, show that he had already deviated from Adam Smith, in the consequences which he drew from the principles laid down by the Scotch economist. The pleasure of proceeding systematically from deduction to deduction, of erecting a series of metaphysical propositions, with the regularity of a mathematician, could not seduce this observing mind, nor blind this practical philosopher, as to how much experience had falsified the conclusions of the learned. He was occupied with results, "the evils of competition, that war of the years of peace; the excess of production, which ceases to be wealth from the moment when it no longer finds consumers."

In the two volumes of his *Nouveaux Principes*, Sismondi gave more development to this first sketch. Since the production of his *Richesse Commerciale*, studying facts instead of books, he now carried to new ground that science in which he has been accused of making retrograde steps. "Strongly moved by the commercial crisis which overthrew the means of life to so many all over Europe, and weighed so heavily on the working class," he had seen, with a feeling of sorrow, the combined efforts of proprietors, of statesmen, and of writers, aggravate the evil they thought to remedy, and in order to obtain a larger *nett* product, reduce *real* product, and change the systems of cultivation, which still spread some comfort and some happiness among the peasants of Switzerland and Italy. "Good persons, full of excellent intentions, caused evil, and lost themselves, sometimes in seeking what might augment population, sometimes what might increase wealth," whilst both, considered singly, are only abstractions, and all abstraction is deceptive. The true problem to find is the proportion of population and of wealth which will secure most happiness to the human kind in a given space; for the object of economical science ought to be to augment the mass of happiness among man, and to equalize the division of it; that of political science, to ennoble the whole nation, by making morality penetrate every class.

The *Nouveaux Principes* might be called the book of economical proportions; they aim particularly at demonstrations; that the social question consists in a due balance. "Income must increase with capital, population must not surpass the income on which it ought to live, consumption should increase with population, and reproduction ought to be in proportion both to the capital which produces it, and to the population which consumes it."

In proving that each of these relations may be disturbed separately, but never with impunity, Sismondi makes it be observed, "that wages are always in proportion to the quantity of labour in demand, which depends on consumption; and this regulates itself, not by production, or by what is wanted, as Ricardo, Say, and their school have pretended, but by income. Each individual buys, in fact, according to his means, and not according to his desires. Systems too often forget that the community is composed only of individuals, and that the public fortune, being only an aggregation of private fortunes, arises, is increased, is distributed, is deteriorated, and destroyed by the same means as that of each individual."

He had not the pride to flatter himself that he could make the world turn on a new pivot, or discover a "universal panacea." To find efficacious remedies, he proclaims continually, the sanction of time, and the concurrence of the most enlightened minds are requisite. As M. Michelet says, in an admirable lecture, the most worthy homage that has been paid to the memory of Sismondi:—"His glory is to have pointed out the evils; courage was necessary for that!—to have foretold new crises. But the remedy? That is not an affair of the same man, or the same age. Five hundred years have been required to set us free from political feudalism; will a few years be sufficient to set us free from industrial feudalism?"

Thus, whilst with the accents of entreaty and of anguish, the writings of Sismondi call on the whole of society to help those it crushes, in his practical and in his private life he sought palliatives, constantly addressed himself to the best feelings of man for man, and rested his hopes and his actions on what is most tender in charity; on that double movement from the heart of him who gives, and from the heart of him who receives."

Q

Independently of his immense work, the "History of the French," (of which two or three volumes appeared alternately every two years,) Sismondi still connected himself by pamphlets, by frequent articles published in different periodicals, with the whole literary and political movement of France, Italy, and England. Everywhere misfortune found in him an advocate, liberty a support, moderation an organ.

In the journey which he made into England, in 1826, before publishing the second edition of his "*Nouveaux Principes*," he saw what he had foretold realized, and shuddered at the fatal effects of "that vital organization, which stripping the working man of all other property, but that of his hands, ends by taking that also from him, and replacing it by machines." Witness of that "progress of industry which tends to increase the inequality of enjoyment among men," recoiling from the aspect "of the hideous convulsions of wealth ill divided," he cries: "No spectacle is more alarming than that which England presents, in the midst of that opulence, which at first dazzles the eye. The great roads are alternately traversed by troops of beggars dismissed from the manufactories, and by troops of ragged Irish, who offer themselves from farm to farm to perform agricultural labour. Both ask alms, only when they are refused work; but every nook is full. The field labourers see with bitterness strangers contending with them for work, which before was scarcely sufficient to maintain them."

"In the towns, in the capital, in Hyde Park, where the most sumptuous equipages succeed one another with the rapidity of lightning, bands of ten and twenty manufacturers, seated motionless, despair in their eyes, fever exhausting their limbs, do not excite a moment's attention. A third of the workshops are closed, another third must soon be closed, and all the shops are loaded; on every side manufactures are offered at a price which can only half pay the expense of production. In this universal distress, everywhere the working man is dismissed, and the English nation gives his place to steam engines."

In the face of such a state of things, "at a period when suffering humanity has the most need that the science which is the theory of the well being of all, should draw near to common intellects, and speak a popular language, political economy is lost in abstractions, and enveloped in calculations more and more difficult to follow."

"What," cried Sismondi, answering Ricardo in a long conversation which they had together at Geneva, a short time before the death of the English writer, "What, is wealth then everything! are men absolutely nothing!"

It was painful to Sismondi, after having repudiated the economical theories which England was teaching to France, still to have to repel the different systems which connected themselves with the demand for industrial organization. He rejected in turn the co-operative system of Owen, the Saint Simonians, the disciples of Fourier. "To attempt to suppress personal interest, and to think that the world can go on without it," he said to some of them, "is sufficiently bold; but to imagine that all the labour of the community, the conducting of all its interests, can be determined at any moment of the day by the plurality of suffrages, is acting like a society of fools." He accused others of ordering a body to walk, after having taken away all the muscles, all the stimulus of individual interest. "They take away from you hope, liberty, family affection," cried he, sorrowfully, "all to make you happy! Alas! there is nothing true in their books but the evil they would remedy."

He stood alone between the masters and the disciples, both of whom he equally disavowed; those, because absorbed by the love of the science which they had created, they neglected the creation of

God; man, the object and end of all science; these, because absorbed in the search of physical well-being, they forget both our celestial origin, and our immortal tendencies; on both sides he repudiated the worship of matter.

The *Etudes* were in great part written at Pescia, whither Sismondi went towards the end of August, 1835, drawn there by the desire to see those who remained of the family of his sister.

The beautiful and fertile fields which had first awakened in him the love of nature, and of humanity, offered anew to the eyes of the economist that association which he continually demanded, that of the owner and the cultivator, the union of capital and hand-labour. He again found the favourable results of the leases for ninety-nine years, the *livelli* which he had formerly studied, and which give to the farmer, married to his farm, as much love for the soil as if it were his complete property. He again entered the cheerful dwelling of the *mezzaiuolo*, the farmer who divides the produce, and who without possessing any thing, lives easy and content, and enjoys, what makes man moral, an assurance of the future, what renders him happy, security, liberty, variety, hope.

This landscape of Tuscany, animated by cheerful labours, intermingled with songs, *fêtes*, and joy, like the small farms which have scattered over them elms, garlands of vines, nosegays of orange and citron trees, forms the most striking contrasts to the oceans of corn, and fields of potatoes of vast and beautiful Ireland; to those flourishing fields where the miserable farmers and the starving cottagers die of hunger in the bosom of abundance.

But when, in 1837, Sismondi traversed the *Campagna* of Rome, which he had visited for the first time thirty years before, vain were the endeavours to make him taste those artistic pleasures which attract the aristocracy and the idle, from all parts of the globe. "Here," cried Sismondi, "I can only hear one voice, that of expiring society, contemplate one view, the decline and agony of Rome. The rapid decay of all I perceive, of all which constitutes a city, monuments, palaces, churches, houses, cottages, pavements, marks, in a fatal manner, the progress of time. The population of the country has disappeared; I cannot imagine how the population of the town can be long in disappearing also. This crowd of parasites, accustomed to live on the crumbs which fall from the tables of the prelates, of the ambassadors of the great, will find no nourishment when these tables are no longer covered. The fields, divided among only a hundred great proprietors, are doomed to become an unpeopled desert, and the wind will there pass over broom and immense briers. The workshops of the cities no longer offer any asylum to the indolent population, for the rich will not consume Roman productions, and the poor cannot buy them; how sorrowful is the spectacle of a great city dying of inanition!"

R

Sismondi had been a witness of historical results and of their causes, and he resolved to write the history of the French. He immediately set about collecting the necessary works. "I look at these quartos with a sort of respect and fear," said he, "when I think that I must go through all that, and that I must make myself as familiar with it as the collection of Muratori is become to me."

Hitherto, having worked by means of borrowed books, and, as happens to most of those who accustom themselves to trust always to their pen, written memory having almost annulled mental memory, he found himself obliged to make numerous and minute extracts. "The purchase of a choice library, formed without regard to expense," wrote he to his mother—"for in fact they are the instruments of my trade" led him to change this mode. Instead of extracting, he composed annals, in which he entered the memorable events of each year, such as he drew them from the original sources. The simultaneous comparison of the different accounts of the same fact cleared up to him what had appeared obscure to the most eminent historians. The historian of the Republics had endeavoured to bring into our view that great number of lives, existing in so many independent sovereign cities, throughout the extent of Italy. The historian of France sought a different point of view. He had to explain a compact monarchy, the most closely united, the most complete organization. He untwisted the threads of this woof so solidly woven, and dividing his narrative into periods, questioned each on the secret cause of a progressive agglomeration, on the strength of a growing centralization; and endeavoured to discover how this indivisible unity was prepared, produced, and consolidated.

S

To elevate his soul still more towards the country to which it was tending, only one step was wanting, suffering, and he was not spared that. He endured it with that unshaken firmness which had been formed by the whole course of his life. A religion full of hope and love, which places prayer in the intimate relations of the creature with its Creator, and in the effort to conform to his mysterious will, added the heroic gentleness of resignation to the strength which had been developed in Sismondi, by the constant habit of making his actions agree with his principles and his writings.

After a violent attack, his illness only left him short and incomplete respites, of which he took advantage to set himself to work again with inconceivable courage. At first living only on milk, his stomach torn by dreadful agony, he did not the less persist in working; soon he dismissed his physicians, lest they should forbid his writing, and because he felt the insufficiency of their art. In 1840, volumes 23 and 24 of the History of the French appeared; in 1841 they were soon followed by the remainder Besides this, Sismondi gave to the *Bibliothèque universelle Génève*, the complete and striking article on penal colonies and punishment. The attention of one who had treated in so superior a manner the greater part of social questions, was awakened by the inquiries and successive reports on the exclusively material prosperity of Van Diemen's Land and Sydney, which was accompanied with its usual consequence, a gross and demoralized social condition. His powerful indignation was excited by the eloquent complaints of the Archbishop of Dublin, Richard Whately; and he treated the subject from a loftier point of view, embracing every kind of punishment, without excepting from the melancholy list, that most fearful of all for the judge—death.

"It is a mournful subject, the evil which men do when they are endeavouring to do good," as Sismondi says. First, he endeavours to discover what are the true conditions of punishment. "Punishment must intimidate, must correct, must reach the guilty, must reach him certainly, quickly, must reach only him; it must be rather intense than long, or else it ceases to be feared; it must not corrupt even the criminal, and must not demoralize society." What then must be said of penal colonies, when the shame of the criminal colonist becomes, through destitution, an object of desire to the day-labourer and free workman; when from these sinks of the community arise new nations, which, born of vice, in the bosom of vice, organize an aristocracy of crime, and carry to a fearful perfection by uniting them together, the depravation of barbarism, and that of civilization. What can be said of penitentiaries, which, after a long and frightful punishment, "like a surgical operation, during which the patient utters an uninterrupted cry of pain," give back the criminal to society, mutilated, not in his body, but his soul; from which has been cut off, by his lonely life, whatever crime had left of intelligence and human feeling.

The profound pity of the historian for social wounds, for vice and misery, of which he had past his whole life in sounding the depths, and discovering the causes, because it is the causes which teach the remedies, found his heart neither contracted nor withered by personal suffering. Whilst in the classification of criminals, in the remuneration of labour, and even in physical suffering, but especially by a continual study of the question, which ought to be a subject of interest to every one, he sought for progressive amelioration, the sure and slow cure which is disdained by the inventors of universal specifics, Sismondi was himself a prey to sufferings of body and mind.

Physical pain had robbed him of those recreations which he had formerly tasted with so much zest, in the rapid exchange of mind and thought. All visits, all society, were become a punishment. "My speech," wrote he to a friend, "is so disturbed and interrupted by hiccough when I have talked a quarter of an hour, that I must be insupportable to others. Even when one writes with a bad pen, one loses half one's ideas, think then how a convulsion which interrupts every sentence two or three times, must hurt conversation." It was only in fulfilling the mission which he pursued with unalterable energy, that he could for a moment escape from his fits of pain: "I forget my suffering when I am writing," said he.

Moral pains, most felt by a soul like his, sometimes softened his heart without lessening his resignation. "I give myself up," he wrote in September, 1841, "to the melancholy which is inspired by a condition like ours, where nothing is renewed, where in one's self and around one, one remarks only decay. . . . Affections leave us, recollections are extinguished" (he had just lost two of his best friends, the illustrious De Candolle, and almost at the same time Chateauvieux, whose funeral he followed, and which preceded his own so short a time). "How melancholy seems this solitude where I remain," pursued he; "sometimes I ask myself what right have I to linger after them?"

It was in 1842, that the radical association, of the 3rd of March, which for nine months had threatened the government of Geneva, and kept Sismondi in anxiety, burst out in insurrections. The national representation was threatened with knives, poniards, fire-arms, and fire. The national guard deemed it prudent to lay down their arms, without having made use of them, the magistrates thought it wise to yield, without having resisted, and Sismondi dying, mounted the breach alone.

On the 30th of March, 1842, he would pronounce, in the Constitutive Assembly, a member of which he had been elected, notwithstanding the alarming state of his health, the last words he uttered in public. This *impromptu* speech, full of good sense, of moderation, of power, was interrupted by painful convulsions, and he was carried home in a state of the greatest exhaustion. Even then he would not be cast down, and as his afflicted widow said, "Standing up as long as there was anything to be done, he lay down only to die."

The conclusion of his history, written on his birthday, five weeks before he breathed his last, is an adieu annexed to the legacy which he left us, to us Frenchmen, for whom he laboured twenty-four years.

"It will soon be two years," said he in his conclusion, "since I have enjoyed a single day of health. Every month, every week, I have perceived that my complaints grow worse, and the advance by which they must arrive at their termination, though slow, is not the less sure They were not common efforts which have been required, not to be diverted one day from my work, that I might devote to it all my remaining strength; but now it is over; it would be impossible to take a step more."

"At the end of so long a task, placed on the threshold of that door which separates time from eternity, I may be forgiven for seeking some satisfaction, in considering what I have accomplished."

"Different powers have been given to different historians: I know what I want, and what have belonged to some of my contemporaries. But there is one testimony which I dare render to myself, and I have a firm confidence that posterity will confirm it; the work which I am finishing, and which I present to the public, is that of a conscientious writer; I have always sought for truth, and I have spared neither labour nor expense to discover it."

"My life has been divided between the study of political economy and that of history; thus, the economist must often appear in this long recital, by the side of the historian; I have endeavoured not to let those lessons be lost which are given by experience, as to what contributes to create and to maintain the prosperity of nations. But above all, I have always considered wealth as a means, not as an end. I hope it will be acknowledged by my constant solicitude for the cultivator, for the artisan, for the poor who gain their bread by the sweat of their brow, that all my sympathies are with the labouring and suffering classes."

"It was in the month of May, 1818, that I seriously began to work at the History of the French; it is in the month of May, 1842, that I lay down my pen, having gone as far as my strength would permit. In delivering this work to the public, terminated with the advantages which I have set forth, with the defects which I do not dissemble, I rest on the feeling that I have done a service to the French nation. I have given her what she had not, a complete picture of her existence, a conscientious picture, in which neither love nor hatred, neither fear nor flattery, have ever led me to disguise one truth; a moral picture in which she may always recognize what bitter fruits are borne by vice, what excellent fruits are borne by virtue; and where, without being inflated by vain glory, she will learn, and may teach her children how to esteem, how to respect themselves."

This task finished, he had only one thought, to go to Pescia and to die beneath the beautiful sky of Tuscany, amidst the flowers, the fruits, the trees he had planted, and with the recollections of the mother who had watched over, and matured the promise of his youth.

But no, his stomach torn by an ulcer, could no longer bear even cold water: nevertheless he corrected proofs, still wrote to his friends, answered historical questions addressed to him by indifferent persons; his patience increased with his tortures. He preserved his soul unchanged, his body was rapidly wearing out.

On the 9th of May he wrote his conclusion; from the 29th to the 31st he drew up a detailed catalogue of his works, which in itself forms a work, the abridged history of his life. On the 7th of June he corrected the four sheets of proofs which terminated the twenty-seventh volume of the History of the French, and rectified the paging of the Index. On the 8th he looked over the four first sheets of the following volume, twenty-ninth and last. On the 10th he wrote two letters, one to the son of his old bailiff, at Valchiusa, to remind him that a small pension which this peasant had engaged to pay to his mother, who was a widow, was due. The other letter, which gave to a Bordelais, employed on a History of the Vaudois, the list which he had asked him for, of the authors which he ought to read, finished with the words of the gladiator to Cæsar, *Morituri te salutant*. On the 13th the dying man still corrected proofs. On the 14th he added a codicil to his will, in which "acknowledging the blessings which Providence had heaped upon him, he surrenders his soul into the hands of God, and begs his wife and all those who bestowed their affection on him, to see him depart with love, but without regret, as he himself quits this world, and all in it which he held dear."

On the 25th of June he continued lying down, motionless, and without speaking till about one o'clock; then he asked to get up. He was dressed and laid on a sofa, where he remained quiet, and at three o'clock in the afternoon he ceased to breathe.

His works remain to us. In one of those hours of moral agony which the most vigorous minds pass through, Sismondi had exclaimed with bitterness, "I shall leave this world without having made any impression, and nothing will be done." He deceived himself. He had chosen France to make his ideas popular; France will apply them. He, whose mind was considered as retrograde, when he said that the opinion of the crowd is not the same as the opinion of the wisest; as a dreamer when he affirmed that the means by which hand-labour is spared should not force men to heavier labour, has done well not to be tired of swimming against the current. His observations, his ideas, have become so entirely a public possession, that those who proclaim them, clothing them in sounding words, often do not even know that they are the ideas of Sismondi which they are proclaiming; his opinions, his principles which they are making popular.

Was it not Sismondi who was first indignant at the *laissez faire, laissez passer*, of political economy? It was only after him that his disciple Buvet repeated, "*Laissez faire la misère; laissez passer la mort!*" Let wretchedness do its work, do not interfere with death!

It was Sismondi who was indignant at the system by which some labour, that others may enjoy.

He it was who cried out that the time will come when our posterity will not deem us less barbarous for having left the labouring classes without any security, than we deem those nations who have reduced them to slavery.

It was he who asked if it is not every where perceived that men are confiscated for the advantage of things? The working men are retrenched, sometimes in one business, sometimes in another. And what signifies the increase of wealth, if it does not serve to feed men?

It was he who demanded for all a participation in the advantages of life: he, who refused to call that riches, which one member of the community took from another: he, who cried that the advantage of all ought to limit the rights of all; that property is the right to use, not to abuse.

Before O'Connell, with as much boldness and more weight, Sismondi exclaimed, "The social order of Ireland is essentially bad; it must be changed from top to bottom. The question is not to give the bread of charity to the famished poor: it is to secure existence, property, to every man whose hands are his only wealth."

Who is the radical who has said with more vehement warmth than Sismondi, "There is spoliation, the rich man robs the poor, when this rich man draws from a fertile and easily cultivated soil his idle opulence, whilst he who has raised this income, who with his sweat bathes every production, dies of hunger without being able to touch it."

It was he who taught the people that the true Savings bank is the land; governors, that to raise the moral character of the people, the future must be given to them, for all our moral ideas are connected with foresight.

He who has been accused of an aristocratic spirit, repeats in all his works, by the examples which he brings, and by the reflections which he makes on them, "that the day in which the aristocracy is uprooted from the country, the day in which it forsakes the soil by which it was nourished, it commits suicide."

It was he who continually repeated, "that all the efforts of charity are only palliatives: of what use are schools to him who has no time? Instruction, to him who sells the most painful bodily labour at the cheapest rate, without being able to get work? Savings banks, to him who has only potatoes?"

No, the persevering study, the warnings, which his heart prompted, are not lost. Facts have gone on; they bring that conviction which he complained of not being able to produce. The day will come when the experience which he laid up will bear fruit in the world; the day will come when both the operative and the labourer will obtain that just share of enjoyment which he never ceased soliciting for them.

INTERVIEW WITH NAPOLEON.

[Inserted in the private journal of M. de Sismondi immediately on leaving the Emperor's presence.]

I HAD already published two articles on the Constitution in the *Moniteur*, when Marshal Bertrand wrote to me on the 1st of May, desiring me to call on him the following morning, Tuesday, at ten o'clock. I arrived some minutes too late, he was just gone out. I waited till noon. On his return, he told me that he wished to present me to the emperor, who had been much pleased by reading my articles in the *Moniteur*. "We have read," he said to me, "your preceding works, and the emperor will be delighted to become acquainted with so distinguished a man." I thought he meant that they had read them together at the Isle of Elba, but he said it was before, and he fixed the following morning, Wednesday, the 3rd of May, before ten o'clock. I found myself, in fact, on the following morning at the Elysée, in the apartment of the marshal; my name had been left there, and a footman immediately conducted me into the great gallery, which served as an antechamber to the reception hall of the emperor.

The marshal came out soon after, and told me to wait some minutes. I had put on a sword with a plain coat; he advised me to lay it down. In half an hour the door opened; I was called. The emperor was in the hall, with several generals and aides-de-camp, among whom I recognised M. de Flahaut, and Labedoyère; he immediately went into the next room, where he called me to him. "Your name is Italian," he said to me, "M. de Sismondi; you are, however, I believe, from Geneva?" I explained to him my origin. "I have read your writings with much pleasure," said he, "and particularly what you have just written on the Constitution." "I am happy, Sire, that this paper has obtained your approbation, but it frankly expresses my thoughts; and in fact, I look upon this Constitution as the best of all that have been given to France." "Let us go into the garden," said he, and he made me put on my hat, and he led me into a large alley of hornbeam, where we walked about for three quarters of an hour alone, *tête-à-tête*. "I see with much sorrow," added I, "that this truly liberal constitution has been received with so much ill humour, and with such senseless clamour." "But I hope that that will become less," he said, "and my decree on the municipalities, and the presidents of the electoral colleges or assemblies [a], will do good; besides, look at this nation, it is not yet ripe for such ideas. They contest my right to dissolve the assemblies, and if afterwards I were to dismiss them by means of bayonets, they would think that quite natural." "What afflicts me," answered I, "is that they cannot see that the system of your Majesty is necessarily changed; henceforward you are become the representative of the Revolution, the associate of liberal ideas. You have so cruelly experienced during the last year the feebleness of royal alliances, the bad faith, and the secret hatred of all those whom you had sought and protected, that you can no longer have any doubt that the party of liberty is here, and throughout Europe, your only faithful ally." "It is indubitably so," answered he, "I feel it perfectly, and I shall never depart from it. The people have felt that very well, and this it is that makes them favourable to me, because, in fact, I have never deviated in my administration from the system of the revolution, not principles as men like you understood them, (*vous autres*). I had then other views, great projects to which

[a] The electors are divided in France into colleges or assemblies.

I was tending, but I have applied it, as for example, in the equality of justice, of the taxes, the eligibility to all places. These are the things which the peasantry remained in enjoyment of, and it is on that account that I am popular among them; but the French, when it regards principles, are extreme in every thing; they judge them with *la furia Francese;* they are distrustful, suspicious. The English have much more reflection; their ideas are more matured on all these subjects; there is a justness of thought found in almost all of them. I saw much of them in the Isle of Elba; many were awkward, had a bad carriage, did not know how to come into my salon; but when once entered into conversation with them, one found beneath this rough exterior a mature man, ideas just, profound, and moderate."

I questioned him about many of the English whom he had seen, about Mr. Douglas, with whom he had been much pleased, and whom he could not conceive to be the same person as he whose violent declamations had been published in the newspapers; about Lady Holland, whom he had not seen, but whose enthusiasm for him he knew. I spoke to him of the embarrassment of their finances, of the sort of nightmare which oppressed them, of the little paper of M. Say. Afterwards by comparison we returned to speaking of France. "The French nation is, however, a fine nation," said he, "noble, feeling, always ready to undertake whatever is fine and great. What can be finer, for example, than my return now? Well, I have no merit in it, none but that of having divined the nation." Then I asked him many questions about his return; he answered them all with complaisance. "People imagined," said he, "that there was a conspiracy, that all was prepared beforehand by intrigues; nothing of all that is true. I had not compromised my secret by communicating it, but I saw well that all was ready for an explosion." "It has been continually said," answered I, "that the revolution was the work of the army, but I was persuaded that the peasantry had concurred in it with no less promptitude." "Without doubt, for I travelled more than fifty leagues without meeting a soldier. The peasants only came to meet me; they followed me singing, with their wives and their children; they had made verses suitable to the occasion, and in my honour and against the senate, which they accused of treason. When I got near to Digne, the inhabitants forced the municipality to come and meet me. It was very ill-disposed towards me; however, it conducted itself very well; I was already absolute master of Digne, I could have hanged a hundred persons there if I had wished. They pressed me to stop in the town, but I wished to go on, and had no time to lose. There is a mountain above Digne, which I ascended, followed by all the population;—at my bivouac, they presented to me successively all the distinguished persons of the country, the police functionaries, the half-pay officers. I had not yet found any troops, but I might have been followed by the whole population if I had wished it."

We resumed our conversation on the Constitution: he said that he thought that these electoral colleges for life would introduce a suitable mixture of aristocracy. I said that in fact some aristocracy was necessary, and that the lasting interests of duration should be represented in the community as well as those of the present moment. "Government," replied he, "is a navigation: two elements are necessary to navigate; two also are required to direct the vessel of the state. Balloons can never be directed, because there is no fulcrum to resist the storms which agitate that element: so in a pure democracy, there is no possibility of directing it but by combining it with an aristocracy; one is opposed to the other, and the vessel is guided by contrary passions." "I entirely feel," replied I, "the necessity of this aristocratic element; I even look upon hereditary distinction as in accordance with our natural feelings; distinction is a quality which is so much the more precious the freer a country is, and when family glory is more connected with national glory. But in the circumstances in which your Majesty is placed, I think it very difficult to establish, and I do not comprehend how the Chamber of Peers can acquire that consideration which it wants. Your Majesty had previously adopted the system of fusing the old nobility with the new, which had succeeded, but which I believe now to be impossible; the old nobility is decidedly inimical; I do not believe that your Majesty can or ought at present to make it re-enter your administration; and I do not comprehend how a new nobility can maintain itself against the old." "For the present, in fact, all idea of fusion must be adjourned: such an association would be impossible." "Then I should have wished your Majesty to substitute an elective for an hereditary aristocracy." "How would you do that?" "I would have left to your Majesty the right of creating new peers, but I would have left to the Chamber the right of filling up, by election, the members it had lost." "Oh no, that would not be possible. Time will be requisite during the first years. I pity these poor peers, because they will meet with much opposition and jealousy; but after some years people will get accustomed to them; the ancient nobility will re-enter this Chamber, and that will at last appear to be the natural order."

He spoke to me afterwards of Italy. "They are also a fine people," said he; "there is stuff there to make a nation of; I had done much for them; I had given them the military spirit which they wanted, and national feeling. They were going on very well, and now they are very unhappy." "In fact, Sire, you have made very good soldiers of them, I believe." "Oh, they were quite as brave as the French; they had the same ardour under fire, and the same steadiness." "I was in Italy last year, when Murat declared himself against you." "Ah, how he conducted himself then! What bad faith!" "Sire, it must be said in his praise, that he saved the persons and property of twenty thousand Frenchmen, who would have been massacred if he had not very actively protected them." "Ah, that is the only thing that can be said in his favour." "I think that there is another still, Sire; seeing the steps he took, and his hesitation, I did not doubt that he was secretly friendly to you, and was only waiting events." "Oh, not at all; even now he has committed another folly by those unseasonable great preparations." "He has, then, been beaten?" "No, he has even had some advantage at Cisene, but he was not the less obliged to draw back. He ought to have kept on his frontier, with his army well disciplined, on the defensive: his exact force could not have been estimated, and there would have been some hesitation in attacking him, whilst by advancing, he has immediately made the extent of his power known." "There is, then, no rising in his favour?" "There has been a little, but he has no means of arming them; he has laid up no store of arms; it would not have been very difficult during a year of peace, especially as he had free trade with England, to buy a hundred thousand muskets, but as they are at present, the Italians can do nothing. They have made me many proposals, and were continually sending me solicitations to Elba, but I always answered them—Be quiet at present, there is nothing for you to do. In fact, in France, it was sufficient to gain the army and the people, and all the depôts of artillery, all the arsenals, all strong places were immediately in my hands. But, however much Italy might have been in my favour, Alexandria, Mantua, with all their arsenals, would not the less have remained in the hands of the Austrians. Besides, all those who have most consideration in the nation, who were most able to put themselves at its head, are arrested." "How is that?" "There has been presented to them a conspiracy in the name of the Duc de Berri, as if he were on the point of entering Italy, to put himself at the head of the French party; it was not true, he knew nothing about it, but they fell into the snare, and those who had seduced them have given their names to the General Bellegarde, who has caused them to be arrested." I told him that I thought Tuscany was less disposed to a revolution than the rest of Italy. "It was so from the beginning," said he, "but now they begin to regret the French tribunals, and to complain of the disorder into which they have been thrown by the abolition of the Code. The other day they followed the Grand Duke to Pisa, saying to him, *Ma non sta bene, Altezza Reale, tutta quella mutazione: non vogliamo più quelle leggi antiche, ne que' dicelli, ne tante stravaganze.*"[a] He spoke Italian very well, and with a very good accent. I spoke to him afterwards of Switzerland, and said how important her neutrality appeared to me. I related that I had sent an article to the *Moniteur*, which had not been inserted; he promised to look at it, and to cause it to appear. I said to him, that if Switzerland wished to maintain her neutrality, it would not be violated. He asked me what I thought of the disposition of the Cantons. I said that the new Cantons were favourable to France; that in the aristocratic Cantons the government was very much opposed to him, but that the people saw with much sorrow the changes of the last year; that the small Cantons were his enemies. "Taking it altogether," said he, "the mass of the population regrets the act of mediation, and I could, with this act, cause a revolution in Switzerland as I have done in France." He asked me how we were pleased with our constitution at Geneva. I told him that the theory of it was very bad, but that it did not act badly, and that we were very much attached to our independence. "The Genevese," said he, "have the spirit of wisdom, and the habit of liberty, but is it then an hereditary aristocracy which has been established there?"

I gave him rapidly an idea of our constitution. On this subject he spoke to me of J. Rousseau; he said he did not like him much, he found much pretension in him, and a style constantly on the stretch. I said to him, that it resembled that of a living author, Chateaubriand, whose style was brilliant, but without simplicity. "Yes," said he, "he aims at effect; one feels that he is occupied about his phrases, and that beneath these there is no maturity of thought. I have not read the whole of the Genius of Christianity; it is not in

[a] But things do not go on well, please your Royal Highness; all these changes will not do. We will have no more of these ancient laws and taxes, and such follies.

my way; it is a system which I do not believe; but, for example, in what he has written against me there is no thought, nothing solid, it is all for effect; however, he is certainly a man of talent." I told him that I preferred his talent and his character to that of another celebrated man of his time, M. de Fontanes. "Ah, as to him," said he, "he is entirely on the system of reaction; he conceives nothing but the ancient *régime;* he sees all that in his imagination, and he has not a mind which can apply itself to real things." He then spoke to me of English novels, of Richardson and Fielding, and asked me some questions about the Italian and Spanish novels, in the same line as Gil Blas, or in that of Pigault le Brun. I showed my surprise at his knowing these things. "It is because I read a great deal in my youth; I worked hard, and read many novels also. In my youth I was much more discreet than I am now; till my first campaign in Italy, I dared not look a woman in the face; I should not say so much for myself now. During that time also I went through a course of law, and when afterwards we were working on the *Code Civil,* the councils of state were quite surprised to find that I knew their business. I told them it was because I had studied it." "Ah," cried I, "that is what makes great men; it is having successively applied their mind to everything; it is because they have struggled hand to hand with difficulties; it is what princes want, and which renders them at this time so incapable of extricating themselves from such perplexing difficulties." "Ah, it is the fault of the system," replied he; "but it is irremediable. The Duke of Orleans is the only one of the French princes who has been put to this proof; during his exile he ceased to be a prince, to become a man, therefore he is the only one who has profited by adversity. So they say." But he then broke off the conversation on that subject. He spoke to me of the popes, who had at all times prevented the Italians from becoming a nation. I said to him, that "people had had at first a great opinion of Pius VII., but that he showed afterwards that he had the obstinacy of a monk, and not the courage of a great man." "Yes, his firmness has been much boasted of; I had the air of persecuting him; he said to me himself that he was, that he wished to be, a martyr to the faith; but, answered I, how is that, holy father?—you are well fed, well clothed, lodged in a palace, and you call that martyrdom; but you are not disgusted with life." Then he laughed. Again returning to the praises of the French nation, and comparing them to another nation, he called the French *we* (*nous autres*) with quite a national feeling. We had already walked nearly three quarters of an hour; at the two last turns he was much heated, he took off his hat, and his forehead was bathed in sweat. At last he turned towards the palace, we entered his room, he said he was charmed to have made acquaintance with so distinguished a man. He bowed to me, and I retired.

THE

PHILOSOPHY OF GOVERNMENT,

AND OF

POLITICAL ECONOMY.

A SERIES OF ESSAYS SELECTED FROM THE WORKS OF

M. DE SISMONDI.

PRELIMINARY ESSAY.

BY THE TRANSLATOR.

The Corn Laws are repealed. After years of strenuous exertion on the part of those who considered that by these exertions they were forwarding the best interests of all classes of society, the period of their complete extinction is fixed. The consequences remain to be experienced. Will they be advantageous to all the different interests in the community, as is expected by those who have carried this great measure; or will they be, as the protectionists aver, destructive of the welfare of one great and most important class, without a commensurate advantage to any other! Will an unlimited trade in corn put an end to those manufacturing crises which have so frequently, during the last half century, been a source of such wide-spreading misery, and of so much degradation to the working classes? Will it increase the comforts and be a lasting benefit to this most important class? Can it, on the other hand, throw our land out of cultivation, make agriculture unworthy attention, and render England, with her generally favourable soil and climate, her skill, science, and industry, unable to compete with those countries where the serf scrapes a seldom renewed soil with miserable implements; or even with those more luxuriant but more distant regions, from which the expense of transit is much greater; and where the more lucrative the growing of corn becomes, the more will be retained at home, to feed not only the cultivators, but all the increasing population which collects around successful agriculture? for the more profitable any production becomes to the great mass of producers, the more will be retained at home for the benefit of those who can, on that account, afford to purchase it. It may safely be assumed that the repeal will neither produce the extent of good on one side, or of evil on the other, that is prognosticated.

One happy consequence, however, there can be no doubt, has arisen from the long discussion on this subject. It has instructed the whole community. It has penetrated the lowest depths of society with a knowledge never before extended to them; it has inspired every thinking mind with a deep interest in the science of political economy, one of the most important of the social sciences, if it be not confined to that comparatively low object of how wealth may be best obtained and secured; but extended to the wider and more philanthropic investigation of how it may, by its acquisition and distribution, produce the least degree of suffering and the greatest of happiness to the whole of the community.

In the study of this most important subject, no man's opinions can be entitled to more earnest consideration than those of the late M. de Sismondi: not only from his possessing the most profound and extensive knowledge of European history of any man of his age; from his having studied the tenures, constitutions, and social relations and opinions of different nations, with the great object of discovering how far they added to or diminished general prosperity and happiness, but also from having had more practical knowledge, both of commerce and agriculture, than can often be acquired by studious men; all his studies and all his opinions being imbued, at the same time, with the most tender and intense interest in the happiness of his kind.

The evils of the system of restriction and monopoly, which had been so long acted upon, were so strongly pointed out by Adam Smith, and the school of political economy of which he was the founder, that it seems to have been thought by his followers that nothing but advantage would result from going as far as possible to the opposite extreme, and little attention has been paid to the consideration of the evils which might attend this also. M. de Sismondi saw them strongly, and had long foretold them, but he might not perhaps allow sufficient weight to their compensating advantages, as, from having witnessed much of the happiness produced under the old system, he was perhaps too unwilling to admit its evils. It is, however, most important in every step of progress, to hear the opinions of wise men taking different views.

It is not possible to read the works of the most eminent professors of the science of political economy without being struck, not only by the different sense frequently attached to the terms they use, but also by the great difference of opinion in regard to its principles, their application, and their results. By the term political economy is, however, generally understood that science which teaches how best to increase and secure the prosperity of a nation by increasing and securing its wealth. And its great maxim to attain this end is by non-interference, what the French economists call *laisser faire, et laisser passer;* that every man should be left at liberty to increase his own wealth by the means which appear to him to be the best, and that in this way the interests of the whole community will be best promoted. M. de Sismondi, however, founds the science upon quite another basis. He affirms that the object of the political economist should be, to ascertain how the happiness and well-being of the whole community are affected by the creation and distribution of wealth, not abstractedly how wealth may be created and preserved; that the principles of political economy should be extended to embrace all subjects which relate to the social welfare of man, and that this ought to be considered as the end, to which the increase and security of wealth is but a means; that the purely economical mode of considering the means apart from the end, the calculating theories in which men are too often reckoned as figures, and considered as means of production, have led to a disregard of their value as men: also, that the theories of political economy, and the legislation founded on them, tend to make the rich, richer, and the poor, poorer. Thus the amount of a nation's wealth being taken as the test of its prosperity, without regard to its distribution, it will be considered prosperous if some of its members are immensely rich; if there is below these a large middle class commanding all the material enjoyments of life, and by commerce and manufactures increasing their own possessions, and employing large numbers, to their mutual advantage; even though by far the majority of its population are earning, by daily labour, an insufficient and precarious subsistence; and there should be still lower a very large and often unheeded class, who, living in vice and misery, have no visible means of subsistence. M. de Sismondi contends that one of the main objects of political economy should be to regulate this very unequal distribution of wealth, which is not only frequently a source of injustice, and a cause of misery to the lower classes, but which causes national insecurity, by tending to produce those revulsions which affect the stability of private fortunes, and by continually adding to that dangerous though despised class who, at any time of difficulty or trouble, are ready to revenge their own sufferings by attacking property and institutions which have afforded to them neither advantage nor protection.

However those who would restrict the science to the limits they have assigned to it, may object to M. de Sismondi including his considerations under this term, they will not, at least, deny their extreme importance. In what way the acquisition, distribution, and employment of wealth affects the comforts, happiness, and morality of the community, is a subject than which few can be more worthy the earnest attention of the legislator, the philanthropist, and the Christian.

M. de Sismondi eloquently points out many of the evils springing from too universal an application of the non-interference doctrine: indeed it is scarcely possible, even were it desirable, to act upon this principle, apart from the considerations of justice, morality, or even benevolence. Slavery itself is only the extreme form of the influence and the power of property, and one can hardly see how he who says you may take advantage of a glut of labour to pay a man less than his labour is worth, and to gather to yourself an undue share of profit, can deny that you are justified in availing yourself of the condition of the slave. Neither slave nor labourer are in their natural position; but alike in one regulated by the laws of property of the country in which they live.

If, in such an extreme case as that of slavery, government would be justified in departing from the non-interference principle of political economy, are there no others in which it may be set aside from considerations of morality and humanity? In all the variety of cases which come under the strictest definitions of political economy, may it not sometimes be called on to protect the poor against the rich, the employed against his employer, ignorance and weakness against skill and power, the rights of man against the rights of property?

And yet in our own country, infringements of the law of liberty, scarcely less cruel than those of slavery, become possible under those ruthless laws which seem to hold life of small importance, in comparison with an uncontrolled exercise of the laws of property.

In the clearances in Scotland, and evictions in Ireland, which have occasioned such dreadful suffering, the principles of political economy were professedly acted upon. The cruelty and oppression, which in such violent proceedings must take place, arose from no ill-will to the poor people who were cleared out; on the contrary, something was occasionally done to lessen their sufferings; and those by whose power and authority these clearances were made, not only considered that they were exercising undoubted rights, but that they were doing what was wise and just, and what would eventually result in the greatest good to the whole community.

But surely we ought most seriously to consider the truth and the certainty of the ultimate benefit to result from principles which justify acts so contrary to the dictates of God and of natural feeling, as those of driving human beings from their homes to scoop out a shelter in the sand, and maintain a precarious subsistence on shell-fish and wild vegetables, or at best by begging; or even those of transplanting whole villages into new situations, breaking local attachments, and forcing the inhabitants upon a mode of life entirely contrary to their habits, for the sake of improving the property of one man, by adopting new modes of cultivation. The efforts made in England to drive the poor from cottages, in order to evade the law of settlement, are in the same spirit[a]. It may be said that the evils are great which it is attempted by these means to put an end to; in some cases they are, in others it is very doubtful; but if these evils have arisen from defects in legislation, bad social arrangements, a false system of political economy, or

[a] "Among the many evils which at this time tend to depress the agricultural poor, the law of settlement is exercising a very unfavourable influence. Settlement, as regards the labouring poor, being now practically confined to the place of their birth, the owners of property are exerting themselves to throw the burden off their own estates, and to fix it upon others. If they can drive the poor from the parishes in which their own property lies, they calculate that they shall be exempted from the pressure of poor's rates. In this object the farmers unite heartily with their landlords, for the payments are made by them, and the occupier is equally interested with the owner in keeping down the burden upon land. There is no settled purpose in all this of oppressing the poor: it arises from selfishness—the caring for none but themselves. But the consequences to the poor are grievous. If cottages are pulled down instead of being built up, if no harbouring is provided for the labouring poor in those parishes where their settlement is, they must either go to the workhouse or find shelter elsewhere. As long as they have health and strength, we know that our industrious labourers will strain every nerve to maintain their families in independence. Hence, they seek the nearest village to their own, where shelter is to be found, however exorbitant the rent. Wherever there are small freeholds in a parish, there speculators will be found to reap a profit from the necessities of these homeless families. Streets of miserable dwellings are erected, where £5, £6, £7, are charged for only two or three small rooms. These villages are perhaps from three to six miles from their own parish, where alone they can find employment; and this distance have these poor men to walk morning and night, in addition to their day's labour, for no allowance is made by the farmer for the distance which his labourer has to come to his work, and unless he is there to his appointed hour at all seasons, he will employ him no longer."—*Times.*

even from the ignorance and recklessness of the poor tenants, is therefore the whole weight of suffering to fall on their unprotected heads?—while those who, from their power and influence, are mainly responsible for the existence of these evils, take no share in the inconveniences of a reform, while they reap the whole benefit of it.

The whole system of the tenures and letting of land is one great hindrance to the improvement of Ireland; tending to create a large and destitute population, producing no more than suffices for bare subsistence; and in times when this bare subsistence at all falls short, entailing immense expense, totally without returns, on the English and Irish nations; fostering, also, that recklessness and idleness in the Irish character, which is the great bar to improvement. Yet, give an Irishman the conviction that he runs no risk of losing the benefits of his labour, bring him to England, and give him a motive to save, and he will work as well in proportion to his strength and skill as an Englishman; and often save more. Above all, were there given him but a corner of his beloved country which he might call his own, and did the right to possession depend on the attention paid to its cultivation, the Irishman would devote to it all his energies of body and soul. Thus, the thousands of acres of waste land in Ireland might be cultivated like a garden. Yet all legislative interference with the modes of letting, and tenures of land, is contrary to the maxim *laisser faire, et laisser passer*, and an infraction on the rights of property. But why does not the government buy up some of these waste lands, and let them in lots to the evicted poor, at a low fixed rent, allowing them after this had been paid for a certain number of years, to become purchasers of the land, by means of yearly payments, if their improvement of the soil proved them worthy to become proprietors?—instead of this, while their native soil lies uncultivated at their feet, they are encouraged at great expense to leave it, and go to reclaim land in far distant countries.

O'Connell calls himself, and is considered by the Irish as a benefactor; but if, instead of abstracting large sums from the poorest and the most miserable, with the vain hope of obtaining what are considered political rights, some of which, if obtained, would probably only make Ireland more miserable than she is, he were to let his estates on a just system, beneficial to tenant as well as landlord, and to use his vast power and influence to counteract the national sin of idleness, to induce his tenants to employ improved systems of cultivation, on a security that their hard earned gains would not be wrested from them, thus showing to Ireland an example of an industrious, contented, and improving peasantry, and proclaiming to the legislature, and to English and Irish landlords, what are the real evils of Ireland, and what their cure, he would be a true benefactor and liberator; a liberator from the worst of all evils—moral evil, and physical degradation.

Unlimited speculation, too, if it be not the direct result, is certainly a vice fostered by the maxims of political economy, and one in which they will not admit of legislative interference. That the spirit of enterprise and speculation has been productive of many advantages cannot be denied; but the evils, both moral and economical, which are also consequent on it, have not, perhaps, been sufficiently attended to [a]. In a great, perhaps the greatest, proportion of speculations, no real wealth is created; what is gained by one is simply taken from others; and often

[a] Some curious accounts of speculation in the iron trade, I received from a gentleman in that business. The iron trade is always a fluctuating one; but in this, as in other trades, when the price rises unreasonably there is a check; persons will not buy at a price beyond bounds, partly from prudence, partly to resist imposition. When so many railways were proposed, it was calculated that it would be impossible to make the quantity of iron required, in any time approaching to that in which it would be wanting. Iron rose. The trade is considered in a prosperous state when it is nine or ten per cent. above the medium price; it rose to thirteen and fifteen. Seven gentlemen came to Liverpool to make sudden fortunes by speculating in iron; they expected to make thirty per cent. on the usual price. One of them was offered a price by which he would have cleared £40,000: he scorned it, and said he should make £80,000; the rest acted on the same principle. Iron did not rise above fifteen per cent. Six of the seven were bankrupts, and one escaped simply from refusing to fulfil any bargain that was not advantageous to himself.

with this additional evil, that the loss to the losers involves a loss to many who are dependent on their industry for their daily bread.

In times of speculation we hear much of the fortunate makers of fortunes: we hear little of the numbers who suffer loss, except when some immense failure precipitates hundreds into distress and ruin, or when some pistol shot reveals the mental distraction of a gambler, not less one because he plays with cotton or shares, instead of dice. The late rage for railway speculations might teach us the evil of the temptation held out to acquire wealth by fortunate chances. Probably but a small proportion of these speculations have been founded on well-considered calculations of the real profits a railway was likely to afford; but the good fortune of some speculators has tempted many to forsake the slow profits of regular business, risking their own property and that of those who depend on them. They have also been a snare to the integrity of numbers, tempting them to defraud their employers, in order to engage in speculations no less dangerous and vicious than if they had carried the money to the hazard table.

But in a prosperous country where wealth abounds, the wave soon passes over those who are ruined by dishonest or hazardous speculations; they are not seen, the nation forgets them, but they are not forgotten before God, who will, in the undoubted and unvarying course of his justice exact a fearful, though it may be long delayed, retribution from all persons and nations who sacrifice moral ends to the pursuit of material wealth.

Any legislative interference in what are called the rights of labour, is also strongly deprecated by the political economists. Any restriction on the manner in which a man may employ his labour, the person to whom he may offer it, the time he may choose to devote to it, or the remuneration he may be satisfied to take, is condemned. So many evils have for so many hundred years arisen from too much interference on these points, and they have been so ably exposed by the writers on political economy during the latter half of the last century, that it was thought that nothing was required to secure the well-being of the working man, but to act on a totally contrary system. Now, however, it is beginning to be felt that evils, neither small nor few, have been the consequence of a strict adherence to the maxim of non-interference, and some steps have been taken in a contrary direction, as in the Factory Bill, the Twelve Hours' Bill, and the Bill to prevent women and children working in mines; all opposed as being contrary to the acknowledged principles of political economy, and all attended with some inconvenience, even to those they are intended to protect, by lessening for a time the products of labour; but all affording hope that the longer they are persevered in, the more it will be perceived that the permanent benefit will outweigh the temporary inconvenience.

Doubtless, legislative interference in private concerns is a great evil, so great that it never can be justified except to avert greater; this must in every case be a question of experience and expediency. It is the part of a good government to weigh each case with wise deliberation; to consider in what way the class which most requires protection may be relieved from any pressure from which it cannot relieve itself; but to be careful not by a rash legislation, founded even on the most benevolent principles, to hazard injuring the real and permanent interests of those it seeks to defend, or to interfere unjustly with the rights of those whose mistakes it would rectify, even should its object be to restrain cupidity, selfishness, and oppression.

The question of legislative interference with the hours of labour was ably argued, on both sides, in the debate on Mr. Fielden's bill, to limit the hours of working in factories to ten hours a day for women, and for children under eighteen. Much was said, and no doubt very truly, on the evils of legislative interference between the employer and those he employs; on the hardships of not allowing a man to make the most of his labour, and to give as much as he pleases of it for his own benefit; on the hindrance to industrial labour if any of those who co-operate in it are limited as to hours; on the impossibility of competing with foreign nations, where it was said the workmen give from twelve to sixteen hours a day to labour; on the loss of profit to the manufacturers. Most of these arguments assume that labour has it in its power to make a fair and just bargain with property for their mutual advantage. But the fact is, that under our present social arrangements and condition, the balance of power is so much in the hands of capital, that labour has no power to make a just bargain. Capital will take every advantage of labour, when unprotected, to buy it at the cheapest rate—a rate often much below its true value; and whenever labour, feeling itself oppressed, has endeavoured to obtain better advantages for itself, it has generally betrayed either its ignorance or its weakness, and the results have been disadvantageous to the employed, as well as to the employer. In many cases, especially in manufactories, the individual operative cannot apportion the number of hours he devotes to work, to his strength, or to the gains sufficient for his wants or his wishes, as is the case in professions, and many kinds of business, which were unfairly compared to the working in manufactories, as affording instances of harder and more continued labour. Had each individual the power to make his own bargain, or to combine with others to work shorter hours, it seems certain by the statements of the operatives themselves, that numbers would find it advantageous to take shorter hours, even with diminished wages. Much would be saved by less sickness, by lengthened life, by more economy in domestic arrangements; and it may be said by more time being given to mental and moral improvement, producing more prudence and self-restraint[a]. But in most manufactories men are bound by im-

[a] At a meeting of the factory operatives, Manchester, December 3, 1845, Mr. J. T. Collins said he had worked in the mill many years, and from sad experience he did not hesitate to declare that the present factory hours were too long for human nature to endure. Such was the state of weakness to which he was reduced by twelve hours' labour in the mill, that he had no taste for learning, or time for the performance of those domestic duties which are so dear to every Englishman.

perious necessity all to work the same hours, or the work could not go on; and not only that, but all manufactories of the same kind must work the same, or nearly the same number of

Among the resolutions were these :—

1. There never appeared to us any substantial reason why factory operatives, who are generally of the most delicate class of workers, including a very large proportion of females, should be compelled to follow the never tiring motions of the machine for a longer period in each day than the athletic mechanic, or the robust and healthy agriculturist, are required to work at their respective labour.

2. Because there is every reason to believe, so far as experience goes, that the present system of long hours is not attended with any pecuniary advantage to you, as our employers, whilst to us it is destructive of health, and materially limits the average duration of human life.

3. Because it deprives us of all mental intercourse with the intelligent portion of society, with whom we might, if we had leisure enough, intermix in our Athenæums, Mechanics' Institutions, and other places of the sort, established for the improvement of the working classes, but hitherto closed against us, because we have neither time nor taste for such intellectual enjoyments, after so much bodily and mental exertion during the present long hours of factory work.

If public parks and pleasure grounds were now open to the inhabitants of Manchester, they would be a dead letter to us without a reduction of the hours of labour.

For these and numerous other reasons, we are convinced that the boon we now seek, if granted, would materially tend to the benefit of us all, by enabling us to improve the mind and morals of the rising generation of factory workers, and thereby, in numerous instances, substitute virtue for vice, sobriety for intemperance, and in some degree restore happiness to our families, self-esteem for ourselves, and gratitude for our employers.

At a meeting of the operatives employed by Mr. Robert Gardner, to thank him for reducing the hours to eleven, an operative spinner stated that the advantage which he had derived from the eleven hours were, that he had better health, and at the end of the week received more wages for his work than formerly.

The book-keeper of the establishment said, that when the system had been in operation a few weeks, he found that the sick list was much diminished, and that very few had to leave work from ill health. On referring to his books, he found that for a period of six weeks, *not a single spinner was off work from sickness, a circumstance which had never before been seen.* On the whole he was fully warranted in saying that the work was *much better under the new* than the old system.

A power-loom worker said his wife was working in the mill, and he had no hesitation in saying that a considerable saving to him had been effected, even by the single hour a day which she could now give to her affairs at home. Many other hands made similar statements.

Preston, March 7th, 1845.

hours, or some would be distanced in the race of competition. This, then, is one of those cases in which man not being a free agent, the interference of the legislature is called for to preserve his rights, his happiness, his life, from being sacrificed to the interests of comparatively a few individuals. The objection to restricting the hours of labour for women and children to ten hours was, that it must necessarily limit those of the men to the same time. Perhaps twelve hours a day, *dinner included*, is not too much for an adult man in health, and would allow time for rest and improvement; but it is far too much for women and children; and it seems a strange subversion of the order of nature, that they must be overworked, in order that men may be sufficiently worked; it would seem more natural that men should work more, in order to allow of their wives and children working less; and it must be considered as a great deduction from the advantages of any industrial employment, when such an inversion is necessary [a]. No married woman should be regularly absent from her family above six hours a day. Have our political economists calculated the waste of public wealth by the sickness, loss of infant life, vice, and crime, occasioned by the want of attention to children, want of economy, severance of family ties, and demoralization consequent on a woman's being absent from her family thirteen or fourteen hours a day—for this it amounts to with meals, and time lost in going and coming?

When the danger of the competition of foreign nations is spoken of, is it meant as regards the interest of the workmen, or the masters? If the superiority in this competition can only be obtained by thousands, millions of human creatures being born to such continuous labour as shortens life, prevents all moral and intellectual improvement, takes away all power of enjoyment except of the lowest kind; this unremitting toil producing often only the bare necessaries of life, not allowing

[a] The returns of the factory commissioners show that of 220,134 persons employed in cotton factories, only about one-fourth of the whole were *males above eighteen years of age.*

enough to lay up a provision for old age; if, indeed, such labour should ever give a hope of attaining to it—can such a life be spoken of as a benefit, or is life itself worth having on such terms?

As regards the real and permanent interests of the employers also, it is probable that the unlimited command of labour has led to that over-production which has of late years caused so many gluts, and so much consequent distress. Ruin to our manufacturing interests has been always predicted, when any legislative interference between the employer and the employed was proposed, even when it was to protect young children from virtual slavery and the greatest hardships; but the evils foretold not having resulted, we may trust that neither would they from a little more restriction. And as it was said by the opponents of the Corn Laws, that there would be no fear of land falling out of cultivation as long as it would maintain the cultivators, whatever became of rent and profit; so may we not say that manufactures will be carried on as long as they will give subsistence to the operatives, a moderate interest on capital, and small but probably steadier profits, instead of the large but uncertain ones now expected?

Should restrictions on the hours of labour diminish the present tendency to over-production, and prevent persons with small or no capital extending their business beyond their means, and have the effect also of creating a smaller but more prudent population, who would therefore have it more in their power to make their own terms, and to obtain their due share of the profits of manufactures; it is manifest that this would be greatly advantageous to the majority, even should individuals no longer be able to make immense fortunes, or to engage in extensive, often ruinous speculations.

An argument much insisted on in favour of the facility which our present system affords of accumulating large fortunes in few hands is, that large profits as well as high rents are necessary to enable the country to pay the interest of our immense debt. On the contrary, a more equal distribution even of less profits would make this more easy; *for the more widely wealth is distributed, the greater is the proportion of it which will be paid to the revenue.* All the returns show that the great amount is not paid by the rich, or even by the middle classes of society, but by the poor and those just above them. All attempts at taxation on luxuries have failed in productiveness: the only sure returns are from those which are laid on the necessaries and comforts of life, affecting the poor in a much greater proportion than any other class; and the state of the revenue depends mainly on the power of that class to purchase these necessaries and comforts [a].

By the wealth of a nation are we to understand only its material riches, or is it to be generally taken as meaning prosperity; and if so, must not the physical strength of those through whose means these riches have been created, and by whom, if attacked, they must be defended, be taken into the account? Will it be said that, according to the principles of political economy, the West Indies in their palmy days were in a prosperous state, because immense wealth was obtained by means of a population so rapidly diminishing that, to maintain its numbers, continual supplies were required from abroad; and will the cutting off of those supplies be in contradiction to the principles of political economy, because it has for the present caused embarrassment, and diminished the aggregate of wealth?

But if political economy will in no case defend slavery, will it defend the principle of non-interference in its fullest extent, where great material wealth is created by the employment of men in a manner, or to a degree, which produces suffering, disease, and deprivation; in which early marriages and early deaths produce a young, sickly, and deteriorating population?

[a] Of the excise and customs, two thirds, or nearly half are paid by the industrious classes.

A labouring man who gets £24 a year, pays £8 of it in indirect taxes.

The Corn Importation Bill may lessen the amount to him, but not the proportion. 200,000 persons with incomes just above £150 a year, pay one-fifth of the income tax.

In this country it appears that there is a great excess of births over deaths, and that the chances of life are considerably increased. This last is calculated upon an average of the whole population, and may be accounted for by the much greater knowledge of, and attention to, the means of preserving health, together with the great number of persons, especially in the higher and middle classes, and many of the lower, employed in occupations which have not a tendency to shorten life; though in one large and important portion of the whole community, the working class in large towns, the chances of life have diminished.

As to the excess of births, it is found that where, from the nature of the employments, from the modes of life, from a degraded state, there is a rapid mortality; yet if it be possible to obtain the means of subsistence of the poorest kind, and there be no prudential considerations, and no wish or power to rise above a state of indigence, there will be an excess of births and an increasing population; but it will be young and weak. Now it is not in the number born, but in the number which arrive at man's estate, that the strength of a nation consists. It is well known, that in our large towns the number of persons between the ages of ten and twenty-five is much larger than the natural proportion, to that of those between twenty-five and fifty.

This is also an economical question. The sanatory inquiries have established two facts: 1st, that a high *preventible* mortality leads to a greater increase of births than a lower rate of mortality; 2nd, that a high rate of mortality is the cause of an increase of cost and waste to the whole community. "In the manufacturing districts, where peculiar causes operate in producing an excessive mortality, an excessive proportion of births is also observed. Early marriages are in proportion; and thus an unhealthy and feeble population is produced, still more liable to be affected by the causes of mortality."[a] It has

[a] Supplementary Paper to the Report on the State of Large Towns and Populous Districts, 1842.

been generally supposed that the mortality caused by destitution, or by unhealthy employments and modes of living, was necessary to restrain an excessive increase of population. The attention, however, which has of late been given to the statistics of these questions shows that sanatory improvements, and whatever tends to lengthen life, are the most effectual means of restraining a too great increase of population. As to the cost of excessive mortality, Mr. Slany states, as the result of his investigations, that "It is within the truth to lay down as a rule that, wherever the mortality closely approaches three per cent., the annual cost, direct and indirect, to the community, of the want of proper sanatory regulations, exceeds *one pound* per head on the whole population, or ten shillings in the pound on the rental of all the houses;" and this vast annual outlay, with the incalculable amount of suffering and guilt, he believes may be prevented by proper regulations, wisely directed and firmly enforced.

Political economy, in pursuing its narrowest object of increasing the material wealth of a country, necessarily allies itself with morality. All vice, all dishonesty, all idleness, all imprudence, all want of truth—nay, even all want of wisdom,—is a waste of the wealth and resources, not only of individuals but of the nation. No subject can be more important, in an economical as well as in a moral point of view, than to discover how to keep down the fearful increase of that class which is in the lowest state of destitution, which subsists entirely either on public or private charity, or by fraud and robbery[a]. Even when the subsistence

[a] In 1836 a Committee of the Liverpool Corporation made a report on the number and earnings of criminals in that town, from which it appeared that £734,240 were annually obtained by unlawful means.—*National Distress, its Causes and Remedies, by Samuel Laing, Jun., p.* 21.

We boast ourselves on being a more moral and religious people than our neighbours; yet the police returns show that in Liverpool there are 7,401 criminals, abandoned and suspected persons. In Paris, with a population of 900,000, above three times that of Liverpool, there are 13,300 of the same class (*Frequier, Chef de Bureau de la Préfecture de Seine*). If they bore the same proportion to the population, as in Liverpool, there would be 22,233.

of this class is provided for by the least objectionable means, where what is taken from the rich is given to the poor, where it is merely money changing hands, it is utterly unproductive; it does not increase the wealth of the country, nor does it go to afford leisure for that mental cultivation, which is the greatest advantage of a non-producing class. On the contrary, it physically, mentally, and morally, debases those who receive it. It is true that as long as bad economical systems and social institutions lead to the formation of a class of persons without either the wish or the power to raise themselves above their degraded state, or to provide for their own wants, their subsistence must in some way be provided for; but the question is, whether such a reform in our economical and social systems be not possible, as may very much lessen, or entirely do away with, a class mainly dependent on others for support; so as to restrict what is called charity to the relief of accidental evils, giving freer scope to the sweeter charities of life, sympathy and disinterested intercourse between the rich and the poor, and affording much larger means for bestowing that only really good gift, education, in the most extended sense of that word.

At this time, when the Corn Importation Bill gives reason to hope for an improvement in the profits of labour, and for a lower price in the means of subsistence, which it is expected will be advantageous to every class, it would be a proper time for a benevolent and enlightened legislature to consider whether it would not be possible to devise some mode of relieving the poor more efficacious and less fraught with evil than the present poor law; a heavy tax on the whole community, and more particularly on the proprietors and holders of land, involving by the mode of collecting and distributing it, expenses very heavy in proportion to the benefit conferred; a source, too frequently, of injustice and oppression to those for whose relief it was established; punishing unavoidable poverty as if it were a crime; tending to widen that gulph between the rich and the poor so much to be deplored; and ever affording a ready excuse to those who, from carelessness, hard-heartedness, or want of generosity, are unwilling to inquire into the condition of their fellow-creatures; having especially the most injurious effects on the character of the poor themselves, by teaching them that there is something to depend on besides their own industry and good conduct, and by accustoming them to claim assistance as a right, and to receive it without gratitude. It is also very reasonably felt as a great hardship by that class of the poor, whom it should be the first object of a wise legislature to encourage; those who, from a noble spirit of independence, are working night and day to keep themselves above the pauper class; that they should, even by these laudable endeavours, be placed in circumstances in which they are called upon to pay poor rates for the relief of distress, too often, they are well aware, brought on by idleness, vice, intemperance or extravagance. It is a cruel injustice, too, that the poorest should pay a much larger proportion of their means towards this tax than any other class of the community; nor can anything be more short-sighted in its consequences than the pressure thus inflicted, often reducing men from the condition of rate-payers to that of paupers. A man can support himself; but because he cannot help to support paupers also, he himself becomes a pauper, and others must support him; and thus he increases the burden on those left, drags others after him, and the evil continually increases [a].

[a] At the *fête* given by the mill people in the employ of Messrs. Courtauld, Taylor, and Co., to their employers, there walked in the procession a hand-loom weaver, getting from ten to thirteen shillings a week. By denying himself from time to time his half pint of beer, he made up his threepence weekly subscription during the three months which his fellow workmen devoted to plan and preparation.

Soon after the procession moved onwards, there came to Appleton's cottage the overseer of the parish, demanding instant payment of the last poor rate, and threatening that a summons should be taken out unless the money was put into his hands by twelve o'clock *that very morning*. Although he was known to be away for the day, the summons was taken out, was served the next morning, with an additional charge of about 6*s*. 8*d*. for fees, &c.

Appleton, who had a sickly wife, and had had nine children, had hitherto been excused from paying poor rates. He understood that this exemption continued as to the present rate. His wife had attended with others before the Bench to represent

The poor rates also fall very unfairly on the other different contributors. Land is burdened with poverty produced by checks to our manufacturing and commercial prosperity, often caused by ruinous or even dishonest speculation, or by the gluts of over-production. In times of agricultural depression, field labourers flock into the towns, hoping to get work which may afford them that subsistence which a total want of employment or very insufficient wages, deny them in the country, being, at the same time, in general the most reckless and idle of the country population. In both these cases, large bodies of men, many of the individuals of which are in very straitened circumstances, are called upon either as ratepayers, or in the form of private charity, to relieve distress caused by reverses in the agricultural or manufacturing interests which they had no share in producing, as on the other hand, they had derived little or no advantage from their previous prosperity.

their inability to pay, and had been told by the magistrates that "they would let it rest." This was, not unreasonably, taken as a remission, to which it seems it did not amount. A subsequent formality, of which the hand-loom weaver was not aware, and therefore neglected, left him technically and legally out of the excused list.

The magistrates hold themselves bound to wait the recommendation of the overseer to put any name on the excused list; and to all pleadings of the unexpected nature of the demand, the exemption in former years, the aggravation of added expenses, the time selected for this abrupt enforcement, the circumstances of the family, and the fact that distraint for poor's rates must bring on distraint for rent, break up the humble establishment of the victim, and consign him with his wife and four remaining children to the workhouse; the cool reply of the overseer is, that a man who can give a dinner to his masters shall pay the rate; and he will excuse him "no, not one farthing."

Loud have been the complaints of a portion of the British Peerage that the poor rates fall heavily on their large estates. We see in this case how they fall on the cottage of the operative. We also see how they can be made the means of punishment—of punishment it may be for no just cause of offence; but for conduct which the well-disposed must generally regard with complacency. In our apprehension, poor-rates ought never to be levied below the line of demarcation drawn by the income tax.

A POOR LAW is, as we understand it, a public charity. There are those who know how to make it a public nuisance, to infuse into it the venom of all uncharitableness, and render it the instrument of oppression and cruelty.—*From a letter by a Correspondent to the Daily News, July 7th,* 1846.

Might it not be possible to substitute for this a system by which the onus of providing against the destitution of those they employ, should be thrown on all employers of large or small bodies of men on daily, weekly, or monthly wages, whether agricultural, commercial, or industrial in every form?

The first Essay in this series, the Preface to the Second Edition of one of M. de Sismondi's early works on the subject of political economy, has been inserted, because it was thought that it would be interesting to see the impression which the state of this country made on M. de Sismondi when he visited it soon after the crisis of 1826. In some points he may be a little mistaken in his view of England; and some of the evils which he points out have been rectified, or may be in the process of amendment. There is still, however, notwithstanding our outward prosperity, a mass of evil arising from our economical system, the causes of which political economists seem at a loss to ascertain, and the remedies for which they appear unable to suggest, differing as they do on both these points. They seem generally agreed, however, that the chief remedy is still to be sought in carrying out farther the great principle of each one being allowed to do the best he can for his own interest with his skill, capital and labour, and that this will result in the greatest advantage to the whole community.

Have, however, these principles, as far as they have hitherto been carried out, produced the expected advantage to the most numerous and most important class? On the contrary, has not our progress in wealth, and in material prosperity, been attended with the increase, in a greater proportion, of indigence and pauperism? The very depressed state of the agricultural labourer has, it will be said, taken place during a system of protection. It scarcely, however, can be said to have its origin in that system, but in whatever has tended to the accumulation of large properties in few hands, and to the extinction of the yeomanry, of small proprietors and tenants on long leases[a];

[a] I am now an old man, and I have been all my life a Norfolk farmer. I have lived in the times when farms were of a moderate size, and when there existed a

very much also to the different mode of paying farm servants, which has obtained of late years [a]. We have at this time a starving agricultural population, who only want to be allowed to gain their bread by the sweat of their brow; land which wants cultivation; and capital which wants investment. Can political economy tell us why these things are so, and how they can be brought to bear on one another for their mutual advantage? Much is said of the evils of a redundant population, and of colonization as a remedy for it. And yet the emigration reports show, to take a few instances, that "In Bilsington pa-

respectable class of people called *small farmers*, who formed a link between the yeomen of the county and the agricultural labourer, but these have all been swept away.

I have witnessed the pulling down of homesteads, the small farmer turned out, and after a period of unavailing struggles, gradually sink down and become incorporated with the labouring mass. I have seen six or seven farms thrown into one, because it was found cheaper to work large farms than small ones; and as fewer labourers and fewer cattle were required, the consequence was that many a poor fellow was deprived of his employ.

This increase in the size of farms was the first blow to the agricultural labourer. —*Letters of a Norfolk Farmer to Sir Robert Peel, in the Examiner.*

[a] Unhappily, while other classes were progressing, the moral and physical condition of the labourer was retrograding. In order to understand this retrogression, and its effect upon agriculture, and a naturally honest and industrious class, we must go back 40 or 50 years, when occupations were not so extensive, when the demand for labour was above the supply, and production more adequate to consumption. At that period most of the farm servants were lodged in the houses, the master and servant often worked together, and hence arose mutual respect and attachment, which mutual dependence and mutual aid almost universally create. The system of weekly wages was the first blow towards weakening the ties which had hitherto bound the farm servant to his employer. Expelled from the long cherished "home of the estate," and thus cut off both from those social communications which insure confidence, and that supervision which imposes a wholesome restraint, the labourer sought a new dwelling, too often an improvident marriage, and his interest centered in his own hearth. As a natural consequence population increased, not at first perhaps, in proportion to the demand for labour, but certainly beyond the rate of wages, which underwent no addition corresponding to the rise of prices in the necessaries of life. In almost all the inquiries which have been made on this point, we have almost invariably found the rate of wages *higher in proportion* when the price of corn was low, than when higher prices have been obtained.—*Bacon's Report on the Agriculture of Norfolk.*

rish, Kent, there are 2,700 acres, and a population, in 1827, of 335, being rather more than eight acres to each individual. And yet the number receiving parochial relief was then 129, being more than one-third of the whole amount." Again, it is stated in the Report, that at Palborough, in Sussex, there are 6,000 acres, and a population of 2,000; and yet, though this is three acres each, Mr. Burrell, the witness examined, says, that the poor rates are about 23*s*. a head. At Mildenhall, in Suffolk, it is stated that there were 268 persons paying rates, and 315 unable to pay, with 124 paupers, making 707; and that the number of acres in this parish was 16,000, being rather more than 22 acres to each.

Now, it has been calculated that an acre, properly managed, will maintain five persons; but taking half of this, Mildenhall, instead of being burdened with 707, would afford sustenance to 40,000 persons; and Palborough, instead of 2,000, to not less than 15,000. It is probable that since these reports were published, some difference in these proportions, and in the rates, may have taken place; it is not, however, at all likely that the agricultural population should be in a less distressed state, or that since so much has been done to drive the labourers from the soil, there should be more in proportion to the number of acres. It should also be observed, that the greatest redundancy of population is found where the number of persons is fewest in proportion to the number of acres. The only way in which these redundancies of land, capital, and labour could be brought together, would probably be by giving more facilities to the acquisition of small properties. Yet the views of political economists are in favour of large farms. No doubt they have many advantages, generally those of more skill and capital, but the much greater good will and industry with which a man cultivates land in which he has a direct interest, than that on which he is only a day-labourer, might compensate for these. Nothing tends to form a happy, contented, hard-working peasantry, attached to their country, its institutions, and its aristocracy, so much as a direct interest in the soil they cultivate.

Nor does even the present condition of our manufacturing and commercial interests, though in some respects they are prosperous, indicate a steady advance to that state which produces the greatest well-being to the greatest number; with crises occurring at periods of about six years, when a sudden stagnation comes upon manufacturing prosperity, and indeed on business of every kind, shaking the stability of the largest concerns, ruining numbers of those below them, and bringing destitution and starvation on those they employ. The cause of these crises does not seem satisfactorily explained. They have been partly accounted for by glutted markets, and over-speculation; but a deficiency in that staple article of food, corn, has been most generally contemporaneous with them, forcing the poor, the great consumers, to spend so much less in manufactured articles, and what may be called luxuries. As regards also this numerous and most important part of our population, is it, as a whole, so happy, so healthy, so well fed, and so well clothed, as it was 80 or 100 years ago? No doubt the working classes, when they are in full employment, have more luxuries in their food, dress in finer if not better clothes, and have more comforts than were thought of at that time; but the much larger proportion of the utterly destitute, and the immense amount of suffering which results from any check or depression in commerce, manufactures, or agriculture, felt still more keenly by those who have been accustomed to comfort, if not luxury, more than compensate for these advantages. And unquestionably the price of provisions is higher, in proportion to the rate of wages, than it was at that time. The great question still remains; can that country be in a sound economical state, in which 8 per cent. of the whole population is mainly maintained by public or private charity [a]? To this waste must be added that of fraud and crime, of which it is the fertile source.

[a] By the estimate of the Commissioners for England and Wales, the number of paupers relieved was 1,300,928 in 1831; per centage of pauperism to population, 9.5. Taking the population in 1841, at 15,911,725, as given by the census, this

Our material prosperity, no doubt, blinds us to the many evils attendant on it. We see, belonging to the aristocracy, splendid mansions and magnificent domains, we see the elegant houses of the middle class scattered over the country, or forming part of small towns and villages, we see substantial farm-houses and cultivated fields; we do not see the miserable cottages of the labourers where a man and his family subsist or starve on 10*s.*, 8*s.*, 7*s.*[a] a week, with no hope, either by industry or economy, of improving their condition[b]. We do not attend to the rows of miserable houses springing up in large and small towns, where those who have been driven from the fields by the large farmers or landowners, live or die no one

gives an actual per centage of official pauperism to population of $8\frac{1}{4}$ per cent., or nearly one person out of twelve.

This proportion far exceeds that of any of the other great civilized countries in Europe, except, perhaps, a few exclusively manufacturing districts in France and Belgium.—*Laing*, p. 9.

[a] See Letters from Dorsetshire in the *Times* of July and August, 1846.

[b] The meeting at Goatacre has attracted considerable attention, and informed the country of the state of the agricultural population in Warwickshire. Their state in Oxfordshire may not be so, well known. Mr. Ferguson, the minister of the Independent Church at Bicester, says, in a letter to the *Patriot*, Feb. 28th, 1845,—

"In the village of Upper Arncott, the mud hovels have been built by the peasantry themselves. The height of some of these hovels, from the floor to the ceiling, is from 4 feet 8 inches to 5 feet. They are cold and damp. In several of them from five to nine persons sleep in the same low attic. On the 15th of January I took an experienced tradesman with me, and visited a number of cottages occupied by field labourers in our neighbourhood. In the second we entered, we found three broken chairs, one small table, and one pot. There was something on the damp floor in the shape of a bed, but not bedstead, on which four persons sleep. In the fifth, we found a mixture of boiled flour and water on the table for dinner. The quantity of flour was one pennyworth. The family are eleven in number, and they all sleep in one room or low attic. They pay 1*s.* 6*d.* a week rent. They had only one young man at work, his wages were 4*s.* 6*d.* a week. On the 20th, we visited some of the parish cottages in villages near Bicester, and in Oxfordshire. The first house at which we called is without a roof. Three poor creatures live there, and sleep just behind the door, on a damp cold floor, catching the rain water, which falls during a wet day, through the broken ceiling, which is the only roof on their devoted heads. I declare solemnly that I never entered so wretched a place, inhabited by human beings, in any part of the Highlands or Islands of Scotland. The second hovel is so small, that a man, his wife, and four children are compelled to do with

knows how [a]; so that if the state of the poor in any town in England be inquired into, the answer will generally be, we have more poor here than formerly, and the poor are worse off. We see a large and industrious population, with full employment and good wages, we forget the large proportion who are very insufficiently remunerated [b], and those who have not the means

one bed and bedstead. All the light to the attic comes from a pane of glass 8 inches square. The poor people live rent-free in these dens of woe and wretchedness, but like the poor at Arncott, they drink the muddy and filthy water the ponds supply them.

"The general rate of wages for men with families, is 8*s.* a week. One of the most frugal, who is in constant work, and has a wife and five children, lays out his wages as follows:—

	s.	*d.*
House rent	1	4
Coals	0	9
Potatoes	0	6
Ten loaves of brown bread	4	7
Lard, 2*d.*; bacon, 2*d.*	0	4
Sugar, 3*d.*; coffee, 1*d.*	0	4
Soap and candles	0	2
	8	0

Thus seven persons must be content with less than a loaf and a half each for seven days; or, if they should get more, the baker must suffer; they sometimes leave him and the landlord unpaid to have a few pence to buy beer to drown their sorrows, or a few yards of cotton to hide their nakedness. Many labourers, particularly in the winter half-year, have only a day's work now and then. A gentleman told me, a few days since, that there are 'thousands starving in Oxfordshire.'"

These are a very few of the cases Mr. Ferguson details.

[a] In the back streets of Blandford, I am credibly informed, there are living at this time as many as 90 labouring families who have been driven into the town from the impossibility of procuring dwellings in the country. In the Blandford Union, the average weekly cost per head of the in-door paupers, (men, women, and children,) for the quarter ending March, 1846, was, food, 2*s.* 2¼*d.*; dress, 5¼*d.*—2*s.* 7½*d.* Now this, for four persons, (and a married labourer's family would not average lower,) amounts to 10*s.* 6*d.*, no house rent included.—*Letter to the Times, July 2nd,* 1846.

An economical mode this of maintaining our poor! Might it not be worth while calculating how much more it costs the nation to keep all these people in idleness, than it would to employ them in agricultural labour, or in great public works?

[b] The following may be taken as a fair and impartial general statement of the condition of the population of above two and a half millions, who appear from the returns to derive their subsistence directly from manufactures, under ordinary circum-

of procuring employment, or who, from being long accustomed to seek subsistence by other means, have lost the wish to find it. We see large and increasing towns bearing every outward mark of opulence, crowded ports, and markets filled with all that can minister to the senses or gratify the taste; we do not see, or we do not heed, the heaps of human misery, of destitution, of every form of physical and moral evil, a mass of corruption in the social body hidden by this splendid and prosperous exterior [a]. On the occurrence of a crisis, all this is im-

stances, and in an average state of trade:—about one-third plunged in extreme misery, and hovering on the verge of actual starvation; and one-third or more earning an income something better than the common agricultural labourer, but under circumstances very prejudicial to health, morality, and domestic comfort; viz., by the labour of young children, girls, and mothers of families in crowded factories; and, finally, a third earning high wages, amply sufficient to maintain them in respectability and comfort.—*Laing*, p. 27.

[a] An enlightened and philanthropic foreign writer, (Eugène Buret—"*La Misère des Classes Labourieuses*,") in describing the results of his personal observation in England, says: "That by the side of an opulence, activity, elegance, and wide spread comfort, of which the world has no example, every great city contains a real *ghetto*, a cursed quarter, a hell upon earth; where the reality of misery, depravity, and every hideous form of human suffering and degradation surpasses any thing that the imagination of a Dante ever conceived in describing the abode of devils."

Dr. Kay, speaking of the district called Little Ireland, in Manchester, says: "This district has been frequently the haunt of hordes of thieves and desperadoes who defied the law, and is always inhabited by a class resembling savages in their appetites and habits."

Captain Miller, Superintendent of Police, in his papers relative to the state of crime in Glasgow, respecting the low districts, wynds, and alleys, says: "There is concentrated every thing that is wretched, dissolute, loathsome, and pestilential. These places are filled by a population of many thousands of miserable creatures. (Mr. Symonds estimates them at 30,000.—*Arts and Artizans*, p. 116.) The houses in which they live are unfit even for sties, and every apartment is filled with a promiscuous crowd of men, women, and children, all in the most revolting state of filth and squalor. In these horrid dens, the most abandoned characters of the town are collected, and from thence they nightly issue, to pour upon the town every species of crime and abomination.

"In such receptacles, as they are permitted to remain, crime of every sort may be expected to abound; and unless the evil is speedily and vigorously checked, it must of necessity, increase. The people who dwell in these quarters of the city, re-

measurably increased; then the cry of starvation strikes our ear, and we say, what can be done to save these people? But it passes away, returning prosperity blinds us to its causes and effects, and we do not reflect that in its progress it has caused numbers to fall back on the large and fearfully increasing class of those who have no visible means of living.

M. de Sismondi, seeing these evils strongly, has perhaps underrated the value of manufacturing prosperity, and of the manufacturing population, which he places below the agricultural in morality and intelligence. In this country at least, it is acknowledged to be unquestionably superior; and operatives, working on weekly wages, will probably be found to be so everywhere, when compared to field labourers paid in the same way.

If large towns produce vice, they also give birth to many virtues which can only be there practised. There is also less ignorance, that great source of crime, in large towns. And never ought this country to forget, that in the last crisis, when one of our largest towns was actually in the hands of a mob, when the country seemed to be on the brink of the most dreadful of all insurrections, that caused by hunger and misery, she was saved by the morality, fortitude, and patience of a starving population. Nor has M. de Sismondi done full justice to the higher class of our manufacturers and merchants, than whom there are probably no men who conduct business on higher and more honourable principles, and among whom are many greatly interested in the welfare of those they employ, and anxious to promote it by every means in their power. It is, however, to be feared, that there is also a very large class employing great numbers of persons who are amenable to all M. de Sismondi's

gard themselves, from the hopelessness of their condition, as doomed to a life of wretchedness and crime."—*Laing*, p. 11.

What strikes us most in reading all these harrowing details is, that there are not more desperate crimes; that, on the whole, life and property are so secure; that we walk with safety. Surely human nature is very good, if it were but managed with wisdom, justice, and kindness.

remarks[a]. It also appears on any great depression of the manufacturing interest, how little can be done under the present system, by even the most generous and considerate masters, to relieve evils from which they are themselves suffering.

What then can we look to as the remedy for our social evils? Would M. de Sismondi have us go back, would he stop progress? It always gave him much pain to be so misunderstood, as to have it supposed that he would stop progress, even if he did not know it to be impossible. But he was anxious to show that progress may be too rapid, and must be attended with its

[a] The following account, taken from the report of F. Tancred, Esq., will serve as an illustration of the fundamental truth, which can never be too frequently or too forcibly impressed on our minds, *that increase of wealth is not* necessarily increase of happiness; and that avarice, or, *as it is now christened, accumulation of capital, when it gets an undue ascendancy over moral considerations, invariably produces misery.*

Most of our readers will have heard of the invention of the hot blast, or use of hot air instead of cold air, in the smelting of iron. In Mr. Macculloch's statistical account of the British empire, a splendid picture is given of the rapid extension anticipated for the iron trade of the west of Scotland, in consequence of this improvement. This anticipation has been more than realized; properties worth a few years ago, only a few hundreds a year, now yield the proprietor upwards of £12,000 annually. The population of the two parishes of Old and New Monkland, where the most important of these works are situated, has increased from 19,447, in 1831, to 40,193, in 1841.

So much for the *economical* results; now for the reverse side of the picture.

"At Coatbridge, where a large portion of this population has been located within the last ten years, no church or clergyman has been supplied till very recently, chiefly at the expense of one of the numerous employers of labour in the district. These efforts came, of course too late, as must always be the case, so long as things of this importance are left to accident and chance. In the mean time a population has grown up, immersed more deeply than any I have met with in the disgusting habits of debauchery. Every thing that meets the eye or ear tells of slavish labour, united to brutal intemperance. I visited many of the houses attached to some of the works, and usually found them in a most neglected state, bespeaking an absence of all domestic comfort and attention to social duties. This domestic discomfort seemed attributable, among other causes, to the crowded state of the habitations which, from the want of buildings to contain the rapidly increasing population, were filled with lodgers. An infatuated love of money, for no purpose but to minister to a degrading passion for ardent spirits, seems the all-pervading motive for action in this quarter. I was informed that almost universally, the higher the wages, the greater the discomfort in which the workmen lived, and the sooner, upon the least illness or other cessation of wages, they become destitute."—*Laing*, p. 43.

disadvantages, as well as its advantages; that if monopoly in labour had its evils, yet that the unlimited power of every man to employ his capital, skill, and labour, in the way that appears to him most advantageous to his own interest, instead of being, as was said and expected, a great advantage to labour, by setting it free from all restrictions, has, in fact, given so great a preponderance to capital and skill, that its tendency is to add to the wealth of the rich, and to the destitution of the poor; encouraging the accumulation of property in few hands, and presenting obstacles to its formation among the lower and middle classes. He saw, too, what few sufficiently consider, that no steps can be made in advance, without bringing ruin and suffering to some. The advantages of progress are obvious, as in railways. All see the facilities to commerce, the many social benefits of increased locomotion, the number of persons employed, the towns rising where stations are established. Little attention is paid to the great shock to existing interests, to the loss of capital invested in roads and canals, to the number of persons thrown out of employment, to towns fallen away, rents diminished. These are not reasons for stopping progress, even if in a free country it were possible; but they are reasons for considering that an advance is not productive of unmixed good, and should lead a beneficent legislation, and all wise and good men to watch progress with a prudent regard to the interests of every branch of the community, so as to direct and soften its consequences, that they may be attended with the least possible amount of evil. The improvement of machinery is the greatest step in progress which has been made during the last hundred years; attended, no doubt, with many and great advantages, contributing to the more general diffusion of many comforts and luxuries, producing great wealth to some, and adding generally to the prosperity of the country, but by its immense power of production leading to overstocked markets, one cause, no doubt, of the frequent stagnation of business. It has also been the means of producing what may be called a glut of population [a],

[a] "Capitalists and speculators without capital, in the pursuit of wealth, congregate in vast masses the vital materials which produce wealth, without taking any care for

so that in the best times it is difficult for all to find employment; and a check in any branch of business throws numbers out of employment, which they vainly seek elsewhere. Before they can find it, many have recourse to pauperism, and others fall into the lowest and most destitute class.

There can be little doubt that we are rapidly advancing to a perfect freedom from restrictions on trade, which, with the cheaper and more regular supply of food consequent on the repeal of the Corn Laws, is looked to [a] as the great cure for our social evils; but may it not be well seriously to consider that even were trade as free as the winds to every corner of the earth, yet if merchants and manufacturers look upon markets as unlimited, or only limited by the wants of the consumers, not by their *income* or means of payment, more will be produced than can be sold and consumed in a sufficiently short time to produce profitable returns; markets will be overstocked; and there is too much reason to apprehend that the commercial

the moral or physical being of these essential implements. Whenever such accumulations become pestilential, or otherwise dangerous, they are rooted out by a summary process under the authority of parliament, which, while it will not be slow in honouring the principles involved in such measures, will employ month after month, in determining on rival schemes of unprincipled pillage, or in some speculation. The great living mass, who are the creators of wealth, are in its pursuit trampled down with as much indifference as so many weeds."—*Times*, Dec. 8th, 1844.

[a] "A still more important consideration is, that a repeal of the Corn Laws, even if it were to be attended with all the consequences which the most sanguine of its advocates predict, would evidently, in a few years, bring us back to the point from which we started, with an increased population, and all our difficulties on an enlarged scale, *unless the system on which we have been proceeding for the last fifty years is radically altered.* The rapid increase of manufacturing industry during the war did not prevent, if it did not rather occasion, the misery and distress under which we are now suffering. All the worst evils of ignorance, demoralization, infant and female labour, increase of destitution, grew up simultaneously with a more rapid advance of manufacturing wealth than it is possible to expect from a repeal of the Corn Laws. The temporary prosperity of the period from 1833, to 1836, when profits were high, food cheap, and when our export trade took a new and extensive development, terminated in the crisis of 1837, and the lingering decline under which we have been since suffering."—*Laing*, p. 95.

To all who would thoroughly understand our social state, its evils, and their remedies, an attentive perusal of Mr. Laing's book is earnestly recommended.

and manufacturing interests will still be liable to convulsions and crises, more appalling in their effect in proportion to the greater number of persons brought into the world by the extension of trade and manufactures. May there not also be just reason to fear that free trade will tend to foster the eager desire after wealth, and that anxiety to make large profits, and yet to undersell in foreign markets, which can only be done by producing at the least cost, and must therefore lead to efforts to cheapen labour to the lowest degree that the amount of population and the cost of subsistence render possible?

From this the operatives can alone protect themselves. It is by personal independence only that men can put themselves on an equal footing with their employers, so as to obtain fair and just wages; and a working man can attain independence through prudence, economy, and good conduct alone.

Though labour ought, on true economical principles, to afford sufficient for a man to maintain himself and make some provision for the future, or for a family, yet it has been found that a high rate of wages, particularly if uncertain, has been more generally productive of vice and extravagance in the workmen, than of any provision against an evil day, or of any improvement in the condition of those who obtain them. So that those, who, when business is prosperous, can get from one to even five pounds a week, which the most skilful operatives in the Birmingham manufactures sometimes do, will not be found at a time of depression to be at all better off than those who only get from twelve to twenty shillings. Frequently, indeed, the economy which is forced upon the latter, and the less power they have of indulging in vice and luxuries, will place them in a better situation. This recklessness is much increased by a dependence on public and private charity, and by there being so little stability in the rate of wages. It might be hoped that the very severe sufferings caused by the crisis of 1842 would teach the operatives a lesson of prudence, but it is very doubtful whether this has been the case, and whether, were the same depression to recur, it would not produce as much misery. Could, therefore, the request of a fair day's wages for a fair day's work be granted on the moment to all men willing and able to work, this alone would not prevent the recurrence of want and misery, unless with this they were more strongly impressed with a sense of their own responsibilities, made to feel that, in regard to all the ordinary circumstances of life, they must depend only on themselves, and taught that they must apportion their outlay to their means, and provide not only for present expenses, and for the future ones which they may bring upon themselves, but for contingencies and old age; unless, in a word, means are provided, not only for instruction, but for education, in all knowledge which tends to make men wiser, happier, and better.

It is to be hoped that one of the best effects of the repeal of the Corn Laws may be, that it will tend to relieve the present very depressed state of the agricultural interest, involving all those who combine to form it; landed proprietors, farmers, and labourers. Certainly protection exercised no beneficial influence for it.

It does not seem possible to point out one period since the Corn Laws were laid on, in which there were not complaints of the small profits, even losses, of farming. Probably this may in a great degree be attributed to the undue expectations which the Corn Law was calculated to excite. Landowners let their land on the high rents which it was expected a high price of corn would afford, and proportioned their expenses to these expectations; which being disappointed, has no doubt led to so much of the land being mortgaged, and to small proprietors being obliged to sell their estates. Farmers took land on the same expectation; those who had capital lost it, and persons who had knowledge and capital not being willing to engage in unprofitable concerns, tenant farming has been more generally undertaken by a lower class, without capital, who, not improving in the science of cultivation, and not able to calculate what rent farm profits would enable them to give, have incurred such great losses, that generous landlords have been continually giving back part of the rent agreed on. To all this must be added the system of tenants at will, adopted for the sake of obtaining political power. Short leases, uncertain tenures, and small capital, must necessarily lead to farming on a system of small yearly profits, without regard to the permanent interest of the land; now, in such an old country as this, its fertility can only be kept up by a system of cultivation which looks forward, by laying out money, the profit of which can only be reaped in the course of a few years. Land, therefore, becomes deteriorated, and each succeeding tenant will give less for land in a worse state of cultivation. All this presses most heavily on the labourers, fewer of whom are employed in cultivation at lower wages, and who are driven more and more from the fields. The repeal of the Corn Laws must lead to such contracts between landlords and tenants as will probably result in greater ultimate advantage to both. Men with more skill and capital will be induced to take land; at least there will be an end to uncertain and over-estimated expectation. It might, perhaps, be worth considering on this subject, whether a small share in the profits of agriculture, instead of mere weekly wages, if it could be arranged, might not be made to do away with much of that want of honesty and want of industry which is often complained of in farm labourers, and in agents and overlookers [a]

[a] If, on a subject on which almost every thinker has his Utopia, we might be permitted to have ours; if we might point to the principle on which, at some distant date, we place our chief hope for healing the widening breach between those who toil and those who live on the produce of former toil, it would be that of raising the labourer from a receiver of hire, a mere bought instrument in the work of production, having no residuary interest in the work itself, to the position of being in some sort a partner in it. The plan of remunerating subordinates in whom trust must be reposed, by a commission on the returns instead of only a fixed salary, is already familiar in mercantile concerns, on the ground of its utility to the employer. The wisdom, even in a worldly sense, of associating the interests of the agent with the end he is employed to attain, is so universally recognised in theory, that it is not chimerical to expect it may one day be more extensively exemplified in practice. In some form of this policy we see the only or the most practical means of harmonizing the rights of industry and those of property; of making the employers the real chiefs of the people, leading and guiding them in a work in which they also are interested; a

Notwithstanding, however, the many evils and sufferings of our social state, we are a wealthy, prosperous, intelligent, and, on the whole, moral people. To what do we owe these great advantages? They existed before the introduction of those theories and maxims of political economy which have only been discovered and acted upon during the course of the last hundred years, and which, though they have brought to light many errors, and relieved the country from some evils, have no doubt, as far as they have been followed out, been productive of others. It is not to them, then, that we owe our advantage, but first to the superiority of our race, combining more

work of co-operation, not of mere living and servitude; and justifying by the superior capacity in which they contribute to the work, the higher remuneration which they receive for their share of it.

In the able and interesting Lettres Politiques of Mr. Charles Duveyrier, some account is given of an attempt which has been successfully made to carry this principle into practice on a small scale by an employer of labour at Paris. The name of the individual is Leclaire, his occupation that of a house-painter, and he has made his proceedings public in a pamphlet, entitled "Repartition des Bénéfices du travail en 1842." M. Leclaire pays his labourers and other employés by fixed salaries or weekly wages, in the usual manner. He assigns also to himself a fixed allowance. The result has been most prosperous both to himself and to his labourers, not one of whom, who worked as much as three hundred days, obtained in the year of which he has published the accounts less than 1500 francs (£60), and some considerably more.

In the mining districts of Cornwall, the working miners are invariably joint adventurers in the concern, and for intelligence, independence, and good conduct, as well as prosperous circumstances, no labouring population in the island is understood to be better than the Cornish miners.—*Edinburgh Review for Oct.* 1845.

Lord Wallscourt has long pursued a similar plan in the cultivation of his estates in Ireland, and its operation has been such as to stimulate the supine Irish peasant into active industry, and to shed prosperity and gladness over a district that was formerly the abode of famine and despair. In reply to our inquiries, Lord Wallscourt says, "I have tried the plan for seventeen years, and have found it to answer much beyond my hopes; inasmuch as it completely identifies the workmen with the success of the farm, besides giving me full liberty to travel on the Continent for a year at a time; and on my return, I have always found that the farm had prospered more than when I was present." Lord Wallscourt's practice is to reckon every man the investor of as much capital as will yield, at five per cent. per annum, the sum paid to him in wages."—*Treatise on the Steam Engine, by the Artizan Club; quoted in the Atlas, July* 18*th*, 1846.

intellectual and physical power than any other nation in Europe, and next, to our having enjoyed for so much longer a period than any other country the blessings of freedom, personal, political, and religious. M. de Sismondi has shown in his Introduction, that the sufferings and low state of the working classes in the middle ages were owing to personal and political oppression, rather than to any defect in the system of political economy. When relieved from this political oppression, the middle and lower classes rose in importance, and acquired wealth with a rapidity and to an extent not known in our days.

It may perhaps be permitted here to advert to some other evils in this country, which seem caused, in some degree at least, by an undoubted confidence in, and great admiration for, the principles of political economy. As the wealth, the prosperity, the happiness of a nation must be made up of the aggregate wealth, prosperity, and happiness of individuals, each individual will consider that in whatever degree he acquires any of these, he is adding something, however small it may be, to the wealth, prosperity, and happiness of the nation. If wealth be taken as the test of a nation's prosperity, as the sign of her greatness, there will be added, in the minds of many men, to the strong natural love of acquisition, the idea, that by a man's increasing his wealth he is performing a duty to his country, adding to her glory and prosperity; or should this be too far fetched a consideration to influence men individually, yet there can be little doubt that wealth being taken as the great sign of national prosperity, has led to the very high estimation in which it is held in this country. It was said by a wise man, Sydney Smith, that in England, "*poverty is infamous*." Without going so far as to say that it is a crime to be poor, yet it cannot be denied, that in this, more than in any other country, respectability is almost universally connected with the idea of wealth; that to want riches according to the station in which a man lives, is to want consideration. To this may be added a very generally received idea, that in this free country, if a man does not improve his fortune it is his own fault. From this arises the unceasing struggle through all classes of society, except those whose immense possessions place them above it, or whose degradation puts them below it, to become rich, or to appear to be so. The respect and consideration of our fellow-men is one great source of our happiness, a natural and laudable object of our desires; what wonder then at the eager pursuit of what most certainly and universally obtains it. Next to being really possessed of wealth, it is important, for the same reason, to seem to command it. To this may be in a great degree attributed the taste for show, luxury, and expense, the continual competition, the eager desire to outvie others and to step into a higher station, the vexation at not being able to make the same appearance as others, the mortification at being obliged to descend, the cruel neglect with which this is often visited, even where it was not occasioned by any fault. How little in proportion do men generally spend on their own tastes, or even on their own comforts, still less to promote their own real happiness, or that of others; how much to purchase consideration! The highest will not be surpassed or equalled in splendour by those they consider as inferior in wealth and station, and if they see themselves approached, increase their expense to keep in advance; though there is perhaps less of this feeling among the nobility than in any other class; having a decided position, they less require the adventitious circumstance of wealth. The lowest imbibe a taste and value for that show which they are taught by the example of their superiors to consider as all-important. This eager pursuit after wealth leads men to the very verge of dishonesty, too often beyond. It might almost be thought, that the great maxim of political economy is, "Be rich, honestly if you can, at all events, be rich." The anxious desire to be so has often led to fraud and dishonesty, spreading wide ruin and desolation, and producing a great waste of real wealth. The necessity, at all events, to appear rich, is one source of the very prevalent and wasteful system of credit. The merchant, the manufacturer, the tradesman, too often, in the eagerness to be rich, engages in business far more extensive than his means and expectations will justify, and then adds to his embarrassments, and the loss entailed on others, by living in a style which he has no fortune to support, in order to keep up appearances; and not only this, but in every class of society how many are there, who, for the sake of external show, are in debt for the very necessaries of life; not few, it is to be feared, who maintain a brilliant exterior on the simple system of never paying a debt when it can be avoided. It were vain to calculate the immense extent of loss, ruin, and misery consequent on the very extended system of credit pervading all transactions of business and private life in this country, a system in which it may be said that those who will so extensively give credit, are often as much to blame as those who require it.

It has been argued that a taste for luxuries is a benefit to the community. Luxuries are no benefit, but an injury, when they are indulged in at the expense of more important considerations; when they lead to expenses beyond means, to deferred payments, to undischarged debts. Besides, the supply of luxuries to the rich employs a very small portion of the working classes of the community; it is the supply of necessaries and comforts to the middle and lower classes which is the great benefit to the producers. In proportion to the greater quantity of these which those classes can command, is the prosperity, not only of commerce, manufacture, and agriculture, but also of the revenue.

The narrow principles of political economy have had another bad effect on our social state. They are applied in every detail of actual business, and men are led to conceive that they are acting according to broad and true principles, and benefiting the community, in seeking their own pecuniary advantage by means which, if deprived of the sanction of this system, would be acknowledged to be harsh and oppressive. Labour is a purchasable commodity, to be purchased according to its value in the market. No doubt, following the strict principles of political economy it is; but by accustoming men to consider it in this abstract point of view, apart from the human beings whose only possession it is, they are led to think they have a right, a right which they can justly and innocently exercise, to take advantage of those who are forced by the most imperious necessity to dispose of this possession, in order to obtain it at the lowest price, and to employ it solely for their own advantage in enriching themselves [a]. This idea has been acted upon in this country to an extent involving extreme cruelty and oppression, the grinding down the most defenceless of our species in manufactories and in trades, to the lowest wants of subsistence [b].

[a] The *Birmingham Pilot* gives a long report of an important public meeting, upwards of one thousand persons being present, lately held in that town, to hear an exposition of the grievances which oppress the journeymen tailors from the unjust and inadequate wages they receive from their employers. The following remarks are judicious, and cannot be too widely disseminated: "The superabundance of labour in the market, no doubt, in some measure accounts for the present depressed state of the tailors' trade, but it cannot be denied that the mammon-worshipping hearts of not a few of the employers are more disposed to screw a penny out of the poor man's labour than a shilling out of the rich man's purchase. The labourer, with a starving wife and family, can ill afford to stand out for a fair price if it be grudged, while the rich man, with his golden purse, can shake it in the merchant's face and beat him down to within an inch of the poor man's life. Bad as trade is, and keen as competition has become, we verily believe that, until the avarice by which our capitalists are now actuated be uprooted, the rich man will get richer, and the one shuts himself up in himself, and leaves the other to realize that oppression which drives even wise men mad."—*Extracted from the Patriot, March,* 1845.

[b] At the meeting on behalf of the Society for the Protection of Distressed Needlewomen, the Chairman, Lord Ashley, in his speech said, he "would press on the attention of the meeting the very great evils arising in all directions from the constant and unceasing efforts to obtain every thing which could be made or executed by a human creature at the very lowest minimum of remuneration upon which it was possible for that mortal and immortal creature to exist within the limits of this side the grave. How did this system work upon this wretched class of persons? He knew one instance of a poor woman having toiled consecutively, day after day, for 20 hours, without intermission, and she desisted only because nature would hold out no longer."

Mr. T. Jeffreys observed, "If the number of needlewomen in London was computed, he believed that, permitting them to work only 10 hours a day, instead of, on the average, 14 or 15 hours, the result would be, that there would be fewer workwomen

The dreadful sufferings consequent on this system which have of late years been brought to light, have led to the attempts to lessen them which are objected to on the ground that all interference between the employer and those he employs are contrary to the principles of political economy, and derange the labour market— the labour market! Alas! by this term are we not too often reminded of the slave market? For though these poor creatures are not slaves bought with money, they are often as completely in their employer's power, shackled by that most imperious of all masters, hunger? It should never

in the metropolis than could do the work; consequently, a 10 hours' regulation would have the effect of curing the evil by raising wages. He thought it would be a good thing if they could get the needlewomen to bind themselves together not to work more than a fixed number of hours. He had understood the large house of Silver and Co, and others had said, 'Force us to pay more, and we shall be happy to do so. If you compel the whole body to comply, we shall be very glad.'"

Mr. Redmayne said, "There was a general movement in the present day to shorten the hours of labour. Shopmen, warehousemen, and even carriers, had all demanded, and to some extent succeeded, in shortening their hours of labour. But the weaker sex were left to toil on unremittingly or starve; and were half-starved, notwithstanding their ceaseless work. They could not spare time even to ask for justice. He should like to see a strike among them."

Such societies as this are objected to on the ground that by relieving a part the remainder are thrown into a worse condition: but it does not appear on the principles of the political economists, why some being employed for shorter hours at rather better prices, should be disadvantageous to those who are content to work more for less remuneration, every one, it being allowed, having a right to obtain work on the most advantageous terms. This objection is of weight when work is done in prisons, schools, and workhouses at *less* than the usual rates. All these evils could only be put a stop to by legislative interference; but it would be very difficult to apply it. The great benefit of such associations is, to call public attention to the evil, and it may be hoped, to inspire employers with a more conscientious sense of their duty to those they employ. The very great competition for work of every kind which can be performed by females, and their utter powerlessness to obtain fair and just terms for themselves, often throw them as completely into the power of their employers as if they were slaves; and it is to be feared that many of these, in not giving sufficient remuneration to support life, act upon the same principle, though probably not acknowledged to their own minds, as the holders of slaves before the abolition of the slave-trade: that it is cheaper to work them out and get fresh, knowing that however great may be the number which every year die from too hard work, or insufficient nourishment, there will always be enough left to take all the employment they can furnish them with.

be forgotten that the labour market is essentially different from all other markets; as regards every other commodity, it is more or less at the option of the seller whether he will dispose of it or not; if he does not think a just price is offered, he can refuse, or he can wait; but the commodity which the working man brings is *life;* he must sell it or die. Why, then, it is said, limit the quantity of this commodity which a working man has to dispose of; why prevent his obtaining as much as he can, by selling all he can find a purchaser for? Because it has been found by experience, that from this simple reason of being obliged to sell it at any rate, a working man has not the power to make such a bargain as will secure an advantage proportionate to the quantity he disposes of. Because it has been found that many men, still more women and children, have consented to work fourteen, even sixteen hours a day, for bare subsistence; and if the legislature steps in and forbids their working more than twelve or ten hours a day, they must gain bare subsistence or they could not work at all. But then, say the political economists, men must be taught not to produce so much of a commodity as materially depreciates its value. Is it possible to make this abstract proposition intelligible to the minds of working men, and if it were, would it not be more impossible to make them act upon it? Was any man, high or low, ever deterred from marrying by the idea that he might reduce the value of the labour market? Besides, this comes with an ill grace from those whose extensive undertakings, and sometimes ruinous speculations, have led to that excess of population, which, when it has served its purpose, or can no longer be employed, is cast aside like a worn out machine. Men, however, may be taught that they bring misery on themselves and others, if they marry without a reasonable prospect of maintaining a family; that a man ought to provide for his wife and children, and not, as is too often the case, depend on their labour for his support; and much may be done to encourage a desire for respectability, and to remove many of the causes which prevent the attaining it.

Probably the present phasis of human affairs, the money making, the wealth creating, if it may be so called, is a necessary step in human progress, as war seems to have been in former times. Till the human mind has made great progress, some strong excitement appears to be necessary to call forth its energies and develop its intellect. For many ages, war, and the love of power, were the exciting principles; gradually the love of money, and of what money will command, have been taking their place. War, with all its evils, had its mission, no doubt. It cultivated that great quality of the human mind, courage, so necessary to the growth of all other high and valuable qualities, and to the defence of all that is dear to man. It sharpened the intellect, it quickened invention. By its conquests it mingled nations together, thus often producing a finer race of men, and developing arts which either nation singly would have been incapable of. It made *man* of value. Men were important as means of attack and defence, and to be secure of men, a certain portion of property was given to them. This is the principle of feudalism, military service in exchange for territorial rights. The requirements of war also led to the invention and protection of many of the arts. The importance of those who invented or improved, and who were occupied in making arms, armour, &c., enabled them to obtain privileges in the towns where they were settled, and this was the origin of municipal rights. Nor was the age of war without its virtues, patriotism, heroism, self-devotion, loyalty, fortitude, the defence of the weak, all those qualities of which chivalry is the beau ideal, and which shows the estimation in which they were held, though so seldom carried out in practice. It is not uninteresting to observe, in reading the histories of the Middle Ages, that periods of peace were in general periods of greater suffering to the lower classes than those of war. Those chiefs who were not called to distant wars, employed their exuberant activity in quarrels with their neighbours, productive of more suffering to their immediate dependants, than when a large body of restless spirits were drawn off and concentrated at one distant point for aggression or defence. When there were no wars, the amusements of kings and princes, and of the high aristocracy, both in large and small states, were more cruel and oppressive to their subjects than their wars. In the short intervals of peace also, men being of less importance, their rights were more wantonly trampled on. Wars of principles, religious or political, led to an inquiry into principles, a self-devotion in their defence, which perhaps no gentler touch could have brought forth. Even the desolating wars of the French revolution, and the flood of Napoleon's victories passing over Europe, have done much good which will be felt when the evils they caused are forgotten. Old institutions which had hung like a dead weight on the progress of society were overthrown. A shaking of heaven and earth, an upheaving of the depths of society, took place, which has taught all governments to have more regard for the interests of the governed. Much remains still to be done, but a fearful storm has cleared the path and brightened the sky.

With those wars, the age of war seems to have passed away; it does not appear probable that Europe can ever again engage in extensive wars: kings may wish it, but nations are opposed to it. Another spirit, not less powerful to excite the mind of man, has taken its place, stimulating exertion, forcing upon almost all men the obligation to labour of different kinds, giving birth every day to new discoveries in science, new inventions in art, opening new roads to intercourse with distant nations, and carrying many blessings, though not unmixed with evils, on the wings of commerce. But this state has also its attendant sufferings; the thousands who die on a field of battle are counted, and the evils of war are proclaimed aloud. The thousands who die in infancy from want of care, in manhood from over work, the devastations of anxiety, destitution, degradation, vice and misery, are not counted, and are generally unknown. The human sacrifices to the love of money may not be quite so great as those to the love of glory, but the worshippers of both consider themselves not only as totally guiltless with respect to the suffering caused by their pursuit, but as deserving the approbation of their country; and that country generally unites in admiring those who have advanced far on the career of fortune, as well as on that of glory, and thinks little of those who have fallen a sacrifice to the pursuit of it.

To what, then, must we look as a counteraction to the evils and sufferings which have seemed necessary to the progress of man? To that spirit of love which was manifested to the world more than 1800 years ago: which, even in the darkest periods of modern history, in the most cruel wars, has produced some alleviations, some gentle virtues, some fruits of love; and in later times has so modified even the spirit of war, that it bears a different aspect to what it did in ancient times. So now only to Christianity can we look to remedy many of the evils of the spirit of this age; of those consequent on the economical principles carried to their full extent. It must penetrate where legislation cannot go; it alone can lead to a full and conscientious discharge of what is due from man to man in every relation of life; it only can insure justice from employers to employed, truth and honesty in the latter, and prevent in every class the sacrifice of these to the pursuit of gain.

We have at the present time every reason to hope that this spirit of love, pervading more and more the whole of society, will eventually prove a remedy for many of its evils. That the well-being of the whole community, and most particularly of that class which is too powerless to assist itself, ought to be the great object of the legislature, is acknowledged on all hands[a]. How that class can be relieved from the state of

[a] "My earnest wish has been, during my term of power, to impress the people of this country with a belief that the legislature was animated by a sincere desire to frame its legislation upon the principles of equity and justice. I have a strong belief that the greatest object which we, or any other government, can contemplate, should be, to elevate the social condition of that class of the people with whom we are brought into no direct relationship by the exercise of the elective franchise.

I wish to convince them, that our object has been so to apportion taxation, that we shall relieve industry and labour from any undue burden, and transfer it, as far

destitution, of physical and moral evil into which it is so deeply fallen, is engaging the earnest attention of society at large. Much is done or attempted wisely, but much more, it is to be feared, with the best intentions, mistakenly. The mistakes seem mainly to arise from our not having yet fully entered into the true spirit of the Christian command, "Do unto others as ye would that others should do unto you." Do *justice:* not *giving* to others of our abundance, not placing ourselves in the superior station of benefactors, and others in the lower one of recipients of our bounty: this is *not* what we should wish others to do to us. We are still too apt to regard those below us as fellow beings to whom we must show kindness, not as fellow men to whom we must grant rights. If, as was well said, property has its duties as well as its rights, labour has its rights as well as its duties. The greatest benefit which can be conferred on the lower classes, is to teach them how, in a truly Christian spirit, to obtain and to use these rights. Let us not deceive ourselves: the age of protection on one side and dependence on the other; the age of alms on one side and humble gratitude on the other; the age of family attachments from the lowly to the great, is passing away. These things in their season brought forth many beautiful fruits, and gave rise to many virtues and good feelings; but any attempt, however benevolent and well-intentioned, to bring them back, is utterly vain. It is an economical age, an age of free exchanges, in order to produce the greatest advantage to both parties. Let it not be supposed that it must therefore necessarily be a cold and calculating age, in which Christian love will die. Does not the purest love, the sweetest affection, spring up where there is equality? not equality of rank, or of wealth, or of intellectual gifts or acquirements, but of *Christian men*, where assistance from those who have to those who want, will be given and received in love; not as now, when alms being too often given in

as is consistent with the public good, to those who are better able to bear it."—*Speech of Sir Robert Peel on the Third Reading of the Corn Importation Bill, May 19th*, 1846.

place of the performance of the higher duty of granting rights, and a general, though perhaps undefined impression of this, having arisen among the lower classes, they are too much received as a right, instead of being accepted as the gift of love.

We already begin to see another field for the exercise of human energy spreading wider and wider every day; another object destined probably to supersede the necessity of the excitement by the love of war, and the love of gain, and to carry on the progress and education of the human mind: another war, affording a grander scope for human effort; another object, demanding as much activity, prudence, and reflection as the love of gain: the war against moral and spiritual evil, conquering the kingdoms of this world, to become the kingdoms of God and of Christ; that combat which was begun by him, and has been carried on by his followers, with varying numbers, and varying success, to the present time; but now the numbers of those engaged in it, and their success, are increasing day by day. Many are making it the great object of gain, to win souls from sin, to produce good out of evil, to carry treasures of moral and intellectual and spiritual light to the dark places of the earth, bringing back no returns, but the sweet hope of having been the means of diminishing human vice and suffering, of having been fellow-workers with Christ.

In the mean time it is well worth serious consideration, whether a stricter application of Christian principle might not be advantageous in an economical as well as a moral and benevolent point of view: whether, instead of the present reckless pursuit after wealth, making it the great object of human energy, more moderation in the desire for it, more conscientiousness in the means by which this desire is to be gratified, might not advance individual as well as national prosperity, with a steadier and more real, if perhaps apparently slower progress; besides diffusing the means of comfort and enjoyment among a far greater number, if in smaller proportions, and saving an immense aggregate of suffering, not only to those who are crushed beneath the wheels of the idol wealth, but to those who, in the rapid race, suffer the alternations of hope and fear, and too often risk all they have on the most uncertain chances: whether greater consideration for the moral and physical welfare of those employed in the creation of wealth would not produce a great advantage to the employer, in work being performed more carefully and industriously, and with a more conscientious regard to his interest, and a saving also to the nation of the great waste caused by vice, destitution, and early death: whether, in short, for nations as well as for individuals, "*godliness be not profitable unto all things, having promise of the life that now is, as well as of that which is to come.*"

PREFACE TO NEW PRINCIPLES

OF

POLITICAL ECONOMY,

AND THE LIGHT WHICH THEY MAY CAST ON THE CRISIS WHICH ENGLAND IS AT THIS TIME EXPERIENCING [a].

It is seven years since I published my *New Principles of Political Economy*, of which I am now preparing a second edition, considerably increased. I do not wish to conceal that this work did not obtain the approbation of men, who are looked upon, with reason at this time, as having made the most signal progress in their science. I must even attribute to their personal respect the delicacy with which they opposed my book. I am not surprised that I have not made a deeper impression. I raised doubts on principles which were looked upon as fixed; I shook the foundations of a science, which, by its simplicity, by the clear and methodical deduction of its laws, appeared to be one of the noblest creations of human intellect. I attacked orthodoxy, as dangerous an enterprise in philosophy as in religion. At the same time I had another disadvantage, I separated myself from friends, in whose political opinions I agreed; I pointed out the dangers of innovations which they recommended; I showed that many institutions which they have long attacked as abuses, had had beneficial consequences; I invoked

[a] Extracted from the *Revue Encyclopédique*, Sept. 1826.

more than once the interference of social power to regulate the progress of wealth, instead of reducing Political Economy to that most simple and apparently most liberal maxim, to *let alone* (*de laisser faire et laisser passer*).

I had no cause for complaint; I waited, for truth is stronger than the spirit of system. If I had deceived myself, the progress of events could not fail to reveal it to me; if, on the contrary, I had discovered new principles, which even in my eyes only then began to acquire importance, facts would not be long in supporting them; and, with all respect for the pontiffs of science, I might say with Galileo, *eppur si muove*.

Seven years have passed, and facts appear to have fought victoriously for me. They have proved, much better than I could have done, that the wise men from whom I have separated myself were in pursuit of a false prosperity; that their theories, wherever they were put in practice, served well enough to increase material wealth, but that they diminished the mass of enjoyment laid up for each individual; that if they tended to make the rich man more rich, they also made the poor man more poor, more dependent, and more destitute. Crises utterly unexpected have succeeded one another in the commercial world; the progress of industry and opulence has not saved the operatives who created this opulence from unheard-of sufferings; facts have not answered either to common expectation, or to the predictions of philosophers; and in spite of the implicit faith which the disciples of Political Economy accord to the instructions of their masters, they are obliged to seek elsewhere new explanations for those phenomena, which diverge so widely from the rules they consider as established.

Among these explanations, those which I had given beforehand have shown themselves entirely conformable to the results. Perhaps to this coincidence may be attributed the more rapid sale of my work, and the demand which has been made for a new edition. It was in England that I performed the task of preparing it. England has given birth to the most celebrated Political Economists; the science is cultivated even at this time with increased ardour; ministers of state, already adepts in the doctrine of public wealth, have been seen attending courses of lectures by the most intelligent professors of Political Economy; its principles are there constantly appealed to in parliament. Universal competition, or the effort always to produce more, and always cheaper, has long been the system in England, a system which I have attacked as dangerous. This system has caused production by manufactures to advance with gigantic steps, but it has from time to time precipitated the manufacturers into frightful distress. It was in presence of these convulsions of wealth that I thought I ought to place myself, to review my reasonings, and compare them with facts.

The study of England has confirmed me in my "New Principles." In this astonishing country, which seems to be submitted to a great experiment for the instruction of the rest of the world, I have seen production increasing whilst enjoyments were diminishing. The mass of the nation here, no less than philosophers, seems to forget that the increase of wealth is not the end in political economy, but its instrument in procuring the happiness of all. I sought for this happiness in every class, and I could nowhere find it. The high English aristocracy has indeed arrived to a degree of wealth and luxury which surpasses all that can be seen in other nations; nevertheless it does not itself enjoy the opulence which it seems to have acquired at the expense of the other classes; security is wanting, and in every family most of the individuals experience privation rather than abundance. If I go into houses whose splendour is perfectly regal, I hear the heads of the families affirm, that if the corn monopoly is suppressed their fortunes will be annihilated, for that their estates, which extend over whole provinces, will no longer pay the expense of cultivation. Around these heads I see families of children, more numerous than the aristocratic class elsewhere affords any example of; many have ten, twelve, or even more, but all the younger sons, all the daughters, are sacrificed to the vanity of the eldest; each one's capital is not equal to one year's rent of the oldest brother; they must grow old in celibacy, and they pay dearly by the dependence of their later years for the luxury of their early ones.

Below this titled and not titled aristocracy, I see commerce occupy a distinguished rank; its enterprises embrace the whole world; its agents brave the ices of the poles, and the heats of the equator, whilst every one of its leading men, meeting on Exchange, can dispose of thousands. At the same time, in the streets of London, and in those of the other great towns of England, the shops display goods sufficient for the consumption of the world. But have riches secured to the English merchant the kind of happiness which they ought to ensure him? No: in no country are failures so frequent, nowhere are those colossal fortunes, sufficient in themselves to supply a public loan, to uphold an empire or a republic, overthrown with so much rapidity. All complain that business is scarce, difficult, not remunerative. Twice, within an interval of a few years, a terrible crisis has ruined part of the bankers, and spread desolation among all the English manufacturers. At the same time another crisis has ruined the farmers, and been felt in its rebound by retail dealers. On the other hand, commerce, in spite of its immense extent, has ceased to call for young men who have their fortunes to make; every place is occupied in the superior ranks of society no less than in the inferior; the greater number offer their labour in vain, without being able to obtain remuneration.

Has, then, this national opulence, whose material progress strikes every eye, nevertheless tended to the advantage of the poor? Not so. The people of England are destitute of comfort now, and of security for the future. There are no longer yeomen, they have been obliged to become day-labourers. In the towns there are scarcely any longer artisans, or independent heads of a small business, but only manufacturers. The *operative,* to employ a word which the system has created, does not know what it is to have a station; he only gains wages, and as these wages cannot suffice for all seasons, he is almost every year reduced to ask alms from the poor-rates.

This opulent nation has found it more economical to sell all the gold and silver which she possessed, to do without coin, and to depend entirely on a paper circulation; she has thus voluntarily deprived herself of the most valuable of all the advantages of coin; stability of value. The holders of the notes of the provincial banks run the risk every day of being ruined by frequent, and, as it were, epidemic failures of the bankers, and the whole state is exposed to a convulsion in the fortune of every individual, if an invasion or a revolution should shake the credit of a national bank. The English nation has found it most economical to give up those modes of cultivation which require much hand-labour, and she has dismissed half the cultivators who lived in her fields; she has found it more economical to supersede workmen by steam-engines; she has dismissed, then employed, then dismissed again, the operatives in towns, and weavers giving place to power-looms, are now sinking under famine; she has found it more economical to reduce all working people to the lowest possible wages on which they can subsist; and these working people being no longer anything but a rabble, have not feared plunging into still deeper misery by the addition of an increasing family. She has found it more economical to feed the Irish with potatoes, and clothe them in rags; and now every packet brings legions of Irish, who, working for less than the English, drive them from every employment. What is the fruit of this immense accumulation of wealth? Have they had any other effect than to make every class partake of care, privation, and the danger of complete ruin? Has not England, by forgetting men for things, sacrificed the end to the means?

The example of England is so much the more striking, because she is a free, enlightened, well-governed nation, because all her sufferings proceed only from having followed a false economical system. No doubt foreigners are struck in England with the arrogant pretensions of the aristocracy, and the accumulation of wealth in the same hands tends continually to increase it. In no country, however, is the independence of every class of the nation better secured; in no country does the poor man, with a deference which surprises us, preserve at the bottom of his heart a greater consciousness of his own dignity; in no country does the feeling of confidence in the law, and respect for its authority, more pervade all classes; in no country is the feeling of commiseration more general; in no country are the rich more eager to assist every kind of distress; in no country are the ministers of state more enlightened, more earnest in seeking the general good, more skilful in discovering it. Are, then, so many means, so many virtues, useless in human society?

Yes, when they have the misfortune to be engaged in a false direction. England, more free, more enlightened, more powerful than other nations, has only sooner arrived at the consequences of the error which she has been led to pursue. Her vital strength and the talents of her statesmen will assist her, when she has a strong wish to do so, to return more easily than any other nation into the good path. But science has its prejudices, nations have their habits, and even at this day, in their distress, the English take no measure which does not tend to aggravate it.

I have endeavoured to establish in the book which I shall soon present anew to the public, that for riches to contribute to the happiness of all, being, as they are, the sign of all the material enjoyments of man, their increase must be in conformity to the increase of population, and that they must be distributed among this population, in proportions which cannot be disturbed without extreme danger. I propose to show that it is necessary for the happiness of all, that income should increase with capital, and that the population should not go beyond the income upon which it has to subsist; that consumption should increase with the population, and that reproduction should be equally proportioned to the capital which produces it and to the population which consumes it. I show at the same time that each of these relations may be disturbed independently of the others; that income often does not increase in proportion to capital; that population may increase without income being augmented; that a population more numerous, but more wretched, may require less for its consumption; that reproduction, in short, may be proportional to the capital to which it owes its returns, and not to the population which demands it; but that whenever any of these relations are disturbed, social suffering ensues.

It is on this proposition that my new principles are founded, it is in the importance that I attach to it, that I differ essentially from those philosophers, who in our time have professed in so brilliant a manner the economical sciences, from Say, Ricardo, Malthus, and Macculloch. These philosophers appear to me constantly to have put aside the obstacles which embarrassed them in the building up of their theories, and to have arrived at false conclusions from not having distinguished things which it gave them trouble to distinguish. All the modern economists, in fact, have allowed that the fortune of the public, being only the aggregation of private fortunes, has its origin, is augmented, distributed, and destroyed by the same means as the fortune of each individual. They all know perfectly well, that in a private fortune, the most important fact to consider is the income, and that by the income must be regulated consumption or expenditure, or the capital will be destroyed. But as, in the fortune of the public, the capital of one becomes the income of another, they have been perplexed to decide what was capital, and what income, and they have therefore found it more simple to leave the latter entirely out of their calculations.

By neglecting a quality so essential to be determined, Say and Ricardo have arrived at the conclusion, that consumption is an unlimited power, or at least having no limits but those of production, whilst it is in fact limited by income. They announced that whatever abundance might be produced, it would always find consumers, and they have encouraged the producers to cause that glut in the markets, which at this time occasions the distress of the civilized world; whereas they should have forewarned the producers that they could only reckon on those producers who possessed income, and every increase of production, which is not met by a corresponding increase of income, causes loss to some one. From the same forgetfulness, Mr. Malthus, in pointing out the danger of unregulated increase of population, has assigned it no limit but the quantity of subsistence which the earth can produce, a quantity which will be long susceptible of increasing with extreme rapidity; whereas, if he had taken income into consideration, he would soon have seen that it is the disproportion between the labouring population and their income which causes all their sufferings. Mr. Macculloch, in a little essay intended to enlighten the people on the question of wages, affirms that the wages of the poor are necessarily regulated by the relation between population and capital, whereas wages being dependent on the quantity of labour in demand, must also be in proportion to consumption, which is itself proportioned to income. In the same writing he exhorts the poor man to apportion the increase of his family to the increase of the nation's capital, of which it is impossible for him to form even the most confused idea; whereas, he might have observed that every man, when he marries, is always bound to regulate his family according to his own income; from whence it is easy to draw the conclusion, that it is enough for the nation, for all men to regulate their expenses by their income, and that nation in which the very poorest have something, and can tell the income which they shall transmit to their children, will run no risk of suffering from an ill-regulated increase of population.

I think, then, that I may re-publish with confidence my New Principles of Political Economy, not such as they were, but such as I have been enabled to complete them, by observing the great struggle among all the interests of persons engaged in industrial occupations. Their somewhat vague title might lead to the supposition that I only intended them to be a new manual of the rudiments of this science. I carry my pretensions farther. I think I have placed Political Economy on a new basis, whether it be the ascertainment of general income, or the investigation of what distribution of this income will spread the most happiness throughout the nation, and consequently best attain the end of the science.

Other principles, equally new, but of less general application, again flow from these. I have shown that territorial wealth is more productive in proportion to the greater share which the cultivator has in the property of the soil; that the laws intended to preserve their patrimonies to old families caused the ruin of these very families; that that equilibrium among the gains of rival occupations, on which modern economists have founded their calculations, has never been attained, except by the destruction of fixed capital, and the mortality of the workmen engaged in a losing manufacture; that, although the invention of machines, which increase the power of man, may be a benefit to humanity, yet the unjust distribution which we make of profits obtained by their means, changes them into scourges to the poor; that the metallic currency of a nation is, of all its public expenditure, the most useful, of all its magnificence the most national; that the public funds are nothing but an imaginary capital, an assignment-mortgage on the income arising from labour and industry; that the natural limits of population are always respected by men who have something, and always passed over by men who have nothing. Let me not then be accused of having wished to make retrograde steps in this science; it is forward on the contrary, to new ground, that I have carried it. It is thither, I earnestly entreat, that I may be followed, in the name of those calamities which, at the present day, afflict so large a number of our brethren, and which the old principles of this science teach us neither to understand nor to prevent.

The criticisms to which the first edition of my new principles were subjected have not been lost on me. I have almost entirely re-cast this work. Most frequently I have endeavoured to elucidate what might have been left obscure, by fixing the attention of my readers on England. In the crisis which she is now experiencing, I wished to show both the cause of our present sufferings, by the connection which exists among the various industrial labours of the world, and the history of our own future, if we continue to act upon the principles which she has followed. But I have also sometimes shown my deference to criticisms which appear to me to be just, by suppressions or alterations. Nevertheless, I think I ought to protest against the often light, often false mode, in which a work on the social sciences is judged in the world. The problem which they offer us to be resolved, involves very different elements from all those which arise out of the natural sciences, at the same time that it is addressed to the heart as well as to the reason. The observer is called upon to take cognizance of cruel sufferings, of unjust sufferings, which proceed from man, and of which man is the victim. We cannot consider them coldly, and pass them over without seeking some remedy. These remedies will sometimes shock the feelings or the prejudices of readers; they will be sometimes superfluous or inapplicable. These are so many errors, no doubt, but they are errors not so much in Political Economy as in the administration of it. The author or the reader may be mistaken as to its application, because all the circumstances which are the basis of this application are not met with in the book. The deduction of principles cannot, however, be shaken by some corollaries open to controversy, or to ridicule. If its principles are true, if they are new, if they are fruitful, they will, in spite of some errors, real or supposed, advance social science, the most important of all sciences, for it is that of the happiness of man.

INTRODUCTION

TO

INQUIRIES INTO POLITICAL ECONOMY.

THE first attention of society must be given to the securing of its material interests, of its subsistence; and we wish to endeavour to discover what path must be followed in order that the material wealth which labour creates may procure and maintain the greatest well-being for all: it is this, which, according to the etymology of the word, we call political economy, for it is the law or the rule of the house or of the city.

Let us not be reproached with lowering man to the level of the brutes by propósing, as the first object of his efforts, the direction of that labour which secures his subsistence, in calling the attention of society, before everything else, to advantages simply material: it will soon be seen that, more than any of our forerunners, we consider political economy in its relations with the soul, and with the intellect. But subsistence is necessary to life, and with life, to all the moral developments, all the intellectual developments, of which the human race is susceptible. Society, as well as individuals, must consider bodily health before any thing else, must provide in the first place for its wants and its development; for without the vigour which this health supplies, without the leisure, which only begins when these wants are satisfied, the health of the mind is impossible. Facts present themselves on every side to convince us that the manner in which society provides for its subsistence, decides at the same time on the wretchedness or comfort of the greatest number; on the health, the beauty, the vigour of the race, or its degeneracy; on the feelings of sympathy or jealousy with which fellow men look upon one another as brothers eager to assist one another, or as rivals furious to destroy one another; on that activity of mind, lastly, which is developed by a happy mixture of leisure, and which puts all on the way of progress in intelligence, imagination, and taste; or that enervating languor which luxury produces in some, and the brutishness which results to others from the abuse of physical strength and from fatigue.

That product of human labour, which, with subsistence, represents all the material good which man can enjoy, and almost all the intellectual good to which he can only attain by the help of the first, has been called wealth. Wealth, or the theory of the increase of wealth, has been regarded as the special object of political economy, an object better designated, since the time of Aristotle, by the name of *chresmatistique* (chresmatistic). Ideas are not made clearer by disputes upon words, and we should not bring this forward, if it did not serve to define precisely the course of the false direction which has been followed, in our time, in one branch of social science. This science has always had, and must always have for its object, men gathered together in society; economy, according to the proper sense of the word, is the regulation of the house; political economy is the regulation of the house applied to the city: these are the two great human associations, the primitive associations which are the object of the science; all proceeds from man, all must relate to man, and to man united by a common tie. But wealth is an attribute, shall we say, of man, or of things? Wealth is a term of comparison which has no sense, if it is not distinctly expressed at the same time to what it relates. Wealth, which is an appreciation of material things, is at the same time an abstraction, and chresmatistics, or the scienc of the increase of wealth, having considered it abstractedly an not with relation to man and to society, has raised its edific on a basis which is dissipated into air.

Wealth, we have said, is the product of human labour, which procures for man all the material good which he wishes to enjoy; it is the representation of all physical enjoyments, and also of all the moral enjoyments which proceed from them. Very well; but for whom? This question should never be lost sight of, whilst, on the contrary, it never presents itself to theorists. For whom? According to the answer which is given to this question, man himself belongs to wealth, or wealth belongs to man

The Shah of Persia esteems himself rich, because he reckons as his wealth all the inhabitants of his vast empire, who are his slaves, and all their goods, which he can take from them whenever he chooses. St. Domingo was formerly called a rich colony, because only the forty thousand whites who inhabited it were considered, and the four hundred thousand slaves who laboured for them were reckoned as their property. The cotton trade in England is called a rich business, for it brings colossal fortunes to the merchant who imports it, to the manufacturer who fabricates it in immense factories, to the seller who sends it all over the world; but no account is taken of the cultivator, who, whilst producing cotton, remains himself in slavery or indigence; of the weaver, who scarcely satisfies his hunger whilst he works, or dies of hunger when work is interrupted. In our eyes, we do not hesitate to say so, national wealth is the participation OF ALL in the advantages of life. It is in various proportions, without doubt, that the members of the community are called upon to divide the product of social labour, but we shall never call wealth the share which one member takes from another.

At the first view of the question, every one thinks he comprehends clearly what wealth is, and the effects of wealth on society; every one thinks he comprehends how it modifies the condition of the poorest and of the richest; but the more closely it is looked at, the more do contradictory phenomena, which to a certain point balance one another, embarrass the judgment. It is because wealth is not an essence, but an attribute, and its nature changes with the persons and the things to which it is attributed. As satisfying our wants, as the source of our physical enjoyments, the idea which we form of it is sufficiently precise, but then it admits of very few degrees. To form a conception of the increase of wealth when our wants are satisfied, we must go out of ourselves and consider the value of things, either by the distinction they confer by marking rank in society, or by the labour which has been devoted to obtaining them; and as these two appreciations are not even commensurable, as our minds continually vibrate from one to the other, we often end by asking ourselves what there is in wealth which is real, and whether, after having enriched ourselves, we do not remain poorer than we were before.

In fact, all artificial productions are valued more cheaply in a rich nation than in a poor nation: thus, whilst we call ourselves richer than our forefathers, all our manufactured commodities cost us much less. Is it true, then, that we have become richer by accumulating more? How shall we compare, for example, the different kinds of stuffs which have succeeded one another in our dress? How shall we decide, by what we spend on them, whether we are richer or poorer? So far as they satisfy real wants, their utility is nearly the same, but since they have been obtained with less labour, they are of less value; since they can be exchanged for less of the means of subsistence, they are also of less value; and under that point of view in which they principally flatter the passions of the rich as a distinction of rank, they are of still less value, for the price of the most magnificent dress is more within reach of the inferior conditions of society than it was at any preceding period. It is asserted, however, that the introduction of a new manufacture enriches the country; that when, with the same labour, ten times, a hundred times more yards of stuff have been produced, ten times, a hundred times more wealth has been created; but what becomes of this wealth in its application to the wants of society? what becomes of it if we endeavour to draw up a balance sheet of the affairs of the nation? Does it really diminish in proportion as its exchangeable value diminishes? and then what is the real utility of all those modern inventions of art, of which we are so proud?

In fact, we lose ourselves whenever we attempt to consider wealth abstractedly. Wealth is a modification of the state of man: it is only by referring it to man that we can form a clear idea of it. Wealth is the abundance of things which the labour of man produces, and which the wants of man consume. A truly rich nation would be one in which this abundance would produce the most material enjoyment, to the poor on one side, to the rich on the other.

Let us endeavour to form a rather more precise idea of these wants, of these desires, of these enjoyments of the human race, to which is attached the happiness of communities. The enjoyments of the poor are composed of the abundance, of the variety, and of the wholesomeness of their nourishment, of the sufficiency of clothes relative to the climate, and of their cleanliness; of the convenience and of the salubrity of their lodging, also as regards the climate and the quantity of fuel which it requires; lastly, of the certainty that the future will not be inferior to the present, and that a poor man can by the same labour obtain at least the same enjoyment. No nation can be considered as prosperous, if the condition of the poor, who form a part of it, is not secure under the four relations which we have just enumerated. Subsistence in this degree is the common right of man, and should be secured to all those who do what they can to forward common labour; and the nation is so much the more prosperous, the more every individual is assured of having a share in these comforts of the poor.

The enjoyments of the rich are composed, in the first place, of these same three wants being satisfied in regard to food, clothing, and lodging, and by the same security for the future continuance of this well-being; but they comprehend a new element, leisure: the subsistence of the rich must be independent of their labour. In satisfying these wants, there is no doubt a sufficiently large latitude. Food, clothing, and lodging may be infinitely better for some than for others. We must not, however, be under an illusion with regard to the enjoyment which is attached to the satisfying of the wants even of the richest. Some are purely sensual, and the philosopher who wishes to appreciate the advantages of wealth to a nation, will not attach too much importance to these, without, however, denying their existence. Others exist only as distinctions, as giving to him who is in possession of them a feeling of superiority over his fellow-creatures. We do not deny this distinction, nor that the respect with which opulence inspires the vulgar, when it is seen displayed on a sumptuous table, in magnificent dresses and equipages, in vast and solid buildings, may not have some political utility; but in appreciating the happiness of a nation, the happiness which wealth gives to the rich, the philosopher will not make more account of the enjoyments of vanity than of those of the senses. He will perhaps make still less account of the third prerogative of wealth in regard to the wants of the human race, that of satisfying its love of change.

But wealth secures to the rich two prerogatives, the advantages of which are reflected throughout the whole of society; one is the employment of their leisure in the development of their intellectual faculties; the other, the employment of their superfluity in the relief of all kinds of wretchedness. It is from these two prerogatives that rich men are necessary to the progress of every nation; whilst a nation which had no rich men, that is to say, no men who can dispose of their leisure and of their superfluity, would rapidly fall into ignorance, barbarism, and selfishness. Let us not be deluded as to the necessarily stupifying consequences of bodily labour and fatigue. Were all the individuals of the nation called upon to exert their muscular force, it would soon be deprived not only of all progress in science and in the fine arts, but in intelligence, taste, mind, and grace. The human cattle might without doubt continually get fatter in their stables, but they would always approach nearer the brutes, they would continually get farther from celestial intelligences. Intellectual progress, however, gives rise to new wants among the rich, and opens a new employment for wealth. Intelligence, imagination, sensibility, require to be satisfied as well as the body, and the search of æsthetic beauty, of moral beauty, of intellectual beauty, attracts towards them a superfluity of human activity, as well as of the wealth which man has produced, and which would otherwise have been unemployed. Charity is another prerogative of wealth, still more important to society than to the poor themselves. It is charity which must repair the accidental disorders which disturb the regular distribution of wealth; but it is charity which, much more, must connect different ranks, substitute affection and gratitude for the contention of interests, spread knowledge with benefits, render all individuals equally participators in the moral superiority acquired by some; lastly, give to the nation that stability which she can only preserve by love among fellow citizens.

To appreciate the influence of the enjoyments of the rich on national happiness, we must take an account not only of their intensity, but of the number of those who participate in them. If we suppose that, after having provided for the necessities of all, the superfluity of the nation is reserved to endow the rich, and if it be then asked in what proportion it is desirable to see them rise above the rest, it is easy to answer, in the first place, that it is better to make many happy than only one; that he who unites ten shares sufficient to secure ease and leisure to ten families, will not himself be as happy as these ten families would have been; but it will soon be acknowledged also, that for the nation, for the social object of their pre-eminence, many moderately rich are worth more than one rich man in opulence. If the vocation of the rich man is especially to develop his intelligence for the good of all, it must not be forgotten that though labour brutifies, it is true, yet that luxury enervates, so that the beneficial influence of the rich on society diminishes not only with the diminution of their number, but with the increase of their wealth, when it goes beyond a certain point. If the second prerogative of wealth is to bind society together by charity, it will be equally felt that the more the number of rich men scattered over the country is diminished, the more distant their residences are by their patrimonies being increased, the more also will they be strangers to the poor whom they ought to assist; the more will the bonds of sympathy be broken by distance of place or of rank; so that even should we suppose that the charities of a *millionaire* would equal those of the ten or the hundred rich men whose patrimonies were united in one, still their moral effect, their social effect, would not be the same [a].

After having thus endeavoured to appreciate at their just value the advantages of wealth, both as regards the poor and the rich, we shall a little better understand, perhaps, what is the distribution of wealth most desirable for happiness and for moral progress, but we shall scarcely have advanced so far as to be able to form a judgment on what enriches or impoverishes a nation, or to discover what effect that which at first appears a progress in wealth must have on general prosperity.

The phenomena which we see before our eyes, far from enlightening our doubts, seem as if they must increase them. In our times, man has made a gigantic progress in industry. With the assistance of the sciences which he cultivates, he has learned to employ as a master the powers of nature; and seconded by the wealth which he has previously accumulated, or by his capital, he produces every year a great mass of things destined for the enjoyment of the human race. The works of

[a] It must have been observed by all who have endeavoured to obtain charitable assistance for the poor, that though there are some whose benevolence is equal to their affluence, yet that generally those are more ready to give to others, and more interested by distress, who feel the pressure of circumstances, than those who are raised above any knowledge of what deprivation is. Those who think most of their own luxuries, think least of the wants of others. "More is given in charity by indigence than by abundance."—*Tr.*

man multiply, and change the face of the earth; warehouses are filled; in workshops we admire the power which man has borrowed from the wind, from water, from fire, from steam, to accomplish his own work; the genius with which he has subdued nature, and the rapidity with which he executes industrial labours which formerly would have required ages. Each city, each nation, overflows with wealth, each one wishes to send to its neighbours those commodities which are superabundant, and new discoveries in science allow of their being transported, in spite of the immensity of their weight and of their bulk, with a rapidity truly confounding. It is the triumph of chresmatistics; never has the art of producing and accumulating wealth been pushed so far.

But is it equally the triumph of political economy? Has this rule of the house and of the city provided for the happiness of both one and the other? Man, for whom this wealth is destined, human society, whose material enjoyments it ought to increase, have these gained in ease, have they gained in security, in proportion to this immense development? At the first aspect of this question, it seems so certain that the more things there are destined for the enjoyments of man, the greater share will each one be able to obtain, that we do not give ourselves the trouble to weigh our answer. Nevertheless, if we look at men, and not at things, if we detail human conditions and the advantages which each one of them can reap from wealth, doubt may perhaps enter our minds. Is each man, in his own sphere, we shall ask, more secure of his subsistence, than he was before this great development of industry? Has he more repose at present, more security for the future? Does he enjoy more independence? Is he not only better lodged, better clothed, better fed, but has he gained by the development of the irrational powers more leisure and more aptitude for intellectual developments? Has the proportion between different conditions changed to the advantage or disadvantage of the greater number? Are those who occupy the lowest steps of the scale more or less numerous than formerly? Are there more steps than formerly between the rich and the poor, or are there fewer; and is it more or less easy for the first successively to pass over them? For example, in the country, is it the number of day-labourers, or of that of *métayers* [a], of small farmers, of small proprietors, which has proportionably increased? In towns, is it the number of those who work by the day, or of masters and journeymen, of small heads of workshops, of retail and wholesale dealers, of intermediates between the producer and the consumer, which has in the same way increased? Let us feel well the importance of all these questions, when it is the sum of social happiness at two different periods that we wish to compare. Wealth is realized in enjoyment; but to estimate the mass of national enjoyment, it is almost always at the number of those who participate in it that we must stop, for the enjoyment of the rich man does not increase with his wealth.

We have infinite difficulty in conceiving a social organisation different from our own, and in seeing a past in which we did not live. However, the monuments alone of a country sometimes speak a language to which we cannot refuse to listen. Those which surround us in the place where we are writing this, revivify the past with a power which presents it entire to the imagination. In Italy, from the most opulent city to the lowest village, there is scarcely a house which does not appear superior to the condition of those who inhabit it at this day; not a house which is not superior to what would be required now, even in the most prosperous countries, for men in the condition of those who have built it. Superb Genoa, the city of palaces, was raised by commerce, but let the palaces of Paris and London, which have been raised by modern commerce, be counted,

[a] The contract which constitutes the *métayer, mezzaiuolo,* is the most common form of letting land in Tuscany. The proprietor entrusts to the métayer a house and a (*métairie*) farm of about ten acres, already in a productive state, with the cattle and agricultural capital necessary to improve it. The métayer in return engages to execute without expense, with his family, all the labour which the estate requires, and to content himself, instead of wages, with half the harvests, whilst he consigns the other half to the proprietor.—*Tr.*

let those in all the provinces of England and France be added to them, there will not be found so large a number as decorate this one city; there will not be found one that has the same imposing character of grandeur and magnificence. The opulence of the commercial men of our days has neither past nor future; thus it does not raise monuments. A single state amongst the republics of Italy seems to have reckoned more rich merchants than the two empires which, at this day, hold the sceptre of commerce. But the palaces of the merchants of Venice, of Florence, of Bologna, of Sienna, rivalled in magnificence those of Genoa; whilst the palaces of the military nobility ornamented Milan, Turin, Naples, Placentia, Modena, and Ferrara, more than Paris or London are now ornamented.

Let us descend to a lower condition; let us enter the smallest towns. Even that near which we are living at this moment, Pescia, enjoys, by a rare exception, all the prosperity of industry; we have seen raised there, in our own time, one of the greatest industrial fortunes of Italy; but what strikes us in Pescia, more than the opulence of those newly become rich, are the palaces of the nobility of the towns: such was their denomination. Pescia is a town containing four thousand inhabitants, and there may be counted there forty of these palaces, which, for the dignity of the architecture, the size of the halls, the noble form of the staircases, the vast extent of the apartments, can only be compared to the hotels which the highest aristocracy of France occupy in Paris. It is true that the interior no longer answers to the magnificence of the first design. On the contrary, the owners of the greater number of them can scarcely keep them standing; the furniture has disappeared, the frescoes are spoiled, and the family have retired to the least imposing part of these vast apartments; but does not their first construction speak sufficiently loud? Does it not say that there was a time when men of moderate but independent fortunes were much more numerous than they are now, and that these men had more taste for grandeur and beauty than they have now in the most prosperous countries of Europe?

Let us descend to a still lower condition. By placing ourselves in an elevated situation, near this same city of Pescia, the eye embraces, at one glance, in a radius of eight or ten miles, ten or fifteen of those small towns (*bourgades*), inclosed in walls, which the Italians call *castelli*. This word answers to that of castle (*château*) in so far as it indicates a fortified place, and is associated with the ideas of resistance and independence. But it differs from it, as the security of civil life was different in the middle ages, in France and Italy. The *château* in France was the residence of the only man who formerly was free in the country; of the gentleman who, behind his moats and his walls, secured himself from oppression. The *castello*, in Italy, was the residence of the free men of the country, who associated together to defend themselves, of freemen who had surrounded their abode with a common inclosure, and who had sworn to hasten at the sound of the same bell, to repulse the same enemies. Let us enter these castles; they are mostly in ruins, and contain scarcely more than twenty or thirty houses. But the solid and strong walls of these houses of three or four stories high, have resisted war during five centuries, as well as the injuries of time. In general only one story is inhabited; those who there hide their humble household seem embarrassed with all that space in which they are lost. These houses had been built for men of a very superior condition to those who now inhabit them. They represent an order of men which no longer exists in the community; which is not found in England, in France, in Holland, in countries where workshops seem overflowing with wealth, any more than now in Italy. These men of a straitened but independent condition worked with their own hands, in gathering the fruits of their fields, and of their vines; but they did not divide them with any one; they reckoned on their own influence to direct the councils of their commune, and on their own swords, when necessary, to defend them; they felt such an assurance of the stability of their own fortunes, and of those of their children, that they wished to build houses that might last for ever. The *Val de Nievole*, where these *castelli* arise round Pescia, their little capital, is not larger than the domain of more than one British peer, on which is seen only the magnificent residence of the lord, twenty large farms, and some hundred cottages of the day-labourers [a].

In no other country, without doubt, can be found the traces of such great former prosperity: so in none of those which now flourish can be found so great a diffusion of happiness. Nowhere are to be seen in proportion to their extent, and to their population, so many moderate but independent fortunes, along with so many colossal fortunes in the hands of those who have proved, not only that they had the power of wealth, but also that love of the beautiful which ennobles the use of it. This fact is very important; for the Italians who were so rich, did not employ those powers of nature which science has given us; they did not produce, they did not create wealth, with that rapidity which strikes us in our workshops.

The monuments of architecture may give us some idea of the wealth of towns in former times, or of all that class of men who had leisure and superfluity. But what would be most important to good political economy would be, to know the condition of the poor, to assure us, that provided he laboured, the community would guarantee his finding abundance and security. In general, the dwellings of the people do not resist for ages the injuries of time; their clothes, their food have much less durability. Scarcely any old author has given himself the trouble to make us acquainted with these vulgar things of his age, which excited so little interest. Besides, the political condition of each country continually complicated purely chresmatistic results; oppression, anarchy, war, continually

[a] The *Val de Nievole* contains 158,000 English acres; the domain of the Duke of Sutherland, in Scotland, covers a million.

struck the inferior ranks of society; and their effects must not be confounded with that produced by the creation of wealth.

It is not, however, perhaps impossible to gather among the historians of the middle ages some traits which have escaped them by chance, and which without completely painting to us the inferior ranks of society, will suffice to make us comprehend how much their state differed from what it is at present.

After the cessation of true feudalism, when the lord no longer wanted the peasant to enable him to defend himself in private wars, the most numerous and most oppressed class in the nation was that of villeins, who alone performed all the labours of agriculture. Their condition was not everywhere the same; in France and in Germany the number of serfs of the glebe was small: the rest owed tithes to their clergy; to their lords, taxes, rates, and bodily service; to the king, the *taille* and *corvée* [a], which took from them the greatest part of the revenue of their lands; but these lands were supposed to belong to them. The *taille*, which was an arbitrary imposition, was regulated according to their apparent wealth, their teams, their instruments of agriculture. Thus it induced the peasants to appear more indigent than they really were; and if they were not content with the rudest and coarsest lodging, clothing, and food, at least carefully to hide all that might indicate some ease. The house which they inhabited, the land which they cultivated, remained to them and to their children; in this respect, the foundation of their fortune was not without security, but they had none for their income; the lord and the tax-gatherers in turns took from them the fruits of the ground which had been produced by hard labour, and reduced them to the most frightful distress. This was not all, the troops of the king were placed among them on free quarters, or often threw themselves upon them against the orders of the government. Then, not only did the soldier eat the peasant's broth, but obliged him to

[a] *Taille*, an arbitrary tax; *corvée*, a certain time required for labour on the king's domain, or in public works.—*Tr.*

kill for him the labouring ox. Often he despoiled him after he beat him, to force a ransom from him, and it may be seen in the archives of the states of Languedoc, during the reigns of Henry the Third and Fourth, that these outrages caused the death of a great number of the families of peasants, and that the number of hearths rapidly diminished in the province.

We cannot think of such oppression without shuddering. So much insecurity, so much violence, so much suffering, must have spread through the whole population the seeds of that hatred which burst out at the revolution. The peasant who produced the means of life for the nation, felt that even the right to live was not secured to him; the community acknowledged that he had a property, but did not guarantee it to him; to the feeling of indigence was continually added that of injustice; for it was by violence, by arbitrary conduct, that what he thought belonged to him was every moment taken away from him. But we must not, in respect to the condition of the peasant under the old *régime*, confound political oppression with chresmatistic oppression. As a citizen, the peasant had no guarantee, as a labourer he would not have been ill off. After having paid the rates, the tithes, and the regular taxes, there would have remained sufficient to maintain him in abundance, and in fact it was generally because he had a superfluity that he was exposed to extraordinary extortions. Troops on free quarters could not be sent among the negroes in the colonies, among the Irish cultivators, among the English cottagers, among the day-labourers of any country, among the lowest order. These last are they for whom it is calculated exactly how much is required to keep a man alive, and to enable him to work. Every day his daily pittance is meted out to him: by any extraordinary extortion his life indeed might be taken from him; there is nothing else of which the soldier quartered upon him could rob him.

In despotic states, rights are respected only so far as they are supported by force; now the inhabitants of cities, even the poorest, were not unprovided with a certain force. Even their title of burghers, in its German etymology, means confederates, one answering for another. They were, in effect, united to defend themselves, to obtain justice; they knew that the nobility detested them, despised them, but that nevertheless they feared them; the city had privileges, and burgher magistrates who administered justice, and its great association was divided into a number of small associations, bodies of trades, corporations, which watched over the interests of their members, and who, in a time of need, knew how to defend them sword in hand. The more general anarchy was, the more powerful were these corporations, and the better did they know how to make themselves respected. They yielded, it is true, sometimes,—then woe to the vanquished; for the conqueror joined to the cupidity and the ferocity of the robber the jealousy and the resentment of the gentleman. The cities of Flanders, and those of the bishopric of Liege, experienced this under the dominion of the house of Burgundy. It was then that the liberty and the security of the burghers were at an end; the government became more regular, but less just; the tradesman, the workman was deceived, humiliated, jeered at, by the gentleman who made him work and did not pay him; the burgherships, the corporations were powers, and the king would leave no power standing but his own; they were continually falling away till the revolution which suppressed them.

The spirit of bodies of men is always jealous and exclusive. The burghers and the corporations of trades wished for justice, liberty, equality for themselves, but they did not extend their attention to the whole nation. Jealous of their privileges, they were unwilling to communicate them. They closed the entrance into their community as much as possible; they drove back the inhabitant of the country who wished to become a citizen; they made the conditions of apprenticeship heavy; they granted the privilege of becoming a master tradesman with difficulty; but on the other hand, they wished that all burghers, all masters of trades, should be equal; they did not allow one master to have a great number of workmen under him; in many trades they limited him to one apprentice and one journeyman, and thus they succeeded in maintaining great inferiority in the industry of towns as to the number of hands employed, but great superiority as to the remuneration received from it, compared to the industry of the country.

The burghers had thus reserved for themselves as many monopolies as the trades which they exercised; and they gained from their fellow citizens the benefit of these monopolies: that is to say, they kept the market always imperfectly furnished, they sold dear and with great advantages, they had little zeal to improve what they produced, for they were secure of always finding a sale. They did not compete one with another, they did not undersell, they never lowered wages by competition; and as they had no poor, except the small number which had been made incapable of work by an accident, they supported them themselves; each trade had its purse, and had rarely recourse to the hospitals. These, founded by charitable men, sufficed for the necessities of the population; the number of beds which were found to be in proportion to the indigence of one generation, were also in proportion to those of the following generation. It was never perceived till the revolution, that charitable relief created poverty.

This system considered in relation to things, in relation to the creation of wealth, and according to chresmatistic rules, was, without doubt, bad. It was at the same time an obstacle to abundance, to improvement, and to cheapness; but with regard to persons, have all the effects of destroying it been well calculated? It powerfully restrained the country people, always eager to flow into the towns, even should they lose there their health, their independence, and their happiness. It raised an almost insurmountable obstacle to the unlimited increase of the industrial population, for the number of masters was limited, and no workman married before he became a master. It maintained equality among the masters, securing to each one independence and mediocrity, instead of permitting a single one, collecting in his workshop a hundred workmen, to swallow up the industry of all others. It assured whoever entered the industrial career of sufficient subsistence as soon as he began to work, of a regular though slow progress towards ease, of a secure condition for himself and his family when he had arrived at mature age.

In fact, historic proof is not wanting to establish the truth that all industrial business in the middle ages, and till the fall of the ancient *régime*, was always amply remunerated. Great well-being prevailed among artisans. Historians, so prolix on war, so brief, so ignorant as regards all the other phenomena of the life of nations, never bring the citizens on the stage, except during public calamities. It is the tumult of the *Ciompi* which brings before us the poorest artizans of Florence; the domination of the two Arteveldes, and the quarrel of the *Whitehoods*, which make us acquainted with those of Flanders; the civil wars of the Burgundians and the Armagnacs, and especially of the League, which initiate us into the different orders of burghers in France. It is after reading the memoirs of these stormy periods that we remain convinced of the consideration which good burghers obtained in the community—masters of trades which are now less honourable; of the hereditary easy circumstances which was preserved in their families, of the richness of their dress, which it was necessary to restrain by sumptuary laws,—in short, of the liberal wages which labour always commanded, and of the certainty which workmen felt that they should be well received and well paid in another town, when a violent revolution drove them from their own.

What then is the end of human society? Is it to dazzle the eyes by the immense production of useful and elegant things; to astonish the understanding by the empire which man exercises over nature, and by the precision and rapidity with which inanimate machines execute human work? Is it to cover the sea with vessels, and the land with railways, distributing in every way the productions of an ever-increasing industrial activity? Is it to give to two or three individuals in a hundred thousand the power of disposing of an opulence which would give comfort to all these hundred thousand? In this case we have, without doubt, made immense progress, in comparison with our ancestors; we are rich in invention, rich in activity, rich in scientific power, rich especially in merchandize; for every nation has not only enough for itself, but for all its neighbours. But if the end which society ought to propose to itself, in favouring labour, and securing its fruits, should rather be to secure the developement of man, and of all men; to spread with a beneficent hand through the whole community, though in different proportions, the fruits of the labour of man, those fruits which we call wealth; if these fruits, which comprise moral and intellectual as well as material benefits, ought to be a means of improvement as well as of enjoyment, is it sure that we have approached nearer the object? Is it sure that in searching after wealth we have not forgotten the order and regulation of the house, and of the city, Political Economy?

In all the military monarchies of Europe, property, as well as all the other rights of the citizens, was ill protected, those of the weak not at all. The possessions of poor peasants, of poor artisans, were subjected to vexations and exactions, now only known in the despotic monarchies of the East: it is not by this state of violence, the fruit of a detestable political organization, that we must judge of the reward formerly secured to labour. We have seen that the lowest rank among the inhabitants of the country, the cultivators, were in general proprietors loaded with dues, it is true, but with dues which would have left them a superfluity, if the rapaciousness of the powerful had not often snatched it from them: the lowest rank among the inhabitants of towns, the apprentices and journeymen, were in general well clothed, well fed, well lodged in the house of the master with whom they worked; and they were sure, by assiduity, of becoming masters in their turn, and being then for the rest of their lives sheltered from want.

The order which we have substituted for this, and which the chresmatistic school considers as its triumph, is founded on quite other principles. This school, pursuing as it were abstractedly the increase of wealth, without asking in whose favour this wealth ought to be accumulated, has proposed as the object of nations the production of the greatest possible quantity of work at the cheapest rate. Wealth, it says, is so much of the useful product of labour as is not consumed, which accumulates on the earth: this wealth accumulates in two ways, by more being produced, and less spent. Each member of the community wishes to enrich himself, each one therefore endeavours to increase what he produces, or to diminish the expense of it; each one, individually, thus tends to the common object of human society. Give to all these individual actions their free spring. Far from restraining men either in what they produce or in what they save, let them on the contrary be excited by universal rivalry and competition; let these reign equally amongst all conditions, and all men of every condition: wealth will then be seen to increase, either by the augmentation of production, or the diminution of expense, with an activity which former ages have never known. From hence, in fact, the chresmatistics, or all those who in our time have become celebrated as political economists, have held out to all industrials, to all the undertakers of work of every kind, discourses in favour of the indefinite liberty of industry and trade, in favour of the most animated competition, which may be thus translated:—"Seek your own interest before every thing else; you will find it in being preferred to your rivals, whether as relates to selling or to working; you will find it in making the most lucrative conditions you can with those who wish to serve you; whether they relate to purchasing from them, or to making them work for you. Perhaps you will thus reduce them to indigence, perhaps you will ruin them, perhaps you will destroy their health or their lives. That is not your business: you represent the interest of the consumers; now each one is a consumer in his turn; therefore you represent the interest of all, the national interest. Thus listen to no consideration, let no pity stop you, for perhaps you will be called on to say to your rivals, your death is our life."

This language will appear harsh, no doubt, but it is not more so than the conduct of those rivals, who throughout the whole of Europe have been called on by this new doctrine to supplant one another, to destroy one another. Two modes of acting, equally encouraged by chresmatistism, have begun, wherever free scope has been granted to individual interests. On one hand the object was to create more wealth, more of those things which labour makes, and which man desires to consume. Now, as things only become wealth when they find the consumer who is willing to purchase them in order to use them, and as wants do not increase with production, each industrial wished to occupy the place of his rival, and to take away his customers. Nations rival one another in production, and glory in it. If a Frenchman can dispose of his merchandize in a foreign market, till then reserved to the English, or if the Englishman can exclude the Frenchman, each praises himself, and demands the applause of his countrymen, not merely as having made a good speculation, but as having performed a patriotic action. The same rivalship exists between towns of the same empire, between workshop and workshop of the same town. Everywhere it is equally war to the death: its consequences are the ruin of the heads, the mortality of the subalterns; it overthrows as many fortunes as it raises, and the branch of commerce which flourishes the most, is probably that in which, taken altogether, there have been the most failures, for new fortunes have only risen from the overthrow of older ones. In fact, before the introduction of universal competition, the celebrity of manufactures belonged to their age; the name of the great fabricators was like a title of nobility which they transmitted with pride to their descendants: now antiquity is a title to distrust, and a prognostic of ruin; it is only beginners who are enterprizing, industrious, and who know how to undersell their rivals.

But if each one labours to increase production, each one labours also to produce cheaper, and one of these is the necessary consequence, the completion of the other. Now wealth, we have said, is the fruit of labour: economy in the expense of production can be nothing but economy in the quantity of labour employed to produce, or economy in the payment of this labour. In fact, from one extremity to the other of the countries in which free competition is admitted, the governing idea which is excited, in whoever undertakes productive labour, or whoever pays for it, is to make more things with the same quantity of human labour, or as many things with a less quantity of human labour, or to obtain human labour at a lower price. Now whenever these two first conditions are obtained, the third necessarily follows, for all superabundant hands are thrown on the market, and are obliged to offer themselves at a cheaper rate. Let whatever is called progress in the arts, in manufactures, in agriculture, be examined, and it will be found that every discovery, every improvement, may be reduced to doing as much with less labour, or more with the same labour; all progress tends also to reduce the value and reward of labour, or the ease of those who live only to labour.

The fundamental change which has taken place in society, amidst the universal struggle created by competition, is the introduction of the *proletary* [a] among human conditions, the name of whom, borrowed from the Romans, is ancient, but whose existence is quite new. The proletaries were in the Roman republic men who had nothing, who paid no taxes, and who belonged to the country only by the *proles*, by the offspring which they produced for it; for the Romans, as well as ourselves, had observed that they have the most numerous families, who having nothing, take no care to rear them. For the rest, the Roman proletary did not labour; for in a community which admits slavery, labour is dishonourable to free men; he lived almost entirely at the expense of the community, on the distribution of provisions made by the republic It may almost be said, that in modern times the community lives at the expense of the proletary, on that share of the remuneration of his labour which it deducts from him. The proletary, in fact, according to the order which chresmatistism tends to establish,

[a] "Of 1500 *proletaries* slain in a battel." *Anatomy of Melancholy*, p. 46, ed. 1804.—*Tr.*

ought alone to be loaded with all the labour of the community, and ought to be a stranger to all property, and live only on wages. The community, according to the chresmatistic school, is divided, as regards that labour which produces wealth, into three classes of persons: landed proprietors, capitalists, and day-labourers or proletaries. The first give land, the second employment, and the third hand-labour; in return, the first receive rent, the second profit, and the third wages; each endeavours to retain as much as he can of the total product, and their reciprocal struggle fixes the proportion between rent, profit, and wages.

The abolition of corporations and of their privileges created the first proletaries, men working by the day, in towns; every one can enter into any trade, and quit it when he pleases to choose another; every one can offer his strength and skill to whoever will employ him; every one, without apprenticeship, without admission into any body, without a workshop or a retail shop, can labour on the capital of another, in the undertaking of another, without having accumulated anything; and he thinks he has gained liberty by losing security. At first the workmen, the proletaries, were a small number, in a situation which was a kind of exception to the trades; but they soon multiplied, whilst the old masters, journeymen, and apprentices almost entirely disappeared, and now the proletaries execute the greatest part of the work of towns.

The revolution produced in field-labour or agriculture was not so sudden. The cultivators, instead of losing any part of their property, on the contrary saw it ameliorated, by the suppression of feudal rights; those who were proprietors, feudatories, and métayers, have continued to unite to their interest as labourers a right in the property which neutralizes it; only the farmers in countries which had adopted cultivation on a large scale, began to find it more convenient to direct labour than to labour themselves, to place themselves on a level with the undertakers of manufactures, and to cause the work which they required, to be executed by the proletaries of agriculture, whom they engaged or dismissed as it suited their convenience. The economical revolution, which has replaced the old peasantry by the proletaries of agriculture, is only fully accomplished in England, but it has already begun everywhere. Everywhere are seen some day-labourers; their number increases, whilst that of the peasants diminishes. The peasant is the cultivator who holds from the country, who has his hereditary right, his share of the country; the day-labourer holds by nothing but the day: he is a cultivator without any interest in the country. The first aspires to perpetuity, the last has neither past nor future.

In the pursuit of, or endeavouring after cheapness in manufacturing, the chresmatistic school has acknowledged as a principle, that there is always loss in the division of a given power; that capitals which represent power in the creation of wealth are so much the more usefully employed the more they are united; that twenty thousand pounds can accomplish more work in one single undertaking, than ten times two thousand pounds in ten different undertakings; that there is a saving in the construction of great machines in their durability, in their friction, in responsibility (*comptabilité*), in inspection; in short, the more wealth is accumulated in one single hand, the cheaper can it execute the work it has undertaken. At the same time that this principle has been theoretically acknowledged, it has been vigorously followed up through personal interest, and it is its application, which, rendering all medium situations untenable, has forced all those who were driven from them into the ranks of the proletaries, so as daily to increase their number. This principle, in fact, which creates an abyss between extreme opulence and extreme poverty, applies equally to all industrial labour, and it gradually drives everywhere out of the field that happy independence, that happy mediocrity, which was long the object of the wishes of the wise. According to the English economists, there is much more profit, and much more economy in practising agriculture on large than on small farms. The inspection of different kinds of labour is easier; less time is lost in going from one to another; the farmer, master of a considerable capital, has received an education suitable to his fortune; he also employs more intelligence and more knowledge; all his tools, his beasts, his buildings, are better and more lasting; he is not forced to sell so soon, so that his bargains are more advantageous. In fact, wherever great farmers have competed with small ones, they have ruined them.

By following up this pretended improvement, an economy of human lives has been obtained in agriculture which the chresmatistics find admirable. Not only have all small farmers descended to the condition of day-labourers, but still more, a great number of day-labourers have been forced to give up field-labour; for we are assured that there was in the system of small farms much labour lost, which is not lost now. But can industrial labour employ the families which are now sent out of the fields into towns? can it give them bread? Has the proportion which must necessarily exist between the productions of the earth, and those of the arts, been considered? And when we see in one country which stands alone, artisans as numerous as labourers, is it not acknowledged that these artisans are so numerous only because they supply the whole world with the things which they make?

In fact, the industry of towns has adopted the principle of the union of power, the union of capital, with still more vigour than that of the country. In England it is only by the immensity of capitals that manufactures prosper. It is only where a manufacturer has much credit at his disposal, that there is economy in the power of machines, in their durability, in the inspection of the work people, in scientific works, in responsibility, in facilities of sale. Great workshops, competing with small ones, have in every market an advantage in proportion to their size.

Whenever great capitals are united, and a great workshop rises up, and different sorts of work are accelerated and concentrated under the same management, so that from the same edifice, the same factory, may be given out cloth made of what was, four and twenty hours before, a fleece on the back of a living sheep, the chresmatistic school utters cheering cries of admiration, it extols to the clouds the prosperity of a country where one man can every day load a vessel with cloths, or hardware, or earthenware, sufficient for many thousands of his fellow men; but what a strange forgetfulness of human kind never to inquire what becomes of the man which the great factory has displaced! For, in short, all the consumers which it furnishes were not before without clothes, nor without tools, nor without earthenware; but they provided themselves from those hundreds of little tradesmen who formerly lived happy in independence, and who have disappeared to make room for one millionaire in the mercantile world.

As by the power of great capital all independent trades have been attacked, and the man who was formerly a master in a trade has been forced to descend to the rank of a man who works by the day, of a proletary, so also have been attacked the domestic labours of the inferior members of the family; and the chresmatistic school has, by its arguments, seconded the power of money, and the seduction of cheapness. Why, it says, should the housewife spin, weave, and prepare all the linen of the family? All this work would be done infinitely cheaper at the manufactory; with much less money the housewife would have more stuffs, and of a finer quality. Why should she knead the bread? she cannot make it so light, she cannot bake it to such an exact point, she cannot make it so cheaply as the baker. Why should she make the pot boil? An establishment on a great scale, with supplies made beforehand, a considerable capital and a common inspection, would procure her better food with great saving of time and fuel. Omnibus kitchens might even every day bring her soup to her door. Why? Why, because reciprocal cares and duties form and strengthen domestic ties; because the wife endears herself to the family of the poor man by the solicitude with which she provides for its first necessities; because love is often in a labouring man only a brutal and transient passion; but his affection for her who every day prepares for him the only enjoyment which he can obtain in the day, thus increases also every day. It is the wife who foresees, and who remembers, in the midst of that life passed so rapidly in labour, and physical wants; it is she who knows how to combine economy, neatness, and order, with abundance. It is in the happiness she gives that she finds strength to resist, if it is necessary, the imperious demands of drunkenness and gluttony. When the wife has nothing to do in the house but to produce children, can it be supposed that the sacred bond of marriage is not more broken, than by the lessons and the example of the most reprehensible immorality?

Manufactures have, however, in those nations which are called the most prosperous, gained the advantage over domestic labours, as well as over independent trades. Their success has been announced as a prodigious conquest of industry, and publicists as well as the heads of the chresmatistic school, rivalled one another in felicitations on the rapid increase of public wealth. But a frightful reality suddenly appeared, disturbing all minds, and shaking all the principles which had been announced in so dogmatic a tone: it was the appearance of *pauperism,* its rapid and threatening increase, and the confession of the oracles of the science that they felt themselves powerless to remedy it. *Pauperism* is a calamity which began by making itself felt in England, and which has at present no other name but what the English have given it, though it begins to visit also other industrial countries. Pauperism is the state to which proletaries are necessarily reduced when work fails. It is the condition of men who must live by their labour, who can only work when capitalists employ them, and who, when they are idle, must become a burden on the community. This community, which gives all its support to the rich, does not allow the proletary to labour on the land, unless the proprietor or his tenant wants him for this purpose. It does not allow him to work at trades, if the manufacturer or his foreman does not want him. Justice and humanity equally proclaim the necessity of legal charity, or of a provision made by social authority in favour of the poor, whose distress would be no less alarming than grievous. No community has believed that it could refuse this legal charity, but it is only very recently that experience and calculation have equally demonstrated that the community has not the power to support such a burden. The Poor Law increases the wretchedness of the poor, their dependence, and their vices, at the same time that it is capable of raising them from indigence only in proportion as it absorbs the clear nett income of the richest nation.

What then is become of this opulence so long cried up? Where is this progress towards prosperity which we are called on to admire? Since nations became richer, are they more in a state to feed themselves? By forgetting men for things, by unceasingly multiplying material wealth, has only poverty then been created? By exciting each one to seek only his own advantage at the expense of all those with whom he has any transactions, have we gained, instead of the equilibrium of all individual powers, only the combined action of each one, for his own advantage no doubt, but to the disadvantage of all. We have long said so, it is true, but writing makes little impression when it attacks a dominant system. Facts are more obstinate and more rebellious. They do not manifest themselves less from its being supposed that they can be refuted without being heard, as if they were only writings; they often increase from having been neglected, and then they fall with their whole weight on the most skilfully constructed theory, crushing and overthrowing it at the very moment when its author was congratulating himself on having victoriously refuted all his adversaries.

ON LANDED PROPERTY[a].

ACCORDING to most of the philosophers who cultivate the social sciences, political economy is a new science, whose origin does not extend farther back than from fifty to sixty years. From this epoch they tell us we are to date the discovery of the theory of the creation and distribution of wealth, and they promise that when this theory shall have been adopted by statesmen, when it shall have become a light to legislation and administration, then human society, guided by this light, will be seen to make a rapid progress in power and happiness. Riches, say they, the source of all material well-being to men, will multiply; then will disappear indigence and its most frightful consequences, contagious maladies arising from bad nourishment, from excessive labour, from being crowded together in unhealthy habitations, from cold and want of clothes: ignorance too will be subdued, that necessary consequence in the labouring class of the constant toil which exhausts the body, and leaves no freedom for the mind: the different ranks of society will be reconciled to each other, because so much happiness and intelligence will be obtained for all as will secure internal peace and the stability of governments. Still more, the passions producing ill-will will be extinguished, and the most formidable temptations removed, and thus the progress of virtue and morality in the human race will be powerfully served. It

[a] Extracted from the *Revue Mensuelle d'Economie Politique*, February, 1834.

required promises thus brilliant of the regeneration and happiness of all men, to prevent our being astonished at hearing the importance of riches preached in the name of philosophy, and the ardent pursuit of them celebrated as public spirit. Unhappily, these same fifty or sixty years which have been devoted to the development of this new system of political economy, have brought the most alarming disturbance into the relations and conditions of the members of society. The collective wealth of those nations which the economists considered as the most advanced, has in fact increased, and sometimes in a very rapid proportion, but, at the same time, the number of rich men has diminished rather than increased, the intermediate ranks have disappeared, small proprietors, small farmers in the country, small artisans, small manufacturers, small shopkeepers in the towns, have not been able to compete with those who direct vast undertakings. There is no longer room in society for any but the great capitalist and the man who lives on wages; and that formerly almost imperceptible class of men who have absolutely no property, has increased in an alarming manner. In fact, all working men, all those who, by the labour of their hands, create the wealth which is spread throughout society, have ceased to have any direct right or interest in the different works which flourish through their means. They are bound to them only by daily wages, by a contract which they and their masters renew every week. Ignorant of those commercial interests which they serve, of the wants of the distant markets for which they work, they are engaged or dismissed in consequence of mercantile revolutions which they can neither calculate nor foresee; they are the victims of all the reverses, of all the mistakes, of all the extravagance of their employers; their own prudence and good conduct are no longer a security to them: their condition is become precarious and dependent, and it is no longer in their own keeping. At the same time, they have been led into a state of continual warfare, either among themselves or with their masters, to fix the rate of wages; want is continually pressing on them, they underbid one another in the price of their labour, the competition ruins them, and forces them to be content with what is absolutely necessary for daily subsistence. If a momentary prosperity, an extraordinary demand for that kind of work to which they are suited, lifts them to-day from this pressure of want, it always threatens them for the morrow. The life of the workman has no longer a future.

All the moral consequences of increased indigence have followed this development of social wealth, which has only augmented the inequality of its distribution. In those places where the eye is most struck with the opulence of some, in England especially, and next in the large capitals of the continent, the number of crimes, against property particularly, has increased in an alarming manner; the number of illegitimate births and foundlings attest the depravation of morals, and the relaxation of family ties; the increasing consumption of spirits reveals that secret intoxication, less noisy than that which used formerly to fill the public houses, but more grievous, more brutalizing, more fatal to health, and henceforth common alike to women as to men. In short, in manufactories, and especially in those of England, the struggle among the poor always offering the most work for the lowest possible wages, has obliged them to devote their children from their earliest age to labour in the production of more and more of that wealth, out of which they are allowed wages scarcely sufficient for life. The latest inquiries on the factory bill have shown that children of eight or ten years of age work commonly twelve or fourteen hours a day; that at sixteen or eighteen, they are often made to work long hours, that is to say, twenty hours a day for two days together, then a night of repose: that the work-rooms are at an offensive temperature; the air filled with mephitic exhalations, and often loaded with deleterious particles of cotton, wool, or metals; that the children, sometimes standing, sometimes creeping among the wheels of the machines, are soon affected by a swelling or weakness of the bones. Then they stoop, their limbs become deformed, and they can no longer walk without pain. To keep children attentive and awake, who can take no interest in their work, recourse must be had to blows, and it has been proved in a court of justice, that death ensued in a few hours to a miserable child who, to keep him awake, had been, in the usual way, but with too much violence, struck on the head. Meanwhile, disease and infirmity seize from their childhood on these feeble labourers; they grow with them, and carry them off, old men at twenty, or if they languish longer, it is to remain in manhood only a charge on public charity, for they have no longer strength to gain their livelihood [a]. Who, then, has had the right to take from all these beings, who have known nothing of life but its sufferings, that portion of happiness which a God of goodness has destined for every creature, as the condition of its creation; who shall restore it to them? Who had the right to deprive them of the joys of childhood, of free exercise and repose, of the sun and air, all necessary to the development of their bodies; of the sight of nature, of hope, of gratitude, of all the affections more necessary still for the health of the soul? Who had the right to make this sacrifice of children, more dreadful even than that which crimsoned the altars of Moloch? For intelligence and virtue, those sparks of the Divinity, are here extinguished before the body.

It has been thought that these frightful evils might be remedied by generous efforts after popular instruction, by extending to all classes the benefit of education; but these efforts, praiseworthy, no doubt, are often ill-directed, and always powerless. It is doing little to teach the children of the people to read and write, if they have not the energy to wish for knowledge, nor the wisdom to choose, nor above all, the leisure to reflect on it and to profit by it; it is doing little to instruct them in trades, to give them some general ideas of the laws of nature, for it is only making them into mere productive machines, and increas-

[a] All this has been much remedied since M. de Sismondi wrote, but it shows the evils to which the system led, until checked by legislative interference.—*Tr.*

ing their power in that contest in which they are all engaged, to underbid one another in the price they receive for their labour. It is even doing little to teach them some of the doctrines of religion, and some of its precepts; to speak to them of a God of goodness, of a love which unites all created beings, of the duties which the desire to approach the Deity and to form ourselves on His image impose on us, if, at the same time, we place under their eyes nothing but sufferings and acts of harshness, if their fathers and their employers, the first representatives of God upon earth whom they learn to know, never appear to them but as covetous and threatening, vigilant to deprive them of all their pleasures, pitiless for the sufferings which undermine their health. The education of life lays hold on them, and it is more powerful than that of their teachers; it destroys in them all veneration, all affection, all gratitude: it breaks the spring of their souls, and leaves them nothing but sensuality and selfishness. The father and mother who have sold their child, who see it perish before their eyes, the young men without hope, the old men without retrospections, have to make themselves insensible to their woes. They seek in the senses a moment of pleasure which the intellect and the heart refuse them; they strive by licentiousness and drunkenness to relieve themselves for some moments from the intolerable weight of a life of effort and privation.

What an account to render to the Deity by those who require only animated machines to produce wealth! What an account of so many intelligent souls created for virtue, whom these men have by their love of wealth driven into inevitable degradation! And if we dare not fix our eyes on this essential aspect of human destiny, what account may not the nation require from these men, of the citizens that have been entrusted to them? Every nation must before all things be strong, that she may defend her independence, but she will not find strength in ricketty, decrepit, degraded creatures, who cannot live in the open air, whose courage has never been exercised, who have not had time to develop thought or feeling, who love nothing, respect nothing, and have only their indigence to defend. Every nation has need of internal peace, of confidence, of love among fellow-citizens; but how shall this peace be maintained, if the production of wealth is based on an opposition of interests in each against all; if the master of any business seeks to undersell others, that he may get their customers; if he seeks to reduce the wages of his work-people, or to replace them by machines to save their wages; if workman contends with workman, and offers his labour at a lower rate, in order to supplant him? A universal contest has been established among all classes, and in every class; every one is forced to contend for the enjoyments of existence, for its necessaries, for life itself. Surely there is room to admire human nature, when even in such an order of things, there is still found in every class, among the poor especially, so much charity, so much sympathy. But the peace, the security of society, how their safeguards have been taken away! And if society is free, if men are told that for the well-being of all, not for the few only, is society organized, what a strange forgetfulness of its object is shown, when the health, the pleasures, the hopes, the security, the intellect, even the immortal life of the greatest part of its members, are sacrificed to the production of wealth? It is the people, the sovereign people, who are thus despoiled of all that gives value, not to sovereignty only, but to life itself. Shall we say, "*Et propter vitam,*" or better still, "*Et propter lucrum lucrandi perdere causas?*"

In England, the country which has advanced more rapidly than any other in the pursuit of this new science, which has outstripped all others in the creation of wealth, which exists only to produce, and maintains herself only by supplanting all others in every kind of production, the disproportion between the opulence of some, and the wretchedness of the greater number, the no less rapid than alarming increase of those who have nothing, and who hope for nothing, the precarious condition to which all those have been reduced who perform the labour of the community, the suffering of children, the destruction of their intellects, or of their lives, the rending of all sympathies among the poor who depend on parish relief, of all ties of blood, of all social duties, the spirit of revolt against oppressive laws, against humiliating distinctions, against even the existence of property, all these have reached a height to make us tremble for the whole order of society. The alarm this inspires is so much the more deep, inasmuch as if offended humanity finds avengers, they will be neither sufficiently enlightened, nor sufficiently virtuous to become afterwards legislators and benefactors. But if all England seem now to be labouring with the fire of a subterraneous volcano, other countries too, who have adopted the same system, who at a distance have followed in her steps, feel the first tremblings of the convulsive state at which she is arrived. These symptoms are the more frequent and the more alarming, the more the first aspect of these countries is prosperous, the more rapidly their collective wealth is on the increase, the more the activity of all is excited, the nearer, in short, their governments have approached to what are called good principles in political economy. The combinations of workmen, now more frequent, are a sufficiently clear manifestation of the sufferings and unsettled state of the poorer classes, ruined by competition; they strive to unite, to drive off the wretchedness which threatens them; but they either fail by their weakness, or lose themselves by their excesses; warning France, however, that it is time to be on her guard against them.

Have then these new philosophers really taught us political economy; that is, according to the primitive sense of the words of Greek origin, the true rule or domestic law of the city, or *l'aménagement* of society[a]; when, whilst showing us how wealth may be created, they have forgotten to show also how it ought to be distributed for the well-being of all? Have they really thought of this house, *οικια*, for which they pretend

[a] This word is used properly only in speaking of the management of woods and forests; dividing them into portions, and cutting down a certain part every year, so as to prevent waste.—*Tr.*

to make laws; of that commonwealth, πολιτεια, which they would teach us to govern? They have forgotten in both, independence, happiness, and virtue; they have fixed their regards only on the theory of the creation of wealth, a science with quite different limitations, and which Aristotle, by a very appropriate name, has named *chresmatistic*. But the Greeks, if we may judge by what remains to us of the legislation of their republics, were acquainted with a more elevated political economy: they did not forget the advantages of an increase of wealth; they only desired that it should secure the material happiness of all; and this happiness was subordinate in their eyes to the moral happiness and perfection of all.

The existence of civilization, the safety of the human race in this our ancient Europe, are closely bound to the triumph of this true political economy, both in public opinion and in legislation; to the development of that science which has for its object man, and not wealth, which asks how this wealth can be employed for the happiness and virtue of all, not how it can be indefinitely increased.

But to return to this high moral science, it will be necessary to combat at the same time the prejudices of the vulgar and those of philosophers, the illusions which language has created and sanctioned, and the difficulties which the subject itself presents, the most abstract, perhaps, the most difficult to seize with precision, of any of the social sciences.

To endeavour to understand what there is yet to be done, to enable us to form some clear and simple ideas on the economy of the social state, we will fix on that condition among men which the new science has caused to deviate least from its former organization, that of cultivators; we will look at the chresmatistic mode of considering it. We will afterwards ask, what true political economy ought to do for it, and though this be of all questions the most simple and the most clear in either form of this science, yet we shall soon see how different is their object, how opposite the advice which they give, and in treating of agriculture, we shall have occasion to set before us all the difficulties of the social state, which are aggravated by making wealth the sole object of consideration, and which can only be removed by fixing our attention on men and not on things.

In the eyes of the chresmatistics, agriculture is a manufacture of rural products. They consider it then like every other manufacture "as a balance of the expenses of production against the products obtained, in which the exchange is so much the more advantageous, as less is given to obtain more. It advances in prosperity whenever more advantage is obtained for the same expense, or the same advantage for less expense."—(Say, *Cours Complet d'Economie Politique*, T. 1me, p. 24.) [a]

Thus, according to M. Say,—and his doctrine agrees with that of all the English school,—the prosperity of agriculture must be estimated by its nett product: it gains either by producing more, or by costing less; either by selling more produce, or at a higher price, so as to get more from the consumer; either by affording less employment, or by paying less wages for the same labour, thus saving what is laid out on the labourer's wages. The proprietors of the county of Sutherland did no more than conform to these principles when, after having discovered that land in that county of Scotland only paid a shilling an acre nett produce, they reckoned for nothing the subsistence which it furnished to many thousand agricultural families. They drove out all these families, destroyed their houses, and put an end to tillage to make sheep-walks: as there was thenceforth nothing to be laid out on the land, its natural produce alone returned them 1*s.* 6*d.* per acre, and they have gained 50 per cent. by what has been done. Among the thousands of labourers thus driven from their ancient homes, some have become fishermen on the shores of the county

[a] "Comme un troc de tous les frais de production qu'elle fait, contre tous les produits qu'elle obtient, troc d'autant plus avantageux, que l'on donne moins pour obtenir plus. Elle est en progrès chaque fois qu'elle parvient à obtenir plus d'utilité pour le même frais, ou la même utilité pour de moindres frais."

of Sutherland, some have gone to America, some have travelled into the towns of Scotland to beg for work, or to perish there from want. (Lord Stafford's Improvements, by James Loch, 1820.) Such is one example among thousands of the increased prosperity in agriculture of the chresmatistics.

The English economists, Ricardo and Malthus, have engaged in a very abstract discussion on the origin of rent. According to the one, *it is a premium on monopoly;* according to the other, *it is the hiring out of the land for cultivation*[a]; neither they nor Macculloch, nor their disciples, have deduced any conclusion applicable to the condition of the man who cultivates it. Say, after having remarked that, by the nature of agricultural labour, there are strict limits to the extent of cultivation of land, or to the quantity of capital that can be employed upon it, renounces, with an expression of regret, any ulterior inquiries respecting landed property, since the progress of political economy, as he understands it, can contribute so little to its development.

Those legislators who occupy themselves about men and not about things, who calculate the mass of happiness to which a nation can attain, not the mass of wealth which it can produce, those who alone deserve to have the name of economists appropriated to them, ascribe a very different degree of importance to agriculture. They see that no employment is more intimately connected with the happiness of men, or acts more directly on the mass of citizens. As consumers, all without exception have need of it, for without land there is no food: as labourers, the greatest number live by it; especially if we com-

[a] *Selon le premier c'est un prix de monopolie, selon le second un loyer du travail de la terre.* In his definitions on political economy, Mr. Malthus defines rent to be "that portion of the produce of land which remains to the owner after all the outgoings belonging to its cultivation are paid, including the ordinary profits of the capital employed;" and Mr. Ricardo, in his Principles of Political Economy, calls it, "that portion of the produce of the earth which is paid to the landlord for the use of the original and indestructible powers of the soil."—*Tr.*

prise, as is usually done, hunters, fishermen, shepherds, and all those who collect the spontaneous fruits of the earth, in the class of agriculturists; the cultivation of the ground employs commonly four-fifths of a nation; as proprietors lastly, the whole soil of the country belongs to them, and they have sometimes arrogated to themselves the right of dismissing the nation from her own abode. Let us consider these three classes, or if you will, these three aspects of society.

In general it has been laid down as a principle in chresmatistics, that it is sufficient to attend to the consumer, and that whatever detriment the producer may experience, society ought to congratulate itself, if it procures everything cheaper. But the economist who does not abstract man to consider only wealth, will say, on the contrary, that the producer ought to be considered first of all. Labour is, in fact, the creator of all the benefits which man enjoys, the source of all his income. Daily labour is the income of the poor; the fruits of accumulated labour give an income to the rich. The division between them is not always equitable, but if the balance must lean, it is desirable it should be in favour of the poor; that is the interest of the greater number; it is at the same time the interest of the weak; the more amply labour is remunerated, so much the more are the necessaries and comforts of life secured to the great majority of the nation. The most desirable state, therefore, is that which secures the greatest advantage to the producers; for by this means the largest share of income, or the largest share of material happiness is distributed among the greatest number of citizens. When the chresmatistics affirm, that each one being a consumer, the interest of the consumer is the interest of all, they deceive us by an abstraction. All things are, in fact, offered to all; but for the immense majority of products, the actual purchasers are very few. In the consumption of the working man, more especially in that of the field-labourer, the only object of primary importance is food; of the income afforded him by his labour, he exchanges a very small part with all other arts, while with nature he exchanges almost the whole of it; *manger*, eating [a], represents all his expenses; he eats to labour, and to produce food for others. The progress of manufactures may offer him clothing at a cheaper rate, but this is no advantage to the labourer, if his wages diminish in exactly the same proportion. If he is the buyer of his own produce, its low price is a symptom of a general reduction of income, from which he suffers with others. Even for the highest ranks of society, cheapness is an advantage more illusory than real. After the first wants of life have been satisfied, the expenses of luxury are calculated in almost every case to afford relative rather than positive enjoyment. What the rich man seeks in his dress, in his furniture, in his equipages, is the elegance which will strike the eyes of the public; it is to impress the idea of his wealth and of his good taste; it is to appear rather than to be; it is, in short, the distinctive mark of the condition to which he belongs. But before the perfection which art has given to the production of manufactures, there was just the same difference as now between what cost an ounce of silver, and what cost only a penny. The rich man choosing among less perfect productions, might show as much elegance and good taste; rank was as much distinguished by dress, or rather far more so; each rank appropriated to dress precisely the same proportion of its income which it does now. It is very difficult to discover how the cheapness of silks has added to the happiness of those who buy them.

The rule adopted by the chresmatistics, to think only of the consumer, and to look upon his interest as the national interest, comes much nearer the truth, it must be allowed, as regards rural productions. All members of society are, in fact, consumers of these productions; and, as food, the poorer a man is, takes a larger proportion of his income, the cheapness of these productions is more important to the poor than to the rich. But whenever the remuneration of labour is given to the

[a] The French expression for expense in general, *manger son bien,* to waste one's estate.—*Tr.*

poor in commodities, the price of these commodities becomes a matter of indifference to him. Now this mode of remuneration is the most just one, for there is a proportion between the goodness and quantity of food, and muscular strength, which does not vary with the price of food. In order that a workman may give all his strength to his work, he will require always the same quantity of corn; in towns it would add to his health and security if he were fed by his master, or received for part of his wages the same quantity of corn annually, for the chances of the market always go against the poorest. This payment in kind is almost the universal basis of remuneration in the country; the husbandman is almost always fed by the produce he has raised, except the day-labourers, whose number hitherto has been very small. The interest of the day-labourer is then opposed to that of the producer: all others, masters as well as husbandmen, have a common interest in good prices. Now it is dangerous for society, whenever the interests of different classes clash, whenever the poor man has to struggle against the producer. There is safety, on the contrary, whenever the poor and the rich are united in a common interest.

In spite of the chresmatistic rule, to regard only the consumer, in spite of the popular clamour for cheap bread, the cultivators of the soil form so considerable a part of every nation, that in England and France they have succeeded in obtaining from the legislature an attempt to secure for them good prices. We are far from approving all that has been done for this purpose, far from advising that an interest so universal as that of the consumers should be forgotten; but we must rank still higher the common interest of society, which demands that the agricultural producer should be amply remunerated; that he who raises the fruits of the earth should retain a sufficient share of them; without this we cannot reckon either on the regularity of production, or on stability of price, or on being independent of foreigners in time of war; and this perfect certainty of subsistence is of more importance than low prices to the consumer himself.

The chresmatistic school has considered the condition of the labourers, who raise the products of the soil, only as a means of arriving at an end, the creation of agricultural wealth. With us, on the contrary, the happiness of these men is the main object of the science, for they form the great majority of the nation. The legislator's aim, then, ought to be to preserve for them as large a part of the wealth which they produce as is consistent with the continuation of their labour; to settle in the country the greatest possible number of persons, for with an equal income the poor man will there enjoy more health and happiness than in a town; to develop their intellect as much as coarse bodily labour will allow; lastly, and above all things, to cultivate and strengthen their morality. To do this, he will feel that he must give stability to the way of life of the husbandman, favour all those contracts which give him a permanent interest in the soil, discourage all those which make his condition precarious, and which leave him uncertain as to the morrow, for morality is intimately united with memory and with hope; it is nourished by duration; it becomes nothing to him who considers only the present moment. This ample remuneration, this participation of the greater number in field-labour, this stability in the condition of the rural population, will appear to him much more important than a rapid creation of wealth; he will attach, perhaps, still more importance to not multiplying motives to strife and rivalry in the most numerous class in the nation. He will regard as the system of cultivation most favourable to the comfort and happiness of all, that which will unite most closely the interests of the landowners and of the cultivators, not that which adds most to the income of the former.

It must not be forgotten that to produce the fruits of the earth, on which all must subsist, hard and prolonged manual labour is required. This labour can only be executed by men who give up the comforts and elegancies of life. The Saint Simonians, and all those who wish to regenerate society by the co-operation system, fall into a great absurdity, when they wish to give by turns to the same men the enjoyment of luxury, and the often rude, sometimes disgusting labours of poverty. He who has been required in the morning to spread manure on the common field, will care little for a ride in a carriage at noon, or for an evening ball in velvet and lace. But the chresmatistics fall into an absurdity of much the same kind, when they say, "The more you produce, the more enjoyment will there be for all." In effect, they reduce the working class to the strictest necessaries; at the same time they cause all the intermediate ranks to disappear; they accumulate in the hands of some landowners, of some manufacturers, of some merchants, colossal wealth; then they multiply without measure those productions of industry which are only suited to those who can live at ease. Where is the use of offering to the nation more sources of enjoyment, if you are to destroy those who are to benefit by them? It is then the happiness and ease compatible with manual labour which should be secured to the husbandman; in his house, in his clothes, in his tools, he should have everything which contributes to health and comfort, but nothing which pretends to elegance, or which nourishes delicacy. He must have them first of all for himself that he may be happy; for other producers, that he may be a profitable consumer; for the revenue, that he may contribute to it without being straitened; for the whole of society, that he may labour. No one ever thought of raising all cultivators above their station at once, but some of them have often been so raised, and this is the system which is favoured by the chresmatistics. They wish to see rich farmers directing a large farm, and contributing to its productions only by the employment of their capital and their skill. They do not work with their hands, but they regulate the cultivation, they inspect and urge on the labourers; they buy, they sell, they keep accounts; they correspond with merchants and manufacturers. At Rome, in fact, they are called *mercanti di tenute*; in England, gentlemen-farmers; but in raising their condition they lower that of their companions in labour. By reserving to themselves the exercise of will, choice, intelligence, they refuse it to their work-people and servants; they ask from them only the employment of their muscular strength; they lower them as much as they can to the rank of machines. It is always a grievous thing to put in competition the interest of those who have intelligence and wealth, with that of those who have only their hands: the first, to secure to themselves profits, stability, a safe futurity, drive the second into a state continually becoming more precarious, and, according to the times and according to the measure of their power, they reduce them to slavery, to serfage, to the condition of day-labourers or servants. The time will come, at last, when they will endeavour through economy to make them disappear altogether.

Agriculture is composed of a series of labours, varying every day, not equally urgent, or equally important, but which require, with a great development of physical strength, constant application, intelligence, and a certain interest in the success of the undertaking. In manufactures, the work is generally the same from the beginning to the end of the year; therefore it is found more profitable to reduce it to a manual operation, always the same: habit makes it more easy, whilst intelligence and good-will become of less value. They may so easily be dispensed with, that a machine takes the place of a man, and a man is only a machine. This degradation of the human species is a great national misfortune, for which no increase of wealth can compensate; but in agriculture it is also a loss of money. The farmer who gives up the intelligence of his labourer, and his interest in his work, makes a bad calculation; for this intelligence and this desire to succeed should direct every stroke of the pruning knife, and almost every stroke of the spade. Thus, for the soil to be cultivated with intelligence and good-will, the labour should be performed by the same person who lays out money on it, and gains a profit. No cultivator, other things being equal, can be compared to a labouring proprietor, who adds to the most direct interest the recollections of experience, and the hope of the future; a tenant with a lease of 99 years, *bail emphytéotique*, has almost the same advantages, for he is insured a perpetuity; then comes the *métayer;* although he has only half the produce, he has as much interest as the proprietor in its abundance, and in the success of his labour. The working farmer has not less interest than the proprietor in the first years of his lease, but his interest changes in the later ones, and then it is that he sacrifices the future to the present, *et taille les vignes en ruine*[a].

The serf does as ill as he can his task-work, *corvée*, on the estate of his lord, but he labours with good-will and intelligence on his own. The farm-servant, hired by the year, has no real interest in his work, but through sympathy with his master, he yet endeavours to succeed; the day-labourer, hired by the week, has no interest, he brings neither intelligence nor good-will to his work. The slave has only an interest in hatred and revenge; he rejoices when the labour which has made him suffer so much, brings no advantage to his master. Thus, the more a system of cultivation raises the condition of the cultivator, the more ease and independence it gives him, and the more will he combine that intelligence and good-will with his work, which will secure its success.

The farmer, who is the head of a family, knowing there are dead seasons in the year, days of rain and snow, when nothing can be done in the fields, reserves for these times any work which is not so urgent, and which hardly repays the labour: that is to say, which might be done by more economical means, were it not most economical of all to do it in times which would otherwise be lost. He has an interest in common with the nation, and in common with the whole of society, in the perfecting of machines, and in all that increases the productive power of man; but he knows very well that were the machine to do the work which he does, in his otherwise wasted hours, it would bring no profit to him, nor yet to society. For example; if a machine to thrash corn, leaves him and his servants and children without work, during the bad days of winter, he knows very well that the use of this machine will be a loss,

[a] Ruins his vines by pruning them to make them bear.—*Tr.*

and not a profit to him; and his interest in this respect is identified with that of agriculture and of society. But if the farming capitalist has his labour done in a press of work, by day-labourers engaged by the week, without caring what will become of them in the winter; if, at the same time he performs by a machine the labour which would fill up the dead season, he really gains by this machine only what he robs from the public charity, on which he throws the charge of keeping his labourers. To make a true calculation of what society gains by any mechanical invention, there must be deducted from it the loss experienced by all the working men who had been dismissed by it, till they have found an employment as advantageous as the one they had before. If we calculate the productive power of the community, the unemployed time of these men is so much to be deducted from what is produced by the machine. If we calculate our income, the wages they have lost should be balanced against the profit made by this fixed capital [a].

[a] "I am far from denying that in the end the country gains, whenever the greatest possible results are obtained by what is called the minimum of labour; but the consequence must ever unavoidably be, that the demand for labour will be diminished in the same ratio. This invention of the thrashing-machine was a proof of this, and it was a heavy blow to the poor labourer. It took from him a large portion of his winter's employ—his employ at a time when he most required it. Allow me, for a short time, to digress and state, as an old practical farmer, my opinion of this invention. I consider that not only has it been the cause of much distress to the poor labourer, but that it has been of serious injury to the farmer, and that no sensible man should use one, if he can help it. This may appear strange, but it is easily explained. In point of expense little is saved by the thrashing-machine. But the great mischief is, that it decreases the quantity of grain produced, as we have no longer the *quality* of manure in our yards that we used to have before its introduction. As much corn is now thrashed, and as much straw thrown out of the barn doors in one day as would give employment to a labourer for nearly a month. The straw is spoilt by the machine, and the cattle will not eat it as they will when thrashed out by the flail. When the flail was used, the quantity of straw thrown out of the barn doors every day was about what was required for the provender of the cattle, and the littering down of the yards and stables; and it came out fresh and sweet. Now it is all thrown out in the early part of the winter, and lies exposed to the weather, which injures it as much, if not more, than the rollers of the thrashing-machine. Before the thrashing-machine was invented, a tenant was obliged to have, besides his stock on the farm, a sufficiency of money to pay his first

The chresmatistic school has represented as an eminent progress in agriculture, the power acquired of doing the same work with a continually decreasing number of hands; this progress has been pushed very far in England, where they have succeeded in driving more than half the nation out of the fields into the towns. The economist of men, not of wealth, cannot behold such progress without extreme sorrow. No manual labour maintains health, vigour of body, and cheerfulness, so well as agriculture; none prepares better soldiers for the defence of the country; none, by its variety, develops so much intelligence; and when the soil is cultivated by small proprietors, or *métayers,* none affords to those who live by the labour of their hands, so much security for the future, so little jealousy among persons in the same employment, so little seduction to vice, and so much morality. As, in our Europe at least, the territory of nations is circumscribed, all that is saved from manual labour in rural employments, sends from the fields into the towns so many families condemned to unhappiness. Even if they succeed in getting employment in a manufactory, they must give up pure air, the light of the sun, exercise, the spectacle of nature, the pleasures of the country, variety in their employments, security for the future; their situation becomes precarious and dependent; their morals get corrupted, because debauchery is the only means of getting rid of the thoughts of the present, and they rarely survive long.

Nevertheless it will not do in the country any more than in towns, for the population to exceed certain limits; for men to be reduced to underbid one another, to lower the rates of labour, to

year's rent; but the thrashing-machine enables him to thrash out the corn of the first year's produce in time to meet the rent of that year. Such is but too often the case at present; a farm is hired without the requisite capital, the tenant struggles on for a few years, till he breaks down; or, should he remain to the expiration of his lease, from want of proper outlay, the land is given up in so impoverished a state, that the landlord has to make an allowance to the incoming tenant, to enable him to restore it. It may be argued that the law and the covenants of the lease will protect the landlord; very true, but it is useless to go to law with a man who has no money."—*Letter from a Norfolk farmer to the Examiner.*

give more labour and yet to produce less, so that they cease to be fully remunerated. The chresmatistic school pretends that this is the fate which threatens countries cultivated in small portions, and alleges, as an example, the cultivation of Ireland; but the cultivation of Ireland, where there are neither small proprietors nor *métayers*, and where parcels of land belonging to absent proprietors are let on the highest terms to day-labourers without capital, is the most deplorable in Europe. The tithes to support the Anglican Church, and the voluntary contributions for the Catholic, the carelessness, and often the extravagance of the great proprietors, the cupidity of the middle men, of whom there are often two or three between the lord and the peasant, the cruelty of the law which makes this last responsible for the debts of the middle men; the universal competition thus established amongst the poor, has deprived this unhappy country of all peace, of all security, of all civilization. The Irish peasant cannot descend lower than he is: he is not afraid of bringing into the world children more miserable than himself; he is the most improvident of all men in his marriages.

On the contrary, in all countries where the cultivator has some security for his subsistence, some present happiness, some future hope, his prosperity itself forms the only really efficacious barrier to the excessive increase of population. Nobody willingly descends from his station, and it is rare in all countries for a son to marry till he is secure of living in some degree like his father. In countries of small farms, no peasant marries till he is secure of a farm, of a *métairie*, where he can take his wife, unless at least he reckons upon succeeding to that of his father. But the son, and all the sons of the day-labourer, marry as soon as they possess a spade or a pick-axe, which they know to be the only property of their father, and which they have as much strength to use as he. Society never ought to wish for a more numerous population than can live honourably, morally, and happily; and whilst labour is amply remunerated, the poor will preserve this honour, this virtue, and this happiness. If the demand for labour increases, the population will not fail to follow it; but there is danger for society if ever it goes beyond it; if children are born before their means of living has been formed: there is danger for society from the moment that it contains a class which possesses nothing, and which, having no fear of falling lower, is not restrained from marrying by any motive of pride, prudence, or paternal affection. The Romans were acquainted with this danger, when they gave to those who had nothing the name of *proletarii*. As this class constitutes in England more than three quarters of the nation, and in Ireland more than nine-tenths, population has increased in those two countries, with as alarming a rapidity as indigence.

The chresmatistic school, to show the creation of wealth, has pointed out how the rent, the profit, and the wages co-operate to fix the price of any thing, being the compensation for the land employed, and the capital and labour laid out on it: the analysis was well made, and these three powers did, in fact, concur in the creation of it; but it does not follow that the land, the capital, and the labour should be furnished by three different persons, nor that there is any advantage in putting these three interests in opposition to one another. On the contrary, almost all the embarrassment which society at this day experiences, proceeds from the fact, that these three interests, instead of being united, are struggling against one another. Thence it comes that the equilibrium between production and consumption is disturbed; for the capitalist does not wait till there is a demand for produce; if he cannot gain at the expense of the consumer, he hopes to do so at the expense of another capitalist, whose customers he will gain, and at the expense of the workmen, whose wages he will diminish. In agriculture, at least, this struggle between the interests which concur in production may be avoided. The soil is never better cultivated than when these three capacities are united, and when the same man is at once landowner, farmer, and labourer; social order is also sufficiently secured when the two last capacities are united, when the same man, farmer or *métayer*, labours on his own account, and not for a master; but the social order is in danger when the greatest part of agricultural labour is performed by day-labourers. The precarious and unhappy state of so large a proportion of the population, their secret hostility against the landowners, and the whole order of society, their want of interest in the work they perform, their proneness to premature marriages, ought to lead the legislator, by every indirect means in his power, to induce landowners and farmers to give up cultivation by day-labourers. To attain this end, the legislator has also two direct means at his disposal, taxes and public charity. He should make the taxes weigh most heavily on estates which call into existence a population whose position makes them enemies of order, and therefore brings more expense on society to maintain peace. The government, as administrator of public charity, has the charge of providing that no individual suffers misery, or dies of hunger. It must begin, if it would be just, by requiring that those, who for their own interest make the poor, should feed them; that those agriculturists alone who employ day-labourers should be called on to feed them when they have no work; these agriculturists will then soon feel that the only profitable cultivation, the only one which will answer their purpose, is that which does not create poor. The principle would be the same for the industry of towns; its application, it is true, is more difficult. It may be thought, from what we have just said of the advantages to society of peasant proprietors, that we would have all cultivators owners of the soil which they cultivate, and all landowners cultivators: this is not our idea; we take society as it is, with poor and rich, and we think this variety of condition most favourable to its development. The class of the rich appears to us necessary, because there are faculties of the soul and of the intellect, which cannot be developed without complete leisure, because physical activity blunts the other faculties, because continual attention to worldly interests contracts the heart, because the noblest employments of the human mind must be followed with disinterested views, and not for gain; because a nation composed of men all equally well fed, well clothed, well lodged, working only so much as is desirable for their health, but incapable of rising to the fine arts, to the highest sciences, to sublime philosophy, would seem to us to be disinherited of the finest gifts of Providence to man; she would not even be in a position to cultivate the social sciences enough to know how to manage herself, and to avoid the loss of all the advantages she enjoyed. Not that those who are destined to enlighten society are born in the class of the rich, but that this class alone can appreciate them, and have leisure to enjoy their works. The rich, according to the language of the economists, are the consumers of all intellectual produce. If there were no idle persons in the nation, whatever might be the well-being of the other classes, there would be no demand for progress in art, literature, and science, beyond that of immediate utility; and those who cultivate in a transcendental manner, if we may adopt the language of metaphysicians, all the noblest faculties of the human mind, would be deprived of the means of subsistence. We will not say that the rich are necessary to assist the miserable, for it would be better if none were miserable; yet the bond of charity binding together different conditions, is one of the beauties of social order, and one of the sources of the virtue and happiness of man; but for this to be efficaciously exercised, misery must be rare and accidental. Where it is produced on every side, and seems incurable, charity abandons her task, and the heart becomes hardened: If it is desirable that there should be rich men in a nation, it is also desirable that some of them should be settled in the country. Above all, this will be their wish; it is natural that those who are not seduced by the pleasures of the world, will wish to enjoy part at least of those pleasures of nature which we have claimed for the poor. But landed property also gives to the rich a character which it is important to preserve in the nation; they are more intimately united with the people, they know them better, they are bound by interest and affection to the province and district which they inhabit. They are more connected with the past and the future; their property, which is transmitted from generation to generation, gives them a feeling of perpetuity which makes them conservatives, amidst the daily innovations of the other orders; they do not run the risks which lead the newly rich into foolish expense and short-lived pleasures; they are less exposed to the rivalries of gain, to resentment and hatred, because their misfortunes come to them from heaven, and not from the intrigues of men; lastly, their presence in the country tends to civilize it, to spread that refinement of manners, that taste and elegance, which to a certain extent may become general; to introduce, not indeed a profound study of the sciences, but their application; particularly, to make agriculture profit by all the discoveries of speculative inquiry. The nation may and ought to wish that there should be rich landowners scattered through every part of the country, but by no means that all the country should belong to them. She may provide, on the increase of wealth, against all the inheritances of the poor being purchased by the rich; she often does it with success. If we are to believe M. Montlosier, who, in speaking of ancient times too often contents himself with affirming, instead of proving, from the beginning of the republics of the Gauls land had its conditions and ranks, the allodial lands, (*alleux*) were for the rich; the feods, (*tributaires*) were reserved for the poor. This would have been a free institution, (*Monarchie Française*, t. 1. p. 9). It is very probable, on the contrary, that it was during a time of oppression that the distinction between the tenure of lands, in fief *de haubert* and in *villenage* was established This distinction had, however, an advantage: the lords left to the villains that portion of the estates which carried with it a sort of degradation. So in England, the lords retained the freehold, and left to the cultivators the copyhold; but since opinion is changed, and the tenure of copyhold does not affect the condition of the owners, all the copyholds have been bought by the rich, and there no longer remains in England any peasants, cultivators of their own soil. In Austria, where legislation sometimes protects material happiness, whilst the government energetically refuses all intellectual development, the law has secured to the peasant cultivator that his share in the property of the soil should not be diminished. The noble who buys the property of a peasant, must sell it again to a peasant, without changing its condition[a].

The nation has in another way an interest in the proportion between the rich and the poor. It is the power to have possession of leisure, and not of luxury, which makes the condition of the rich useful to society. It demands a refined mind, a relief from care, but not opulence. Besides, it must not be forgotten that landed property is a given quantity which cannot increase; we must inquire, then, whether this quantity is to be divided amongst a thousand, or ten thousand families. Even if we consider only the rich, the quantity of happiness which wealth affords is increased by dividing it; ten thousand families in easy circumstances present far more of it than a thousand in opulence, more than a hundred with the colossal fortunes which we see in England. Among the landowners of this country, some not being able to spend their enormous incomes, are continually buying the patrimonies of their neighbours, and end by possessing provinces; others fling themselves into extravagance, and with incomes of £100,000 a year are straitened, in debt, anxious, and suffer, in extreme opulence, the disquietudes of poverty. It is then for their own interest, as well as for that of the nation, that the law should favour the division of fortunes, for the industry and cupidity of men always tend to re-unite them.

The class of rich landowners, of owners who are not labourers, lives without working, on the nett produce of the land; the only result of agriculture which the chresmatistics have considered. Labour applied to land, produces more than it has cost. The often debated origin of this surplus, is an idle question; its existence is a fact which is not contested. This surplus is divided between the producers and the owners of the soil: the more the first retain for themselves, the less will there remain for the others.

[a] See notes at the end of this Essay.—*Tr.*

By the chresmatistics, the producers are considered only as ciphers; they make no more scruple of displacing and getting rid of classes of men who, they think, can be dispensed with in the production of wealth, than in displacing the unknown quantities in a problem of algebra, in order afterwards to get rid of them. We would not forget that producers are men, still more, that they form by far the majority of the nation; and in the division of the surplus of agricultural produce, we would call for the superintendence of sovereign authority. In fact, this surplus represents for the labourer all the material enjoyments of life, good food, good clothing, good lodging, and the good health which is connected with physical comfort. It represents also a mixture of repose which is necessary, in order to mingle some cheerfulness and some pleasure with his life; in order that a little time may be given to the cultivation of the affections, a little to the cultivation of the mind. The chresmatistics wish the poor man to do all the work possible; the true economists, on the contrary, make it an object to reserve to him some leisure moments.

Since, in the struggle between the rich and the poor, it is the first who make the law, if authority does not interpose, the rich preserve for themselves all the surplus of the produce, all the enjoyment, and all the leisure. The rich class, in fact, being the most enlightened, is in a position to direct and secure itself: the nature of landed property, invariably limited, whatever may be the demand of the producers or consumers, gives it the power of a monopoly. The small number of proprietors, and their rank in the state, allows of their meeting and acting in concert: lastly, their wealth gives them the means of waiting without inconvenience till those with whom they treat submit to the conditions which they wish to impose on them. Thus, in every country, the share assigned to the labourer is most frequently only just what is sufficient to support his existence.

Authority has, however, interposed in different ways between the landowners and the labourers; religious authority, by consecrating one day in the week to repose, to worship, and to moral enjoyments, to the development of the heart and the mind, in short, to social pleasures, has taken away from the rich one seventh part of the surplus which they would have appropriated, to bestow it on the poor. In Greece, political authority, by calling the Athenian during a great part of each day to the public assembly, left him much less time to produce an income for the rich, and accustomed the whole nation to seek after the public luxury of arts, taste, and intelligence, whilst it was ill-fed and ill-clothed. It gave to the moral development of man all that we give to the trifles of fashion. Military authority, when, as among the ancients, it summoned all men to gymnastic exercise, as among us to militia service and exercises in arms, subtracts also something from the total product of labour, and from the income of the rich, to give it back to the poor in address, strength, valour, and a feeling of dignity. Educational authority, when, as in Prussia, it obliges the children of the poor to devote the first fifteen years of their lives to acquiring moral and intellectual instruction; at the same time obliges the rich to leave to the labouring poor a sufficient share to enable them to bring up their children without exacting from them lucrative labour. Sacerdotal authority in Egypt, in India, in Europe, in the middle ages, by employing the surplus of the product of labour in creating those gigantic monuments of religion, which we admire without being able to imitate them, has also taken something from the rich to pay wages to the poor; it has given to society the luxury of monuments instead of the luxury of elegance; above all, it has preserved the poor from their present calamity, that of competing with one another, so that the more they produce, the less their labour is in demand. The Egyptian never knew the misery of our manufacturers, for neither the pyramids nor the temples of the Thebans were sold in the market.

After having made all these deductions in favour of the poor from the share of the rich, it remains sufficiently large, as much so as is advantageous to society. Some English economists, however, require that the legislature should abstain from laying any restrictions on the rights of the rich over their property, from regulating by law, testaments or inheritances, the portions of children, or the predial services imposed for the benefit of the public, lest men should become disinclined to accumulate wealth, and should dissipate it as soon as they had acquired it. It will be time, we think, to guard against this calamity when the history of human society shall have furnished at least one example of it.

We stop, however. The corollaries to be deduced from the principles which we have only indicated, would be matter for a long work; though we have confined ourselves to the most simple and the most limited portion of political economy. The inquiry as to what must be done for the happiness of the classes who are jointly engaged in producing in the towns, is more complicated and more delicate. The true idea of political economy, however, will never have been attained until the distribution, more than the creation of wealth, has been followed up to the point where it is really most advantageous to the happiness of all.

NOTES

TO

ESSAY ON LANDED PROPERTY.

M. de Sismondi devotes a long chapter to an examination of Mr. Loch's book on the improvements made in the domains of the Marquis of Stafford, from which the following extracts are taken.

Many readers will perhaps refuse to believe that it can ever have been proposed as an amelioration of an agricultural system, to get rid of the peasants who made the land of value, and to drive them from their country. The experiment has, however, been made at various times, and in different parts of the British dominions, in England, Scotland, and Ireland.

We think, therefore, that we ought to fix our attention on the calm and methodical exposition which has been made of this great operation of agriculture, *the clearing of an estate*, by the person who has executed it on the largest scale, and who was employed by the great lord to whom he was attached, to justify them in the eyes of the public. But it is not this personal cause which occupies us in analyzing his book; we endeavour to find there the true history of the great revolution to which, at that period, the population of the mountains of Scotland was subjected, by the application of the chrematistic principles to their cultivation; and we are willing to believe all Mr. Loch affirms as to the humanity with which this was executed, according to the commands of the powerful family whose agent he was.

During the time which has elapsed since the commencement of this century, the nation of the Gaëls, the remains of the ancient Celts, now reduced to 340,000 individuals, has been almost entirely driven from its hearthstones by those whom it regarded as its chiefs, by the lords to whom it had shown, during a long course of years, an enthusiastic devotion. All the properties which it had cultivated from generation to generation under fixed dues, have been forcibly taken from it; the fields which it tilled have been devoted to the pasturage of sheep, and given up to foreign shepherds; its houses and its villages have been razed, or destroyed by fire, and the mountaineers of the expelled nation have been left no other choice but that of cabins on the sea shore, where they might support their miserable existence by fishing, in sight of the mountains from which they had been driven, or to cross that sea to seek their fortune in the deserts of America.

The author of this work endeavours to prove, and does so successfully, not only that the Marchioness of Stafford only made use of rights which the law recognises as belonging to her, but that in the exercise of them she did not lose sight of the preservation of the existence of her vassals, for which she considered herself responsible. What we consider as worthv of attention in this work, is not that the conduct of a great lady has been more or less skilful, more or less generous; it is the spirit of the legislation which has abolished the ancient limitations of property, established by custom; it is the application of the principle that the proprietor is the best judge of his own interest, and of that of the nation, as far as relates to his property;—it is, in short, a great experiment of the application of chresmatistics to agriculture, and of its results.

The ancestors of the Marchioness of Stafford, as the book of her agent informs us, were sovereigns in the most northerly part of Scotland, over about three quarters of the county of Sutherland. Their possessions were about a million English acres. This extent is larger than that of the department of the Upper Rhine. When the Countess of Sutherland inherited these domains, the population did not exceed 15,000 inhabitants. It cannot be said exactly what was its size in ancient times, but we know that the Gaëls made the south of Scotland tremble, and that battalions of soldiers descended from the mountains, which the exhausted nation would be far from being able to furnish now. Reduced as it was, the population of Sutherland appeared too numerous for its lord, as he no longer required military service. All, in fact, was military in the ancient organization of the country. Only thirty of these gentlemen held immediately under the earls: they were called tacksmen, and the district which was assigned to them to govern and to cultivate was called a *tack*. The tacksmen were the judges of their peasantry in peace, and their captains in war; but their obedience was softened by the persuasion that they only formed one family. All called themselves relations of the chief, and bore his name. The income received by the Earl of Sutherland from the *tacksmen*, and by these from their vassals, was so small that it ought rather to be considered as an acknowledgment of sovereignty than as a rent.

But, on the other hand, every man who was born on the domains of Sutherland, in every degree of the feudal scale, was bound to lavish his blood and his life in defence of the sovereignty and the honour of the family of which he formed a part.

After the revolution, private wars became in Scotland more rare and less dangerous, and the kings of England, without ever extending their real authority to these distant provinces, wished that at least the power of their great men should appear to be an emanation from their own. They encouraged the raising of family regiments, which they granted to the Scotch lords, combining this new military establishment with the national system of *clans*. The 93rd regiment was granted to the Earl of Sutherland, and the gentlemen of the county received *tacks* according to their rank, as part of their pay.

Thus the tenure of the estates lost its ancient character of liberality. They were no longer given as an act of munificence on the part of the chief of the family, but as a pecuniary bargain, by which the Mhoir Fhear Chattaibh, *the great man of Sutherland*, endeavoured to get something. In fact he required it; he was called to court, and found himself very small amidst the luxury and opulence of London; he felt himself humiliated by the penury with which his nation was proverbially reproached by the English. All his officers, all his tacksmen, were obliged also in their garrisons to compete with the ruinous expenses of England; and at the same time acquired a taste for luxury which they had not known before. They redoubled their efforts to obtain all they could from the cultivator. But at the same time they ceased to encourage the industry of the country; they were no longer content with the tartan and plaid woven in their family, with the claymore forged in their mountains, with the oatcakes which had been their bread; food, drink, clothes, arms, furniture, all began to be furnished by commerce, and no longer by domestic industry; they had very little to offer in return, for their productions were of little value, and scarcely worth carriage. When the chief and his officers required money to procure the objects of luxury which they could no longer do without, it was necessary to produce not for consumption, but to export to sell, and to sell only.

All the local industries disappeared; in a country where scarcely one dry day between two of rain or snow can be reckoned on, there was no longer any profitable work which could be done under cover; the poor man ceased having an occupation for every season of the year for all the members of his family; idleness increased indigence; the population rapidly decreased, but not enough to satisfy those who wished to improve these great domains.

This population was spread pretty equally over the surface of Sutherland. Each valley contained its hamlet, the alluvial land was destined to the cultivation of barley and oats. The mountains, covered with thick herbage, were given up to the flocks which furnished milk, meat, wool, and leather. All the wants of the population had thus been satisfied, as long as it was content with these rude products.

Between the years 1811 and 1820, the 15,000 inhabitants, forming about 3,000 families, were driven, or according to the softened expression of Mr. Loch, *removed* from the interior of the county. All their villages were demolished or burnt, and all their fields turned into pasturage. (*Improvements, &c., by J Loch, p.* 92.) A similar operation was performed nearly simultaneously by the seven or eight other lords who possessed the rest of the county of Sutherland, or an extent of more than 25,000 English acres. Mr. Loch, however, assures us that the Marchioness of Stafford showed much more humanity than any of her neighbours; she occupied herself with the fate of those she had removed, she offered them a retreat on her own estates; retaking from them 794,000 acres of land, of which they had been in possession from time immemorial, she generously left them 6,000, or about two acres to each family.

These 6,000 acres, which were to serve as a refuge for the small tenants, had not been cultivated, and yielded nothing to the proprietor. They have not, however, been conceded gratuitously: they were subject to a medium rent of 2*s.* 6*d.* an acre, and there were no leases for more than seven years, with a promise of renewal for another seven years if the land was well cultivated. (*Ib.* p. 107.)

The 794,000 acres of which the Marchioness of Stafford thus retook possession, have been divided by her agent, Mr. Loch, into twenty-nine great farms, very unequal in extent. Some are larger than the department of the Seine. These farms, destined solely to the pasturage of sheep, are each inhabited by only one family, and as the industry which they introduced into the country is new, they scarcely employ any Scotch, but only farm-servants from England. 131,000 sheep have already taken the place of the brave men who formerly shed their blood in the defence of Mhoir Fhear Chattaibh. (*Ib.* p. 147.) No human voice resounds in the narrow passes of these mountains, formerly distinguished by the combats of an ancient race; no one recalls glorious recollections; the valleys have no hamlets; no accent of joy or grief disturbs these vast solitudes.

We have no doubt that this overthrow of the property, of the habits, of the affections, of the entire existence of a small nation, has prodigiously augmented the fortune of the Countess of Sutherland. But Mr. Loch is desirous of showing that it has also augmented the wealth of the county; that there is more money, more activity, more industry, more of the enjoyments of luxury; that all Sutherland has been from that time in a progressive state of prosperity, after having been stationary during centuries. We believe, indeed, that judging of the state of the county after the principles of the chresmatistic school, calling that prosperity which it calls by that name, Sutherland has made progress. Many roads of 40 or 50 miles in length cross the whole of the county; bridges of stone and iron have been built at the expense of the countess, dikes and embankments prevent inundations, ports have been opened to commerce, coaches cross the county as far as the small towns built at its extremities; inns and posting-houses have been built by the Marquis of Stafford; and since the year 1820 the exportation of 415,000 lbs. of fine wool show how much wealth it may be expected in time will be sent out of a county which has been made valuable by such an admirable economy of inhabitants, of labour, and of happiness.

Mr. Loch assures us that the lot of these thousands of families exiled from their country, has not been so deplorable as their fears and their regrets predicted. Some, it is true, would hold nothing under her who had driven them from their dwellings. The clan Gunn, or the Mac Hamishes, abandoning the mountains of Kildonan and the valleys of Naver and Helmsdale, all left the country, and Mr. Loch does not tell us what became of them. But except this tribe, and thirty-two families of Strathbora, which went to America in 1818 and 1819, the others, we are afraid, *almost all* accepted the lots which the Marchioness of Stafford offered them. Driven to the borders of this immense domain, between the sea and the foot of the mountains, they found land proper for cultivation, and Mr. Loch affirms what must appear very strange, that it is only in a band half a mile wide, till then uncultivated, that Sutherland can obtain any profit by the cultivation of corn.

Mr. Loch concludes, after enumerating the advantages, that the projects formed by the Marchioness of Stafford to ameliorate her estates in the county of Sutherland have been fully successful. Not only has she obtained great advantages, but she has made the county which depended on her, pass rapidly from barbarism to civilization. If she caused the most grievous anguish to the little nation whose destiny was confided to her, she has opened a more vast field for their industry, and she has endeavoured to soften their regrets by offering them the hope of more ease for the future. We cannot help remarking how much this way of pressing onward the march of civilization resembles what Mehemet Ali employed at the same time in Egypt; and he also was much celebrated for a time by the chresmatistic school, as the restorer of commerce and of the arts; he also mingled in his own person the rights of sovereignty with those of property; he also judged of the prosperity of the state, not by the security or abundance which its inhabitants enjoyed, but by the activity of traffic, the value of exports, the profits of rents; he also laid down roads, opened canals, raised bridges and dikes. He covered Egypt with the works of art; he attracted there learned men, engineers, operatives; he also, wishing perhaps to do good, had especially in view the increase of his own revenue. In his calculations the lives of men appeared only as cyphers; in his accounts he put them on the same line with bales of cotton, as the Marchioness of Sutherland does with bales of wool. He calculated; but the affections, the recollections, the hopes of the unhappy people he disposed of, are not elements subject to calculation.

Admitting with Mr. Loch, that the marchioness executed her projects with as much humanity as prudence, still we must shudder at the idea that the law, as it is interpreted in England, permits the expulsion of a whole nation from its hearthstones, without providing in any way for its subsistence and its future fate; that the government should, when necessary, have lent the strength of a military force for this expulsion, and that it has done so more than once; that in short, as Mr Loch allows, other proprietors in the county have not been so humane. "The population of the Gruids on Lochshin," says he, "was considerable; it does not appear that any lot of ground was assigned to these people, or that they received any compensation at the time of their expulsion, which was effected in the winter of 1818."

This expulsion of the Gaelic people from their ancient homes is legal, but shall we dare to say that it is just?

It is by a cruel abuse of legal forms, it is by an iniquitous usurpation, that the *tacksmen* and the occupiers or copyholders, (*tenanciers*,) whether of the county of Sutherland, or of the rest of Scotland, are considered as having no right to the land which they have occupied for centuries, and that their former leaders are authorized to violate the contract which united for so many centuries the cultivator with his lord.

The English lawyers have constantly assimilated all political rights to properties, and have defended them under this title. They wished to recognise a property in the political rights of the lords, as they pretended to see one in the exclusive rights of certain burgesses to elect members of Parliament, or municipal magistrates; as they pretend to see one in the right of the church to its dignities and revenues; forgetting that when functions are instituted for the advantage of the people, to the people belong the funds by which they are remunerated. English lawyers have scarcely been willing to admit that the community, when it makes progress, has had the right to suppress powers which were burdensome to it; at least they wished that if the functions were suppressed, the remuneration attached to them should be retained. At the same time, instead of giving attention to institutions different from their own, in order to guard equally the interests of all those affected by them, they would consider only the single person who obtained by them a pecuniary profit, and they placed this profit in the same class as the possession of a field, or of a house.

The vast extent of seignorial domains is not a condition peculiar to England. In all the empire of Charlemagne throughout the west, whole provinces have been usurped by warlike chiefs, who obliged the conquered, slaves, and sometimes their companions in arms, to cultivate them for their advantage. In the ninth and tenth centuries, Maine, Anjou, Poitou, were for the counts of those three provinces, three great farms rather than three principalities. Switzerland, which in so many points resembles Scotland, in her lakes and her mountains, in her climate, which so often prostrates the hopes of the labourer, in the character, usages, and habits of her children, was at this period divided among a small number of lords. If the counts of Kyburg, of Leutzburg, of Hapsburgh, and Gruyères had been protected by English laws, they would have been now precisely in the condition in which the earls of Sutherland were twenty years ago: some of them, perhaps, might have had the same taste for improvements, and many republics would have been driven from the Alps to make room for flocks of sheep. But whatever might have been in its origin the right of the counts, the legislation of the whole of continental Europe has not ceased guaranteeing and ameliorating the condition of the feudatories, of the vassals, of the serfs, strengthening the independence of the peasant, covering him with the buckler of prescription, changing his customs into rights, sheltering him from the exactions of his lord, and by degrees raising his tenures to the rank of properties. The law has given to the Swiss peasant the guarantee of perpetuity, whilst to the Scotch lord it has given this same guarantee in the British empire, and left the peasant in a precarious condition. Compare the two countries, and judge of the two systems.

It must not be forgotten, in fact, that the Highlands of Scotland have never been subjected to the yoke of a foreign invasion, that the feudal system never became the law of the country, though the national customs which have been there observed from the most ancient times, have been assimilated to this system adopted in neighbouring countries.

We cannot hope to find in a barbarous nation, which had not the use of writing, authentic documents as to the manner in which those great family associations were formed, known in Scotland by the name of clan, any more than the successive uniting of many clans into one single sovereignty, as in Sutherland. But their name Klaan signifies in Gaelic, children. All their usages, all their reciprocal relations, all their affections, are founded in fact on the tradition which persuades them that they are children of the same family; all their rights, in fact, were those of the children of the same father, on a common patrimony. They were not subject to any other subordination but what the common defence made necessary. The instability of the division of the land did not weaken the rights of property of the great family to which the district where it was established belonged. Such were the public rights of the Celts, as also of the Germans; and among these last, who were organized much more for war than for cultivation, lest the families should become too much attached to the fields which they cultivated, the lots were changed frequently, even annually. All had a right to all among the Scotch, but the field of each one might pass to his neighbour, whether assigned to him by lot, whether extended or restricted according to the power of the family to cultivate it, or that different portions of land were assigned as a reward for services rendered to the country. There is not, indeed, any country in Europe in which may not be found even recent traces of the temporary and variable division of the common domain. In Scotland, it was an object of these divisions and subdivisions of the land to indicate and maintain the subordination of the soldiers to their chief. The *great man* of each clan exercised, perhaps had usurped from the community, the sole right of making these distributions; he gave to his officers the different *tacks* of land, and retook them, according as they showed themselves more or less useful in war. But though he could thus reward or punish militarily the members of the clan, he could not in any degree lessen the property of the clan itself. The favoured individual was different, but the obligation of service was always equal. The military magistrates established for the good of all, acquired at last a more or less considerable share of the national domain, without Sutherland ceasing to belong to the men of Sutherland. The tenure of land was always the same; their contribution for public defence, their dues to the lord who led them to battle, and who maintained order among them, were never augmented.

When civilization began to make progress, the lords, with the language and dress of England, began also to adopt the usages and the manner of thinking of the English. They did not understand, or they no longer cared to understand, the national contract of the Celts, and to give it the form used in civilized nations they reduced it to writing; at the same time they granted to their vassals the *tacks* or portions of land, for a determinate time. Thus they appeared to have conceded much to them, for formerly they could dismiss them at will. It was, on the contrary, an usurpation as to the community, since formerly, when they dismissed them, they must always replace them by others on absolutely the like conditions; whilst when they began to give these lands for rent, they insinuated into the contract that at each renewal of the lease they might make new conditions or increase the dues of their tenants.

By this usurpation, the lords of the Gaelic lands, who properly had the right only to an unchangeable rent on the property of their clan, changed it into an unlimited proprietorship of the domain which paid them this rent. At all events, they were far from foreseeing, or their vassals were far from apprehending, that the day would come when they would take advantage of the renewal of leases, not to increase the dues of the cultivators, but to drive them out. Before forming so barbarous a resolution, the lord must absolutely have ceased to partake of the opinions, the feelings, the point of honour of his countrymen; he must not only have ceased to believe himself to be their father or their brother, but even to feel himself a Scotchman; a base cupidity must have stifled in him that feeling of consanguinity on which their common ancestors had reckoned, when they entrusted to his good faith the destiny of his people. It is as soon as such a change takes place in the opinions, in the interests, in the respective position of the different members of the community, that the legislator ought to interfere, that the whole nation may not be delivered up to the mercy of a small number of greedy and imprudent men. The question is not to solicit the pity of the lords, but to establish the rights of the Gaelic people; it is to prevent for the future a lord from concluding, according to the principles of the chresmatistic school, that man may be troublesome in human society, that there may be economy, progress, prosperity, in cutting off man from his country; or at least not to allow him to act in conformity with these principles. If the Marchioness of Stafford had a right to replace the people of a province by twenty-nine families of foreigners, and some hundreds of thousands of sheep, no time should be lost, as regards her and all others, in abolishing so odious a right.

It is already a great misfortune for a state to have allowed many small properties to be united in few hands. When one single man possesses a territory which would suffice for many hundred families, his luxury takes the place of their comfort, and the revenues which would have nourished their virtues are dissipated by his follies. But what will become of the state if the proprietor of a province imagines that his interest is in opposition to that of its inhabitants, and that it suits him to replace men with sheep and cattle? It was not for this end that territorial property has been established, or that it is guaranteed by the laws. Nations acknowledged it in the persuasion that it would be useful to those who had nothing, as well as to those who had something; but society is shaken when the rights of property are put in opposition to national rights. An earl has no more right to drive from their homes the inhabitants of his county, than a king to drive out the inhabitants of his kingdom. The most despotic of monarchs, if he made the attempt at this day, would soon learn what it would cost him to go beyond the bounds of his authority. Let the great lords of England take care! The less numerous they are, the more dangerous it would be to them to put themselves in opposition to the nation, and to prefer themselves to her. Let them not say, when the question concerns their own interest, like the agent of the Marchioness of Stafford, "Why in this case should a different rule be adopted from what has been followed in all others? Why should the absolute authority of proprietors over their property be abandoned and sacrificed for the public interest, and from motives which concern the public only?" (*Loch*, p. 41, *note.*) If once they believe that they have no need of the people, the people may in their turn think that they have no need of them.

CLEARANCES AND EVICTIONS.

In May, 1845, eighteen families in Glen Calvie gave bond peaceably to leave on the 24th; after which their stock was to be given them, and they might go where they wished. These eighteen families, consisting of ninety-two individuals, supported themselves in comparative comfort, without a pauper among them; they owed no rent, and were ready to pay as much as any one would give for the land, which they and their forefathers had occupied for centuries, but which it seems is now to be turned into a sheep walk.

Behind the church, in the churchyard, a long kind of booth was erected; the roof formed of tarpauling stretched over poles, the sides closed in with horse-cloths, rugs, blankets, and plaids.

A fire was kindled in the churchyard, round which the poor children clustered. Two cradles, with infants in them, were placed close to the fire, and sheltered round by the dejected-looking mothers. Contrasted with the gloomy dejection of the grown-up and the aged, was the melancholy picture of the poor children playing thoughtlessly round the fire. Of the eighty people who passed the night in the churchyard with most insufficient shelter, twenty-three were children under ten years of age, nine persons were in bad health, ten above sixty years of age; twelve out of the eighteen families have been unable to find places of shelter. With the new Scotch Poor Law in prospect, cottages were everywhere refused to them. Each family had, on an average, about £18 to receive for their stock. This sum is sufficient evidence that they were supporting themselves respectably. It will, however, soon be spent, and in the search for places and employments in the south, it is a moral certainty that most of these unskilled men and their families will be reduced to pauperism. This is the benefit the country derives from such proprietors and factors as have owned and managed this glen.

The course pursued in Sutherlandshire, in turning the whole county into a sheep walk, is impolitic as regards the population, as evidenced by their condition; impolitic as regards the country, as evidenced by its stationary or rather retrograde appearance, and by the unimproved rent roll. What then is the condition of the people and of the county in Caithness, where a totally different system is pursued? The great bulk of the county is let in small farms from £15 to £50 a year rental. Instead of the wretched bothies crowded in clusters, and then some twenty miles without a cottage, which is the characteristic of Sutherlandshire, and scarcely a man to be seen employed; throughout Caithness there is scarcely a bothie to be seen, but every five or six hundred yards there is a good stone cottage, often with a little garden to it, and evidences of comfort about it. The whole land is cultivated, and there is scarcely a field without men and horses in it labouring, and women weeding and stone picking.

In the sheep-farming and clearance county of Sutherland, the annual rental assessed to the property-tax in 1815 was £33,878, in 1842-3 it was £35,567, being an increase of about $\frac{1}{20}$ in twenty-seven years. The population in Sutherland in 1801 was 23,117; in 1841, 24,666, or an increase of about 1,500 in forty years. In Caithness, in 1815, the land rental was assessed to the property-tax at £35,469; in 1842-3, the land rent was assessed at £65,869, and the house rent at £10,500. The population in 1801 was one third less than that of Sutherland; in 1841, it was one third more.

I see, the Spectator writes, that the extensive sheep-farms and fishing villages support a larger population than was supported in a chronic state of pauperism under the tenant and tacksman system.

It is scarcely possible, in three lines, to collect a greater number of fallacies, to make more assertions directly contrary to the truth. The "larger population," where is it? I rode over an "extensive sheep-farm" yesterday. It extends over twenty miles, is in the hands of one man, who employs twenty shepherds, one man to a mile. The "fishing villages;" I have been all round the coast of this country, and I have not seen one fishing village. I have seen several collections of wretched huts on the coast, the male population of which migrate to Lewis and Wick to the herring fisheries carried on there, leaving their families to subsist on the credit of what they may earn. But not a "fishing village," where fishing is carried on as a regular trade and means of living, have I seen in one hundred miles of coast. In only two places have I seen a boat of any kind—the people are so wretchedly poor that they have no boats, much less a market or a trade to "support a larger population" than formerly, in "greater comfort," by their fishing. And their former "chronic state of pauperism;" why, imagination cannot conceive their situation to be worse, a more universal state of "chronic pauperism" than that which now exists. Three fourths of the people, if not actually paupers on the roll, live by begging. They have nothing on earth to do, or that they can do. The bits of land they have will barely supply them with potatoes, and they have to migrate south as day labourers the greater part of the year, in order to pay their rent. It is impossible to conceive, generally, wretchedness more abject than this "greater comfort."

The system of driving out the people has been here tried without compunction. The population has been destroyed, and there is a starving refuse left behind without any means of employment. The peasantry have been thinned and thinned till they are almost isolated, and yet they starve. And who prospers by this system? Not the gentry apparently—the landowners—for they are most of them over head and ears in debt. It is, however, manifest that the people and the nation lose by it.

On the evidence before the Commissioners of Poor Law Inquiry, it was stated that W. Donald McDonald, with 30,000 acres, only kept eleven shepherds. The Rev. W. McKenzie, speaking of the clearance system, said, "I am very positive, and have not the least doubt, that the condition of the people has been very much deteriorated by the change."

The Rev. W. Findlater, of Duirness, said, that while the population of the parish continues much the same as formerly, the number of paupers on the roll is just about doubled. While the population were settled in the interior, though they were more liable to be affected by unfavourable seasons, yet from the numbers of sheep and cattle which they kept, they could generally, by the disposal of part of their stock, purchase the meal requisite for their families. And though they have now the additional resource of fishing, yet, from the nature of the coast and boisterous character of the Western Ocean, it is very precarious; they cannot purchase boats or drifts of lines for white fishing. The Rev. Daniel McKenzie, of Foir, said, "I remember very well the change which took place on removing the small tenants from the interior to the seashore. In my opinion, the people have been decidedly losers by the change. They cannot command the same amount of the comforts of life as they did formerly."

See a long and very interesting series of letters on the condition of the poor in the highlands of *Scotland* in the *Times*, May and June, 1845. Also the debate as reported in the *Times* of July 4th, 1845.

On the third of April, 1846, Mr. O'Connell entered into an explanation of the causes of the disturbances and crimes of Ireland. He read a mass of evidence to prove that one of the main causes was the clearance system, and mentioned as an appalling fact, that within five years 120,000 persons had been evicted in the county of Tipperary alone. (Not contradicted.)

EXTRACT FROM THE *ÉTUDES*, VOL. II., P. 169.

Whilst ancient Europe was divided among small free agricultural nations, their prosperity was increasing with wonderful rapidity; cultivation extended from the plains even to the summits of the mountains, all the means of increasing the fertility of the land were successively discovered, all the productions of the soil which could satisfy the tastes of man were, by turn, called into existence; that Campagna of Rome now so desert, made wholesome by the breath of man, was covered with so close a population, that five acres were supposed to be amply sufficient for the support of a family; in spite of frequent wars this population increased continually; as a hive of bees gives out a swarm every year, so it was necessary for every city after the development of one generation to send out a colony; and this colony recommencing social progress after the same principles, with peasant proprietors, and expecting every thing from agriculture, rapidly advanced towards the same prosperity. It was then that the human race spread itself over the face of the earth, and that in reciprocal independence, in the bosom of abundance and of virtues, those nations grew up, whose fate it was, at a later period, to become the sport of politics and of war.

That rural happiness, the picture of which history presents to us in the glorious times of Italy and Greece, is not unknown in our age. Wherever are found peasant proprietors, are also found that ease, that security, that independence, that confidence in the future, which assure at the same time happiness and virtue. The peasant who does, with his children, all the work on his little inheritance, who neither pays rent to any one above him, nor wages to any one below him, who regulates his production by his consumption, who eats his own corn, drinks his own wine, is clothed with his own flax and wool, cares little about knowing the price of the market; for he has little to sell, and little to buy, and is never ruined by the revolutions of commerce. Far from fearing for the future, it is embellished by his hopes; for he puts out to profit for his children, or for ages to come, every instant which is not required by the labour of the year. Only a few moments, stolen from otherwise lost time, are required to put into the ground the nut which in a hundred years will become a large tree; to hollow out the aqueduct which will drain his field for ever; to form the conduit which will bring him a spring of water; to ameliorate, by constant attention, all the kinds of animals and vegetables by which he is surrounded. This little patrimony is a true savings-bank, always ready to receive his little profits, and usefully to employ all his leisure moments. The everlasting power of nature makes them fruitful, and returns them to him a hundred fold. The peasant has a strong feeling of the happiness attached to the condition of proprietor. Thus he is always eager to purchase land at any price. He pays for it more than it is worth, more than it will return perhaps; but what a reason he has to esteem at a high price the advantage of thenceforward always employing his labour advantageously, without being obliged to offer it cheap; to find always his bread when he wants it, without being obliged to buy it dear.

It is Switzerland particularly that must be gone over, that must be studied, to judge of the happiness of peasant proprietors. Switzerland must be known, to be convinced that agriculture, practised by those who gather the fruits of it, suffices to procure great comfort to a very numerous population; great independence of character, the fruit of an independent situation; great exchange of what is consumed, the consequence of the well-being of all the inhabitants, even in a country where the climate is rude, the soil moderately fertile, and where late frosts, and uncertain seasons, often destroy the hopes of the labourer. Whether we pass through the cheerful Emnethal, or bury ourselves in the most distant valleys of the canton of Berne, we cannot see without admiration, without being affected, those wooden houses of the least peasant, so vast, so well closed, so well constructed, so covered with carvings. In the interior every detached chamber of the numerous family opens into large corridors; each room has only one bed, and it is abundantly provided with curtains and with coverings of the whitest linen; furniture, carefully kept, surrounds it; the closets are full of linen; the dairy is large, well ventilated, and exquisitely neat; under the same roof are found provisions of corn, of salt meat, of cheese, and of wood; in the stables are seen the most beautiful cattle in Europe, and the best attended to; the garden is planted with flowers; the men as well as the women are warmly and properly clad—the last preserve with pride their ancient costume, and bear in their countenances the marks of vigour and of health; they are striking from that beauty of feature which becomes the character of a race, when for many generations it has suffered neither from vice nor from want. Let other nations boast of their opulence; Switzerland may always with pride place its peasantry in opposition to it.

The peasant proprietor is, of all cultivators, the one who obtains most from the soil; for it is he who thinks most of the future, as well as being the most enlightened by experience; it is he also who makes the greatest profit of human labour, because dividing his occupations among all the members of the family, he reserves some for every day of the year, so that there is no waste time for any one; of all cultivators he is the happiest; and at the same time, in a given space, land, without being exhausted, never produces so much food, or employs so many inhabitants as when they are proprietors; lastly, of all cultivators the peasant proprietor is the one who gives most encouragement to commerce and industry, for he is the richest.

Shall we conclude from this, that all proprietors should also be labourers? No: we take society as it is, with poor and rich, and we believe this variety of its conditions most advantageous to its development.

ON THE

CONDITION OF THE WORK PEOPLE

IN

MANUFACTORIES[a].

WE have, in a preceding article, endeavoured to fix the attention of civilians, on what appears to us the most important of all questions in Political Economy, on the share of happiness which wealth ought to diffuse among those who contribute by their labour to its creation. With us it is a fixed principle that social order ought never to sacrifice one class of men to another, and that, whilst admitting divers conditions, poor as well as rich, these differences are only protected for the common welfare of all, this inequality is only legitimate, because it secures, even to the humblest, a portion of comfort, which he could not find in savage life. The gifts of a just and beneficent community may be unequal; but this community becomes iniquitous and oppressive, if it takes from some to give to others; if it demands from the poorest, labour which the savage is not acquainted with, and does not secure to him in return that comfort, content, and security as to the future, which he could not find in the woods.

The progress of civilization and industry has multiplied all the products of human labour applicable to the uses and habits of man: the poor man, in exchange for his labour, ought to obtain his share of these products; and this share ought to comprehend food, lodging, and clothing, sufficient for the preservation of

[a] Extracted from the *Revue mensuelle d'Economie politique.—July and August*, 1834.

health. Civilization has developed in man the love of society; the poor man, who labours, has a right to a share of social pleasures; he has a right to those relaxations and enjoyments without which life is a burden. The application of science to the arts, and the invention of machines of continually increasing power, have multiplied indefinitely the results of the employment of human strength for the common advantage; the poor have a right to their share in this advantage; they have a right that the development of mechanical power should procure them more rest. Civilization has developed cultivation and power of mind; it has raised the intelligence of man; it has placed him likewise on the way to obtain a higher moral state. The poor man has a right also to his share of the enjoyments and virtues acquired by intelligence; he has a right to education for his children; to a share of instruction in his riper age, that the progress of thought may not increase the distance which separates him from his fellow-men. Sensibility, also, is developed with civilization; by it are increased the importance and the charms of domestic life; the poor man has also a right to have his share in the happiness of domestic ties; he has a right that his wife and children should multiply his chances of happiness, rather than those of suffering. Social order considers it of the first importance that stability, security, that tie which cements the present with the past and the future, should be guaranteed to the citizen. The poor man who labours has a right that his future also should be secured to him; that his condition may place within his reach also, those two feelings equally essential to happiness, confidence in the advantages he possesses, and the hope to ameliorate them still more. We repeat it, it is this participation of the poor in the advantages of progressive civilization, which appears to us to be the object towards which all political economy should tend; an object completely neglected, completely wanting in the school which we have called chresmatistic; an object from which social order in modern times is every day receding more and more, instead of advancing towards it.

In the eyes of the moralist, in the eyes of the true legislator, the fundamental idea of civil society is the right of every man to improve his condition, resulting from this simple fact, that each man forms a part of this civil society. Men have associated together, only from the hope of improvement and happiness: to purchase these, they submit to the authority of one another; on this condition only is social power legitimate. But to give some value to their inferiors in the eyes of the powerful, of those who profit by the present state of social order, it is perhaps necessary to direct the attention to another consideration—their own safety; we must tell them that if sovereign power is not efficaciously employed for the happiness of all, their own happiness, their wealth, their life, run the most imminent risk. They must perceive that there exist in society an already numerous class, and which has a tendency to become more so every day, to whom the present order of society does not give the enjoyment of any of the fruits of the association; these are men, who, creating wealth by the labour of their hands, never participate in it. Not only have they no property, they have no certainty of a livelihood; habitually reduced to the commonest food, to the most miserable lodging and clothing; if sometimes an unexpected demand for labour, (which seems to be the case at this present time,) an unexpected rise in wages should procure them a fleeting abundance, on the other side they know that any day all demand for labour, all wages may cease, and then the wretchedness into which they fall is frightful; and if they are fathers of families, the despair of their wives and children redoubles their own.

That class of working men to whom has been given in our time the name used by the Romans, *proletarii*, comprises the most numerous and energetic class of the population of large towns. It comprehends all those who work in manufactories, in the country as well as in towns; it continually encroaches on those kinds of business formerly known as master trades, whenever a manufactory can be established, when all together, in one place, under one head, but by many hundred hands, those common utensils and tools can be made, which used to be made in the places where they were wanted; lastly, it encroaches on agriculture when the system of great farms cultivated by day-labourers is introduced, and which has, in England, almost entirely superseded the formerly independent and happy class of yeomen, or labouring small landowners. The proletarii are cut off from all the benefits of civilization; their food, their dwellings, their clothes are insalubrious: no relaxation, no pleasures except occasional excesses, interrupt their monotonous labours; the introduction of the wonders of mechanics into the arts, far from abridging their hours of labour, has prolonged them: no time is left them for their own instruction or for the education of their children; no enjoyment is secured to them in those family ties which reflect their sufferings: it is almost wise in them to degrade and brutalize themselves, to escape from the feeling of their misery; and that social order which threatens them with a worse condition for the future, is regarded by them as an enemy to combat and destroy. This is not all; whilst their own distress is increasing, they see society overcome, as it were, by the weight of its material opulence: they are in want of everything, and on all sides their eyes are struck with what is everywhere superabounding. At the same time, the information which is not given to them, comes, however, to great assemblies of men; higher principles as to the destiny of the human race are spread abroad; feelings of liberty and equality ferment in their hearts; they know that they have rights which are violated, which are invaded, and even their ignorance of the nature and limits of these rights increases their resentment, and the danger with which their victory would threaten every other order of society; in short, in the course of late years, they have acquired courage, a powerful sentiment of honour, and a confidence in themselves, which was not formerly found in the inferior ranks of society—what motives for the rich to think of the poor, from a regard for themselves, and care for their own safety, if they will not do so from virtue, from justice, from charity! The rich and the powerful know, that notwithstanding the disproportion of numbers, they can maintain a contest with the poor, because those who have money can always find soldiers; because science opens her resources to destroy men, as well as to create wealth, but they ought not the less to tremble at the idea of a servile war—a war now preached by eloquent tongues, pointing out to the vengeance of the oppressed, "*him whose name is only known in hell.*"[a] Victory might be theirs, but their wealth might be annihilated, and floods of their own blood might flow during the contest.

The events of the month of April of this year have given a frightful degree of reality to these forewarnings. People wished to look upon the crisis at Lyons only as the efforts, and perhaps last agony, of the Republican party. Although those who took arms assembled in the name of the republic, it was much more a question of property than of a political constitution which inflamed them. Republics, as well as monarchies, admit not only of the distinctions of wealth, but of those of rank, and those who, calling themselves republicans, recollect the history of the world, do not found their ideal republic on an equality which has nowhere existed. A party, however, which calls itself republican, irritated against the present disorder, instead of reforming, would destroy the edifice from top to bottom. As far as their theories can be understood, they attack the distinction of fortune as well as that of rank; and there can be no doubt that this party looks upon the proletarii as their forces, and that their strength consists in this numerous mass of men, who suffer, to whom the future looks threatening, who feel themselves unjustly deprived of their rights, and who

[a] "And the wicked man who had lied to his brothers amassed more wealth than the wicked man who had enchained them. The name of this last is Tyrant, the other has no name except in hell."—*Paroles d'un Croyant*, viii.

It is impossible to lay open with more clearness, and at the same time more eloquence, than M. de la Mennais has done, the double action through which the labour of the operative increases, and his wages diminish; but a believer (*un croyant*), a charitable man, should not have supposed a wish to injure in the master manufacturer, and called down upon him the vengeance of the multitude, when he only saw the invincible power of things.

demand vengeance. If war, declared against established order by the proletarii, must inspire us with well-founded alarm; it must be said that the way in which the defenders of order have triumphed over them, is not calculated to inspire less terror. The historian, whose studies have led him to compare the explosion of popular fury at different periods, is able most strongly to express his reprobation of that character of ferocity with which anger and fear have impressed this contest. From the first shock, there has been no wish to appease, to conciliate, but only to destroy; to be sure of reaching the guilty, the innocent have been sacrificed, the stranger who passed through the streets, those whom the most urgent need of bread, of water, of help, forced to come down into them: houses and warehouses were battered down; though it was well known that the proletarii had neither houses nor shops. In short, the Rhone from its confluence with the Saône, as far as Arles, carried down eight hundred dead bodies of Frenchmen, killed by Frenchmen; the same number with which it was clogged on the day of St. Bartholomew; but then these civil wars had already divided France into two camps, which had terrible reprisals to make against one another; besides, religious fanaticism, formidable as it is, is a nobler passion than fear and the love of money.

At the same time, other events took place in England of a totally opposite character, which, however, taught almost the same lesson to both nations at the same time. The workmen of all the manufactories who employ a great number of hands under one head, formed themselves into a kind of mutual insurance society, which they called a *trades' union:* it extended from one end of England to the other, and was said to consist of a million of members: all, whilst in work, were to pay a weekly subscription into the common purse, and from this fund allowances were granted to maintain the workmen, when, after a consultation among themselves, they decided that their wages were insufficient, and therefore refused to work—what they called a strike—in order to oblige their masters to increase them.

The procession of the trades' union in London, about the same period as the contest at Lyons, struck terror into the capital. It only manifested, however, the power of one idea, when it brings union, the order and discipline which it maintained, its respect for peace and law; and on the other side, the admirable mixture of moderation and firmness which the government displayed. The assemblage separated without being satisfied on any point, and without having committed the least disorder.

The state of social order is, in fact, exposed to risk throughout Europe; the juncture is serious; the multiplying of proletarii threatens the most civilized countries with a war which the English have first called servile, and which may, in fact, present all the frightful characteristics of that, which, under the direction of Spartacus, placed the Roman republic in the most imminent danger. The position is serious, no doubt, but by no means desperate. If, instead of uniting our efforts to accelerate our movement down the rapid slope along which we are rolling, we would contemplate the precipice at its foot, and have the strong determination to stop, we should soon become masters of the impulse which hurries us on.

We have established in the first place, in our article on landed property, that the great mass of working men who labour in the fields are not customarily driven into the class of proletarii; in most countries they are in some manner attached to property; they are the allies of the rich instead of contending against them; they enjoy a certain degree of comfort, they may obtain more; they have a security not only for the future, but almost for perpetuity. Those countries which are so unfortunate as to have converted their agriculturists into day-labourers, ought to lose no time in returning to a better system in the cultivation of their estates: even their existence depends on this. As to France, it is calculated that four-fifths of the population are devoted to agriculture; there is no necessity to change their condition; only to ameliorate it. It is easy then to give a prospect of future welfare to four-fifths of the nation, and to make them attain it in time.

There is no reason to expect that this proportion, which appears to be general throughout Europe, should change. It is much more difficult to apply the great discoveries of science to agriculture than to the industrial arts. If in the most barbarous ages one man in five was sufficient to clothe and lodge all the five, whilst four were required to till the ground to feed themselves and the fifth, this fifth assisted by all the powers of mechanics, and all the powers of nature which man has learned to command, must be able to accomplish the same task, and henceforth to do it with more perfection and more taste. This primitive exchange is the basis of the prosperity of all nations, for their own consumption ought to equal their production; they may work for foreign markets that they may produce by exchange what they want, but if they reckon on doing the work of foreigners, on labouring that foreigners may consume their productions and pay their wages, they make a false calculation, by which, as we shall show further on, they will inevitably be disappointed.

By an approximating calculation, four-fifths then of the nation belong to the country and to agriculture, and the fifth to towns and other occupations. There would be danger to the state, the balance of productions would be overthrown if this fifth became a quarter or a third, but it does not follow that this fifth should go to increase the ranks of the proletarii. One part of the products of industry is prepared by trades, another part by manufacturers. Now the life of men who exercise trades is in general happy, and affords all those securities which we have demanded for the poor who work. A trade always requires an apprenticeship; and even where the ancient regulations which fixed the duration of this apprenticeship are abolished, it is not possible at the same time to abolish the necessity of a preparatory education to make carpenters, masons, locksmiths, farriers, cartwrights, shoemakers, tailors, bakers, or butchers. This apprenticeship, which requires a sacrifice of time and of money, and which does not begin till after childhood, necessarily limits competition; it does not offer the dangerous temptation to tradesmen which it does to manufacturers, to bring children into the world to employ them in gaining something, even at six or eight years old, to the great injury of their health and of their moral development.

The master tradesmen do not willingly take apprentices when their trade does not flourish in their locality, a second obstacle to imprudent competition, to a creation of products beyond the demand. The apprentice enters his master's family according to a contract which often binds him for many years; if he is not always sheltered from the effects of the rude manners and want of education of his master, he can, however, only be subjected to moderate labour, with hours and days of relaxation; and almost always time is allowed for moral instruction, because there is equality of condition and sympathy between him and his master. After his apprenticeship he becomes a journeyman, and engages with a master for a salary; he travels from town to town; his mind becomes enlarged; he is accustomed to independence; he learns the proportion between population and the demand for work; he finds out the place where he can establish himself with advantage, secure of sufficient work. It is then only that he settles; becomes a master; employs the little capital which he has been accumulating, in purchasing tools and furnishing a workshop; engages a journeyman and an apprentice; then lastly, he marries, for his means of living are now secured; he is in port. Before this time, even if he should have had the imprudence to seek a wife, it is probable that he would not have been able to find one, for he had nothing to offer; but thenceforward his life is independent and happy; he knows exactly how much employment there is a demand for in the district, and how much of it he can do. His wife does not assist him in his work; she has the care of the housekeeping, of keeping their house clean, and of the education of the children. The entrance of life may have been difficult, but from that time every step which he has taken has brought him nearer to a better condition.

If among those who began life with him some have not succeeded, they do not marry, and do not transmit their poverty. If some discovery in mechanics can be useful in his trade, he profits by it; he does not run the risk of being superseded by a machine, or of his work being stopped by the prohibitive laws of a foreign country with which he has no quarrel.

It is in the midst of these trades, exercised by the freemen of towns, which formerly did all the industrial work in all nations, that manufactories have arisen. The masters of manufactories in towns hold the same place in the industry of towns that great landowners do in the country. Like them, to make their own great fortunes, they must cause the disappearance of one or two hundred small independent properties: like them, they afterwards, by agreeing together, reduce all the men who work under them to a state approaching to servitude; like them, by the great means at their disposal, the employment of scientific assistance, the more complete division of labour, the economy of time and of inspection, whilst they make an advance they cause the condition of men to recede; like them, in short, they experience a reaction when those they employ begin to suffer, for after all, those who have must feed those who have not, and they are themselves ruined by the false system of labour which they have adopted, with the object of enriching themselves.

One has great reason to be astonished that a system which tends to destroy small properties in mechanical arts, as well as in agriculture, and to substitute for them, indigence on one side and opulence on the other—a system which creates for some, power unbounded, and for others absolute dependence—a system whose tendency is in opposition to the governing idea and passion of the age, equality—should exactly in such an age, have been received with so much favour. Nevertheless, it is a fact; and industrialism has been proclaimed as being the tendency, as well as the glory of our age, by persons who would equally have paid homage to the feudalism of the twelfth century. Still more, the Saint Simonians have almost made a religion of it. The prodigies of the mind of man subduing the elements have made them forget that the character of true prodigies, of those which come from God, is to be useful to man. Industrialism, or the substitution of one great workshop for many small ones in the common arts, has been considered to be one of the benefits of civilization, in consequence of many illusions. It was natural that at the movement of the establishment of a great and scientific manufactory, the eye should have been struck with admiration at the power of man, and at his triumph over nature, at the multiplicity of productions heaped up in a few hours, remembering the few processes by which they had formerly been obtained. Had it been possible, however, to see with a glance, the hundred or thousand families who had been deprived of their livelihood, or whose independence had been destroyed, it is probable that what society gained by the change might have been calculated more scrupulously. Thus, when a Scotch nobleman sends a whole clan to the other side of the Atlantic, in order to subject to a more scientific cultivation the estates from which he has expelled his former vassals, it is not sufficient for him to show his harvests or his flocks to prevent its being asked what he has done with the men. But manufactories are scarcely ever established in places, where the trades which they have replaced, were disseminated. These trades were established as near as they could be to the consumers; this was the true means of knowing the demand, and of proportioning their labour to the quantity of productions which they could dispose of. Thus nearly each village had its miller, its potter, its shoemaker, its locksmith; but if capitalists, profiting by the progress of science, propose to grind corn, and to make earthenware by steam, to make locks, to cut out shoes by complicated machines, in large quantities, and supply the whole country at a time, they will leave their consumers that they may go where fuel is abundant, or the raw material of the best quality, or where wages are low. In the place where they establish themselves, they will do only good; they will disperse a great deal of money; they will give a value to raw materials and to provisions, which before it was difficult to dispose of; they will be surrounded by people to whom they give a livelihood; to whom they give wages for work; to perform which even an apprenticeship is not requisite. It will be said that these capitalists carry prosperity with them, and no one will go into unknown villages to count the master millers, potters, shoemakers, and locksmiths, whose means of living have been destroyed by the new manufactories. But it is for the statesman to count them, and to have always present to his mind the sum of evil by which any advantage is purchased.

The struggle between old trades and new manufactories has nearly terminated in the victory of the last, as respects all those articles in the production of which the two methods can enter into competition. The only way in which we can form an idea of the independence of the master tradesmen and of the prosperity to which the workman formerly attained at the end of his career, is to look at those trades where the business, varying according to circumstances, cannot be transported and must be in direct demand; such are those of the carpenter and mason. But a new struggle has arisen between the manufacturers who possess the most capital and those who have least, and a new illusion has hidden from the eyes both of those engaged, whether in business or legislation, how much there is that is odious and cruel in the nature of this struggle; this illusion bears on the extent of the market.

The economists mean by these words, *extent of the market*, not only the distance to which the producer can carry his products with the hope of selling them, but the power and the will to purchase of those comprehended within this circle. In order to occasion no remorse to those who might fear that they were raising themselves on the ruin of their rivals, the promoters of industrialism pretend that the extent of the market is unlimited. Produce boldly, say they, for the more abundance there is, the more people will enjoy and consume; and a Scotch economist, who likes to clothe his reasoning in several abstract forms, has said, exchanges will necessarily increase with the increase of abundance: thus the field A has produced one year a hundred sacks of corn, and the workshop B, the same year, a hundred yards of cloth. The following year the same field has produced a thousand sacks of corn, the same workshop a thousand yards of cloth; why should they not also exchange one against the other? Why should not the same exchange be made if it were ten thousand or a hundred thousand? As usual, the Scotch philosopher has forgotten man in this reckoning; if instead of a field and workshop he had recollected that two men, one a farmer and the other an artizan, must exchange that surplus of their products which they did not use themselves, he would have perceived that he was saying an absurdity. One of these two men, after having purchased as much corn as he wants for food, is no longer hungry—wants no more—whatever may be the quantity produced on his neighbour's field; the other having bought cloth enough to clothe himself, is no longer cold—wants no more—whatever may be the activity of the manufacturer.

The extent of the market is, in effect, always limited by two things very independent of one another, the need or convenience of the buyers and their means of payment. It is not sufficient to be hungry in order to buy bread, unless there is wherewithal to pay for it; thus, however, the population may increase, its consumption will not increase unless its income increases also. Again, for a man to buy bread it is not enough to have an income, he must also be able to eat it; now not only is the quantity which the rich eat limited; the quantity of all manufactured productions which they can use is limited also. The luxury of opulence can never affect manufactured articles; but the productions of the artist only, from the embroiderer or lacemaker to the sculptor. It results from this important and too much forgotten rule, that to increase the sale of the produce of the industry and labour of man, it is not the income of the rich but the income of the poor that must be increased. It is their wages that must be increased, for the poor are the only purchasers who can add greatly to the extent of the market.

But *the extent of the market* for a new manufacture is composed not only of all the new purchasers, who, feeling new wants, and having acquired more income, present themselves to consume the new production which is offered to them. Unfortunately it also reckons much on the old purchasers, who may be drawn away from rival manufactures; it also calculates the power of *underselling*, a word which I must be permitted to borrow from a nation where it is made the basis of mercantile policy. It is assumed, that the market for any manufacture extends to every purchaser to whom the articles it has produced can be offered at a lower price than can be done by rival manufactures. All those which can be undersold are driven from the market, and then the one which has been able to do this prospers, and makes no account of the loss of those over which it has triumphed; circulating capital is dissipated, fixed capital remains unemployed and soon falls to ruin; workmen are dismissed; they suffer in indigence or perish from want. The manufacture which has been undersold makes every effort to recover the market. It defends its very existence, and the combat is to the death. The master is content with less profit; often he goes on, even at a loss, to maintain his credit; he gives up making a rent on his buildings and machines; he engages his famishing workmen to be satisfied with the lowest wages, rather than be dismissed and lose everything; after having worked in the day, they work also in the night. If however their rivals owe the advantage of selling at lower prices to the discovery of a new machine, of which they retain the monopoly, ingenious men torture their minds to discover the secret; if the producers belong to two different nations, learned bodies will occupy themselves with it, government will second them; national vanity would be wounded to be, as is said, tributary to foreigners, or more properly, to pay wages to foreign workmen whilst their own are perishing with hunger; the secret will be at last discovered;

patriotism will collect the necessary capital; the two rival manufactures will strive against one another in order to gain purchasers, who are only sufficient for the consumption of what is produced by one of them ; the market is glutted to the ruin of industry, and in the midst of this contest, the manufacturers proclaim the disastrous principle, that the basis of all manufacturing prosperity is the low rate of hand labour.

The low rate of hand labour is, however, the way in which they designate the contract which gives to the workman in exchange for his labour the least enjoyment possible. Whilst the master manufacturers are aiming at taking away one another's customers, by continually lowering the prices of their fabrics, they drive their workmen into still crueller poverty. First they deprive them of even the humblest comforts and pleasures, then of their hours of repose; the workman must work for the strictest, most absolute necessaries; he must give every hour of the day for reduced wages; but it is discovered that by greatly exciting his interest it is possible to obtain from him more employment of muscular strength; he has the offer of working by the piece; soon, however, competition reduces the price of labour, and he gets no more by working by the piece than he formerly did by working by the day. Then, in order to live, he must call upon his wife to assist in the manufactory. The business of the wife in the poor man's household ought to be the preparation of food, domestic arrangements, keeping the clothes in order, but especially the education of the children, whom she should inspire with the virtues of their condition, and with the affection which binds them to their parents. But at this point of the workman's degradation there is no housekeeping for the poor man, no domestic arrangements requiring neatness and care; public kitchens prepare food for all, cheaper and cheaper; infant schools receive children just weaned till they are six or eight years old, when they are required to contribute to get bread for the family by labour, which destroys their health and brutalizes their minds. Such is the frightful progress of wretchedness produced by the competition to obtain hand labour at the lowest price. It has taken from the poor all enjoyment, all family ties, and the virtues of which they are the source, all gratitude from children to their parents. It does not, however, stop here; the poor man cannot live for less than his master gives him, but he can die; a new machine is invented which can, henceforth, do with a hundred hands what formerly required a thousand, and all these supernumerary hands are then dismissed. Such is the fatal course of every manufacture, founded, not to satisfy new wants, but to create a market for itself by underselling the old producers. The reaction against the workmen is equally cruel, whether the new manufacture endeavours to undersell natives or foreigners; neither will consent to give up all work, all income, all wages; they will not do *something else;* first, because neither their tools nor the skill which they have acquired prepares them for something else; then because the ruin of their own employment is no reason why some other thing should be in demand, and because all labour, which is not in demand, produces the same glut, the same ruin. The reaction is equally cruel, whether the competition be between productions of the same kind or between those which may be substituted for one another, as when cotton fabrics took the place of those of wool or silk.

It is as unjust as it is dangerous to the public peace to accuse the master manufacturers of wishing to reduce the poor to this distress. No doubt they committed a serious error when they undertook to manufacture anything which the public did not demand; for the first rule of prudence, as well as the first duty of the manufacturer, is to study the state of the market, and never to contribute to glut it; it is to proportion their products to the means of the purchasers, to live by serving them, not by hurting their fellow manufacturers. But this lesson, so loudly enforced by reason, so long well understood in commerce, and which has been the basis of its prosperity till the end of the last century, every one now strives to forget. The cry of monopoly is raised against all those who endeavour to keep up prices; those are violently applauded who, by a fortunate competition with their fellow producers, procure for the consumers unexpected low prices; universal competition is preached; we are to believe that the interest of the consumer is above that of the community, forgetting that the consumer must have an income before productions can be offered to him, even at the lowest price. Can we be astonished if the manufacturer has fallen into an error accredited by all writers, common to all the world, and now the reigning idea? Once entered on this fatal course, the manufacturers have been drawn on by an irresistible fatality. Their whole capital is quickly engaged in their manufactory; then, to pay their workmen, they must sell; to sell they must lower their prices; to lower their prices they must offer their workmen insufficient wages, whatever may be their humanity, their generosity; they submit to the law before imposing it on others. Undersold by their fellow manufacturers, they have only the choice of offering to their workmen a miserable pittance or nothing at all, and closing their workrooms.

This fatality, which governs the manufacturers, renders vain all efforts that the workmen can make against them in order to ameliorate their condition. The chresmatistics had announced that the power of the masters who desired to lower wages, and that of the workmen who wished to raise them, was equal, so that their opposition would fix the rate of wages at a just medium. This equilibrium was a primary error; in a contest of this kind, he who can wait the longest is sure of victory; the capitalists do not suffer much from suspending works for six months—for the workmen it is death. But when once a glut in the market has begun, the contest is no longer between the workmen and the masters; it is between the workmen and inflexible necessity. The great association, known in England by the name of *Trades' Unions*, has been a melancholy experiment of this kind. With a remarkable agreement in their design, the men were able, by refusing to work, to force their masters to close their workrooms, but not to raise their wages, for they could not procure them a single customer; still more, it is impossible to think without deep sorrow of these poor men, obedient to the law in their distress, dissipating in a vain but just struggle the savings of their labour, and obliged at last to yield.

If the legal resistance of the English Unionists was not efficacious, the armed resistance of the French could not be more successful. It is not the point to inquire whether the sufferings of the proletaries in France, the famine which threatened their wives and children, gave them the right to take arms, but whether resistance or even victory could ameliorate their condition. Now, conqueror or conquered, the master of a manufactory can only get interest on his capital by selling its products; he can only pay his workmen's wages with the money which he receives from his customers; burning his warehouses and his machines—robbing him, killing him—far from raising wages will entirely dry up their source. The suspension of work does not even cause a void in the shops which require to be filled up; the suspension of one manufactory only makes another flourish the more rapidly, which, secure of a temporary sale, will hasten to increase its machines; the convulsions of Lyons only redoubled the activity of manufactories in Switzerland, Germany, and England. It is not therefore in the name of morality and law, it is in the name of their own interests that we should unceasingly call upon the workmen to refrain from coalitions—to refrain from risings.

At the moment when these coalitions and these risings spread so much alarm, we heard it repeated that the workmen were unpardonable, for that their wages were sufficient; and in fact we know that, at this moment of excitement, many workmen made unreasonable demands; many others, intoxicated by false theories, thought less of their subsistence than of the sovereignty of the people, and demanded, under the name of a republic, not that form of government which in Greece, in Italy, in

Switzerland, in Holland, and in America, has been signalized by wisdom, steadiness, and virtue, but that turbulent democracy whose short existence has always been marked by blind fury. But if we reflect on the state of ignorance, distress, and danger to which the workmen in manufactories are reduced, we shall not be surprised either at their bad conduct, or at their hatred of established order; we shall not reproach them for not having waited for the extreme of penury before engaging in the contest to which they attached their last hopes of safety; for when the extreme of hunger is felt, resistance becomes impossible; it enervates body and mind, and death alone remains for him who suffers it. Very few workmen experienced this extreme of suffering, but the example of those who did was sufficient to alarm the others; all felt that their lives, and those of their families, were subject to all the chances of a lottery; that, without enjoyment for the present, they were without security for the future; and that the hardest work, joined to the most enlightened foresight, was insufficient to secure them from the torment of being surrounded by the objects dearest to their hearts asking in vain for bread.

Is this then the condition to which civilization should reduce the most active, the most energetic part of a nation? Should the triumph which science and art have obtained over nature, have for its result to reduce the producers of all our wealth, and of all our enjoyments, to a state in which they know neither enjoyment nor repose? No: this great wound of the social body, if it cannot be cured by the sole efforts of those who suffer most immediately, is not, however, incurable, if the government, if the whole of society would endeavour to close it. No doubt the chronic maladies of the social body, those whose origin is very distant, are not susceptible of a rapid cure; retrograde steps will be as slow as the progress of the disorder. But we must, at least, begin to change the system; governments and nations must be addressed in the words spoken by St. Reunz to Clovis, at the moment of his baptism, "*Mitis depone colla, Sicamber; incende quod adorasti, adora quod incendisti.*" [a]

If our eyes were not fascinated by the mystical words which certain economists have pronounced over us, the first thing we should acknowledge would be the glut of all the markets, and the sufferings which all producers experience from the difficulty of selling. Is it not evident, that instead of making a virtue of industrialism, that is, of the effort which all are making to glut the markets still more, society and government should endeavour to give another direction to human activity, so that, as machines will henceforth do the work of men, men should no longer do the work of machines? When man first became in some degree civilized, every thing was wanting to satisfy his necessities; whatever interfered with profitable labour must have been regretted; feasts, political employments, gymnastic and military exercises;—now, on the contrary, every thing should be encouraged which forces upon men employments not industrial; there will be time enough left to produce more than there is the means of consuming; and the hours which the community will require to take them from labour, their masters will still be obliged to pay them for. Formerly it might be regretted that prejudice kept out of industrial occupations those who held the highest rank in the state, and who had most capital to dispose of. Now, on the contrary, we may regret that this prejudice no longer exists: it would temper, at least, the feverish activity which torments the whole of society.

It is neither the increase of population, nor the increase of labour performed by that population, which constitutes the well-being of society, but the proportion between population and

[a] "Bow thy head, oh Sicamber, with humility; adore what thou hast burnt, and burn what thou hast adored."—*Gregor. Turon.*, liv. ii. § 31, p. 177. The object of political economy seems to be to make the entrance into every career easy, without examining how all can be followed; formerly it was thought desirable to make it difficult to enter upon any career, but once entered, progress was certain. Instead of making it easy for the poor to be born, and difficult to live, social organization ought to make it difficult to be born and easy to live.

property, and the equable distribution of that income whose source is labour. Society is happy when each one, according to his condition, can enjoy content and ease; it is happy when wages are high, because wages are the income of the poor; it is happy when wages are high, because the poor, not being obliged to work every hour of the day in order to exist, abstain from mutual competition by not producing more than can be sold.

It is exactly this end which we propose to ourselves, have long said the promoters of industry; we have encouraged the invention and construction of machines more and more ingenious, that while blind force was executing the work of man, man might rest; we have thus encouraged the erection of manufactories, more and more numerous, that by offering more work, and outbidding one another for workmen, wages might rise. Some contradiction might be discovered between these two objects: however, the reason appears logical, and might have been held as conclusive, if experience had not fully contradicted it. We have already shown how these two simultaneous efforts, tending to produce continually more articles without any proportion to the demand of the market, have lowered the price of every thing; consequently wages, consequently also, the consumption of the poor; but another effect of industrialism has been to increase unlimitedly a necessitous population. The first establishment of a manufactory does, in effect, raise wages. The manufacturers arrive with great capitals, great hopes, and a determination to collect workmen at any rate; these give themselves up to the same delusions which deceive their patrons; they live in plenty, and they think that this plenty will last. Young men and young women work most frequently in the same manufactory; temptations multiply; restraint and modesty do not long resist example and intimate contact; in the course of their lives they have no progress to expect, they will never be better off than they are; the birth of children does not frighten them, for from the age of six or eight years the manufactory offers them wages; they marry, but scarcely do their family and their wants begin to increase, than that reaction which affects every manufacture in turn, is felt by this, and wages fall.

For the rest, though the manufacturers expect to gain credit for spreading money in a country, and giving bread to the poor, this is rarely the determining motive of their undertakings; they hoped to be able to establish themselves, and to undersell their rivals, because they had discovered some new application of the powers of nature of a kind to spare human labour, and could, at the same time, dispose of sufficient capital to put it in action. Formerly, rich men, gifted with sufficient activity to run such risks, were not numerous; at the same time, the church and the prejudices against usury, made lending on interest very rare: now, there is not a crown, in whatever hands it may be, that does not find its way towards the most profitable employment. To the rich, who wish to be exempt from care, is offered the temptation of shares in anonymous companies; often the directors of these companies care little for their final success. With the command of a vast capital which does not belong to themselves, they make expensive machines, they throw sand in the eyes of the public; they sell their shares advantageously; soon, however, the company cannot pay the interest of the shares, the machines bring no profit: no matter; they are worked, and compete fatally with the workmen; and this losing undertaking contributes as much to lower wages as if it had been well conceived.

Still more in England and in America another cause is perceived to tempt projectors to engage in undertakings which prove disastrous to them, or towards what the English call *over-trading*. It is the invention of banks, always eager to furnish capital. Banks, in fact, make a profit in proportion to the circulation of their notes; thus they are as desirous of lending their fictitious capital as in other countries borrowers are desirous of obtaining advances. The mechanism of a bank consists in borrowing the value of the circulating coin of a country, and giving notes in exchange, on which it gets interest.

It adds, no doubt, to the income of all a sum equal to this interest, but for this slight advantage it deprives the country of the security given to all value by the circulation of coin. At the same time, it deprives it of that vigilance with which a true capitalist would be on his guard against hazardous investments and foolish manufacturing undertakings. Thus many seductive interests combine to urge capitalists, men who are making discoveries, and projectors, towards a feverish *industrialism,* not proportionate to the wants of the country; on every side they are eager to produce, without ascertaining whether what they produce can be consumed. Is it not fit that the country should secure itself against an inconsiderate spirit of speculation, the fatal effects of which are felt on every side? All the products which labour annually creates, and brings into the market of a civilized community, ought to be purchased by the collective income of that community. This sum of the income of the community is no doubt very difficult to calculate, but it is not on that account less precise and determinate. It results from this, that whenever the income of the community does not increase, and the product of the labour of the community does increase, it is at the expense of the producers; they give more labour in exchange for the same quantity of the income of the consumer. It is true, that neither the interest of the producer nor that of the consumer are necessarily identical with that of the whole community. If the producer gives too little labour, or too little of the fruits of labour in exchange for income, those consumers who do not labour enjoy too little for their money;—with respect to those who do labour, their gains as producers will perhaps compensate for their loss as consumers. If the producer gives too much labour in exchange for income, the consumer who does not labour obtains what he enjoys cheaper, but this cheapness is not a compensation to him who labours, for his consumption diminishes. Instead of saying to the government, let things alone, the recommendation ought to be to hold the balance even between these two interests, and its attention should be always awakened when it sees the producers and the operatives suffering. For a considerable part of the last century the legislature, in industrial countries, gave all the advantage to the producers. It made the entrance into industrial arts difficult by the statutes of apprenticeship; it organized the heads of different trades into corporations, and gave to the corporation a jurisdiction over all its members; it authorized manufacturers to forbid the establishment of rival manufactories; to protect trades against manufactories, it did not permit several kinds of trades to unite together; in many towns it did not allow a master to hire for wages more than one or two *compagnons* or journeymen, to keep more than one or two apprentices.

It was not justice which dictated these regulations: they were all directed against the consumer, and for the interest of the producer. The rich had a double cause for complaint, as making them pay dearer for every thing, and preventing them making the most of their money by manufacturing; but it is the poor who have complained, and their clamours are still so great, that it is scarcely possible to think of re-establishing such regulations. Nevertheless, they exist in some towns of Germany and Switzerland, who hold to their ancient prejudices; and it is remarkable that exactly in these towns are to be found at this day accumulated capitals which would purchase all the provincial towns in France; at the same time that the citizens of the middle class, elsewhere destroyed, have preserved an honest independence; no proletaries are to be seen there, and yet the conveniences of life are not dearer than in other places[a].

[a] Manners and customs which are now looked upon as merely picturesque, preserve, in the Swiss cantons, in many districts of Italy and Germany, that local industry which has not yet been absorbed by great manufactures. Each little district had its national costume; head-dress, the form and colour of the clothes, ornaments, shoes, all was rigorously fixed; it is so still in that part of Switzerland which is not manufacturing. These costumes are rich and durable, and it is very well for a girl to know that she cannot decently show herself, consequently not marry, without having amassed the little capital represented by these best clothes (*habits de fête*); but at the same time these costumes, unknown in the towns, are manufactured in each district. It is the way in which the women of the villages

Without returning to the municipal institutions of our forefathers, we may at least conceive that the authority which they exercised for the advantage of monopoly alone, might be put into hands more impartial and more just, who would exercise it for the benefit of the whole community. Let the principle only be agreed upon, and the means of applying it will not be wanting, particularly now that we are enlightened by the double experience of monopoly and of universal competition. Even before having recourse to such direct means of restraining industrialism, instead of continually exciting it, the aspect of society would change, if the government were persuaded that it was not advantageous, either to itself or to the nation it governs, to direct its efforts towards extending manufactures, to favour great manufactories at the expense of small trades, or the agglomeration of fortunes preferably to their division. The cessation of the indirect but daily encouragement which society gives to that system, whose dangers it is now experiencing, would perhaps suffice to restore the equilibrium, especially if, whenever a crisis occurred, an enlightened government should labour to diminish the glut instead of increasing it.

Already governments have frequently been called upon to support a manufacture which was threatened with ruin; and the more gluts in the market increase, the more the embarrassment of the manufacturer increases, the more frequently will this assistance be called for. Now, the suspension or the absolute cessation of work in a manufacture for which there is no longer any sale, is a first step towards the diminution of general suffering; the government ought, in fact, to come to the assistance of men, and not of industry; it ought to save its citizens, and not business. Far from making advances to the master manufacturer,

earn their bread, weaving the stuffs and hats, the dress-makers and modistes of the village, working for a market which they very well know, and are in no danger of encumbering. All this employment would disappear, all these industrial resources would be taken away from the women of the mountains of Appenzell, of Schwitz, of Entlibuch, and of Emmenthal, if the inhabitants of these valleys got accustomed to cover their bodies with the calicoes of St. Gall, and their heads with the handkerchiefs of Glarus.

to encourage him to manufacture to a loss, it ought largely to contribute funds to take the operatives from an employment which increases the embarrassment of all their fellow citizens. It ought to employ them in those public works whose products do not bear upon the markets, and do not increase the general glut. Public edifices, town-halls, markets, public walks, are native wealth, though not of a kind that can be bought and sold. Immense quantities of land may be recovered from water, on the sea-shore, along rivers, and by draining marshes; the fertility of whole provinces may be doubled, quadrupled, by works of irrigation, which by means of canals circulate over the plains water borrowed from rivers; and to make these improvements throughout the whole extent of France, and which would cover it with a network of running water, might well employ, not only her industrial classes, but a quarter of her inhabitants for a long time to come.

But in assisting the workmen in any depressed industrial business by public works, government must adhere principally to the following rules:—not to compete with an existing business[a], and thus bring fresh disturbance into the markets; not to make of those works which it orders and pays for a permanent occupation, to which will be attached a new class of day-labourers—*proletarii*,—but to make them perceive how long it will last, and where it will end, that they may not marry in this precarious state, but may keep up the wish to disperse, and to establish themselves; in short, never to forget that these public works ought to be a preparation and an apprenticeship for a new situation, particularly as agriculturists, either in the new land which these works will have made fertile, or in some colony. A workman detached from a great manufactory, where, thanks to the division of labour, he filled, perhaps with superior skill, one single function, is like one of the wheels beside which he worked, of no value detached from the machine. An English workman,

[a] It would be well if this rule were attended to in every attempt to give employment to those who want it, or are selling their labour too low, lest by assisting some, others are more distressed. *Tr.*

employed by his parish in breaking stones on the highway, is degraded even below a machine; but a man who has been made to work intelligently at works of irrigation or clearing, and who has again become a peasant, a tradesman, a weaver, mason, carpenter, or blacksmith, is become a complete being; he may go to Algiers, become useful to his country wherever there is a demand for his labour, and regain complete independence. It will be said, no doubt, that these immense works require treasure, and that the abandoning of industrialism will dry up the sources of the public revenue. We might ask in our turn what sacrifices of the national fortune has not industrialism already cost; what ruinous laws, both for the revenue and those who contribute to it, have not been made to secure to our manufacturers, sometimes the monopoly of the home market, sometimes a preference over foreign markets; we might say that this new sacrifice is also imposed by industrialism, for it is this, which having created proletarii, has reduced them to die of hunger. Now the fundamental condition of society is, that no one shall die of hunger; it is only on this condition that property is acknowledged and guaranteed. But we do not know on what grounds industrialism pretends to be a source of the public revenue. Since nations, instead of working each for itself to provide the things it wants, have desired, each one striving against the others, to become sole providers of the whole world, we have seen all those old fortunes overthrown which in manufacturing countries had been transmitted from generation to generation as part of the glory of the country. It is, in some sort, a necessary consequence of the system, that every new discovery in the arts should enrich the first who made use of it, by ruining his predecessors: his opulence lasts ten or twenty years, while he can preserve his secret, or till another comes, who, more skilful than he, ruins him in his turn to rise in his place. It may be said that by these rapid vicissitudes, art, considered abstractedly, flourishes and becomes continually more perfect; but the fortune of manufacturers has lost all stability; they must themselves give up all trust in the future, which is more than half our happiness. The violence with which all capitalists in these times engage in gambling in the funds is, in fact, the consequence of old and honest industry having become as hazardous as gaming.

Even had manufacturers remained much richer than they are, it has never been easy to tax any considerable part of their profits. The two great sources of revenue to the state are taxes on land, and taxes on consumption. These last never produce abundantly, except when they reach the enjoyments of the poor, and when the poor have no enjoyments they produce almost nothing. All efforts of financiers to obtain a product at all considerable by taxes on the luxuries of the rich, have been vain. Thus, fiscal science, as well as all other branches of political economy, requires that the poor should be liberally paid for their labour, that they may contribute largely to public expenses.

On whatever side we look, the same lesson meets us everywhere, *protect the poor*, and ought to be the most important study of the legislator and of the government. Protect the poor; for, in consequence of their precarious condition, they cannot contend with the rich without losing every day some of their advantages; protect the poor, that they may keep by law, by custom, by a perpetual contract, rather than by competition—the source of rivalry and hatred—that share of the income of the community which their labour ought to secure to them; protect the poor, for they want support, that they may have some leisure, some intellectual development, in order to advance in virtue; protect the poor, for the greatest danger to law, public peace and stability, is the belief of the poor that they are oppressed, and their hatred of government; protect the poor, if you wish industry to flourish, for the poor are the most important of consumers; protect the poor, if your revenue requires to be increased, for after you have carefully guarded the enjoyments of the poor, you will find them the most important of contributors.

ON THE

NATIONAL INCOME,

OR THE

INCOME OF THE COMMUNITY[a].

As in the administration of a private fortune a knowledge of the income must direct the economical arrangements of the family, so in political economy the question which ought to govern all others, from its importance, and from the consequences which result from it to all the members of the community, is to determine the amount of the social or national income, to discover how much all the different members who compose the community have to spend a year. There is no man who does not feel that in a private fortune his expenses must all depend on his income. We take this word, income or revenue, in its largest sense, as comprising all that part of a fortune which is reproduced annually, so that whoever has the disposal of it, may consume the whole, and employ it entirely for what he wants, without being poorer. We call income, not only the profits of land, and of capital lent, or of houses let, but the profits of all industry, of all commerce, of all agriculture, the wages of all labour, the salaries of all servants, of the public or of private persons; we call income annual gains, whatever they may be, and we repeat that the first question in domestic economy is that which in fact is always asked, how

[a] Extracted from the *Revue Mensuelle d'Economie Politique:* May and June, 1835.

much has this man to spend, by the year, or by the day? It ought to be the first question in political economy also, how much has this nation to spend, by the year, or by the day?

In the management of a private fortune the income is the only reasonable rule of expense or consumption. Every one knows very well that it is the way to ruin, if a man spends his capital with his income. Every one calls ease in his circumstances only the sum of what his income enables him to enjoy, and considers as extravagance whatever exceeds each one's means, and as what will bring inevitable poverty. It is the same with a nation, or with the whole of human society. Its wealth is only the aggregate of all private fortunes, its capital is the capital of all, its income the income of all. And it is as true of a nation as of an individual that it is going to ruin if it spends its capital with its income; that the sum of what it consumes does not indicate ease unless we are assured that there is no waste, that expense does not exceed income.

Every father of a family knows that he can only become rich by economy, by adding to his capital a part of his annual gains. He knows also, that he does not become rich by the fruits of his industry, unless his gains increase with his labour; he knows that there may be a profitable production and one that is not so. The shoemaker knows that if he made a hundred pairs of shoes the last year, by which he gained 3*s.*, and two hundred pairs of shoes this year, on each of which he gets 1*s.* 6*d.*, his income is the same, but his labour is doubled; so that the increase of what he has produced has not been profitable to him: if on each of these two hundred pairs he only got 1*s.*, he sees that his labour has doubled whilst his income has diminished one-third. It may be the same with a nation, neither production nor consumption are the certain sign of prosperity, which is increased only by the increase of income.

Every head of a family very nearly calculates the difference between real profits and those that chance may give him. He reckons the first only as his income, and places the second among those happy chances, of the return of which he has no certainty. Real profit costs no one any thing: he who pays finds his advantage as well as he who receives. Such is the increased quantity which a man obtains from the land by agriculture, when he sows one sack of corn and reaps five; or the amelioration of quality by industry, when a bale of wool is made into cloth; or the great conveniences which he obtains by commerce, when he brings into towns salt made on the sea shore. But gambling profit, that of speculation, is a loss to him from whom it is taken. The gambler, either on the cards, or in the public funds, or in merchandise, knows very well that he enriches himself at the expense of him who bargains with him; that there is in fact no increase of fortune, only a change; he knows, though in fact it is not of much importance to him, that though the profits of his game add to his own income, they add nothing to that of the nation for they must be deducted from that of his adversary. But the father of a family understands better, because he is more interested in it, that he can give to him who makes real profits a confidence which he refuses to the gambler; for the gambler either plays with equal chances and he must lose as often as he gains, or he plays with an advantage on his side, and he is dishonest. This man understands also, or he learns by experience, that he who pursues chances, loses successively all the qualities essential to the good ordering of his fortune. Uncertain of the future, he seeks his pleasures in the present; he does not distinguish his capital from his income, for he has really no income; he does not provide for the future with wisdom, for he has no future. For a nation the distinction between real profit and chance profit is still more important than for an individual. Its income arises from the first alone; the second presents positive and negative qualities which balance one another; but the second at the same time spreads vices among the population which destroy industry and foresight, and which lead as certainly to ruin as the dissipation of capital.

Every economist knows also that by his income he ought to

regulate the formation and increase of his family; that he ought not to take a wife if he has not enough to keep her as well as himself; that he ought not to wish for children if he has not a sufficient income to divide with them, if he does not believe that he shall leave for them an income equal to his own. The most vehement of human passions may, no doubt, create an illusion as to this, but the more precisely his income is fixed, the more he has stripped it of all increase from chances, the less will this illusion be possible. Every workman knows, at the birth of his children, that they not only will be many years incapable of getting any thing, but will prevent their father and mother from giving all their time to labour, and will consequently diminish their income. The family cannot increase without increasing expenses, and diminishing the means of providing for them. However, if the father of a family has sufficient to meet these without infringing on his capital, he must sacrifice other enjoyments for that of being a father. If he is secure of finding profitable situations for his children as soon as they are old enough, he sees without anxiety the increase of his domestic circle; the education of his children is as a chest where he puts his savings; they form a capital from which he expects some day to receive an income. But if, on the contrary, he perceives that his annual gains are not enough, if he sees too that business does not prosper, and that he will not be able to secure to the beings who are so dear to him sufficient income in exchange for their labour, the birth of each fresh child is a calamity. If he is in easy circumstances, he is careful not to expose himself to this; but if he is in one of those unfortunate positions in which men cannot ascertain their future income; if it depends on circumstances over which he has no control, on that terrible game which society sometimes plays at the expense of the poor, then most frequently he gives himself no concern about it, but lets premature deaths repair the excess of births.

Income is the measure of the increase of population in a nation as well as in a family. Income is the measure of subsistence and ease to each; the income of the whole is the measure of the subsistence and ease of the whole. The more young children there are in a nation in proportion to the whole number of its population, the more expense increases and income diminishes; on the contrary, the more individuals it contains between twenty and fifty in proportion to the whole population, the greater is the working power. Now population increases whenever labour is sufficiently compensated to increase the income of the working classes. Then there are more births; fathers can make advances for the education of their children, in the hope of future advantages; there is also more longevity in all the working class, for comfort is a cause of good health, and comfort is the consequence of a demand for labour. But if, on the contrary, income diminishes whilst labour increases; if in particular wages diminish; if the poor, to make up for this, force themselves to do more work, they are worn out by labour and privation; they die young, or they languish in sickness; then the number of effective men sensibly diminishes. Perhaps the number of births will diminish also, if habits of prudence and order prevail in the nation; perhaps, on the contrary, they will increase, if men are so much degraded as to think only of the present moment, and of their sensual appetites. Thus it is seen that the disposition to drunkenness increases with indigence, but the children are the first victims of this wretchedness; the more there are born the fewer will there be preserved; as when more are preserved fewer are born. The numerical quantity of the population may in this case be maintained; it may even rise in spite of the diminution of income, but the population arrived at the age of manhood will be diminished, the chances of life will diminish, and the great number of births, which is accounted a sign of prosperity, will only indicate the great number of those who are born only to die, without having known either the pleasures or duties of life.

Malthus has assigned subsistence as the limit of population. Mankind, said he, increases in a geometrical progression, and subsistence only in an arithmetical progression; the first then proceeds towards a frightful famine. There is no doubt that there are limits beyond which subsistence cannot increase in a geometrical progression, that there are even limits beyond which it cannot advance at all; but we are at an infinite distance from these limits. There is room on the earth for an immense development of culture, and those of its products which we appropriate for our subsistence, animals as well as vegetables, multiply in a geometrical progression infinitely more rapid than man. He is, in fact, gifted with such a power of multiplication, that the number of men might be doubled or quadrupled every twenty-five years; he partakes of this power with all organized nature, though of all animals and vegetables he possesses it in the smallest degree. But man is not destined to make an habitual use of this power, and never does. It is only in very rare cases, after a great destruction of the population, or when man is transplanted into a virgin soil, where, great need of labour being felt, a great income arises from this labour, and population rapidly proportions itself to it, because the life of those who would have died in indigence is preserved by easy circumstances. As soon as the level is re-established, population increases in the slowest manner, and this slowness is often even an indication of great prosperity. Where middle life is the longest, where each one who is born has the greatest chance of arriving at advanced age, there also, as at Geneva, the number of births approaches nearest to a perfect equality with the deaths. Still more, where the number of marriages is proportionably the greatest, where the greatest number of persons participate in the duties, the virtues, and the happiness of marriage, the smaller number of children does each marriage produce. At Geneva the average is below three; two children represent the father and mother, and will receive the income which sufficed for their parents; the fraction below the complete third represents the individuals who do not live to a marriageable age, or who die in celibacy. The subdivision of inheritances with which we are continually threatened by the English economists is unknown, for the population proportioning itself to the income, maintains itself in the same or increasing ease, without its being possible to say whether its progression is geometrical or arithmetical.

The law which Malthus imagined, with its two progressions, one geometrical and the other arithmetical, and the danger of famine with which he threatened the human race, would only find their application at some hypothetical time which the human race will probably never see. Whereas it is now, it is every day, that the increase of population ought to be regulated by the increase of its means of subsistence. When the population suffers, it is not because corn and meat fail in the market, but because there are not means to purchase them. When it feels at ease, it is not because new supplies of provisions are spread out for sale, but because it has a sufficient income to command what it wants in greater abundance. Malthus himself, though he only expressed the gross and material limit of subsistence—the only one to which his theory of the two progressions can relate—appears to have had a vague idea of the proportion of the population to income; he has explained that by subsistence he understood all the wants of man relative to his condition, which is destroying at the base the reasoning on which he relies.

But if income is the measure of the ease and prosperity of all, if it is the regulator of consumption, if it is the regulator of population, how happens it that Malthus has not expressed it, that none of the economists have pointed out its importance, have even mentioned its name? How can this omission be explained, when Adam Smith, the true renovator of this science, owes all the progress he has enabled it to make to his care in constantly comparing public wealth with a private fortune, by the judicious application of all the rules of domestic economy to all the problems of political economy. It is because all dogmatic writers, all those who wish to raise a system, must attach it to some striking idea which can be understood by all; and that the idea of the social income, of that power which gives the impulse to all the social mechanism, becomes more confused the more they strive to fix it: it escapes them by the infinite multiplicity of its relations, by its continual transformation, by the daily exchange which is made, either in production or in consumption, of the income of one with the capital of another. The economical philosopher looking at all the different kinds of social wealth can never say, this belongs to capital, that to income, without some one being ready to answer; what you call capital is my income, and what you call income is my capital. This impossibility of finding in material things any character by which they may be arranged in either class; this necessity of considering the division in an abstract manner, and as only existing in the appreciation of each person, has caused it to be judged more easy to deny it altogether; to consider only what society produces instead of its income, what it consumes instead of what it spends. The experience, however, of every day ought to teach us, that a nation as well as an individual sometimes sees its circumstances become less easy in proportion as its production increases; that sometimes also the increase of consumption, far from being an expense, is a means of wealth; and that whatever has been used is reproduced in so much abundance, that in consuming, capital is amassed.

The recent sufferings of society will never be truly explored, and it will not be possible to remedy them, till there is some idea affixed to the division of income and capital, however abstruse and intangible it may be. It is useless to open saving banks for the people, without being assured that they have an income out of which they can save; it is useless to labour at their education and instruction, without being first secure, that the time they are obliged to employ in securing an income will leave some little repose for thought, some little vigour for meditation: it is useless to push a new production without being assured that from this production will arise an income proportionate to the efforts which this will require; it is useless to open foreign commerce without being sure that by selling to foreigners income will be increased; that in buying from foreigners, the saving that will be made of one part of income will not annihilate at home another part more important. Population, production, consumption, accumulation, profit, prosperity, indigence, all is connected with income, all is explained by income.

Will it still be asked, what then is social income? It is the sum of the income of every man. What is that sum? We are ignorant of it. Of what material part of wealth is it composed? We are ignorant of that also. We can only seize on the idea of this income as being what is in the hands of each one; we can only recognize it according to the calculation which each one makes for himself. Science points out mysteries which she cannot succeed in enlightening. The management of a fortune is reduced to conjecture, when an exact calculation cannot be arrived at. Now, whenever the question relates to public wealth, where so many positive and negative qualities are imperfectly balanced; where the prime cost, the market or competition price, the price estimated in days of labour, in subsistence, or in money, continually mix together so many opposite ideas, it is not possible to make a valuation which can be expressed by numbers, to arrive at any quantity other than conjectural.

The mercantile system made the wealth of a nation to consist in the gold and silver which she possesses, and which, according to its supporters, she is continually accumulating; the system of the physiocrats only acknowledged as wealth what is derived from land. Both have been victoriously refuted by Adam Smith; both, however, yet maintain an influence which misleads many minds; because, to the question, What is wealth? they can give a positive answer, false, it is true, but one easily remembered, whilst Adam Smith has been able to answer only by an incomplete and vague enumeration, the idea of which, even if it has been well comprehended, soon fades away.

Public wealth, according to Adam Smith, is all that which constitutes the fortune of each one; houses, fields, tools, cattle, man himself, with the skill that he has acquired and his faculty of labour; then all the products of the industry of man, though some of them are so fugitive that they are not susceptible of accumulation. This enumeration appears very vague, yet it is sufficient to dissipate many errors. By comparing in the fortune of each person these different possessions with the quantity of gold and silver which each one has, it will be acknowledged, that money makes a very small part of wealth, either private or public. It will be acknowledged also, that the mutual debts and credits of two individuals make no part of public wealth, for they are two quantities, negative and positive, which balance one another. The public funds will also disappear, for they are credits of the lenders on the possessions of the taxpayers. Paper money will also disappear, for it is a promise to pay in money, or a mortgage on the precious metals in circulation. This list alone of the public fortune will suffice to dissipate the error of those who attribute to credit a creative power, whilst it only gives to one the disposal of what belongs to another without augmenting either its quantity or its power.

The enumeration of the income of all will be, perhaps, still more vague, but it may serve to dissipate some illusions.

Whether man dedicates his labour to agriculture or to the industrial arts, whether he makes land produce fruits or gives to those fruits a form more adapted to the use of man, he increases the value or the quantity of the materials on which he employs himself; he makes wealth by them, and this wealth is superior in value to the advances by means of which he obtained it. The superiority of the annual product of the labour of man over his annual advances, comprises all the income of the community; but this surplus value has two different valuations, according to the labour which it has cost, and according to the wants of those who use it.

When a family lives completely isolated, when, however numerous it may be, it is always directed by a common interest, which proportions the labours to the wants of each of its members, there is no work done without being demanded, without its destination being known. There is no money price, because there is as yet no exchange; and nevertheless the idea of income is more clearly developed than in our complicated societies, where the idea of giving a special security to the general interest is given up, and where individual interests contending with one another by means of exchanges, it is believed that the same end will be attained. In this isolated family, which we will suppose numerous, it is known that there will be required annually a determinate quantity of food, clothes, and furniture. The members of the family have already materials, provisions, and tools, the products of their former labours; some may be considered as capital which they have accumulated, such as corn for seed, the fleeces of which they mean to make cloth, the tools which they will use; others are the income of the preceding year, which they will consume whilst they are producing for the next—these are food and the clothes which they are wearing. The members of the family set to work; they divide their labours; some plough and sow, some prepare leather, some weave wool; they collect and finish all that it is necessary to provide for the coming year. In this provision we recognize three parts: one is capital—it is replacing those advances which had been made to agriculture or industry, the seed of the tiller, the wool and flax of the weaver: the other participates in the nature of capital and of income—it is the subsistence of the family during the year they have been at work, the food they have consumed, the clothes they have worn out; it was income as the produce of the preceding year; but as an accumulated product which must be in existence at the commencement of each year to recommence labour and to make it productive, it is capital. The last part is pure income; it is the material quantity of the product of this year over the preceding one, or the profit of labour.

It will be seen that, even in this most simple state of society, income has something in its nature mysterious and intangible; it is converted into capital; capital is consumed like income; it is the blood which nourishes the human body, which is converted into its substance, and which, notwithstanding, is continually renewed. In this state, however, some of the laws of the community are more clearly understood than when the complication is increased. It is acknowledged that the product of labour is more considerable, in proportion as the means of producing are perfected, as the machines are better; but it is also felt that all increase of production is not profitable. The wants of society are limited; all that cannot be consumed is useless. The quantity of food that a given number of individuals can eat is soon attained; thenceforward there would be a loss of labour in increasing it, and all the superfluity of labour bestowed on food must be employed in increasing its quality, not its quantity, in making food more wholesome, or more delicate. The quantity of clothes which a given number of individuals will require in a year is a little less precise; though the same dress may suffice for a year, it will be more agreeable to have a new one four times, eight times a year, so that the same dress only lasts six weeks, but we must stop there; all the clothes supplied beyond what are wanted, cost useless labour, without advantage to the community, without producing income. If the productive power goes on always increasing, by the increased perfection of skill and instruments, it soon arrives at a limit where it must cease to augment the quantity, and employ itself only in perfecting the quality. There is not one of the products of human industry to which the same rule does not apply. At the same time, the perfection of the quality has its limits; they are laid down by that labour itself which society is called on to perform; all the productions which can only be enjoyed by those who have leisure, are useless unless this leisure can be reserved.

Thus, there are limits prescribed to production which it cannot go beyond. It is only when contained within these limits, that the redoubling of its power is an advantage. The quantity must be regulated by the number of the population, the quality by its leisure. Should man succeed in calling to his aid the highest sciences; should the progress of mechanics permit him to accomplish infinitely more work in infinitely less time, he must also longer suspend his productive powers; he must reserve much more leisure; for the most exquisite aliments, the most costly clothes, and all works highly perfected, are only used by persons of leïsure.

Those rules which are understood and clearly seen in a family, however numerous it may be supposed to be, are equally true in every state of society, though it may not be directed by an intelligence which comprehends all the relations of its members with one another, by a will which makes them all concur in the common welfare. Individual interests have broken the bond which united them: men have been permitted, by the assistance of exchange and of money, each to satisfy his own wants apart from the rest, without caring for the public good; they are all found to be in opposition to one another; but philanthropists have found it easier to say and to believe that their reciprocal opposition restraining all, tends, by their combined action, as much to the advantage of all, as if it were really the object they had in view.

The interest of production is considered as independent of the interest of consumption; and this interest of production is divided among a great number of rival interests. Those who have in hand a certain quantity of accumulated wealth, have taken upon themselves in general the direction of annual production; they are divided into two classes, one guards the interests of agriculture, the other those of industry. They say to the landed proprietor, give to us up the use of your estate, of your buildings, of your improvements. We will direct all the labour, and out of what it produces we will reserve for you a portion always the same, rent of land or of houses: that will be your income. They say to the labourer, let us take the direction of your labour; we will collect the fruits of it; and before you could obtain them, we will pay you day by day, wages which we will take from our capital, and which will form your income; we will advance on our part new capital for different improvements; the product of your labour will be more considerable than if you directed it yourselves; but that will be our profit. Then comes the government and the church, who take from rent, wages, and profit, a new share, which they distribute as income to every class of public functionaries.

At the same time, other capitalists undertake the direction of industry; they secure wages to workmen, rent to the proprietors of mills and machines, interest to other capitalists who are content with lending their capital without wishing to give themselves any trouble; they pay taxes to government; they keep a profit for themselves: they are thus the distributors of an annual income to four or five classes of persons; but this income, whether obtained in the country or in towns, is never anything but the surplus of the value of what labour has produced above the advances that have been made to produce it.

Production would always be proportioned to demand, if labour were always performed in concert with the consumers. But the farther commerce extends, the more exchanges with foreign countries are multiplied, the more impossible it becomes for producers to measure exactly the wants of the markets for which they have to provide. Besides which, they care very little about it, and instead of asking whether their efforts will really increase the income of the community, each one labours to appropriate to himself the greatest share at the expense of others, and often the shortest way to do this is to diminish the portion of each.

The capitalist who undertakes any business, will certainly see his income increase, if the demand of the consumers for the products of his industry is increasing in the market which he supplies; but this increase, if it is common to the whole of society, is singularly slow and gradual. In order that there may be a greater demand for food, it is not alone necessary that there should be a great increase of births; for this circumstance by itself, being accompanied by an increase of expenses and a diminution of gains, the mass of the population will be worse fed, and the greater number of children will die in infancy;

but there must be increased means, particularly for the poor; for food makes three quarters of the expenses of the poor, whilst it is scarcely a tenth part of the expenses of the rich. Increased means will prolong life among the poor, and more children will arrive at manhood. In countries where population has increased most rapidly, either by births or by longevity, it has never yet, except in colonies, been known to double itself in a century, though it has been calculated sometimes, that if it continued to increase at the rate of such or such a year, it would double itself in much less time. In general, in really prosperous countries, it does not increase in a sensible manner. Its progress is, however, the limit which agriculture ought to impose upon itself in the production of alimentary substances. Laying aside the oscillations of good and bad harvests which balance one another, the quantity of subsistence should not be increased more than a hundredth part in a year; for it is the most rapid rate at which population increases in Europe; and as each improvement in agriculture gives more considerable and rapid produce, each ought to be followed by abandoning those kinds of cultivation which give the greatest weight of alimentary substances; a certain number of fields of potatoes, for instance, to produce corn, fields of corn to produce flesh meat, or fermented liquors, fields cultivated for alimentary substances to produce flax, hemp, madder, raw materials for the industry of towns. It is, in fact, what is generally done, except that many substances cultivated at first for man have afterwards been appropriated to animals, which comes to the same result.

In detached districts which have little communication with their neighbours, the quantity of alimentary substances which can be consumed every year is sufficiently well known to the producer to prevent his cultivating and throwing into the market a quantity of substances which cannot be sold; but when the farmer is near a large town, a seaport, a canal or a railway, or any market in fact whose extent he cannot calculate, he pays no attention to this. If he can, he doubles and redoubles his harvests, and calculates that he shall sell them by disposing of them at rather a lower price than other producers. To lower the price, he begins by endeavouring to diminish the income of those who compete with him in production, by giving less rent to the proprietor, less interest to those who have lent him money, less wages to his labourers, less taxes to government. By taking more corn to market than he could sell, he necessarily produces this effect, for the price of corn becomes lower, all the farmers make the same complaints to the proprietor, to the capitalist, to the labourer, to the government; rents diminish, interest becomes lower, wages are reduced.

He reacts at the same time on all other farmers. If his methods of cultivation are better, he can, with the same labour and the same advances, produce a greater quantity of food, and gain at a price at which others lose. Thus he continues to enrich himself whilst others are ruined. Then he wishes to take the farms of others with his own, and he finds capitalists who will facilitate his doing this; the trouble of inspection will not be doubled, though his undertaking is doubled; it answers better to get 4 per cent. on £20,000 than 5 per cent. on £10,000. Small farmers disappear, and nothing is seen but cultivation on a great scale.

Thus all incomes arising from land are diminished by this exaggerated production. The proprietor consents to lower his rent, the capitalist is content with 4, instead of 5 per cent. interest, the farmer with 4, instead of 5 per cent. profit, the labourer with 1*s*. a day wages instead of 2*s*. All are, however, consumers of commodities, and joined together they form themselves the great mass of consumers. The diminution of income will to every one of them be followed by a diminution of consumption, in quantity or quality; the poor will give up meat for bread alone, or bread for potatoes. The effect on the rich will be more complicated; in consequence of the diminution of income, more capital will be required to live, more land to obtain the same rent, more money must be lent to get the same interest, larger farms to get as much profit; and as the rich pay great attention to keeping up their families, and not to make improvident marriages, the number of old rich families will decrease, as it does every generation, and consequently inheritances will be more considerable. As a result of this, the consumption of the rich class, taken in a mass, will diminish, not only in proportion to the diminution of income, but also by the diminution of the number of persons. This double action is very apparent in England, though the number of roads open to fortune maintain probably a greater number of opulent families there than elsewhere. The total number of landed proprietors has there sensibly diminished, that of farmers has perhaps diminished still more. The quantity of corn, meat, and beer consumed must have diminished also; as to the day-labourers, they are gone back again from meat to bread, from bread to potatoes; their consumption has diminished in quantity and quality.

We have fixed our attention preferably on agricultural industry, because the relation between production and consumption is here most easily perceived; but exactly the same thing takes place in regard to the manufactured productions. Thus to produce a greater demand for clothes, it is not only requisite that there should be more births, but more ease in the circumstances of those who are to wear them; more income in every class of the nation, for all employ part of their income in dress. The increase of births may only increase the number of deaths, and make no difference in the consumption of any kind of wearing materials. The increase of vitality, by prolonging life after manhood is attained, a period when more is laid out in clothes, has a much more sensible effect. However, as we have seen, neither the multiplication of births, nor longevity, will double the population in a hundred years. Ease in their circumstances will increase more rapidly the consumption of clothes, and particularly among the poor. It is an advantage to health, to cleanliness, to enjoyment, to change the clothes frequently. The sultanas of the Great Mogul made it a point of honour to tear their dresses every evening that they might not wear them more than one day; perhaps some European women have thirty dresses in a year; their caprice may not extend to a consumption beyond this, but as a matter of health and cleanliness, an average of four new suits of dress a year is probably the highest term to which national consumption will attain. As soon as the manufacturers have produced this quantity of fabrics they cannot usefully go beyond it. Then they must fix their attention on the quality, and not on the quantity; they must vary the materials of their fabrics, their fineness, their elegance, and then at last they must stop; supernumerary hands must be employed in something else than in manufacturing articles of clothing, or they must perish for want. Now the increase of productions in manufactures is infinitely more rapid than in agriculture. Such a machine, with a given quantity of labour, doubles the products in a year; such another quadruples, even multiplies them ten-fold. The quantity of materials sufficient to dress every one has soon been produced; the limits to the improvement in quality, at least as far as regards working men, is also soon attained. Labour is incompatible with fine and elegant clothes; a workman looks upon duration as the most precious quality in his clothes; but this quality dispenses him from renewing them often, and diminishes his consumption; as to the substitution of cloth for serge, of cotton for wool, it is not an increase of consumption, it is often a diminution when the second costs less, and requires less labour than the first.

But the manufacturer, like the great farmer, within reach of a large town, does not know his market; he is lost in what is vague, he figures to himself buyers without number; or without caring for his rivals' losses, he thinks only of attracting his customers. He thinks himself a patriot when he ruins only a foreign manufacture by the development of his own industry; then he is vain of it; but indeed he has no more regard for those of his countrymen. All his labour, all his skill, consists in underselling; sometimes in substituting a more perfect, more expensive, but more productive machine, for those already in use; sometimes renting his buildings, obtaining capital at a lower rate, thus diminishing the income of the rich who are idle; sometimes lessening the wages of his workmen, and the income of the industrious poor; sometimes reducing the profits of his own business, which he can do profitably if he pursues it on a greater scale; sometimes attracting the taste of the consumers by offering them new productions, or by the invention of new fashions. Thus he increases his production by diminishing the incomes of capitalists, of the proprietors of mills, of his fellow-manufacturers, of himself, and in short of his workmen. To many this operation is fatal; when he raises what he manufactures from £5,000 to £50,000 annually, he destroys the nine manufacturers, his rivals, who with £5,000 each competed with him; when he reduces the wages of his workmen, or obliges his rivals to dismiss theirs, he first causes the weakest among them and their children to perish for want, and then the greatest part of the rest. His prosperity is fatal to things as well as to men. His new manufacture, his new machinery, have made the old useless, which are ruined by his rivalry, and all the capital which had established them is annihilated. It is a loss of income to society by the diminution of interest of money, by the diminution of the profits of industry, by the loss of rent on all buildings, on all machines that are become useless, by the diminution of the total number of workmen, and of the wages of each. There is then diminution of consumption in all classes; and whilst the manufacturer exerts himself with all his power to increase the quantity and improve the quality of the fabrics which he has to sell, his exertions tend as actively and as efficaciously to diminish the number of purchasers of both quality and quantity, and to lead all those who are impoverished to make their clothes last longer, and to content themselves with coarser qualities.

We should fatigue the reader in vain by following this out in regard to the fabrication of the other products of industry, utensils, arms, furniture; everywhere we should find that consumption cannot go beyond a certain limit, difficult to trace, without doubt, but no less certain; that whenever production oversteps this limit, exuberant production, far from augmenting income, diminishes it, and that then the increase of material wealth, of apparent riches, produces throughout all society only straitened means and poverty.

We believe that by this analysis of the income of the community, we have sufficiently answered the difficulty which we have raised; we think we have made it understood how there may be too much, of even the best things. In effect, labour is a good thing; but too much labour may be offered, if it thus lowers wages, and if it consequently diminishes the income of the workman. Capital is a good thing, but there may be too much capital, if that, and not the demand for consumption, excites production. Then, in effect, production is superior in value to the income which ought to purchase it; this disproportion lowers the value of all there is to sell, and consequently diminishes the incomes of all those who have something to sell; the proprietors of these incomes are, however, in their turn, consumers, and the loss which they have undergone will render them so much the more incapable of purchasing the production of the following year. Production in itself, in short, is a good thing, but there may be too much production, either by means of a superabundance of labour or of capital, or by the too powerful assistance which science has given to the useful arts; for when production has not been regulated by the desires of the consumers, and by their means of satisfying them, means which must be measured by income, production remains unsold and ruins the producers.

Another proposition results from what we have shown, and it contradicts the received doctrines: it is, that it is not true that the contest of individual interests suffices to produce the greatest good of all; but that as the prosperity of a family requires that in the mind of its head expenses should always be in proportion to income, and production be regulated by the wants of consumption, so in the administration of the fortune of the public, it is necessary that sovereign authority should watch over and restrain particular interests to make them subservient to the general interest, that this authority should never lose sight of the formation and distribution of income, for it is income which spreads ease and prosperity throughout all classes; that this authority should especially take under its protection the poor and labouring class, for it is that class which is the least in a state to defend itself, which is more likely to be sacrificed to every other, and whose sufferings form the greatest national calamity; in short, that it is not the rapid increase of national wealth or income which sovereign authority ought to have in view, but its stability and equality; for the duration of an invariable proportion between population and income is always attended by general well-being, whilst whenever they are subject to variable chances, the unexpected opulence of some cannot be considered as a compensation for the ruin and miserable death of others.

THE

COLONIES OF THE ANCIENTS,

COMPARED WITH THOSE OF THE MODERNS,

AS REGARDS THEIR INFLUENCE ON THE HAPPINESS OF MANKIND[a].

WHEN we endeavour to give an account of those causes which have contributed to diffuse among men all the advantages of social life, the first, the most important, which is especially pointed out by the study of antiquity, is the foundation of colonies. The history of the colonization of the countries situated on the shores of the Mediterranean may be called also the history of the civilization of the human race. This history, without being known to us in all its details, is sufficiently taught us by the historical movements which antiquity reveals to us, to enable us to have an idea of it as a whole. Almost from the earliest times we find a powerful nation, the Egyptian, arrived at great wealth and great glory by events which escape our investigation. Its history is enveloped in clouds, but the domestic life of the inhabitants of Egypt, their customs, their arts, their manufactures, their agriculture, have been submitted to our inspection; the image of them has been preserved by indestructible monuments, which quite recently have been carefully explored. The *civil* life of the Egyptians, their life as members of the *great city* of society, is represented by pic-

[a] *Les colonies des anciennes comparées à celles des modernes, sous le rapport de leur influence sur le bonheur du genre humain.—Tiré de la Bibliothèque universelle de Genève, Jan.* 1837.

tures, which makes it present to our eyes. We there see that, without the shadow of a doubt, they had already made in those arts by which nature is subjugated, that progress which appears to us most suited to render a numerous population happy; that they were highly civilized two thousand years before the Christian era.

The Egyptians have no historians which are come down to us, they have no philosophers known to us who have studied the march of human society; their influence, however, on their neighbours has been revealed to us, for the people who have given us the most admirable models in the art of writing history, the people who have best understood the art of constructing human society, the people who have studied with most advantage the action of interests, opinions, and passions, the Greeks, begin their history precisely at that period when the immense picture of Egyptian civilization, which has been recently placed before our eyes, was composed. The Greeks tell us, that at this epoch they were themselves completely barbarians, and that they owe all their progress, all their development, to Egyptian colonies.

The Greeks could only know very imperfectly this figured history of Egypt, which the art of engraving has multiplied in all our libraries, and which, till our times, had been concealed from all eyes, in those sacred asylums from whence the profane were excluded. They did not endeavour to make their own history agree with these monuments of ancient Egypt; they were occupied with themselves, and not with the pictures of Thebes with its hundred gates. Although vain, although endeavouring, as all nations do, to shed a halo of glory around their own origin, it is they who have told us that their ancestors had not risen above the savage state at the arrival of the Egyptian Inachus on their coasts, nearly eighteen centuries before Christ. The Greeks, they say, the Pelasgians had no settled habitations; they were hunters and shepherds at the same time, but their country, intersected by arms of the sea and by mountains, did not admit of the extended pastoral life of the Scythians, the Tartars, and the Arabs, nor of the formation of great communities. They were not acquainted with all the domestic animals; the horse was brought by sea, it was a present from Neptune; they were acquainted with no modes of culture, the vegetable kingdom only supplied them with acorns and beech mast, on which they fed without planting the trees which produced them. The introduction of the three great cultures, the wheat by Ceres, the olive by Minerva, the vine by Bacchus, points out, under a mythological veil, the progress for which they were indebted to strangers. None of the three were known in Greece before the time of Inachus; all the domestic arts were equally unknown, and men were clothed only in the skins of the animals which they had eaten.

This social state of the Pelasgians is inferior to that of all the inhabitants of Asia, of all the negroes, inhabitants of Africa, who practised arts and agriculture, to all the pastoral nations in both these parts of the world, to whom agriculture is forbidden by the nature of their country, but who have, however, made some progress in civil society; it is inferior even to the hunting nations of America, who knew at least maize and potatoes, and who fabricated some kinds of stuffs, and it can only be compared to the state of the savages of Australia. Nevertheless the Egyptian colonies brought the inhabitants of this country to a state of the highest civilization; they taught them all the arts of life, all the means of subduing nature. They did not drive them away, they did not exterminate them, but they admitted them into their new communities, they united them with the colonists in their cities; they did not make them into Egyptians but into Greeks; religion, language, manners, dress, all was Greek, all belonged to the new country not to the old; especially the political organization was Greek. There only were seen to arise liberty and patriotism; there was lighted the torch which was to enlighten the universe.

About three hundred years of the history of the Greeks, from the arrival of Inachus, who founded Argos, to that of

Danaus, who was called to reign over the same city, are filled with stories half traditional, half mythological, of the arrival of all those chiefs, Egyptian or Phœnician, who each in their turn founded a new city, and brought with them an endowment of new arts, of new knowledge. Greece transmitted to posterity the names of those who taught them the different kinds of agriculture, the working of mines, the art of weaving, of navigation, writing, coining, commerce and music. Three hundred years rolled over, but at the end of that period the Greeks were more advanced than their instructors, the Egyptians; forming so many separate states, and engaged in continual struggles, they were less powerful, no doubt, they were less wealthy; society was less stable, but there was more life in them; all classes of the nation were drawn nearer together, more mixed together; there was more happiness for all.

Scarcely had the aborigines and the colonists which came from Egypt melted into one nation, Greece, when she began in her turn to spread along all the coasts of the Mediterranean the civilization she had received. Colonies of Ionians, Æolians, Dorians, bent their way to Asia Minor. Others founded new cities in Italy, in Sicily, on the borders of the Pontus Euxinus, on the coast of Africa, and on that of Provence. Everywhere these colonies exercised on the indigenous inhabitants the happy influence which the Egyptians had exercised on the Greeks. Everywhere they civilized them, everywhere they taught them the arts of life, everywhere they admitted the ancient inhabitants to an intimate union with themselves, and everywhere, thanks to this union, they soon outran their mother city in population, in wealth, in all the arts, and even in development of mind. Troy, a Greek colony, was more powerful than any of the Greek cities which leagued together for her ruin. The colonies of Greeks in Asia Minor were richer, more advanced in the arts and in philosophy, at the period of the war with the Persians, than the Peloponnesus, though their situation did not permit them to resist that powerful monarch so long. The south of Italy took the name of Græcia Major, because it surpassed, in fact, ancient Greece in its extent, in the number, the riches and the power of its cities. Sicily was covered with cities still more prosperous. Syracuse not only surpassed Corinth, which had founded it, but its population equalled that of the whole of the island at this day; it is said that it contained 1,200,000 inhabitants. So Marseilles surpassed Phocæa, which had founded it, and Cyrene the island of Thera, which had sent out the first colonists.

Rome was not a colony of Greeks, but Rome owed her civilization, her laws, her language, her religion, to the nations of Italy, educated by the colonists from Greece. Rome was not content, as the Greeks had been, with only carrying from country to country her arts, her language, her religion, and her philosophy; she would reign wherever her arms had penetrated. The Greeks sowed their coasts with new and independent nations; the Romans aimed at unity, they also spread their colonies as far as they carried their arms; but these colonies, although an image of the great city, were only garrisons from the great nation, not germs of new nations. They also, however, were intended to mix with the aborigines, to communicate to them all the progress which Rome had made in the arts and in the social sciences, and to initiate them in civilization; and the colonies of the Romans, in all the ancient world, completed the first education of the human race.

It will be thought, perhaps, that a picture of the progressive civilization of the modern world by the colonies of Europe would not yield in grandeur to that of ancient colonization. In fact, during the three last centuries, Europeans have sent colonies into almost every part of the habitable world. They have subjugated countries infinitely surpassing in extent those they have left, and they have founded empires and republics proportionably larger than those of the old world. Nevertheless, we cannot for a moment compare in our minds the colonies of the ancients and those of the moderns, without the first impression, even before reflection, informing us that the colonies of the ancients renewed the human race, tempered it afresh, and began political existence with all the advantages of youth; ours, on the contrary, are born old, with all the jealousies, all the troubles, all the indigence, all the vices of old Europe; that the colonies of the ancients, in every point of civilization, constantly rose above those who had given birth to them; that ours as constantly descend below their founders; that our colonies, already so large, are destined to become larger, but that in vain will be sought for in them, the virtues, the patriotism, the vigour, which belonged to the first age of the world.

More attentive observation makes us feel still greater differences. The Greeks, and before them the Egyptians, founded a colony that it might be complete in itself; we, that it may be a part of another empire. They had constantly in view the welfare of the colonists; we, the advantage of the mother country. They wished the colony to suffice to itself, with respect to its subsistence, defence, internal government, and all the principles of its development: we wish it to be dependent in every way, to subsist by commerce, and that this commerce should enrich the mother country; that it should be defended by her arms, obedient to her orders, governed by her lieutenants, and that these new citizens should receive even their education only from their elder brothers.

A profound study of the colonies makes us perceive another difference, still more afflicting. The colonies of the Egyptians, of the Phœnicians, of the Greeks, and even of the Romans, brought benefits to the countries where they were established; ours, calamities. The first, by their contact, civilized the barbarians; the modern Europeans have, wherever they have settled, destroyed all civilization foreign to their own manners; they have barbarized (if this expression may be allowed) the nations whom they called barbarous, by forcing them to renounce all the arts of life which they had themselves invented. They have in their turn barbarized themselves; for here Europeans have descended to the manners of pastoral nations, there to that of hunters; everywhere, in all their transactions with the aborigines, they have sullied themselves, by deceit, by abuse of force, and by cruelty; everywhere they have gone back in the arts they brought from Europe; their agriculture is become half savage, all their tools more rude, all their knowledge more incomplete, distinguished men more rare; and the general level of intelligence, as well as of morality, has descended instead of rising.

Perhaps to this will be objected the success of the United States, whose prosperity appears so brilliant as to leave no cause for the moderns to regret the system of ancient colonization. The United States, however, owe perhaps their principal advantages to their first founders having approached much nearer to the Greeks and Romans in their ideas and opinions than we do now. The pilgrims of New England, emigrating in search of liberty of conscience, proposed to themselves, in the first place, to create a new country, as the Greeks had formerly done; all other colonists, sent by Europe, took with them, as their only principle, the love of gain, as their only theory, the extension of commerce; thus they always sacrificed the future to the present, and sowed the seeds of dissolution in the new colony from the moment of its birth. We shall have only too many occasions of remarking that these seeds have also been developed in the United States.

Let us endeavour to observe better the contrast between the principles of the Greeks when they founded a colony and ours. The Greeks, when they transported themselves into a new region, wished their colony to represent the original type of their own community, the city; when we found one, it represents the original type of ours, an empire. They concentrated their political existence on one point, we disseminate ours over a territory. This is not the place to inquire which contribute most to virtue, to happiness, to the progress of intelligence, the small republics of antiquity, or our great monarchies. Each nation is led by circumstances which govern the whole race, to aim at a certain degree of strength and independence proportioned to the power of other nations, who for want of this balance might be tempted to abuse their power. But at the origin of nations, at the beginning of associations, there was more liberty to profit by the lessons of experience; to colonists only can it be said that, in order that mutual wants may unite them, and that a fraternal tie may be established among adventurers, often brought together by chance alone, they must begin by being small, they must feel weak among strangers, for power would only make them arrogant and threatening; their situation must force them to conciliate the aborigines, they must strive to associate them to themselves instead of treating them as savages, and especially to be careful not to bring among them, as the only mark of civilization, the art of war to exterminate them.

In founding a colony, the first attention of the Egyptians, the Phœnicians, then of the Greeks and Romans, was the choice of the site where they would build their city, for it was in cities that they wished to live, it was by means of cities that they spread the arts of the life of towns, or civilization [a]. The site of the city should be naturally so strong that its inclosure might be easily defended, and that its inhabitants might, without the assistance of the mother country, resist the sudden attacks of those in the midst of whom they had first established themselves. But this resistance supposed also that the colonists could easily be assembled to take arms, that the call of the trumpet, which answered to our alarm bells, would make them run from every part of the territory of which they had taken possession. From this circumstance alone was derived important modifications in their whole economy. First, their territory must be very circumscribed. Most frequently it was a desert which they had legitimately acquired from the aborigines in a pacific manner, and this first contract was not, as in modern colonies, continually interpreted, continually modified by fraud or violence. The colonists felt that they could not, that they

[a] From *civitas*, city, we have the words *civis, civilis, civilizatio.*

ought not, to go far from their city, from their only retreat; they had no temptation to usurp a greater extent of land, and that cupidity which continually involves Europeans in war with the aborigines did not act on them.

The colonists, weak, few in number, and completely abandoned to themselves, for the mother country did not think of defending them, took care to build all their houses in the narrow inclosure of the city. At night they reposed under a common guard, in the day only they could go abroad into the fields to their rural labours From this circumstance their agriculture took the character of that of Provence or Spain, where there are no farms, no houses dispersed in the fields, and where all the cultivators with all their cattle are shut up in the towns. This system of agriculture has certainly heavy inconveniences. It increases the work of the labourer and of his beasts; it scarcely permits of his attending to his land, or expecting abundant harvests: it does not encourage him to plant his fields, to ornament them, to feel an attachment to them. But the influence of this system on man is more important than on the creation of wealth. Now the sentiment of social life, of civil life, is what it is most important to keep up among colonists, and the rural inhabitants of towns will continue much more civilized than if they were scattered over the country. In itself the undertaking of founding a colony relaxes the social tie. It is always the most independent spirit, the most proud, the most intractable, who engage in these adventurous projects. Often it is those who cannot support the yoke of the laws in the mother country, notwithstanding their ancient authority and the power of custom. These men are still less disposed to obedience in a perfectly new state, where no prejudice lends support to order, where no habit is deeply rooted. Great care must be taken not to allow them to disperse themselves in the deserts; for if they can fix their habitation at a great distance from their comrades, they will soon acknowledge no law but their own caprice, no judges but their resentments, their offended pride, and their other passions. Each father will be a little tyrant in his family; a stranger to the society of his equals, he will exact implicit obedience from his wife and children; the art of persuasion will be useless to him, the art of conversation will present to him neither charm nor reward; he will know no pleasures but those of the senses, and intoxication will take the place of all mental development. If by chance there arises a quarrel between him and one of his neighbours, he knows that no neighbour will see them, no peace-maker will come to his assistance, no inquest is possible; he will then endeavour to get rid of his adversary, or if he is without arms, to tear out his eyes in the American mode, to have done with him, that he may not be tormented by his complaints, and that he may not be condemned by his testimony, even supposing he would submit to tribunals which cannot reach him. Whatever may have been originally the cultivation of his mind, or the mildness of his character, he will very soon arrive at the condition of *backwoodsman,* the colonist of the distant forests, such as are seen in America, in that solitary existence, brutal and violent, which destroys all true civilization, all sympathy with other men, but which preserves all those qualities by which a fortune may be made, such as strength of body, address, the spirit of enterprise, and especially the spirit of calculation and cupidity.

But in the Greek colony, man was always in the presence of man; he had to give to his fellow-citizens, his companions in adventure, an account of all his movements. He could not run the risk of going to any distance without his absence being remarked; he could not give way to any excess without his intoxication, his rage, his acts of tyranny being known to all, and subjecting him to public animadversion; he could not commit homicide, and flatter himself he should escape the law, whether his victim were a fellow-countryman or a native. The colony, it is true, had no force to pursue him out of its territory; but he had himself such constant need of the colonial government that he constantly returned to place himself under its wing, and this government which knew its own weakness and its want of neighbours, looked upon a quarrel with the natives as a public offence. If the delinquent adopted the plan of not returning at night to his own house, of withdrawing himself from the tribunals of his own country, he must go away for ever, and eternal exile was looked upon as the greatest of punishments.

In modern colonies, an immense extent of fertile land seems abandoned to the first occupier; and the colonist, reckoning on the powerful protection of the mother country, takes a portion of it for himself, out of all proportion to his physical strength to cultivate, to his capital to improve, to his wants to consume the produce. The colonist of antiquity, who only depended on himself, and on his companions in the adventure, did not wish to possess fields from whence he could not hear the trumpet of war calling him to defend the city; and on this principle, colonial authority founded the division of the land that had been acquired. All must have nearly an equal share, for all must be within reach of the walls; the divisions extended like the sections of a circle, the cultivated fields were nearest the fortified enclosure; beyond, the colony possessed a zone of pasturage, from whence the approach of an enemy might be perceived at a great distance. Thus, whatever might be the inequality of wealth among the associates, a superior interest, the safety of all, brought them to an equality in territorial division. Each head of a family was not required to purchase his new land; the distribution was gratuitous; or at most, it was proportioned to the power of each family to cultivate and defend it, and to its numbers to consume its productions. Thus, from the time of their arrival, the colonists, limited in space, were obliged to introduce into their fields the culture which was suitable to land of the highest value; they brought with them those modes of cultivation which the most advanced state of rural science in the mother country had led to the practice of, and thus they taught their art to the savages. Ours on the contrary learn theirs from them; masters all at once of an immense extent of land, which they hold by right of the sword, or by a purchase of a share from a company, they do not husband any of the benefits of nature. They clear the forests by fire, or by barking the trees, and leave them to decay where they stand; they abandon every system of manuring, of improvement, of the rotation of crops; they apply themselves to benefit by some of the natural advantages of the soil, to which they sacrifice all others; they exhaust the soil by a succession of the same crops, and they soon reduce the richest soil to sterility. All the vast and beautiful countries which border on the Atlantic, whose fertility astonished the Europeans when they landed for the first time, have been ruined in this way by the cupidity of the cultivators, who sacrificed the future to the present. The colonists, instructed by the native Americans in the arts of destruction, did not even think of imitating them in the art of preservation. The same fault is repeated at this time, at the Cape of Good Hope, in New Holland, in Van Diemen's Land; in these new colonies land is distributed by four hundred and eight hundred acres. They wish to begin with farms as extensive as those which the richest English farmers cultivate in a manner which requires great advances, and yet they give them to men almost without capital, who are therefore almost necessarily obliged to cultivate them as those who went before them did, on the borders of the Atlantic; regarding only the present, and with no thought for the future. So in the projects of colonization for Algiers, we hear only great companies and great farms spoken of, whilst what ought especially to be considered, is the customs of the Arabian cultivators, the means of associating them with the European, and of making this association profitable, by improving the industry of the country, and not overthrowing it. If, in fact, the land conquered in Africa is taken from the native cultivators to be given up to speculators, to people éager to enjoy, eager to destroy, and incapable of creating any thing, agriculture, far from advancing, will go back from the point to which the Arabs had brought it.

The Greek colonies were composed of men whose condition was free, but who came from every rank of society, and they were led, in the heroic ages, by the sons of kings, and in later times by *eupatrides*, or citizens of the most illustrious birth; yet the necessary consequence of their enterprize was to establish the greatest equality among the colonists. Those who engaged in the adventurous expeditions took no fortune with them, nor did they think of making a fortune. It was not that they renounced ambition; they hoped to distinguish themselves in the first rank among their fellow-citizens in council or in war. They hoped to become great, by their eloquence, their prudence, or their valour, never to become rich. On the soil of their new country, they expected to subsist only by the labour of their hands; they received, like all the rest, their share of the colonial fields, they must cultivate them without servants, without day-labourers, without slaves; for the new community, surrounded by enemies, by rivals, could not consent to assemble in its bosom domestic enemies. Among the small nations of antiquity, at the time of their mutual independence, slavery was only an accident of the rights of war, and not an industrial organization; it had not therefore yet made labour dishonourable. The greatest citizens of the colony did not refuse to perform manual labour, but it was necessary that this labour should not fill up all their time, for they must devote part of it to the administration of their new country, to its instruction, and to its defence. In a country where the cultivator has no rent to pay, where the state has no debts, where one share of the product of the labour of rising generations has not been mortgaged or sold in advance by their parents to their creditors, in a country, at the same time, where manners are simple and tyranny is unknown, rural industry always produces much more than is necessary for the support of those who are employed in it. If, even now, the cultivator can live upon half his harvest, and give up the other half to his landlord, formerly the cultivator being the proprietor, could live upon the labour of half a week, or half a day, and consecrate the other half to the service of the public.

Thus, those who were rich in the mother country were no

longer rich in the colony, but on the other hand the poor were no longer poor; both lived by the labour of their hands, but a labour liberally rewarded by nature. Both were called upon for an habitual exercise of all their corporeal faculties, but they did not the less habitually exercise all the powers of their minds. The government of a colony had a greater share of democracy than existed in any ancient state; it ought, and it could do so without danger. The different conditions of the citizens in such small nations did not act as with us, or in our colonies, by a universal rivalry of one another; but on the contrary, all felt a common interest, which had relation also to the aborigines. Intercourse with them could alone feed the colony at its commencement; the means of gaining their friendship, of obtaining their confidence, of establishing between them and the colonist common signs, a conventional language, was the business of all, the urgent interest of all: at the same time, it was from these aborigines that all danger arose; watchfulness of them, defence against them, in case of any sudden quarrel, were also interests equally felt by all. When they left their mother country, some sons of illustrious men, some sons of rich men, had probably brought with them some pride of birth or of family, some feeling of superiority, and if this superiority was united to a more careful education, to the habits and experience of the world, to the traditions of their fathers, to talents; it was acknowledged and appreciated, for it was useful to all. It even flattered the popular imagination, for it is in a country where all is new, where all is first springing up, that the recollections of antiquity are most dear. But the lowest colonist, the lowest cultivator, had the same identical interest as the nobleman. Like him he served his country by his vigilance, and defended it by his arm, like him he was admitted into the councils where the new born nation deliberated on the existence of all. The more restricted the circle was, the more close and intimate their confidence, so much the more did the man of the common people receive from the well-born man with whom he was associated, the powerful education of common circumstances and common action. We are accustomed in these days to confound instruction with the influence of books; but the greatest instruction, fruitful instruction, is the action of man on man. All social interests were in turn debated in the *Agora*, every example was placed before the eyes of all; all characters were in some sort developed in public, and the study of man, the philosophical study of human passions and human interests, was accessible to the poorest as well as to the richest. The delicacy of language and modes of expression did not mark different conditions, for all studied to speak with the same purity of language: if from time to time some books increased the fund of public instruction, their effect was popular; it was to assembled Greece that Herodotus read his history. In our times, also, we have pretended to democracy; but the first element of the Greek cities was wanting, that equality of condition which resulted from their economical organization, an equality which was nowhere greater than in the newly born colonies.

The community of interests, the close approximation of all the citizens, their constant action on one another, made the colonies of antiquity resemble a school of mutual instruction. The information which some superior men had brought, soon spread through the whole mass of the little nation, by continual contact, by a daily exchange of all their observations and of all their ideas. What one knew, all knew, all practised, all taught to the natives: it is thus that the culture of wheat, of the olive, of the vine, working in metals, weaving, the alphabet, and the aid of writing, a knowledge of coins, of calculation, of music, were successively introduced into the new countries, and tradition or mythology preserved the traces of these great benefits: each was attributed to one hero, to one semi-fabulous being, but all his companions became, with him, the instructors of nations; because the talent, the superiority, the beneficence of each chief was reflected by all the members of the growing community associated with him.

What an afflicting contrast do our modern colonies form to

those of the ancients—the civilizers of the human race! Our colonists, when they leave the shores of the mother country, do not form a chosen society, associated together to run the same risks, united by the confidence that all will be ready to expose themselves, each for all, all for one. There is among them neither fraternity nor confidence; there cannot be. The colonists are for the most part men who have experienced in the world either reverses, or at least great sorrows. They leave Europe with ruined fortunes, credit shaken by misfortunes, which the world is always disposed to attribute to their imprudence; they go to seek a new world, where they may forget the old, and where they may themselves remain unknown. There are also restless spirits, who reject with bitterness the forms of the old world, and who cannot be content in the place to which they are there restricted. There are also adventurers greedy of gain, who not being willing to trust to the ordinary chances of agriculture or industry, consider fortune as a game, and risk their lives and property on chances, which because they are unknown, appear to them immense. This mixed troop, already so little worthy of confidence, is increased by the scum of the old community, which it casts with aversion upon the new. Bad individuals, whom their family would save from the ignominy of judicial proceedings, obtain as a favour to be allowed to go to the colonies. The garrisons sent there are composed of regiments recruited by soldiers who have been expelled from other regiments for their follies, their vices, and sometimes their crimes. The managers of the finances, the officers of justice, even the governors, are often sent to the colonies as an honourable exile. The more eminent have been sent because they were in less credit at court; others from the legislative chambers, because their opposition was feared. Some have been taken from before the eyes of the public, to whom they were becoming odious; others have been sent away, to prevent inquiries which would have ruined them; all have been chosen not as being most fit for the colony, but as being inconvenient in the old country. Lastly, in this afflicting enumeration of so many elements of disorder, of vice and of crime, we have not yet comprised that class, which Europe could not add to them without a cruel offence to humanity, those who are transported,—men branded by a sentence which makes them infamous, and who are sent to inoculate with crime a new nation, constituted and designated by a name which makes one shudder,—*a penal colony.*

Is it strange that men, known to one another as belonging to certain classes, all suspected, though in different degrees, should avoid instead of seeking one another;—that as soon as they arrive on the vast continent open to their enterprises they should disperse over its whole extent? Those who feel in their hearts the love of honour and duty know well, that any contact with the companions of their adventures may contaminate them, may compromise them, but can teach them nothing good. Those who wish their past lives to be forgotten avoid the observation of men; those who feel that their present conduct will not bear examination avoid it still more. All the beneficent influences of human society are lost upon them all, but its corrupting influences remain, for the colonists do not live absolutely alone. The richest, the most civilized, are obliged to associate with their inferiors in the manual operations of their establishment, and they always acquire something of their language, of their coarseness, and of their vices. Even in the penal colonies, whatever may be the repugnance of the proprietors to mix with the convicts, as almost all labour is performed by them, they must communicate with them, they must place some confidence in them; and estimating them according as they are more or less hardened in crime, they almost consider as an honest man one who has only been led into it once or twice. The corrupting effect of the habitual presence of corrupted beings is inevitable; the poison spreads equally to those who hate and those who excuse them. The man who should see in these convicts, by whom he is surrounded, only objects of disgust and aversion, would soon lose all sympathy with the human countenance, all pity for suffering, all faith in the expression of feeling,—would undergo a moral contagion even more grievous than he who had been accustomed to look on vice and crime with indulgence. Thus these degraded beings, who can only be produced in the mire of great cities, who have lost all moral feeling, who cannot distinguish what is just and honest, introduce into the places where they are transported a focus of corruption, which will continue to develop itself as long as they live. Ages will not stifle these fatal germs of vice, barbarously carried to establishments destined to rapid increase. We have grafted the most poisonous of fruits on the young shoot, which grows vigorously, and promises to become a large tree in future generations.

It is not only by penal colonies that the crimes and vices of countries which have passed through civilization have been transplanted into virgin soils. The history of European colonies shows everywhere civilized man abusing the superiority of his powers and of his intelligence to despoil the aborigines, to force them into war, to corrupt them, and to exterminate them. The Greeks, by their colonies along the whole extent of the coasts of the Mediterranean, settled wandering nations; led to agriculture, then to arts and commerce, hunters and shepherds; taught them the science of government and the love of liberty, substituted for a gloomy and bloody worship, for the jealous and oppressive power of bodies of priests, the worship of heroes, benefactors of humanity, who were the gods of Greece; opened their minds to a philosophy which was at a later time to purify and reform an already reforming religion. By all these benefits the Greeks called into existence an increase of population, and of a happy population, which passes our comprehension. Græcia Major, Sicily, and Asia Minor, reckoned thousands of cities to which no provincial towns of our greatest empires can be compared. At the same time, the population of the natives, enriched by the arts of Greece, increased with a not less surprising rapidity, and civilization extended into regions which the civilizing nation had never trod. Now, on the contrary, wherever Europeans have established themselves they have destroyed the pre-existing civilization. By their contact have disappeared, first, all those of highest rank in the indigenous society, then all the improved arts and the agriculture which was practised by the natives, then their virtues, and at last the race itself. It is a fact, which at this time does not admit of doubt, which is even presented to us as a law of nature, as a necessity, that wherever a white race comes into contact with an indigenous race, that race must disappear in the course of a few generations.

When the Spaniards landed on the coasts of the new world, they found them pretty equally divided between natives still barbarous, and natives which had already made great progress in civilization. The most advanced among them were the inhabitants of the Antilles, and those of the two great empires of Mexico and Peru. These shewed what development the red race which peoples America was capable of acquiring by itself and without foreign assistance. Tribes formerly wandering had long been settled. They had found in the new world very few species of animals capable of being tamed; thus they had not tried the pastoral life; but they had had more success in extending their dominion over the vegetable kingdom: by means of agriculture they had obtained a very abundant subsistence; in fact, a numerous and happy population covered and fertilized the country, whilst a class devoted to the arts had built large cities. Between the tropics, a space of much less extent than is required in temperate regions, suffices, with less labour, to furnish man with food. In the *tierras calientes* (the hot regions near the sea), as well as in the islands, a plantation of bananas, a *platanar*, which does not occupy more than one hundred square metres [a], affords each year more than four thousand pounds' weight of a nourishing substance, whilst the same space would scarcely produce thirty pounds of corn in France. A plantation of

[a] A metre is a little more than a yard.

manioc, from which the cassava is extracted, requires, it is true, more labour and more time, but it furnishes a substance as abundant and more nourishing than the banana. The culture of all the productions of the tropics was practised in the islands with skill; it supported a population prodigiously numerous, which with few wants and much leisure, passed life in feasts and joy. The population of Mexico and Peru, especially in the *tierras templadas* and the *tierras frias* (the temperate and cold regions of the mountains), were obliged to employ more constant labour, either to subdue nature, or to support the political and religious luxury of these two nations. Maize and potatoes formed the basis of the nourishment of the people, but at the same time an infinite variety of fruits and flowers multiplied the enjoyments of man. The boats of the gardeners, who came to Mexico by the lake, displayed, as they do now, all the pomp of that rich vegetation. The plantations of maguay (*Agave Americana*), from which they extract the *pulque*, or wine of Mexico, filled the place of our vines. Manufactures adapted to the wants of the people were multiplied in the towns; a court which loved splendour, grandees proud of their wealth, and a religion surrounded by pomp, had directed industry towards the production and the enjoyment of luxury. The red race, as well in Mexico as in Peru, wished to perpetuate the memory of its great deeds and of its discoveries, and for that purpose had invented a kind of writing by hieroglyphics. It had also discovered the art of extracting from the mines, and of working some of the metals, and for its misfortune used ornaments of gold and silver, which excited the cupidity of the first Spanish colonists.

We have no intention to retrace here the frightful conduct of these Spaniards in the new world; public opinion has branded it for ever. It is enough to say, that if we consider the number of their victims, and the duration of the torments inflicted on them, their crimes surpassed all the crimes which sully the history of the human race. In the intoxication of victory, some Tartar conquerors gave the dreadful order to massacre all the inhabitants of a town, of even a province, to raise hideous pyramids of their heads, in remembrance of their victory; but the avaricious ferocity of the Spaniards cost humanity many more lives; they were destroyed by torments much more atrocious, much more prolonged, they were sacrificed without provocation by the calm calculations of avarice. The peaceable inhabitants of these countries were all equally condemned to the labour of the mines, they were forced upon exertions which were beyond their strength, whilst they were not allowed sufficient nourishment; they were driven by the whips of their inspectors, in spite of weakness, wounds, sicknesses, and they were relieved from these horrible torments by death alone, which soon released them. Depopulation went on with such strange rapidity, that in the course of a single generation the red race disappeared from the Antilles: the population of St. Domingo alone was, nevertheless, more than a million inhabitants; Cuba had at least as many; all other islands in proportion. Among the Caribbees, some thousands of this unfortunate race escaped extermination; but it was only those, who initiated by suffering, and losing all hope, did not continue in any fixed abodes: they abandoned agriculture, renounced their civilization, and cast themselves upon savage life. The inhabitants of Mexico and Peru had been subjected to an oppression no less frightful; but whether it was that the race of the inhabitants of the mountains was more vigorous, or more accustomed to hard labour, whether it was that the *corvée* [a] imposed upon them, the *mita* which called them by turns to the mines, was exercised with rather more equity under the eyes of the viceroy himself, or whether time was wanting to finish the work of destruction, a part of the ancient inhabitants survived the most atrocious measures, and it is they who are now renewing that part of the population. At the time of the journey of M. de Humboldt, they were not subject to any kind of *corvée*, their labour in the mines was voluntary and well

[a] Statute labour, which a peasant had to do for his lord.

paid, and they had resumed the pursuit of agriculture with spirit. In Mexico, the red men, who still form a population of 3,679,000 souls, are alone distinguished by their industry in the cultivation of land, and their activity in introducing it into new districts. But this race is now only composed of labourers; all the grandees of the city-empire have disappeared, and with them all the wealthy, all the priests, all the learned men, all the citizens of towns, and all the merchants. None of the old civilization is to be found among them. The labourers form the lowest steps of a Spanish and Christian civilization which is not their own; none of their ideas are prepared to profit by it, no progress is possible to them, no European development penetrates to them. In Peru, the red race has suffered more: it is nearly extirpated, and nothing remains of the ancient civilization of the Incas, but negroes and mulattoes have taken place of it, and are employed in the most fatiguing labours. In Chili, where the native race was more remarkable for its warlike virtues than for its civilization, it has been driven out of European society; but the savage tribes are excited by the Spaniards to continue wars with one another, and intoxication has deprived them of all the qualities which formerly distinguished them.

Never, we hope, will Europeans, will Christians recall the conduct of the Spaniards in the new world, without horror and indignation. With some reason, no doubt, it has been attributed to the spirit of the sixteenth century. The old Spanish bands of Ferdinand the Catholic, of Charles the Fifth, and of Philip the Second, distinguished themselves during this century, in Italy, in France, in Germany, and in the Low Countries, by their ferocity, and we cannot be surprised if the same character was still more manifested in the new world, where these fierce warriors found themselves completely withdrawn from the restraint of public opinion, and had, at the same time, no feeling of brotherhood for another race. But without pretending to excuse the Spaniards, it is particularly the modern system of colonization that we must condemn for such horrors. It is this system which drives to foreign lands adventurers without honour, without probity, without restraint, which encourages their cupidity, which celebrates their robberies as exploits, and which, abandoning to all their most shameful passions, men of another race, whom they began with calling savage in order to excuse themselves from any feeling of pity towards them, and to consider themselves authorized to despoil them; gives to the aggressors all the support of a powerful nation advanced in the art of war, furnishes them with arms, with ammunition, and, when requisite, with soldiers, to enable them to exterminate their inoffensive neighbours. In continuing our review of modern colonies, we shall soon find that the arrival of colonists from every other nation of Europe has been not less fatal to the aborigines than that of the Spaniards. Besides, the Spaniards are the only nation that have admitted the natives into their social union, to occupy at least the inferior ranks of it. Among them alone the red race of America multiplies: everywhere else it is on the point of being exterminated.

It is indeed only in the old Spanish colonies, in Mexico, in Peru, and in the Philippine Islands, that the devouring activity of adventurers has given place to sedentary habits, and that the inhabitants think of enjoying life instead of having no object but to get rich rapidly. There, only, is the universal competition to acquire, to accumulate, by means honest or dishonest, moderated, at least, if not suspended; there, only, have the subjugated races also obtained, if not equality of rights, at least some consideration and some protection. In Cuba, the Spanish colonists continue to make their profits by men [a], instead of things; they are manufacturers, and they are given up to the mercantile spirit in all its harshness; they cultivate the sugar cane, and they make sugar in the true system of the chresmatistic school, seeking only to save as much ex-

[a] *Exploiter*, to make the best of any thing by working it. *Exploiter ses terres*, to improve his estate. *Exploiter une mine*, to work a mine. *Exploiter une forêt*, to fell a forest.

pense as possible in the subsistence of the men who produce it. Thus in all slave countries, there is not one in which the treatment of slaves is more barbarous than at the Havanna, none where the slave trade is more openly exercised. In all the rest of the half desert possessions of the Spaniards, in New Mexico, in California, the Andes, in Paraguay, and countries watered by the Maranon, wherever, in short, a career has been opened to adventurers, the creoles act in the old spirit of colonists, and their influence in making the country barbarous, is as constant, as cruel, as it has ever been. All the neighbouring tribes have been abandoned to them like the game of the forests and savannahs, to make a profit by their life or by their death. They go to hunt *Indios bravos* (Indian savages) with as little scruple as they would hunt wild boars. If they can ensnare them, they take them by nets, by traps, or chase them with dogs. If they surround their villages, they massacre all who resist, they drag the remainder into slavery. By their continual pursuit they have forced these Indians to live wandering lives, to subsist by hunting; and wherever the Spaniards take these Indians captive, they oblige them to continual labour, beyond their strength, under which they soon perish. Along with these odious hunters of men, there were formerly, it is true, colonies of missionaries, who followed these same *Indios bravos* into the woods, and endeavoured to convert them to the Christian religion, and to a life of agriculture. God forbid we should refuse our admiration to such great virtue, such ardent charity, such self sacrifice. Missions however have never had the beneficial effects of the ancient colonies; not that the Indians were inferior to the Pelasgians or less capable of instruction, but because the instruction which the Padres gave them was too little prepared, was too little suited to their nature. They did not begin their education by the material world, but by the invisible world; they wished to bring them to confess, but not to understand, those mysteries of divine and human nature, which the strongest heads in the most reflecting nations can scarcely grasp; and forcing them to renounce their own language, they taught them in two new languages, the Castilian and the Latin, which to the poor Indian were only sounds devoid of sense. In consequence of this sacrifice of understanding to memory, the *Indios reducidos* (subject Indians) are become in the hands of the missionaries only great children, hearing without understanding, and obeying without knowing why. Besides, almost all pleasures have been represented to them as sins, so that they live without motives; they have lost all interior spring; they present the image of European society divested of its activity, of its intelligence; they are incapable of progress, and the effect which European instruction has had upon them, confirms the prejudice against the red race which the European race originated.

It is also difficult for the *Indios reducidos* to escape the molestation of the Spaniards, who are jealous of the efforts of the Padres to convert them. Whatever progress the missionaries make takes away a certain number of individuals or families from that fund of human creatures, which the colonists consider as reserved for their rights of chace; it impoverishes the slave market; and the faster the captives die, the more important do the colonists consider it to keep up the stock from whence they are taken. In general the missionaries had established themselves at a great distance from these aggressive colonists, but as these are continually advancing, the missions soon find themselves in contact with these hunters of the *Indios bravos*, who on their side make a wish for conversions the pretext for their hostility. The Spanish government, full of prejudice as it was, oppressive as it often showed itself towards the interests of the colonies, had at least no sympathy with those hunters of men, and the object of its general orders was most frequently to protect humanity and religion. But in the new republics, the local authorities have been entrusted to men who partook of the passions of the district by which they were elected. In general they have shewn themselves very unfavourable to the missions; sometimes they have forced the *Padres* to emigrate with all the *Indios reducidos;* numerous bands have gone to English Guiana, whilst M. Pœppig, when he crossed Upper Peru in 1832, found in the middle of the ancient missions of Cuchero, Pampayaco, and Tocache, only silent deserts; the rapid vegetation of the tropics had left no perceptible trace of the yet recent labours of man. The republics, by the expulsion of the missionaries, expected to get credit for their liberality; they wished, they say, to restrain the formidable influence of the clergy, and to oppose the progress of superstition: few persons at some thousands of leagues distance will in fact comprehend, that the true object of this liberality was to extend the hunting of men over new districts.

The white race, in exterminating the red race throughout the greatest portion of America, have, it is true, multiplied in their place. All the continent of South America is now open to Europeans, particularly to the descendants of the Spaniards. But it must not be supposed that with their race, civilization has extended itself into these deserts. The great plateau of South America is covered with troops of cattle and horses which have been introduced there from Europe. In New Grenada, in the republics of Rio de la Plata, Bolivia, Chili, there are many proprietors who possess fifteen or twenty thousand head of horned beasts, but the *vaquero* who lives amidst these herds becomes wild, and all the population of these central regions, or those which they call the *Llaneros*, have descended rather to the level of the hunting tribes, than to that of the pastoral tribes of the old world. Far from subjugating or taming these wild animals, as the Tartars and Arabs have done, they abandon domestic animals to a wild state, and obtain nothing from them except by destroying them. The Arab, by his care, his intelligence, his affection, his study of the instincts of animals, had succeeded in attaching to himself, in rendering obedient, the proudest and the wildest: the Llanero considers beasts, sheep, goats, swine, only as game which afford him the pleasures of the chace, and which he takes pleasure in tormenting with unspeakable ferocity.

What we have said of the Spanish colonies, may in many

respects be applied to the Portuguese. These, instead of bringing civilization, have spread everywhere robbery and desolation. In Brazil, where the Portuguese found themselves in contact with the red race, in the earliest state of barbarism, that is to say, when wandering hunters are just beginning to settle and cultivate the ground, they forced them to give up this cultivation, and to bury themselves in the woods, where the colonists pursued them in order to exterminate them, or to reduce them to slavery. They have endeavoured to replace them by negroes, of whom they import into Brazil every year a hundred thousand, although the time may come when these, becoming the strongest, will massacre them all. In the two kingdoms of Congo and Mozambique, where the Portuguese have established themselves on the eastern and western coasts of Africa, the colonists of European or mixed blood have so entirely descended to the level of the natives, that they cannot be distinguished from them; all trace of civilization has disappeared from among them, and the sovereignty of Portugal over so vast a portion of Africa, is only remarkable in modern times by the pretensions of the Portuguese nation to continue the slave trade when it was disallowed by the rest of Europe, because, said the Portuguese diplomatists, their merchants had the exclusive right to sell the inhabitants of these regions, inasmuch as they were born subjects of the king of Portugal.

The expeditions of the Portuguese to the East Indies recall those of the Spaniards to Mexico and Peru: there is the same mixture of cupidity and chivalric bravery, the same religious fanaticism joined to perfidy and ferocity. But the Portuguese came among more civilized nations, more wealthy, and especially more advanced in the art of war, than those which the Spaniards conquered. It was necessary to employ with them the greatest discretion; they more frequently went as merchants than as soldiers; besides there were no mines where they settled, so that they could not conceive the dreadful idea of sending whole generations of the conquered nations into the bowels of the earth to get gold and silver. However, in reading only the

Portuguese historians, there appears no doubt that in all their quarrels with the Indians it was the Portuguese who were in the wrong, so that on them must always fall the reproach of being the aggressors, of being treacherous and barbarous; that their wars have cost torrents of blood shed with heartless gaiety, and that their dominion in India, now happily reduced to two great cities, has contributed much to make the country fall back into that state of anarchy and military oppression, that domination of adventurers, which, substituted for that of the ancient governments, have since that time desolated the country.

The colonies of the Dutch were founded on the ruins of the Portuguese empire in India: the system was changed; a mercantile spirit took place of the religious and chivalric spirit which had spread a sort of brilliancy over the Portuguese cupidity and ferocity, but humanity gained nothing by the change. The Dutch thought no more than the Spaniards and Portuguese had done, of carrying civilization with them. Though republicans and Protestants, though they had experienced among themselves all the advantages of the spirit of inquiry, and of the co-operation of all for the benefit of all, though they had attained to liberty and independence by a confederation of provinces and of cities, of which each one guarded with care the local interests to which they were attached, they carried with them no sentiment of liberty, no mental progress, no thoughts of local advantages to be afforded to their conquests. They kept at an immense distance from the beneficial colonization of the Greeks, and wherever they extended their dominion, did not even think of disguising the cold and avaricious calculations of selfish speculators, who referring everything to themselves, estimating every thing by money, never asked themselves whether the regulations by which they protected their monopoly would carry misery, desolation, and mortality among the natives, whom, without provocation, without pretext, they had subdued by force of arms.

During a long time the Dutch have been distinguished in the

world for that low mercantile cupidity which made them burn all the spices in the Moluccas, preferring to destroy them rather than allow their price to be lowered in the European markets. Equally well known are their yearly expeditions into all the islands of Sunda to seize the cinnamon, cloves, pepper, and nutmegs which might have escaped their monopoly. But it is especially in the life of Sir Stamford Raffles, that virtuous governor who succeeded the Dutch, first at Java, then at Bencoolen, and who had afterwards the grief of restoring to the Dutch this island of Java, over which he had diffused so many benefits, that we can learn all which this immoral and avaricious government permits even to this day, in order to drive back into barbarism its industrious subjects in India; what a scourge to the magnificent archipelago of the isles of Sunda is the Dutch dominion, and how guilty that minister was who lightly and foolishly gave back, by the treaty of Vienna, millions of prosperous subjects to the detested masters who oppressed them so cruelly.

The Dutch government, which has driven back towards barbarism all its possessions in the Indian seas, will appear, perhaps, at the first glance, to have been more successful in the great colony of the Cape of Good Hope, which it founded in 1652, with a handful of Europeans, and which is at present a large empire in extent, taken by the English in 1795, and since retained in their possession. It was only in 1672 that the Dutch bought from the Hottentots, amidst whom they were settled, the district of the Cape, and established there some Dutch peasants, *boors*, to cultivate fresh provisions for sale to the vessels which stopped at the Cape in the passage between India and Europe. It could scarcely have been expected that these boors, the peaceful and industrious cultivators of the *polders* of Holland, famed for their slowness and methodical habits, would be transformed in one single generation into a pastoral and warlike people, not less quarrelsome, not less formidable to its neighbours, than the Mongols and Tartars. But the boors had before them vast countries particularly suitable for pasturage, and which the natives of the country had already covered with their flocks; they had behind them a sea-port, which offered a rich market for all the products of pastoral industry; they were in contact with tribes for whom they had been inspired with no sympathy, who were abandoned to their use, and over whom their fire-arms secured to them an incontestable superiority. In all their quarrels with them, they were sure of the powerful aid of the government of the Cape, which could neither inspect nor direct them in their deserts, and which did not pretend to judge them, but which always thought itself obliged to defend them. The Dutch boors could not fail to abuse such advantages.

The country where the Dutch had founded their colony was inhabited by a mild and inoffensive race of men, divided into small tribes, and incapable of opposing any effectual resistance; these were the Hottentots, whom Europe has chosen to distinguish only for their ugliness, their dirt, and their superstitions; nevertheless these men had made the first and most important steps in civilization; those which make all others easy. They were surrounded by domestic animals, and they cultivated the ground. Man has already exercised much intelligence when he has studied and learnt to perceive in wild animals those qualities which would make them useful when domesticated, and the affection by which their obedience might be obtained; when he has discovered in the plants of the forest the properties useful to man, and the means of multiplying them. The Pelasgic nations were not so far advanced when the Egyptians and Phœnicians landed among them; the Italians and Gauls had scarcely made these first steps when the Greeks led them to make every other. With kindness, with persuasion, with good faith, the colonists might have brought the Hottentots into civilized habits. Their population was already very considerable; by this time they would have become a powerful nation; but the boors did not think themselves bound by any moral duty towards them. Under pretence of trafficking with them, they deceived them in their bargains, and after having excited their resentment by fraud, they found, even in this resentment, a pretext to make war on them. Associating in bands of from 80 to 100, they threw themselves on a neighbouring tribe, killed those who defended themselves, reduced others into slavery; took away from those who fled, the cattle which was their only wealth, and exposed them to die of hunger. The population of the Hottentots cannot be estimated at less than 200,000 at the time of the first European establishment: now they are not reckoned at more than 20,000, and three-quarters of these are the children of Europeans, whom their fathers have left in the same condition as their black mothers. In the year 1771, the Dutch were alone masters of all the country as far as the Snowy Mountains (*Snieen Berghen*); they possessed an extent of 100,000 square miles, or ten times the surface of the United Provinces, but the human race had almost disappeared from this vast territory.

After the extermination of the Hottentots, and the occupation of their country, the Dŭtch colonists found themselves in contact with a more warlike race, more united and more formidable, which they designated by the name of Caffres, from the Arab *Kafir*, unbeliever, for this name is unknown to themselves: the Boors attacked them in the same manner, but to do this they were obliged to assemble more forces, and to call out the national militia, called a *Commando*.

"Thus, according to our view of the history of the Cape colony," says a writer in the Edinburgh Review, Jan. 1846, "the Boors alone were the conquerors of South Africa. The government of the Cape, as well as in Holland, did its utmost, by threats and declamations, to keep them in check, and to protect from aggression the aboriginal owners of the soil, but in vain; the Boors marched onwards with continually increasing herds; wherever they found pasture they made themselves masters of the country, and the colonial government had no part to choose but to follow them and claim the sovereignty of their conquests." (Edinburgh Review, vol. 62, p. 457.)

When this colony passed into the power of the English, it

was not possible to change this system; in spite of themselves the English were led on by their Dutch subjects to conquests continually more extended, to wars more bloody, to the expulsion or destruction of all the aborigines. The last war against the Caffres, terminated by the treaty of the 17th of September, 1835, was distinguished by such ferocious acts as ought to bring the severest reprobation on European soldiers: it extended the frontier of the colony as far as the banks of the Ky, and of the Keiskamma, giving it, at the least, a surface of 200,000 square miles; but in this immense empire, the Europeans only reckon 130,000 inhabitants of their own race; the numerous nations which inhabited it are destroyed, and the small number of free blacks which the last treaty has again intermixed with the Europeans, will before long disappear.

The history of the colony of the Cape of Good Hope, leads us from the Dutch to the English administration, but it does not give us cause to celebrate an amelioration in the lot of the aborigines. The English, however, are the only nation who have felt any true sympathy for the people among whom they have sent their colonies, who have acknowledged their rights, who have seriously proposed to protect them, to civilize them, to make them happy. This sentiment does them honour; it is found in the government, in parliament, in British writers, but it is not found among the colonists. These, brought up in the midst of that animated competition in all professions, of that eager desire to become rich, which characterizes the present age, and England particularly, embark for the colonies, penetrated with the idea that their first business ought to be to get money, and looking upon the universe and its inhabitants as given up to their speculations. The cupidity of the English does not resemble that of the other nations who have preceded them in this career: the Spaniards, the Portuguese, taking the sign for the thing itself, thought only of heaping up gold and silver; they sought for the precious metals with inordinate passion, they seemed to become intoxicated by their possession. The Dutchman was more calm; he united the character of the usurer with that of the merchant; he calculated more coolly the interest, the profit, the advantages of monopoly, and what the ruin of another might bring to himself. The Englishman wishes to gain that he may spend and enjoy; in his career of fortune he never deprives himself of the comforts of life; more than any other nation he joins luxury and elegance with cupidity. No government is so expensively served; and the salaries of its officers in India, equal to the revenues of princes, are entirely employed in procuring for them, not ease only, but luxury. This elegance keeps the Englishman at a greater distance from the natives than all the other European nations; it exposes him less to private contests, to malevolent passions; but it leaves on the other side less room for sympathy, for friendship, for those intimate communications which forward the progress of nations less advanced. The English, especially the young, in their relations with the gentle and timid inhabitants of Hindostan, think they must keep in obedience and fear *the black fellows, the natives*, who might forget the difference of their nature. Such as they are, however, the English are still the best masters that India has ever had. Wherever in this vast continent their dominion is direct, it is a real benefit. They have re-established security and justice; they have given the people a feeling of duration, and of something to look forward to; and exactly because they keep themselves apart, because they did not wish to direct every thing, to change every thing, they have permitted Indian civilization under them to resume its natural progress. Agriculture is flourishing; the arts are cultivated with care; population and riches begin to increase; intelligence makes some progress; and European opinions ingraft themselves naturally and gently on the old ideas of India: in short, the conquered people have learnt to defend the foreign rule; the native army is formidable, and there is little probability that if the road to India were open to the Russians, they could sustain a struggle against the English. The presence of Europeans has, however, exercised its fatal influence on that part of India not subject to them; it has hastened its demoralization; the adventurers spread through it have shaken off all respect for public opinion; all the princes, feudatory or neighbours of the Company, give themselves up to more shameless exactions, and their subjects are more unhappy, even by reason of the fear which the English inspire, and from the tributes and presents which these require from them.

In their possessions in Canada, the English find themselves in contact only with the least advanced of the nations of the red race; these are tribes of hunters who have receded continually before the English colonists, and who are so much diminished in number, that it may be foreseen that the time is very near when they will be entirely destroyed. The immense continent colonized by the English, and which forms at this time the United States, was, as well as Canada, formerly occupied as far as the shores of the Atlantic, by tribes of hunters and warriors, who practising no industrial arts, and scarcely any cultivation, and possessing no domestic animals, required a great space in order to subsist. The new population, of European origin, which inhabits this continent, without doubt infinitely surpasses in number the aboriginal population which it has destroyed; but is this advantage sufficient to excuse their usurpation? The Americans of our times often present to us in their works of imagination rather a fanciful picture of the virtues, the happiness, the address, the development of the corporeal faculties of the natives of these countries before the arrival of the Europeans: without giving absolute credence to these recitals, we must acknowledge that the natives were much more advanced in civilization than they are now. Their ancient arts are lost; it suits them better to buy their clothes, their arms, their utensils, from Europeans, than to make them themselves; they are eager, therefore, in the destruction of wild animals to procure furs, their only merchandize, and thus they continually increase their wretchedness. Those which have remained in the midst of the English possessions have scarcely ever been willing to submit to agriculture; those who have been driven back towards the west, forced continually on a more wandering life, have lost the few agricultural habits which they possessed. The French, the English, and the Americans, involving them in their wars, have furnished them with more murderous arms than what they had formerly possessed, so that the flower of their warriors have been everywhere cut off; but above all, the Europeans have poisoned the half savage nations with brandy. It is a great crime to have offered this fatal liquor to men whom it must necessarily brutalize. The red man, who feels himself humiliated by the superiority of the whites; who is driven to indolence whilst all is agitation and animation around him; who feels the melancholy present, and still more the melancholy future, cannot resist the seduction of artificial excitement; he sacrifices all he possesses to procure brandy, he plunges into the most disgusting intoxication; even when he recovers from it he is brutalized, he is incapable of all labour, and he soon dies. It is brandy which has depopulated the new world, it is brandy which has first killed the richest, the *Sachems*, chiefs of the nation, and which impresses on the countenances of the survivors that character of indolence and degradation, so contrary to that of the ancient warriors; it is brandy, which, in fifty years, will not perhaps leave a single survivor of the aborigines. Drunkenness is a vice, no doubt, and a misfortune for all nations; but when wine, beer, cider, *pulque*, are the only liquors which they can obtain, their effects are temporary. Brandy, to make which requires chemical knowledge, is a product of civilization; but why have not civilized nations felt that it was a strict duty in them, not to carry to barbarous nations drugs which would irretrievably destroy their health and their reason? can they justify themselves for having taken opium to India and China, coco to Peru, brandy everywhere? Every colony which takes brandy with it, is necessarily a destructive scourge to the region where it is established. Brandy destroys the red race with so much rapidity, that the United States might have spared themselves those acts of fraud and cruelty by which they have recently expelled some nations of this race from the territory of the Union. It would have been enough to wait some years the effects of the poison they administered.

The colonies of the English in Australia find themselves in contact with a race much behind the red race of America, more thinly scattered, and as it is said, more ferocious in their habits. It cannot be doubted, however, that, especially in penal colonies, provocations are continually given by the whites to the natives, by the powerful to the weak, and that the near and imminent destruction of the first inhabitants, is a crime to be added to those which have been produced by modern civilization.

Some generous men, animated by the spirit of religion, have left England to spread civilization by colonies which have a little more resemblance to those of antiquity; for like those, they seek success only in the progress of the aborigines. These are the missionaries who have spread themselves among the islands of the South Sea. But, perhaps, these men, occupied with the thoughts of heaven, were not very well suited to teach the arts of earth; perhaps, filled with the importance of certain formularies of faith, they have paid too little attention to the progress of ideas; perhaps they have undertaken a too rapid transformation in this desire that the inhabitants of the Friendly Islands should become English Methodists. The reports on the missions are, it is true, contradictory: however, what appears most certain, is the introduction into the South Sea Islands of imposts, police, uniforms, and fire-arms; and, on the other side, such a rapid diminution of the race, that it is not probable that it can last two generations.

The French, also, have had colonies; still more, of all the nations of Europe, they have perhaps shown the most sympathy for the nations called barbarous, and seem, therefore, most suited to civilize them. On account of the inferiority of their marine, the French in other parts of the world have always had to fear the hostilities of rivals more powerful than themselves; therefore, except with neighbouring nations, they have never been able to assume that arrogance on the superiority of their bayonets, which they have so often put in the place of right, of justice, and of affection; on the contrary, they have sought the friendship of their hosts of another race, and they have almost always obtained it. Less attached to their opinions and their prejudices than any other nation in Europe, less proud of their nationality, they have been the most flexible of any of them in adopting foreign manners and customs; their activity, their spirit of enterprize, have made them enter heartily into the pleasures as well as the occupations of the wandering tribes. Less avaricious than others, they sought for success and excitement, rather than profit, and when they were not within reach of the society of their countrymen, their sociability made them eagerly seek friendly connections with savages. In Canada, in Louisiana, a strict alliance was formed between the French and the red men; they became companions in life and in death, in war, and in the chase. French names and French sentiments are found among the most formidable tribes which infest the frontiers of English America. The Frenchman become half a savage, had learned more from the American than he had taught him. He had adopted his opinions and his habits; he had only communicated to him his arms and his pleasures. The gun and the violin had penetrated into the most savage retreats; and even now the French villages, a small number of which may be found disseminated in the midst of the vast colonies of English origin, may be known from afar, not by their opulence, not by the good cultivation of the surrounding country, but by the accents of gaiety which are heard to issue from them, by the Sunday dances, when the red men unite gaily with the whites. The violin, like the lyre of Orpheus, would have done more to civilize the woods of America than commerce or philosophy; it would have taught the men of the two races to unite together, and to love one another.

The colonists of Canada and Louisiana were cultivators; they preserved the character of the most amiable and most estimable part of the nation. The colonists of the French Antilles, of Guiana, of the isles of France and Bourbon, had gone from towns; they belonged to a more calculating class, more greedy of gain, more infected with the vices of commerce; with its vices only, for it was in general those whose ill conduct had brought reverses on themselves, that went to the colonies. There they found a population, founded on what remained of freebooters and buccaneers. These wild adventurers had been actuated by their ferocity, as much as by their cupidity, in founding shelters for corsairs in the isles of the Antilles, from whence they went out to pillage the Spaniards. They obtained new recruits during a long time among those who were transported, stained with crime; for the government then considered these rich sugar islands only as penal colonies. The French, however, had no share in the extermination of the inhabitants of the Antilles; they had all already perished under the Spanish yoke. The first conquerors had transported them to the continent to work in the mines. The French were not so exempt from crime towards the African race. In the islands which they possessed on the east of Africa, they first caused all the aborigines to perish in slavery; then they recruited their workshops by importation, and they took miserable wretches carried away by robbery from Madagascar, and the coasts of Mozambique, to continue labour which they refused to perform themselves. The crimes of the slave trade and of slavery have yet more deeply stained the Antilles and Guiana. Not only have Europeans never civilized these regions by their colonies, but still more, after having caused all the inhabitants to perish, they have, two or three times in the course of two centuries, renewed the whole population, which has as often perished under protracted sufferings. However, among all the Europeans stained by these horrors, the French have been the least barbarous. Less avaricious than other planters, less wealthy, living themselves among their negroes, instead of entrusting them to agents and factors separated from them by a vast ocean, they have been acknowledged as the least cruel of task-masters.

France possesses only a very small part of her ancient colonies, and her children are no longer in contact with the aborigines. But the conquest of Algiers at the present time has just opened to her a new career for civilization. The moment is arrived when the European race may redeem its debt to human kind; when it may carry liberty, justice, agriculture, philosophy, all the arts of peace, from port to port, from shore to shore, along the coasts of that same Mediterranean Sea which the Greeks formerly covered with their colonies. The Arab and Moorish race with which the French find themselves in contact, has shown itself capable of the highest civilization. It has already made the most important, the most difficult steps in this career. It has been for a long time oppressed; it has suffered much; it will therefore feel more sensibly the advantages of security, of equity, of beneficence. Under a just government it may in a little time multiply with rapidity, and cover, with the wonderful agriculture which it formerly introduced into Granada and Valentia, a region not less fertile than Spain, and scarcely less extensive. Three times has civilization been carried to this same race, in this same country, by the Phœnicians and the Carthaginians, by the Romans, and by the Arabians, and each time it has produced the most valuable fruits. Nine centuries ago, arts, letters, science, all which makes the glory of Europe, flourished at Cairo, whilst our fathers were plunged in barbarism. Will the French show themselves more incapable of restoring order, peace, happiness, and the cultivation of mind, to the north of Africa, than the successors of Mahomet? Instead of scattering benefits, will they pursue that war of extermination which they have already begun? By provoking the Moors and the Arabs, will they force them to fight, will they burn their towns and villages, and will they drive into the desert two millions and a half of inhabitants who were under the regency of Algiers at the moment of their invasion, and which under a paternal government might become the seed of a great nation? After so many fatal examples which are presented to us by European colonies during the three last centuries, the choice which the French nation is on the point of making between the career of benefits and that of crimes, makes one shudder; and the alarm is redoubled when the denunciations against acts of rapine and cruelty are received at the tribunal of the public by the cry, *You dishonour the nation!* Ah! he who would dishonour the nation, is he who should show any indulgence towards the crimes of oppressors.

It is not transporting some thousands of French colonists, some thousand adventurers to the coast of Africa, which is here in question; it is not founding some experimental farms in the plain of Mitidja, or giving a value to the shares of some companies of speculators: it is to make two millions and a half of French subjects re-enter the career of happiness and improvement; it is to restore to the cultivators of Algeria the security they have so long lost; that they may again claim from these fertile plains the rich products which their fathers formerly obtained from them, at the same time that they are enlightened and directed by French science, which uniting with them will teach them to do better still. It ought to be the business of France to raise again to prosperity all those towns, all those villages, which were formerly the abode of a great nation; to reanimate those arts, that industry which formerly offered so many objects of exchange to Europeans, and to assist the Moors, whom they have subjected, to profit by the progress of science, so as to improve their manufactures. It should be the business of France to give back to the towns and villages of Mauritania the local powers required by the ancient customs of the country; to secure to those who have so long inhabited the country the benefits of municipal administration and of prompt justice, enlightening them in government and jurisprudence by the social sciences cultivated in Europe; to revive ancient studies, and the brilliant Arabian literature, by putting them in relation with the progress of mind among the Franks; in short, it ought to be the business of France to maintain among the Mussulmen the beneficent influence of the religion of Mahomet, by disengaging it from the gross fanaticism which has been introduced by despotism and ignorance, by making it co-operate with the charity and philosophy of Christians, to unite men by their religious sentiments, instead of putting them in opposition to one another. If such could be the fruits of the conquest of Algiers, humanity would be under an eternal obligation to France; and France would reap from it, not glory alone, but the most important and most durable of material advantages.

ON UNIVERSAL SUFFRAGE[a].

FROM the title of this little essay, it may be supposed that we are preparing to leave the restricted field of political economy. We think, however, that without going beyond the limits of this science, we may seek for the origin of social power even in the houses of simple citizens, and inquire to what point all may and ought to concur in the expression of the national will. The security which every condition ought to enjoy, the not less important security of the prosperity of all, concern public wealth as well as public liberty. Indeed, in entering upon this inquiry, we fear much more that we shall not make ourselves understood, and that we shall shock the sentiments and prejudices of all parties, than that we are leaving the circle to which this journal ought to restrict itself.

If there be a truth demonstrated by the experience of every age and of every nation, it is, that whoever exercises political power is disposed to abuse it; that on the other side, whoever is deprived of every political power and right, is in danger of being oppressed; whether this portion of the nation, which is despoiled of these securities, is separated from the rest by birth or by race, by wealth or by indigence, by the religion which it professes, by the territory it inhabits, or merely by the spirit of

[a] *Du Suffrage Universel. Extrait de la revue mensuelle d'Economie Politique. Mars,* 1834.

party. But what are the defensive arms which can be given to each class of society, which each class will know how to use? What are the political rights which can be attributed to all the citizens, and which will be adequate to secure themselves, without injuring the nation of which they form a part? It is indeed the fundamental problem of political organization, the problem which all legislators, friends of man and of liberty, have proposed to themselves to resolve by balanced constitutions, but which, however, is not yet resolved.

It is true that in the eyes of ignorant and presumptuous youth this problem, which the sages of antiquity confessed their inability to resolve, is one no longer. We find on every side publicists without reflection and without study, ready to affirm boldly, that the electoral right is a sufficient security for all and for each. They protest that Universal Suffrage is the essential prerogative of a free people, and they stigmatize with the name of monopoly every limitation to the right of all men to co-operate in elections; at the same time, they decide that from elections should proceed every social power.

It is not everything to have a popular government; it must accomplish its task; and far from its being so simple, so easy to every one, it is, on the contrary, the most important, the most complicated, the most difficult of any task to which men can devote their efforts. An old maxim of the French economists, Let things alone (*laissez faire, et laissez passer*) which they gave as a rule to governments in commercial legislation, and for the advancement of national wealth, has too much disposed the public to think that the action of social power ought to be negative; that destined only to prevent evil, its best part is to remain quiet. It has been too readily decided, that it is enough to retrench the power of government: the action for which this power is designed, and the knowledge which ought to direct this action, are too much forgotten.

What is the end of man? What is the end of human society? The happiness and the progress of all. Do not let us forget that these objects of our wishes ought to be united, that prosperity without improvement is not enough. We desire these two things for all, and for each ; we desire them for the whole nation, and for every family, and for every individual of which it is composed.

To attain this double end, the knowledge of existing laws and of jurisprudence, which constitutes the celebrity of many eminent men, is not enough ; we must rise to the philosophy of law, to the theory of the manner in which the administration of government and justice acts on men. In order to lay open to the young the way to acquire this knowledge, it is not enough to be acquainted with various sciences, or to know what has been done in different communities; we must rise to the philosophy of education, to the theory of the distribution of moral and intellectual light, so as to make it more vivid, and to diffuse it more and more. It is not enough to be attached by the heart and the conscience to the religion we profess ; we must rise high enough to judge the religious spirit of men, the good and the evil that may be expected from it ; we must place ourselves above the narrow and intolerant spirit of sects, and even in religion open the door to progress. It is not enough to understand chresmatistics, *de laissez faire, et laissez passer*, not to interfere with the acquiring or disposing of wealth ; it should be known how to direct its distribution, so as to procure for the poor the greatest material comfort and the most leisure, allowing them time to exercise the intellect and to develop their virtues, more knowledge of their duties, more zeal to fulfil them. In short, it is not enough for social power to have endowed the nation it directs with all these advantages; it must provide against their being taken from it by other nations. Thus is required the knowledge of the comparative strength of nations, of their interests and of their attachments ; that of the obligations they have contracted by their treaties, and of their public rights ; finally, a knowledge of all means of defence, of finance, and of national resources, of chrysology, or the theory of money and credit, of strategy, of the marine, and of all the art of war. Certainly when one measures the whole circle of the social sciences, one is frightened at all which they require, study, talent, genius, and elevation of character.

There exists an opinion, Madame de Staël often said, which is more acute than that of the most acute man of the world; it is that of the public, for public opinion collects all the most distinguished opinions, it enlightens them, it renders them more acute by collision, it is the sum of the best, and not the mean proportion of the most advanced and the most absurd. So there exists in public opinion a social science, entire, developed, and more profound than any publicist has ever attained to. It is this opinion which we call into power and action when we proclaim the sovereignty of the people. We invoke this sovereignty, but it is that of national intelligence, of the enlightened, virtuous, and progressive opinion which has been formed in the nation. In order to conceive a better state of society and to realize it, and in order to develop the progress of all, it is necessary to be in advance of all; not only talent, but genius is required. The nation can only be well governed by the most enlightened and the most virtuous of her citizens. It is not that they have, by reason of their virtue and intelligence, any right to sovereignty; it is that the nation, as sovereign, has a right to the intelligence and virtue which they possess. If they were set apart to form a governing aristocracy, it would be giving them an interest of caste, which would probably destroy this virtue and this intelligence; but if from the fear of giving them an equal share in the sovereignty, they are left in that minority where they must necessarily originate, all the advantages of this virtue and of this intelligence which belong to the nation are lost, and the object is not obtained.

Certainly the direction of a state is more difficult than that of a ship; nevertheless, if a ship on an unknown sea had on board with a thousand ignorant persons one skilful pilot, these ignorant persons would be mad if they did not give up the helm to him, or if they pretended to regulate his navigation by the majority of suffrages. It is not the pilot who has the right to direct the ship; it is the right of all those who are running a common risk, to profit by the skill of the most skilful for the safety of the lives and property of all. The object of association is, in fact, to bring forward the greatest talent and the greatest virtue, in order to employ them for the greatest good of all. In a time of great danger, of deep feeling, the instinct by which to discover greatness is not wanting to the masses, and genius often takes its true place without trouble. But it is rare that political questions inspire the people with the sentiment of danger and the necessity of confidence at the same time. Most frequently, if we asked each individual for his opinion, we should be far from obtaining in reply the expression of the national opinion. The ignorant populace, given up almost everywhere to retrograde prejudices, will refuse to favour its own progress. The more ignorant the people are, the more are they opposed to all kind of development, the more they are deprived of all enjoyment, and the more are they obstinately, angrily attached to their habits, as to the only possession they have left; like horses, which in a fire it is impossible to force out of a stable in flames. Count the voices in Spain and Portugal, they will be for the maintenance of the Inquisition. Count them in Russia, they will be for the despotism of the Czar. Count them everywhere, they will be for those laws, for those local customs which most require to be corrected, they will be for *prejudices*: it would seem that this word, appropriated to opinions adopted by vulgar minds without discussion, says enough; it suffices to teach us that the masses hold to opinions ready made, that only the small number of thinkers rise above them to consider them anew.

In fact, the national will, that is the sum of all the wills, of all the intelligence, of all the virtue of the nation, a sum in which each quantity counts for what it is, and negations count for nothing, is almost always absolutely opposed to the doctrine of universal suffrage, which makes those who have no will prevail over those who have, those who know nothing of what they are deciding upon, over those who do know it. How is it possible, in endeavouring to discover the national will, to reckon as nothing the intenseness of the will of those whose suffrages are counted? Do we not know that as soon as a question presents some obscurity, most men have in regard to it only a suggested will, thousands of which often represent only one suffrage, one individual choosing and making others agree with him? Do not we know that when the ignorant are sincere, they prefer not voting at all, for they know their vote is a falsehood? Between two names equally unknown, they decide either by the intrigues which recommend to them the candidate of a faction, or by chance. Is this the suffrage which is represented as an indivisible unity, as precisely equal to that of a great citizen whose will is firm, enlightened, and virtuous? "Which way shall we direct our course, to China or to California?" we will suppose is asked of every sailor on board a vessel in danger in the middle of the South Sea. "But I do not know where we are," answers he, "I do not even know whether there is a China or a California: I will not vote, for I cannot make a choice, I have no will in the matter."—"That is of no consequence," is the reply; "you must vote, and your vote will have as much weight as that of the most skilful among us."—"China, then, the name is shorter, and I shall remember it better."

The national will rises as high as the most elevated point of the intelligence, will and virtue of the nation: universal suffrage, on the contrary, (and according to its principle, women and children should share in it,) by lowering all that is elevated to an illusory equality, is just as far removed from all pre-eminence as all pre-eminence is rare in society. If the decision is to be made by the patriotism, the disinterestedness, and the courage of a country, can we reckon on a majority of men like Regulus or Aristides? If it is to be by the extent of knowledge, shall we more easily find a majority of Montesquieus? If it must be by the energy of the will, is there a nation in which Napoleons form the greater number? Can we arrive, in short, at that expression of public opinion which comprises all that is great and good in the nation, by reckoning all these eminent individualities as simple unities lost in the crowd?

The most that can be hoped for from universal suffrage is, that it should give the proportional mean among all differences; that the eminent minorities should succeed in modifying the vulgar majorities, precisely according to their respective numbers; that if, for example, there are among those called on to vote nine ignorant for one wise man, the result of the vote should only be nine-tenths nearer the ignorance of the first than the wisdom of the latter. But most frequently the two portions of the assembly, instead of reciprocally modifying, will clash against one another, and there the ignorant will triumph by an immense majority. In both cases, universal suffrage, which considers men as simple figures, as so many equal unities, and which counts them instead of weighing them, strips the nation of her most precious possession, the influence of her greatest men.

We need only ask what would be the decision of the majority on all questions already decided by science, by national will, or by virtue, in order to enable us to acknowledge this complete opposition. France, England, and Germany, know doubtless that the earth goes round the sun. Consult the majority in these three countries, by universal suffrage, it will no doubt answer that the sun goes round the earth. Let us descend from this scientific idea to a decision to be made in a common case: a drowned man is taken out of a river; consult the majority by universal suffrage as to what is best to be done; they will answer, hold him up by the feet, that he may throw up the water he has drunk. During the death-struggle of Poland, all the virtue, all the energy of France and England would have wished to save her at the price of the greatest sacrifices; it might have been said that France and England willed a war, for the amount of the wills of the most energetic, the most reflecting, and the most virtuous, is really the will of the nation. But universal suffrage would have given the sum of apathy, that of indifference and of personal interest. The apathetic and indifferent knew too little of what Poland was to have a will; the others repelled the ideas of conscription and taxes, with too much egotism to make sacrifices. By consulting the greatest number, we hope to arrive at the exact medium. Universal suffrage may throw the nation by turns into the two extremes, but her true resting-place is the exact medium.

We have been accustomed, in our modern Europe, to governments which have not been founded with a view to the good of all, to governments inherited as a patrimony, where the people were only considered as property, more or less profitable; their masters only thought of getting the most advantage from them, not of making them advance towards prosperity, intelligence, and virtue. When these nations began to know themselves, to feel what they were, to make their voice heard, their sovereigns, astonished or affrighted at this new sound, only thought of imposing silence. Sometimes they deceived the public voice by priests sold to authority; sometimes they corrupted it by frivolity and pleasure, or by the bait of false glory; sometimes they imposed silence by terror and punishments; never did they consent to listen to it, and to conduct themselves by its advice. This hostility of power to public opinion has accustomed us to see only the physical obstacle which represses it. We have invoked the sovereignty of this public voice, and have not given ourselves the trouble to inquire how this public voice is formed.

The ancients had much more experience than we have in free governments, and in all republican forms. Those who appeal to their authority in support of what they call principles, great principles, must be astonished if they should ever open, not only Aristophanes, but Plato or Aristotle, to see them declare themselves so strongly against pure democracies. All the Greek philosophers who had seen them in action, had remarked the constant increase of the dominion of the retrograde over the progressive principle, of the low tone of the greater number over the virtue and knowledge of the smaller. They had seen the habitual oppression of the minority by the majority, the harshness of masters towards their subjects when the city commanded the country; or when democracy was supreme, popular favouritism not less formidable than that of courts, and the rapidity of revolutions produced by the violent but fugitive enthusiasm of the multitude. We shall not stop to discuss their testimony, but we cannot help asking, with astonishment, the partisans of universal suffrage, not where is their experience, but where is their theory? They reject what is old, they would change the face of the world, and they not only do not bring forward a legislator, but not even a philosopher, a wise man, a great writer, who has admitted and developed what they call their principles.

For ourselves, when we look round, there is no want of examples, even in our own times, to show us the retrograde spirit of the masses. It is a very melancholy lesson in human nature, which Spain and Portugal have not ceased giving, ever since the people have been called into action in the Peninsula. Among the inhabitants of these two countries, the worst governed in Europe, all those who have any soul or intelligence, and they are in great numbers, ardently desire fundamental reform, and have not feared manifesting this desire in the midst of the greatest dangers, and by the greatest sacrifices; but the masses, confounding the remains of past time with its trophies, and attributing the ancient national glory even to the abuses which destroyed it, have shown a not less energetic determination to maintain everything which is the disgrace of Spain. The population, raised and led by priests, the most dangerous of all demagogues, fought with fury against the progress of knowledge, against liberty, against clemency. Insurrections broke out in 1832, at Toledo and at Leon, to repel the amnesty offered by the queen. They were renewed in 1833, because this princess was suspected merely of liberal intentions, and an absolutist revolution would have succeeded against her if her adversary had not wanted courage and capacity, to a degree rare even among royal families. The most ignorant, the most fanatical, but the most numerous party in Portugal, remained faithful to the monster Don Miguel, after he had lost two capitals, his treasures, and his arsenals, and in spite of the scarcely disguised hostility of France, England and Spain. We should think this constancy heroic, were it possible to admire violence against all that is good and honourable in human society; devotion to all that is criminal and disgraceful. The Italian patriots, who make such generous efforts to restore to their country that liberty which formed its independence and its glory, who, on a soil watered with the blood of so many martyrs, still press forward every day to offer the sacrifice of fortune, happiness, and life to their country, are for the most part too young to have seen, as we have done, insurrection burst forth everywhere in their beautiful country, to cries of *Viva Maria, morte alla libertà!* the populace pursuing, pillaging, and murdering the patriots, and receiving with transports of joy the colours of their Austrian oppressors. Now, however, the Italians say that this foreign yoke has undeceived the people, that their feelings are changed in many provinces, that in others the inhabitants of the country might be attached to the liberal cause by the abolition of certain imposts; a melancholy way of bribing an opinion proclaimed as being sovereign. Nevertheless, the majority is not with them; on the contrary, Rome might still *lâcher contre eux la grande lévriere*[a]; it was the phrase which the same party, the party of *obscurantism*, employed in France, in 1562, when it let loose the populace and the inhabitants of country places against the Protestants: the reformation, already dominant among the noblesse and the citizens of towns, triumphant in the states-general of Orleans and Pontoise, was then attacked by all the rude and ignorant men in France, and was almost everywhere drowned in blood.

[a] "Let slip the dogs of war."

But it will be said that slavery debases men till they love it, and this is true: we shall be required to take our examples from free countries, where the citizens have received the vigorous education of public assemblies, where they have been enlightened by experience as to their interests, purified by virtue, inflamed with noble sentiments. Certainly we shall not deny the superiority or the excellence of a republican education; we shall not cast a doubt on the power of such institutions to imbue the mass of the people with more intelligence and virtue, and greater interest in public affairs. It is by associating all the citizens in the national power, that the most noble object of all social science, the improvement of all, can alone be hoped for. But if it is supposed that in republics the masses are progressive, it is an error contradicted by the history of all ages: we arrive at an absurd contradiction in terms, if we choose as a guide to progress the majority of suffrages; for when all the votes are considered as equal, the majority must stop at a mean term between the most advanced and the least informed voters.

The new publicists would usefully employ their time, if they gave some attention and some study to the republics of Switzerland. For five centuries this country has gloriously preserved her independence, her attachment to popular forms, her ancient manners, and her love for the name of liberty. Thanks to her republican and federative constitution, Switzerland is reckoned among the second rate powers of Europe, while her population and her wealth would scarcely assign her a place among the fourth. Switzerland has sought her liberty, with more or less success, with more or less capacity, in balanced constitutions: if she has not always succeeded, she wished at least to give public opinion the means of forming itself into masses, by uniting all conscientious and enlightened individual opinions, the means of maturing itself by discussion, and at the same time of pointing out eminent men, in order to place them at the head of the state, instead of dragging them after it. But in Switzerland there are also many republics where the democratic principle has prevailed in all its rigour, where each intellect, as well as each will, is reckoned equal, and where universal suffrage has stifled public opinion.

In the centre of Switzerland the three little cantons of Uri, Schwitz, and Unterwalden are pure democracies; among shepherds, almost equal in fortune, as well as in intelligence, it was not thought necessary to preserve greater influence for opinions resulting from mere deliberation; the elections as well as the laws, as well as all public resolutions, are carried by the votes of universal suffrage, by all the male inhabitants above the age of 18, assembled in the Landsgemeine; it is really a will of their own, which the citizens of these little cantons express in these assemblies of all the people; but this will is constantly retrograde. In spite of their confederates, in spite of the clamour of Europe, they have continued the use of torture in their tribunals; they have kept up the custom of contracts to enter into the service of foreign powers; and these men, so proud and so jealous of their liberty, are the most eager to sell themselves to despots, to enable them to keep other nations in chains: every year, in short, and at every diet, they solicit their confederates to proscribe the liberty of the press. We must not suppose, however, that there are not in Uri, Schwitz, and Unterwalden, men whose more enlightened intellect, whose more elevated character, recoils from torture, trading in men, and the censorship of the press: no doubt they would form public opinion, if time were given them; but before every discussion, universal suffrage decides, by a majority, in favour of the gross ignorance of the great number, against the virtuous intelligence of some few.

Must we accuse our young and presumptuous publicists of ignorance or bad faith, when they endeavour to escape from the consequences of these notorious facts by a singular juggling trick? They have given the name of *aristocrat* to the democratic party in Switzerland, they have talked to the public of the aristocratic faction, which at the conventicle of Sarnen separated itself from patriotic Switzerland. There never was in the world an example of a more absolute democracy than that of the three little cantons, of the *dixains* of the Valais, and of the communes of the Grison league. Without doubt these democracies have their demagogues, their leaders; it is the necessary consequence of such a government: almost always these leaders are nobles or priests, and it must be expected, that at the head of a democracy they will preserve all their prejudices, all their attachment to their orders; without doubt, they labour unceasingly at confirming the people in their illiberal sentiments and prejudices; but the little cantons would not be democracies, if ambitious men did not there endeavour to rise to power by seducing and corrupting the people.

To these democracies of the mountains were associated at the conventicle of Sarnen the democracies of the cities of Basle and Neufchatel, in which the exercise of the rights of the city belonged almost exclusively to the freemen of these two cities. The shoemakers and butchers of Basle and Neufchatel must smile to see themselves reproached in the journals with their pride of ancient nobility, but they complacently admit this reproach; whilst it was the privileges derived from their shops, exercised often with revolting rigour in order to enable them to sell dearer and buy cheaper, which frequently embroiled them with the inhabitants of the country. The heads of the burgesses of Neufchatel, enriched by commerce, have obtained titles of nobility from the king of Prussia, and think themselves great lords: those of Basle, though as opulent, have remained more modest and liberal in their sentiments, but they have not been able to conquer the narrow spirit, the mean interests of the burgesses in their companies; and when afterwards their self-love was engaged in the quarrel between the democracy of the city and the democracy of the country, their obstinacy drew them into the greatest imprudences. On the other hand new democracies, but equally blind, equally illiberal, interfered in this quarrel, and all Switzerland blushes at the arbitrary sentence which destroyed the University of Basle, and divided its possessions between the town and the country. This opposition between the towns and the country is the scourge of pure democracies; with men employed in mechanical labour, the interests and the jealousy of trade influence them more than all social considerations. Thus it is precisely in these republics, where the inhabitants of the towns exercise all the power, where the constitution appears most liberal, that the sovereign citizenship has most oppressed the peasants, and excited the most bitter resentment, as at Zurich, Schaffhausen, and Basle. In military aristocracies, on the contrary, which have passed through a revolution, as at Berne and Lucerne, the country forming the great majority is thoroughly counter-revolutionary, and keeps the liberal party in continual alarm. In general the present fermentation of Switzerland, and the dangers which threaten her, arise from the endeavours which the friends of progress are making to gain entrance into the different constitutions for a little liberality, a few general ideas, a little application of the first notions of political economy, of religious toleration, of law proceedings, of criminal justice, and lastly, of hospitality, not only to foreigners but from Swiss to Swiss; and from those endeavours being everywhere opposed and resisted by the democratic spirit, or the supremacy which universal suffrage gives to those who know nothing, and who do not understand what they are deciding on, over those who wish for the advance of true liberty.

Among those who know these facts, some think they give sufficient answer by calling all the demagogues *aristocrats*, without trying to find out how there can be a democracy without demagogues, and how they can be prevented abusing the power which they owe to popular caprice. Others refer us to the progress of knowledge and to the care that will be taken of the education of the people. We eagerly accept the augury; we hope that really free governments will feel that their first duty is to give to all citizens, not the power of leading and governing others, but the power of conducting and governing themselves; that they will not relax their efforts to put knowledge within the reach of all, virtue within the reach of all;

that they will fix their attention on increasing the comforts of the poor, on one side to keep them from temptation, on the other to give them more leisure, and more means of exercising their intellectual faculties as well as their hands. But whatever may be their efforts, as long as there are rich and poor there will be men who cannot devote all their time to meditation and study; there will be others who can only give up to them some moments every day, and that with a body fatigued by manual labour, and a mind distracted by the cares of life.

Would it be expedient to level all conditions, to divide equally all possessions, and afterwards to maintain the equality of these divisions? But supposing that this order of things were possible, it would not do away with the necessity of manual labour, and even then this must fill the greatest part of the existence of all: it would only be to forbid a life of study and meditation to every one; the nation would only be so much the less elevated, when every one was forbidden to raise himself; and yet it would not be possible to level native talent. Even in a nation equal in wealth, universal suffrage would always leave virtue, talent, and genius in the minority. Shall a more reasonable plan be followed? Shall the development and the progress of all be favoured without disturbing the differences of rank? Then every rank of intelligence will be more advanced than it is now, but the distance between them will be always the same. It cannot be, it never will be, that a majority can be composed of superior men.

The wisest will say, perhaps, that they are not partisans of democracy, but of representative government. It is a great concession, and we ask no better than to accept it with all its logical consequences; we believe that representative government is a happy invention to bring forward the eminent men of a nation, to give them an opportunity of gaining, and above all, of deserving the public confidence, and of placing them at the helm of affairs. We believe that it is a still more happy invention to bring into notice different interests, different feelings, and different opinions, by giving organs of utterance to each, so that they may be discussed, light thrown on each, one weighed against another, in order ultimately to form one focus which may be regarded as national interest, thought, and feeling. We think it is a happy institution to form public opinion, to make it advance; to make it triumph at last, so that when collected from those who know and feel, elaborated by the discussion of those to whom the nation listens, it may re-descend to the masses and penetrate them with a common opinion before being transformed into a law. We believe that happy though difficult combinations, may, with the assistance of representative government, protect all localities, all opinions, all classes of citizens, and all interests. But if such is in fact the object, if such is the office of representative government, all the scaffolding of abstractions and vain suppositions which are every day presented to us as principles must be thrown down.

In fact, those who will see in representative government only an expedient invented to make the democracy govern in large states, do not wish to give the sovereignty to public opinion but to the plurality of voices. They adopt as a principle which they scarcely give themselves the trouble to declare, much less to discuss and establish, that all the individuals of a community know, feel, and will, equally, so that they must all be reckoned as simple unities. They believe that if all the decisions of the community were made according to the greatest number of voices, they would all be conformable to its interest, to its progress, and to its virtue; they believe that the sole motive of the community in delegating its powers, is the impossibility of assembling a great nation to exercise them itself; they believe, in short, that the minority is free, when it is bound by the will of the majority, and that the majority is sovereign, when instead of commanding itself it commands by its representatives. There is not one of these pretended principles which is not contradicted equally by reason and by experience.

We have already endeavoured to make it understood what immense differences there really are among these pretended equalities, how wretched a nation would be which allowed itself to be led by a majority without intelligence, without knowledge of the thing on which it decides: instead, therefore, of pointing out the double vote as a scandalous violation of equality, we should be disposed to see in it an invention susceptible of a happy application, to make all the population take a part in public affairs, but yet to leave the decision to the most independent as well as the best informed. Experience has confirmed our doubt as to the equal value of suffrages; the farther the right of voting has been extended, the more have electoral assemblies been deserted. Why should the nation make so great a point of the suffrages of citizens who themselves do not attach any importance to them, who will not submit to the slightest inconvenience to go and vote? In this way the pretended vote of the people is often a falsity, for a small minority of those present often carries it over an immense majority of the absent.

It is not because the nation is identical with its representatives, it is not because they will do precisely what the nation would do if it could be assembled altogether, that the representative government appears to us to have been instituted, for persons can only delegate what they have, and if the masses are ignorant and retrograde, they will not transmit to their deputies progressive knowledge and will. If pure democracy is a bad government, representative democracy cannot be worth more. It is something else which has been sought for by means of popular elections; partly the dignity and the guarantee which the exercise of some political power gives to every citizen; partly that tact in discovering eminent men which great meetings of men almost always manifest. It is said that in great political crises genius almost always takes its place; in calmer times, virtue and nobility of character gain suffrages by the sympathy which they excite. The people, it is true, know men of action better than men of theory, and I do not know whether the Athenians had not a better chance of choosing their generals well by public assemblies, than the French their legislators. Besides the advantage of elections by the people is, that they are generally free from corrupting interests; they choose according to the value of the thing itself; whilst governments and ministers are often directed in their choice by personal advantages in opposition to public interest. Now this purity of popular elections cannot be maintained when the citizens, by their suffrages, distribute dignities, power, or riches. Then, and whenever the people open or close the career of ambition at their pleasure, they are the object of every act of intrigue, of all the baseness of flattery. The language which is addressed to them, the principles which are gloried in before them, are only the white robe of the candidates, which is laid aside when they mount the curule chair. To please the people, to flatter them, to corrupt them, are the arts which ambitious men study above all others; but when by these means they have arrived at power and riches, they only think of keeping them for themselves, and of preventing others from rising by the artifices which they have themselves employed. As soon as they have obtained power they change their maxims and their conduct; according to the advice of St. Remy, they burn what they had adored, they adore what they had burned; and their jealousy of their prerogatives, their distrust of their rivals, are the more active and vigilant from knowing so well the means by which they have themselves risen.

Thus, with respect to popular elections, we must not say, *it is a principle*, but *it is expedient;* we must not speak of the right of every citizen, of every individual, to be represented, but of the right of every individual to be well governed, of the interest of the community that in every case the best possible choice should be made; of the right also of every individual to be respected, to have entrusted to him by the community some participation in political power, which may serve him as it were as a defensive arm, without exposing him to too much danger from his inexperience or his imprudence. In fact, political institutions are only good in as far as they attain this end.

It is not, however, only poor and obscure citizens who require to be furnished with defensive arms to protect their rights; all classes, every fraction of society should possess them. Those publicists who have founded universal suffrage on the sovereignty of the people forget that there is no pre-existing contract by which the minority are bound by the will of the majority. This rule for deliberations has been introduced into the laws as expedient, by virtue of precise stipulations in different constitutions; it is by no means inherent in human nature, or in the formation of all communities; it may easily be changed into a frightful tyranny, and examples of this are not wanting in countries which consider themselves free. Sometimes the minority forms a class by the circumscription of its territory,—a province is oppressed by a larger province, or a nation by another nation. Thus Holland was oppressed by Spain, America and Ireland by England, and in the smallest republics, the conquered bailliages by the democracy of Schwitz, and the Lower Valais by the democracy of the Higher Valais. Sometimes a race is proscribed by the race which dwells with it. Thus many of the American constitutions grant the right of suffrage to free negroes and red men, but both are always thrown into the minority, and the dreadful laws which have been during the last three years passed against them, and against all who give them any instruction, will long be a scandal and shame to the American Union. Sometimes one religion is proscribed by another religion; and the atrocity of St. Bartholomew was less the crime of Catharine and Charles IX. than of the demagogues who demanded it and the people who executed it. Sometimes material interests are armed one against another. In pure democracies, where power rests with the mechanical trades, arises the opposition between the towns and the country. At Basle, at Zurich, at Schaffhausen, at Neufchatel, the peasants were at first subject to the shops; now that they are accounted the strongest, and find themselves to be so, they abuse their power, being the majority, as it was formerly abused against them; they talk of razing the fortifications of the towns because the fields are not fortified, of unpaving the streets of the towns, because the country roads are not paved.

If it is absurd to say that a minority is free because it only obeys laws made against it by a majority, it is no less so to say that a nation is free because she only obeys laws which those whom she has elected make contrary to her interest: it is the nature of the laws, it is their conformity with public opinion, and not the deceptive idea of a representation, which must prove that they are really the expression of the will of a free nation. It is false that the people obey what they have themselves willed when they obey the will of their regularly chosen representatives, for most frequently, on the legislative questions which these decide, they have neither will nor opinion; still less can it be supposed that they have transmitted their will through their deputies, for the questions which those have to decide upon are, most frequently, posterior to their nomination. Besides, as we have seen, if the people had a will in these questions, it would almost always be behind the common rate of information. Still more, the poor and labouring classes of the population experience a difficulty in the exercise of their right of election, which renders their representation always illusory. They have, in fact, not theories on public order, but sufferings, interests and wants, to which it is of consequence to them to give utterance, that they may be heard. By whom shall they get themselves represented? By their equals;—peasant by a peasant, working men in a manufactory by working men? But these ignorant and illiterate men, not being able to seize the whole of social organization, nor to arrange their ideas, nor to express them in a way to lead others, would come unarmed on that political arena where others combat with so much advantage; they would be deceived, they would be intimidated, they would exercise no influence. Shall poor men be represented by men who are also poor, but who are strangers to all trades, and who follow the profession of letters, perhaps that of intrigue? There would be no identity of interests among them, no knowledge even of what the poor desire and what they ought to desire, and striking, daily examples, so numerous as to be almost without exceptions, show us that this class is, of all those which constitute society, the one most easily seduced, the most easily intoxicated by drawing-room success, the most accessible to the baits of vanity, luxury, pleasure and riches. Shall the poorer classes address themselves to the rich and the powerful? But then how could they be represented by persons differing so completely from them, communicating so little with them, who neither understand them, nor feel what they have felt? In all the democracies of Greece, Italy, Germany, Holland and Switzerland, the working classes have tried in turns these three kinds of representatives. Sometimes the rude good sense of the peasant or the mechanic, seated among statesmen in his coat of coarse cloth, has been praised; but the utmost that this rude good sense could do, was to prevent him from compromising himself; it had no influence on public decisions. Then came poor and clever intriguers, such warm patriots before their election, so jealous of the people afterwards, and thence arose the proverb, *il n'est oppression que de parvenus;* upstarts are the greatest oppressors; then last, the people threw themselves into the arms of the noble and the rich, and the longer a democracy has lasted the more certain it is to see these in possession of power.

If we have established that democratic elections, that popular representation, are not in themselves sufficient guarantees of liberty, how much more reason have we to reject the deceptions of a constituency named by primary assemblies, or of a constitution voted by the people. How can the people, in fact, transmit to the men they have delegated a knowledge which they do not themselves possess, of what is most high, most abstract, in the science of legislation? It is not the people alone, it is philosophers and civilians, men most eminent in social science, who can only understand a constitution by experience, who ought only to judge *à posteriori non à priori.* A community receives its constitution, or its mode of existence, which preserves it in life, and which that life is continually modifying, from all the chances embraced by the past. By combining its habits, its manners, and its laws, by resting written rules on recollections, and confirming them by precedents, it comes by degrees to distinguish the vain clack of the words of charters from really leading principles; it finds out what injures it, what improvements its wants require. Then only the most eminent men in the nation partially arrive at the most sublime of all theories. They point out the modifications to be made, by degrees they triumph over the resistance of the people, who defend every abuse foot by foot, who in Poland claimed the *liberum veto* as the palladium of liberty; they correct by degrees ancient disorders, and they arrive at last at an organization, each part of which has been preconceived by genius, adopted by enlightened men, sanctioned by experience, and lastly, placed under the guarantee of national usage. It is in this way only that a constitution is willed by the nation; but to pretend that the will has emanated from her because it has emanated from deputies which she has chosen, without being able to transmit one idea to them, or yet more, because she has at last accepted it without comprehending it, and without its authors comprehending it, is the most cruel mockery.

We have said that we consider the questions relative to the participation of simple citizens in political power as among the most complicated, the most difficult and the most obscure that the social sciences present. Thus we have not the presumption to offer a solution of them; besides, we do not think there is any one which can adapt itself to all nations. We have desired only to point out the end to be attained; it consists in bringing out the true will of the nation; that is to say, accelerating the formation of public opinion, maturing it, and then only, causing its authority to be acknowledged. We ask from national representatives not to divide themselves into two or three camps, under two or three banners, but to come penetrated with the virtuous wishes and opinions of all the localities, all the bodies, all the sects and all the employments of those who send them; to be prepared to defend them, but also to modify them, in order to make them agree with public opinion. We attach much more importance to the deliberations of these representatives than to their votes. We believe that in defending the interests which they represent, in making it their ambition to shine by the development of national opinions, they get to the bottom of abstract questions, they form themselves, and they enlighten the nation. We believe that the first principle of all liberty is respect for independent opinion, the protection of the minority, that it may investigate every thing and keep up discussion to the last. We do not know which to condemn most, orators who indulge themselves in sarcasm, who aim at provoking and abusive modes of speaking, or majorities who, provoked, close the discussion and crush by votes those whom they have not been able to convince. We have very little respect for assemblies which decide instead of deliberating; their knowledge appears more than doubtful, and they belie their moderation when they refuse to listen. Finally, we look upon no decision of the legislature as definitive as long as it continues to be a subject of discussion in the opinion of the public.

By looking at the system of elections which has been adopted in France, we may discover how incapable even the most profound thinkers have been of forming a judgment beforehand as to the effect of the sanctions which they introduced into the constitution. After the revolution the French legislators wished at first to make all the nation concur in the nomination of its representatives; it gave to primary assemblies the nomination of electors, who, collected in electoral assemblies, were to choose the members of the legislature. They thought that by thus doing they preserved the whole sovereignty to the nation. The citizens, much better informed, soon perceived that the deputies named by them in this way were strangers to them, had neither respect nor gratitude for them; that their wishes had no influence on the will of the legislature, that their share of the sovereignty, which at the most could only be estimated at a six-millionth part for each citizen of an age to judge, was really reduced to nothing. They did not come to these primary assemblies, and the elections fell into the hands of a small number of intriguers.

True philosophers, true publicists, returned then to the more simple idea, that the people could only have a real participation in power by direct elections, and that for every citizen to feel the importance of his suffrage, the right of suffrage must not be too much multiplied. Elections by one step were introduced into France for the first time after the restoration; and its effect has been to give to the nation the means of expressing its will, very energetically, more than once.

If, however, the proportion of electors to the mass of the population were as large as in Schwitz or Basle, which have been so absurdly called aristocracies, there would be six million electors in France, and not one of them would give himself the trouble to go out of his way to exercise a six-millionth share of influence on the elections. The framers of the law of elections only gave the electoral right to Frenchmen who paid 300 *fr.* direct taxes. Their number it is said was not much above a hundred thousand citizens. This classification at first gave universal satisfaction; the electoral right was not a privilege, for it was accessible to all; each one could, without litigation, without expense, establish his own; and it was agreed that the rate paid to the taxes might be received as a presumption of the education, the intelligence, and the independence of each elector, for it was only a presumption of these qualities which was sought for in establishing electoral rights.

When the English still more recently were occupied in reforming their electoral system, the simple, equal, regular system of the classification in France, was put in comparison on both sides the Channel with the ancient English system, both before and after the Reform Bill, as being more rational, more perfect. It is by use only that it has begun to be perceived that the multiform system of the English, in spite of its rights being subject to litigation, in spite of the flagrant inequality between one citizen and another, between one town and another, connects the national representation with all classes of the nation, and that the French system, in spite of its simplicity and equality, left the population, and especially national intelligence, out of the representation, and ended by exciting universal censure.

In the English parliament are seen seated together, deputies from counties, deputies from towns, deputies from universities; the first are elected by the freeholders, proprietors in the country, of that kind of property which was formerly looked on as the best guarantee of independence. The second are elected by the citizens of towns; in certain towns, the number of electors is so limited that the election is decided by a strict coterie; some other towns extend the right of election to all the male population, and then it is the work of a pure democracy. Whoever has received his education in one of the universities and has taken his degrees there, concurs in the election of the deputies for that university. Far from the double vote being considered in England as a violation of the equality of the citizens, the same man can frequently vote as master of arts in one of the universities, as a freeholder in two or three counties, as a freeman of two or three towns; so that towns consider it an honour to give their freedom to eminent men.

In France, after the revolution of 1830, it was wished to make the elections more popular, and as there was only one class of electors, it was thought that this object would be attained by lowering the rate of 300*fr.* to 200*fr.*, and now a new clamour demands a much more considerable diminution; at the same time, to relieve the electors from an expensive journey, which would prevent those who were poor from coming to give their votes, the elections were transported from the chief places of the departments to the chief places of the districts. But far from the electors being found to be more numerous, they have become much less so; the assemblies remain deserted; the spirit of locality and the jealousies of neighbours have only been strengthened, and have become even obligatory on half the deputies; thus the Chamber has been filled with men whose celebrity only extended to districts and villages; and by persisting in the same course, by still farther lowering the rate, the elections will become still more estranged from the nation.

It has not been sufficiently considered that the electoral rate has the effect of giving a prodigious advantage to the inhabitants of the country over those of the towns, because the land tax is much the most considerable of all direct taxes, though it forms less than a third of what the people are called upon to pay; as it takes from the proprietor nearly the fifth of his revenue, the country elector paying 200*fr.* has only for himself and his family, which may be estimated on an average at five individuals, 1000*fr.* income, so that he must labour with his hands to live; but in towns there is no family working with their hands who pay nearly 200*fr.* in direct taxes: there are a great number, on the contrary, who enjoy some advantages of education, who have the sentiment of independence, and a lively interest in public affairs, but who having their money placed out at interest or in the funds, or in business, would not be called on to exercise the electoral rights, even by another lowering of the rate. Now, although we believe that agricultural labour is best suited to man, most advantageous to his health, his morality, and his happiness, we believe also, that it is what least prepares him for an acquaintance with the social sciences. The inhabitant of the country lives very little in society, scarcely ever hears political interests spoken of, does not read, and remains a perfect stranger to the experience obtained by study. In workshops, conversation, newspapers, and books, habitually excite political fermentation. The ideas of the working man may not be just, but they are his own; those of the peasant are only a reflection of the ideas of his curé, of his lord, or of the attorney of the village.

In fixing the electoral privileges by the direct taxes, the more the rate is lowered, the more the man who labours with his hands is secure of an overwhelming majority: he who works only with his mind is thrown into a minority which is reckoned as nothing. The uniformity of the rate, the uniformity of the electoral right, have been adopted by the nation with blind fanaticism as a result of equality, and by the minister with calculating skill, for he had well remarked that the country electors were much more tractable, and much less restless than those of towns. But mind is power, its restlessness is power also, and the government may find that it has injured itself by giving this power to its enemies.

Certainly, we have not the penetration to propose an electoral law, and if we allow ourselves here to make some calculations, it is only to make it understood how, by adopting the complicated system of the English, instead of the simple but deceptive system of the French, a much greater part of the nation might be associated in the elections, and still that share preserved to the national intelligence which it ought to have. We will propose, for example, to give two-fifths of the national representation to the democracy, two-fifths to the most enlightened and intelligent part of the nation, who inhabit towns, and there develop material prosperity; a fifth to that part occupied in intellectual interests. We will lower the census to 100*fr.* in obedience to the present clamour; and giving to 84 departments (Paris not included) two deputies for each department, to be elected in the chief place, we shall have 168 deputies, representing particularly the democracy of the country, perhaps, more probably, the nobility, who will seize on it. We will add 42 deputies elected by the 21 greater cities in France, in purely democratic assemblies, such as those of Westminster and Preston in England, giving a vote to whoever can read and write. We would give an equal number of deputies, 210, to the burgesses of towns requiring for their admission to the freedom a complete education in the secondary schools, and a degree of fortune which places them above manual labour. We would reserve at least 105 deputies for learned professions, in which all those who had received a superior education and taken degrees, should have the honour of being inscribed, and we would allow these last elections to be made by letters, that they might point out the most eminent persons, not in the provinces only, but in France. We should thus have a representation of 525 members, to the election of whom a very considerable part of the nation would have contributed, but in which, however, the share of intelligence and real will, would have been preserved.

We would not ask for any rate of eligibility, for in democratic elections great eminence would be necessary, in order to fix on any man the attention of all the inhabitants of a department or of a great town; besides, those whom they would elect, not forming the majority of the assembly, would not be corrupted by their own power, or detached from the interests which they ought to represent. As to the deputies from the middle class, and the highly educated class, the guarantee to the community would be found in the condition of the electors. By making a separate body of the highly educated class, and giving to it a direct power of election, the personal suffrage of each well educated man would have more value than if confounded with the masses, and at the same time the well-founded objection of the ministerial party would be avoided, that an extension of the right of suffrage would only be in favour of those who have not succeeded in their business or their profession.

We again repeat, this is not a project but an example, to make ourselves understood. We do not wish that the deputies of France should all have the right to enter the Legislative Chamber by the same title, but on the contrary, that there should be different qualifications: we would willingly multiply them much more. We should wish them to think of the different interests which they have to defend, instead of being ranged under three banners, bearing the deceptive names of carlists, patriots, and ministerialists; for, among these hostile battalions, exasperation has made all discussion impossible; each one prides himself to his own party on bitterly insulting his ad versaries, and the exasperated majority reply to the insults by scandalous clamour, and overwhelm their enemies by their votes.

It would not be very polite to tell the present Chamber what France, what Europe thinks of it; history will take care to do this; but there is one thing which it ought to perceive without being told of it; it is that the representative system is beginning to be considered as a great deception; the ministerial party see in it a convenient form of protecting their own ease and advantage, the liberal party a cruel cheat to deprive them of their liberty. The first have rejected the very modest pretensions of the intellectual professions to be admitted into the electoral college by the same title as qualifies them to be on juries; they have restricted as much as they could participation in municipal elections, which ought to be so much the more extended as political elections are less so: the second, by their cry for universal suffrage, labour at their own annihilation. The Chamber is, however, a pretty true representation of the just medium of the intelligence, energy, and virtue of those who have chosen it. The object of the true friends of liberty ought to be, to infuse into it a greater portion of that knowledge, and of those elevated ideas and sentiments, which constitute the true citizen. The counter revolutionary party, on the contrary, should desire, and does, in fact, desire to bring into it a greater portion of ignorance, personal interest, and low passions, so as to lower the level of the just medium among all the electors. It desires universal suffrage, and it has a very good reason for doing so, for it knows that whilst we would go forward, the masses are retrograde; it knows that every passion will in its turn make a step backwards; it knows that while civil and religious liberty might in France play at universal suffrage, priests and kings would win the game, and liberty would soon be lost.

ON

THE PRINCE,

OR,

EXECUTIVE POWER IN FREE COUNTRIES [a].

It is only the hope to make the experience of past ages useful to coming generations, which gives a great interest to the study of history. If we could learn nothing of the art of making nations happy, or if we could never make use of what we have learned, it would be wiser to turn away our eyes from the calamities without number which have afflicted our race. That oppression, those vices, those massacres, those tortures, those foolish passions, the pictures of which we so often find in every age and in every country, would then be portrayed only to rend our hearts by the recollections of the past, and to make them tremble for the future. The Asiatics, who be-

[a] We begin the publication of our essays on the fundamental questions of social order by this little treatise, printed in the year 1823, but which has never been published. It was designed for the Annals of Legislation and of Political Economy, which had just been established at Geneva, and which were almost immediately suppressed by their authors, out of deference for the government, when the threats of all the neighbouring powers obliged the Swiss to restrain the liberty of the press, at the period of the *conclusa*. Circumstances have changed; the allusions no longer relate to the present time; experience has thrown new light on the subjects here treated on. We shall make use of it in the following articles, but we have only made slight additions to this first essay, that its date as well as its spirit may render it foreign to any thing polemical.—Extracted from the *Revue mensuelle d'Economie Politique*, Vol. v. 1834.

lieve in fatalism, who regard all improvement as absurd, who renounce all influence on the social body to which they belong, are consistent when they shut themselves up in the present. To their eyes history is a royal and not a national science. The Gengis, the Timours, may contemplate with interest the monuments of ravages on the earth; they may demand a chronicler to relate their battles, in the same spirit which made them raise pyramids of heads in those places where they had destroyed a nation; but the Arabian turns away his eyes from the chronicles of Abulfarage, as he turns away his plough from these heaps of bones.

It is not thus that the European judges for himself of the past and of the future. He thinks he sees that even the blood with which the earth has been so often soaked produced sometimes good fruit. He compares ages, he follows the human race extending and multiplying on the globe; and though he has often the grief to see it make retrograde steps, it seems to him, however, that he can also perceive a general progress. The European congratulates himself that he has been called into life in the nineteenth century, and not in any of those which preceded it. He acknowledges the numerous conquests that have been made over barbarism, the numerous and crying abuses that have been destroyed, the odious causes of crime and suffering which it does not seem likely will be repeated; and though even the progress of social science and of civilization have been sometimes endangered by the vigorous resistance of what may be called the spirit of darkness; although posts which seemed gained have been sometimes retaken by the enemy, yet the European dares to believe that a better future is approaching, and he supports with more fortitude the ills he suffers in the hope that his descendants will be delivered from them.

It is true that to the European this confidence in the future is, perhaps, only a flattering dream, but to the American it is become in our time almost a certainty. The nations of the European races, established on this rich continent, with all the inheritance of our civilization, of our science, of our philosophy, of our dearly acquired experience, are there destined to recommence social life, without any of those burdens with which we are so heavily laden. They know all the improvements of our agriculture, and they will have for a long time to come abundance of virgin lands, which at present belongs to no one. They know our trades, our machines, all the powerful assistance which science has given to human industry, and they are not loaded with an immense class of day-labourers, who ask for work, and who seem on the point of perishing if a machine is made to supersede the labour of their hands; they know our systems of taxation, our modes of finance, our credit, and they have scarcely any debts. They know all the developments which our skilful civilians have given to the laws which regulate property, and they have much fewer subjects of litigation; they have adopted all those guarantees which the friends of humanity have secured to those persons brought before criminal justice, and they have no men forced to rob by universal poverty; they have profited by our discoveries in the construction of arms, of vessels, and of fortresses; they know our tactics, they have strength to defend themselves, and they have no neighbours, no natural object of ambition. May they equally profit by all which our long experience has put us into a situation to learn of the difficult science of government, without being led into error by the necessary falsehoods to which European politicians see themselves reduced, without being prevented from looking at those fundamental questions from which we so often turn away our eyes.

It is at this moment, when Columbia, Mexico, Chili, Buenos Ayres, Brazil, are employed in raising the social edifice from its foundation, that it appears to us important to classify, to analyze the political experience of Europe, of which we may offer, as it were, an inheritance to our younger brothers[a]. We

[a] It is twelve years since this was written, and the new states, formerly Spanish, have advanced no farther in the reconstruction of social order. Perhaps no real progress can be expected, till the whole of the generation accustomed to civil war, to

cannot be accused of presumption in endeavouring to be useful to them; the theories of which we wish to speak to them are not the creatures of our imagination; it is not by reason of any superiority that we are the depositaries of them; if we possess them, it is because we have paid for them with our blood, and with that of our fathers and of our forefathers. We have suffered enough to have a right to say to them, Behold the precipice, avoid our steps, and profit by our example. What nobler object of ambition, however, can be offered to those who have studied the fate of the human race, than that of assisting nations, destined to cover a third part of the habitable globe, to avoid some fatal errors? What a moment is that in which the fathers of nations are weighing resolutions on which will depend for many ages the fate of millions of men! What an imperative duty to speak the truth, when we know that it has been so often perverted, and that weak compromises, sometimes for the sake of power, sometimes for popularity, have gained credit for a crowd of errors which no one any longer thinks of contradicting.

The editors of the Annals of Legislation published at Geneva were in favourable circumstances for taking into consideration the highest questions of constitutional policy. Citizens of a republic, and writing under the protection of its laws, they were authorized even by the nature of the government of their country, to inquire what is the essence of power, and what are its foundations in public utility. To them it was permitted to lay aside all prejudice, all pretence to sympathetic affections, in order to rest only on realities. Whenever they entered on constitutional questions, they addressed themselves by preference to nations who were then labouring to give to themselves fundamental institutions; they fixed their eyes more particularly on the citizens of those new states which the revolutions of

violence, and to disregard of law, shall have retired from active life: a melancholy example to add to so many others, of the inability of men who have destroyed, to reconstruct. It should not make us renounce revolutions when they are necessary; it rather teaches us how dearly we purchase liberty by their means.

America had left as a clear field, and where the legislator is fettered neither by the rights of families, nor by those of orders, neither by powerful prejudices, nor by hereditary affections. At this moment circumstances allow French writers almost as much liberty of opinion. Whenever a part of the ancient edifice subsists in all its strength, it is not the time to think of the best means of superseding it. The nations of Europe are completing their institutions; the Americans are raising theirs from the foundation. In regard to the first, time may have established rights; for the second, it has left only experience. The citizen of an old state must study the ground on which to combine its peculiar affections and recollections with the rights that it has acknowledged. For the founders of the new states which we see unfolding themselves, it is sufficient to have present to their thoughts the result of what experience has taught Europe in regard to the first of all sciences.

We propose, at this time, to employ ourselves in considering Executive Power, because it is that part of constitutive policy respecting which Europe has acquired most experience, whilst, at the same time, the writings which this experience has produced may have given authority to the greatest number of errors. In fact, in our old states which have succeeded other old states, there have not always been sufficient guarantees, as respects legislative and judicial power; there has always been a government, but the public good has not been always kept in view: it has always been an object to make the government solid, prompt, and energetic; it has not always been one to make the laws the expression of the general will, to make judgments the application of the principles of eternal justice; but the great object has been to secure command and obedience. Men have always wished to oppose the perpetuity of the state to the ephemeral life of man, and to the fluctuations of his will. The construction of what J. J. Rousseau called the Prince, or what is now called the Executive Power, makes the distinctive character of monarchies and republics, and Europe can compare them in her history; she has seen all kinds of hereditary monarchies, with the infinite modifications of hereditary rights, primogeniture, and a division among all the children; the exclusion and non-exclusion of females; a testamentary right to the crown, or the imprescriptible right of the princes of the blood: she has also seen numerous elective monarchies; with the right of election confided to the whole nation, as in the ancient Teutons; to armed warriors or the equestrian order, as in Hungary, in Transylvania, and in Poland; to those whom the nation considered the wisest, as in Venice; to a small conclave of princes, as in the Germanic empire; to the heads of religion, as in the Pontifical states, and the sovereign bishoprics of Germany; to men who had made a vow to renounce the world, as in the sovereign abbeys of Fulda, of Kempten, of Musbach, &c.; to women rigorously shut up in cloisters, as the abbesses of Quedlinbourg, Lindau, Herforden, &c.

Again, with respect to republics, Europe can in her history compare executive power confided to one man, which may be regarded as an elective and temporary monarchy, with that which was exercised by two or more colleagues, and with that which was delegated to councils. Among these there are some of which the members were elected for life; others where they were all renewed at once; others by rotation. If the executive power has never been constituted in a completely national manner, it is not certainly because a variety of combinations have been wanting; and if our history presents us no model worthy of imitation in every respect, it is rich at least in lessons of what ought to be avoided.

Nevertheless, no subject has been treated in a more superficial manner by political writers, nor more frequently disguised by false reasonings, which through the power of repetition are confounded with public opinion. No part of political science has been more carefully excluded from controversy. Thus, for example, at a time when Europe contained far more elective than hereditary monarchies, there can scarcely be found one writer who has dared to appreciate their comparative advantages: the question between them has been supposed to be decided by allegations, the examination of which has never been allowed. In the same way, in half Europe the monarchical crown may descend to females; in the other half, females and their descendants are excluded in perpetuity. Numerous writings, where the succession was disputed, had for their object to found the right on the fact; no one has dared to enter on the principle. History is full of the consequences of these fundamental laws; wars of succession, countries united by marriages, the loss of independence which had been defended by seas of blood, and afterwards abandoned to hereditary chances, are related in every page; yet no publicist, as far as I know, has endeavoured to compare the advantages resulting to nations from the order of succession established in France, with those of that established in England.

This voluntary blindness does not prevail among slaves only; in free countries, where all political subjects have in their turn been the subjects of long debates, these alone have been constantly avoided. In fact, discussion may precede the establishment of legislative and judicial power: it cannot begin till after the establishment of executive power, and as soon as that exists, it will not permit it. From the first day, from the first hour of the existence of a nation, it must have chiefs to direct its efforts, to regulate what it must sacrifice, to secure its defence. These chiefs, who have in general existed before national deputies, and before all political writers, became, to these last, facts which they were obliged to admit, and by which alone they could regulate other political institutions.

We are not in this situation; we endeavour to discover sincerely, but with perfect freedom, what is the constitution which it is best to give to power, that it may be truly national, and that its interests may be identified with those of the nation whom it represents. With this object, after some preliminary reflections on the institution of social power, we shall pass in review, with all the impartiality of which we are capable, the different forms of this power which Europe has experienced.

ON THE INSTITUTION OF THE SOCIAL POWERS, AND ON THEIR BALANCE.

Men who, reduced to their individual efforts, found themselves unable to contend with the powers of nature, obtained more happiness and more security by associating together. The spirit of association distinguishes the species, and the essence of their reciprocal engagements, whether tacit or expressed, has always been to aim at one common end, and to submit their reason, their will, their power, to that general will, in which they all concur. As soon as men begin to unite and act on a common plan, we see the same beings who before were the slaves of the elements, and of all their inclemency, subdue nature, and change the face of the earth. Men associated together in their labours have, by opening the inundations of the Nile, created Egypt; by forming dikes against the ocean they have created Holland. Countries now infected by pestilential vapours, will, by the spirit of association, be restored to salubrity, and become populous and rich; the vast regions which are watered by the Orinoco, and the Maranon, will one day rise from beneath the waters; whilst despotism, which isolates man, has changed into a desert Asia Minor and Greece: it has made the vegetating earth of mountains disappear, it has covered with gravel the loam of the plains in countries once famed for their fertility; everywhere nature is stronger than isolated man, whilst human society can always subdue nature. Of all associations, that which constitutes nations is the most vast, and the most energetic; it has more strength, it has more wealth, it has more duration, it has more stability, than any of those created by individual interests; the opinion of all is of more value than that of each one. If government were only the expression of this general will [a], if its power were only the national power, and

[a] We have elsewhere explained that we understand by general will the sum of what is best in all the most eminent opinions, and not the proportionate mean between the most advanced and the most absurd. (*See Essay on Universal Suffrage, ante, p.* 290.)

acted without any obstacle, we should be astonished at the wonders which it would be able to accomplish. Then we should without fear confide to the government all that is most precious to us, even to the care of our own reason, the direction of the education of our children, the worship of our churches, the employment of all our faculties. Now we suspect, not without reason, that what it would have us do, is for its own interest; but how strong would the human species become, if it executed in common what it willed in common, and what wonderful progress would it be seen to make, if it was not necessary to distinguish between confidence in its government and confidence in itself!

It has ever been one of the first principles of constitutive policy, that all absolute power becomes tyrannical, to whatever hands it may be confided. In fact, what is called the will of all is always a fiction, since this expression supposes in the first place that all have a will, which is very far from being the case; afterwards, that all these wills are unanimous, which is impossible. Wherever it is thought that the expression of the public will can be found, it is always supposed that the majority bind the minority, and still more that all those who have not given themselves the trouble to reflect on the question which is submitted to them, or who cannot comprehend it, are bound, and even bind others, by their formal or tacit assent to the *will* which is expressed in their name. Nevertheless, the majority may impose upon the minority the most unjust and most cruel sacrifices, and those who give a vote of confidence may, if they allow themselves to be deceived, fatally sacrifice their own rights and those of others. Thus, even should all the members of a community vote, and the majority alone make the law, this community itself would not be secure from tyranny.

The community would not only fail to secure itself against tyranny, if, instead of throwing upon government the charge of willing for it, it were to attempt to govern itself; it would soon perceive the ignorance, the carelessness of many members of the community to whom it could not refuse equal rights, consequently its own incapacity, the imprudence of its resolutions, the precipitation of a numerous assembly, and if the community is really powerful, the impossibility of assembling all its members. Thus, even should the nation (which has very rarely happened) be formed calmly, without opposition, without danger, still it would find itself reduced to seek the expression of the general will elsewhere than in the majority of all the members of the community; to consult different interests, different classes, instead of every individual; but the more indirect is the manner in which this will is expressed, the greater becomes the chance that this will, supposed to be general, should not be so in fact; that those who have the charge of willing for all, would consider their own advantage, and not that of the community; that they would endeavour, perhaps, to oppress this community, and that those who really do *will* would tyrannize over those who are supposed to will.

When it is thought desirable to confide the sovereignty to the general will, it is supposed that nothing is more simple than to know it, that it is sufficient to propose the question to be decided on, then to count the voices: this is a mistake. Three quarters of those who answer *yes* or *no*, are incapable of well understanding the question, have not thought about it, have no will respecting it; to save even themselves from their precipitation, it is necessary to give the minority the means of resisting the majority for some time, that those who are consulted may have time to enlighten themselves, and to form a distinct conception of that which they decide upon before they command, or are obeyed.

Such is the origin of that system, of a balance of power, which has been established with so much care in countries where less than a thousand individuals under the names of king, of ministers, of peers, and of deputies are supposed to express the will of many millions of citizens. The more difficulty these citizens experience in speaking for themselves, in their own persons, and in setting right the will ascribed to them, the more necessary is it to demand the concurrence of many constituted wills, for the purpose of changing what exists, because what exists is supposed to have obtained general assent. If the citizens can only manifest what they think of the labours or of the policy of their representatives by a general election, and this only returns every seven years, the more necessary is it that a double security should be given to what has been done in past times, and all change made so much the more difficult, the more it is doubtful whether this change is brought about by the general will.

Above all, it was important for a community to choose him, or those, who were to act in the name of all, or to direct the action of all, for their common defence, whether against the enmity of nature, or that of men. It was important to find in these, vigour, secrecy, promptitude, prudence, economy. Society depended on them for her defence against whatever is foreign and may become hostile, and for the security of the community against all private interests. To these first proxies has been given the name of Prince, either in regard to rank as the first of all; of government, as taking part for the whole; lastly, of Executive Power, because administration was regarded as the execution of the will of the whole community.

But all the qualities which society sought for in the Prince, contributed to separate him from the nation, and to make him dangerous to her if he once came to have a different will from hers. It was required that he should be vigorous, but only against the enemies of order; secret, but to foreigners alone; prompt, but only to execute the national will; economical, but not to amass treasures except for the nation. The Prince was subjected to the surveillance of a body of men, who were to represent the people, and always to continue to belong to the people, who should declare the national will, but who, not exercising power, should not be corrupted by flattery. It was required that these representatives should express the variable will of the moment, and the national interest at the time of their election. But as this variable will is not the only one which ought to be consulted, and as besides the interest of the day there is also in nations a permanent interest, which may be in opposition to that, recourse will be had to divers artifices, to combine a representation of the past with that of the present, to make other voices speak besides those of the people, to whose deputies will be given only a share either in the *legislative power*, or in the body charged with the expression of the national will, to which the prince must conform.

From this watchfulness ascribed to the deputies of the people, from the remembrance also of the ancient struggle which in almost every place has successively wrested national securities from the depositories of power, has arisen a dangerous prejudice, which all the polemical writers of Europe at this time have a tendency to confirm: it is that executive power is an enemy against which it is necessary to contend; it is that there is a constant opposition between the government and the people, between the Prince and liberty. Legislators never having created power, that power has never been the true organ of the national will, the true representative of the people; all the friends of liberty have constantly laboured, if not to destroy, at least to counteract and limit it. Its action has been unceasingly restrained, retarded, reduced to indirect means; even its existence has been often compromised, and the depositories of power, their will thwarted, their safety threatened, their self-love humiliated, have felt as much hatred of the friends of liberty, as the latter have had distrust of them; if they cannot crush them at home, they fight against them in every other part of the world; they end by having interests opposed to those of the nation, and passions still more opposed to it; and the struggle which difference of position had begun, is envenomed by every kind of animosity.

Government, however, must go on; of all the necessities of the social state, this is the first. This necessity preponderates over distrust and discontent. Hence it is concluded that the struggle between the prince and the people is the essence of free government; that an opposition is necessary to watch over administration, to criticise it, to keep it active, in order either to prevent it through shame from going too far, or to arrest in their birth culpable projects; but that it is also necessary that the administration should constantly triumph over this opposition till the moment when it is overthrown; that it should have sufficient force to resist these daily attacks; that it should be surrounded by riches, pomp, and an immense patronage, not to attain the objects required by the nation, but that it may not yield under the first attacks of the deputies of the nation. In the system of modern legislators, States maintain a kind of parliamentary gladiators, whose combats no more serve to change the constitution than those of the circus formerly did to defend Rome.

When a thing has existed for a certain time, man soon arrives at the belief that it exists necessarily. He always presents to himself ingenious reasons, plausible reasons, to persuade himself that those effects of chance which are always before his eyes, are equivalent in advantages to the sublimest combinations of human intelligence. All modern publicists have regarded government as the born enemy of liberty; but they have not seen the evil of so regarding it. They have directed, with more or less ardour, attacks against this government, and they have sanctioned the opinion that the less a state is governed the more it will prosper; that whenever the citizen can act without being influenced by government, it is a conquest for liberty; that government in short, is a necessary evil, like taxes, and that every effort of the liberal party ought to tend to having as little of it as possible. Others, at the same time, to save the administration from annihilation, justify in turn its vast patronage, the ministerial influence which is exercised over opinion, and even parliamentary corruption.

Nevertheless, antiquity has shown us States, we have seen them in the middle ages, and we may see them afresh among the Anglo-American, where executive power is only an emanation of popular sovereignty, where the will of the prince is one with that of the people; where no opposition is organized, and no distrust would be legitimate; where no public strength is spent in struggles not even known; where the government, having no separate interests from those of the nation, has no arms of its own; where its power, in short, is equal to that of the nation to do what the nation wills, and null to do what it does not will.

We should not consider ourselves as refuted, should it be denied that such governments as we have supposed have ever existed. In the science which we are entering upon, facts, still more than theories, are subject to the empire of passion, and perverted by the eyes of those who observe them. It is enough that the imagination may conceive a constitution where the prince always obeys the national will, in order to prefer such a constitution to those whose essence it is that he should always contend against it. The continual struggle in which the representatives of the prince and those of the people are engaged, by nourishing intestine hatred, preparing resistance to the legitimate action of all power, and paralysing national strength, which is consumed in the oppósition of one power against another, is the abuse of constitutions founded on the system of balance. The same observations apply to the contest of the press against social power, to its criticism on all persons and things, to its outrages against whoever commands. There may be a social state in which such an evil is necessary, but it is a strange error to take this evil for a good. The system of balance in the degree even in which its inventors have conceived it, that is to say, as a means of ripening deliberations, of guaranteeing existing rights, and of giving each power the means of defending itself, rests entirely on the supposition that the established order is sufficient to secure the welfare of all, and that it has general assent; that tyranny, on the contrary, can only be introduced by innovations, and that the door to these should always be opened with extreme difficulty, since they have always against them the prejudice of not having been brought forward by the general will. Thus there is a sort of absurdity in beginning a revolution by establishing a system of balance; it is putting drags to the four wheels at the moment of starting the carriage on its career. When a nation determines on a revolution, it proclaims loudly enough by that, that the order which has been long established has not general assent, that it fears tyranny from its institutions, not from innovations, and that far from willing what is, it submits to immense dangers and immense sacrifices, that what is, may cease to be. More than one European nation has not perceived that in adopting British institutions, they were transporting defences which had been raised to preserve the rights of a free people, to surround abuses which an enfranchised people wished to destroy.

Still more, the system of balance must be considered at a time of danger as employing the strength of a nation to a complete loss. Distrust is already too much excited by a foreign attack; and at the moment when a new constitution is established, at the moment of a revolution, if the foreigner joins one of the parties which will not fail to be formed in the interior, the public and legal struggle of the constituted powers will leave no force to oppose to the enemy without. When a nation is aiming at establishing its independence, and at shaking off a yoke which all the creatures of power throughout the universe will think it their interest to strengthen, it has need of all its force: the slowness of parliamentary discussion, the resistance of hereditary interests which are opposed to the interests of the day, the habitual mistrust excited by power, and the struggle of patriots against the administration, will be so many auxiliaries in the enemy's camp. At such a moment, all struggle must cease; the national will, which has decided on the revolution, must execute it, the representation must emanate from the people, and power must emanate from the representation; the government, in short, must be only the accomplishment of that will which the deputies of the people have manifested.

It is then, especially, that a man is necessary to the revolution, a man who, identifying himself with it, puts his will in the place of that which the nation cannot yet express; a man who brings every thing to a common centre, who foresees, who combines, who keeps every thing secret, who orders without discussion, without rendering any account, and who by rapidity of thought compensates for all the disadvantages of his position.

Monarchy is born of revolutions. It is in the midst of the dangers of a mortal struggle that it becomes the refuge of nations; whether it be a chief of barbarian warriors, called by the talent which he has displayed in battle to be the sole director of the conquerors he leads, as the Germanic founders of the monarchies which now cover Europe; or whether it be a hero, who having snatched a free people from the yoke, has been constituted the representative of the will of that people by his glory or his talent. Sweden, crushed to the earth, had no time to combine a legitimate representation when she acknowledged Gustavus Vasa for her organ; Scotland was enslaved when she committed her destinies to William Wallace, or to Robert Bruce; Holland was almost annihilated when she called upon William of Orange to be her liberator.

It is true, that the more the power of a man is energetic and prompt, the more dangerous is it for the liberty which he has undertaken to found. He is not an ordinary hero who, having united all power in his own hands, for the national defence, consents to lay down whatever is not necessary for this defence as soon as the danger is past; he, who raised to the place of despots, listens to nothing which would recall despotism, and remains deaf to the suggestions of his own vanity and to the servility of courtiers. Too often the defender of the people thinks only of defending his own rank, and he turns against those who had raised him the arms which had been entrusted to him to fight for them.

Thus revolution is the foundation of monarchy only when time is wanting for combinations; because the people, called to defend themselves at the moment when they are beginning to exist, can only choose their representative by a sort of acclamation, because national confidence, acquired by a popular name and acknowledged talents, is the only possible manifestation of the will of all. If the nation is already represented, if an assembly of deputies freely elected is already in possession of the confidence of all, she will take care not to relinquish a power which will be indubitably turned against her: whilst the revolution lasts, whilst the struggle and the danger are prolonged, social power ought to be administered by it, or by its delegates which are only one with it.

The crimes of the Committee of Public Safety, sullying the name of liberty, endangered her cause; it is, notwithstanding, to the close union of the Committee of Public Safety with the Convention that France owed all her means of defence. In the crisis she was experiencing, with Europe armed against her without, and so many enemies within, she would have yielded, if the executive power had been anything but an emanation of the power of the Convention; if one had not been blended with the other; if the legislature had been ever seen to command the ministry in vain, to resist them, or to experience any resistance from them.

But, it will be said, this is to establish that absolute power which becomes tyranny, in whatever hands it may be lodged; and if we must bend under tyranny, we may as well keep what we had before. It is true; and the example which we have chosen makes us conceive all the danger of it. But war is itself a tyranny; and when existence is compromised, the rights and enjoyments of life may be sacrificed to its preservation. During a calm, it is in the combination of different voices that the national will should be sought; during the storm, one only is listened to, and that one speaks in the name of the nation. The struggle for existence calls for dictatorship, the character of which is, that it is not the less an emanation of the legislature because it is raised above the laws.

In short, when these same principles are applied to periods of repose, it is not strictly true that the security of liberty can only be found in the balance and opposition of constituted powers. Antiquity, the middle ages, modern times, have seen governments really free; where opposition was not constituted, where there was no struggle between the legislative and executive powers, where the magistracy only fulfilled what councils had willed, where one mind, one way of thinking, seemed to animate the prince and the representatives of the people.

What secured liberty in such circumstances was, that the whole of the governing powers were always in the presence of the people, who had a prompt and efficacious action on them. It was not that a balance was established between the constituted powers, but that they were all and wholly in the hands of the people who reigned as the true sovereign. In the republics of Greece, or in the monarchies of Germany, the people, not numerous, and always armed in the face of a government without arms, assembled altogether on the public place; they were directly informed, *vivâ voce,* of all their dearest interests, and the strength was so evidently in their hands, that the archons of Athens in Greece, the kings of the Franks in Germany, would never for a moment have thought of resisting their will.

It was only a very small nation, easily assembled on the public place or the *Champ de Mars,* which could exercise this continual influence on its government: thus liberty was formerly considered as the peculiar privilege of nations whose city was their country, or where the *heriban,* the convocation of the army, was equivalent to a general assembly, the *comitia.* The invention of the representative system extended to larger states the prerogatives of free men, and allowed the union of national power with the greatest dignity of man.

The representative system required a balance among the representatives for the safety of the represented; from it sprung opposition among the constituted bodies and the balance of their reciprocal rights. But a new progress in civilization, a progress which dates only from our own times, has placed, as formerly, the government in presence of the whole nation: with the diffusion of intelligence by printing, by newspapers, and by the complete publicity of all administration, the servants of the nation may become as completely dependent on the nation,—even when it covers an immense space, as in America for instance,—as they formerly were on the people of Athens. Henceforward, opposition is only a means of discussion; separation of the different powers does not suppose resistance: the president or the temporary king may be without pomp, without treasure, without patronage, without means of corruption; the senate without an aristocracy, without territorial power; the elections of deputies may be annual, or every two years, and suffrage universal; the judges may be removeable; it is no longer their independence which constitutes liberty; it is wholly found in their constant and necessary submission to the general will.

However, the more the other guarantees of liberty seem to be depressed, to be, as it were, annihilated by this guarantee of publicity, the latter may, on the other hand, present dangers which were not suspected before its introduction. The English speak sometimes jokingly, sometimes with real anxiety, of this *fourth estate of the gentlemen of the press*—the newspaper editors. They know, they have first taught us that a nation cannot attain to true liberty but by developing national intelligence; that to do this it is necessary that individual ideas should be brought forward, should be enlightened one by another, should be matured by discussion; that there is no power in the state to whom can be confided the right of putting bounds to thought, whilst, on the contrary, thought must control all other power. Such are the principles of the liberty of the press; but by the side of the elaboration of thought, which is a right and a necessity, is placed journalism, which is a trade. All power which is exercised with a view to lucre should excite distrust, for it is in the way of being corrupted. The daily press is a power, and its object is not public good but to get the largest number of subscribers. It is not for the advantage of the country, it is that it may be read, that a newspaper attacks the institutions of the country, lessens consideration for those in power, plants thorns on every public career, drives from it all those who have not by intrigue acquired a front of brass, spies out the secrets of the state, proclaims its weakness or its irresolution, and reveals its projects to the enemies of the country as well as to its readers. Publicity is no doubt an immense progress in social science, but venal publicity is often an advantage obtained by crime.

In endeavouring to discover what is the most advantageous manner of constituting executive power, we are brought to ask first, whether it is better to confide it to one man or to many. If to one man, what are the comparative advantages of elective royalty, hereditary royalty, or royalty for a fixed time or presidentship? If to many, is it better to preserve the advantages of individuality by placing at the head of government two colleagues, two consuls for example? or, on the contrary, is it best for the man to disappear, and only a council, a directory, or a seigniory (body of nobles), to appear? Again, should the executive power be one or divided? Should it act alone or be subordinate to legislative councils? We shall endeavour to collect, with fidelity, the different solutions which history offers to these questions; and perhaps we shall arrive at the conclusion, that there are a thousand ways of being free for those who are worthy of freedom.

ON ELECTIVE ROYALTY.

It seems that elective royalty was the first known form of government. In the small states of Greece and Italy, in those of Arabia and Germany, among all barbarous nations, or those who were making the first steps towards civilization at the origin of society, power has been uniformly seen divided among an elective chief, who had the office of commanding the nation in war, and of being its judge in peace; a council of old men, or men acknowledged as superiors, to second him; and an assembly of the people who in their turn gave advice before they obeyed. Absolute power is not an idea natural to man; it is always by some accident that it has been established, and in almost every dynasty it may be shown where it has begun. All small nations have at first seen in their chiefs, what they were in fact, the first servants of the state:

they chose them for their own advantage, and supposing that they might afterwards find that there would be more stability by renouncing their free choice and trusting to the chances of heirship, it was at least not a combination which could present itself to their minds from the first. There is, perhaps, not one hereditary monarchy which has not been elective.

In the same way elective monarchy has preceded a republic as being a more simple combination. In the infancy of society, a state of war is, in some sort, the habitual state; and in war the superiority of a chief over a council is so evident for secrecy in discussion, for promptitude in decision, for the influence of example, for enthusiasm, much better excited by a man than by an abstract idea, that there is scarcely an example of the command of an army being given to the collected wills of several men. To choose a king is to choose at the same time a general and a judge; in no other respect did barbarous nations think they had any need of government. On the contrary, to choose an executive council was to oblige this council afterwards to delegate the functions of generalship to a man, who perhaps would not be always disposed to obey.

But elective kings often wished to seize on all power, and to transmit it by inheritance to their families. When they succeeded, they founded hereditary monarchies; when they failed, they had inspired so much distrust that royalty was abolished, the power which had been intrusted to them was divided, its duration was limited, and assemblies of the first men (colleges), were substituted for individuals.

Thus the primitive form of government was abolished almost everywhere; only those nations which have remained in a state approaching barbarism have preserved the too simple organization of an elective king, sharing the sovereignty with a council of old men and an assembly of all the citizens. The motives which caused it to be adopted no longer subsist among civilized nations and in modern times; war is no longer in the power of small nations; they require from their magistrates more prudence than bravery: thus they entrust their destinies to a senate rather than to a general. This primitive form, so distant from us and so little known, does not seem to deserve any further attention.

We need not, perhaps, give much more to the small elective monarchies belonging to ecclesiastics, which have been preserved to our times in so great a number in Germany, and all which we have seen destroyed; whilst the pontifical sovereign at Rome exists on the same basis, as a specimen of a social order scarcely credible, if we did not see it exist. How is it possible to conceive, in fact, that to form a statesman, a legislator, an administrator, a warrior, to obtain the union of all these qualities, not less necessary to a bishop-prince than to any other prince, of those qualities which ought alone to deserve the confidence of nations, of all that knowledge which makes the science of government more difficult, and at the same time more noble, than all other human sciences, it should be required from him who in his old age is to end by being a monarch, that he should in his youth abjure the world and all commerce with men; that he should renounce active life; that he should abhor, above all things, the trade of arms, and that he should consecrate all his time, all his energy, all his faculties, to a study which has not the least relation to the functions which he will have to fulfil; that after this education has been given to all the aspirants, the choice of the monarch should be confided to men as completely ignorant as himself of all affairs of government, that his council should be formed of those who, like himself, have abjured the world, and that even to the lowest of those employed in his administration, the fundamental condition of being in their places should be that they are not suited to such a situation?

This character of the elections in sovereign prelacies cannot be applied without some exceptions to the papacy: the importance of the dominion over conscience throughout Christendom has called statesmen to the government of the church. Popes and cardinals were not recluses, nor men who had renounced worldly policy; and, in fact, the court of Rome has shown in a certain line an address and an energy, which perhaps no other court has equalled. However, the talent which it is most requisite for nations to find in their chiefs, is that of administration; and among all the popes, distinguished by their character or their genius, there has not been one single good administrator.

It seems as if the election of a prince-bishop should be considered as the last term of political absurdity; however accustomed we may be to find the people reckoned for nothing in the constitution, these governments seem more openly than any other to announce that they were instituted for the advantage of the prince, and not for that of his subjects. This is not all, however; there were monk-princes, princes of religious orders. In Germany, alone, were reckoned four sovereign archbishops, twenty-one bishops, twenty-nine abbots or priors, and fifteen abbesses; besides a grand master of the Teutonic order; in all, seventy elective royalties reserved to the members of the church.

These governments have all been suppressed in our times; but, what is well worthy of remark, they have all been regretted. The conditions of the election were such, that one would not have chosen for the lowest employment, a carpenter or a mason, in the way a prince was chosen; it was sufficient, however, that there was an election, to secure some kind of constitution. At each new reign, the contract between the prince and the people was renewed; the old creatures of power were changed; some ancient abuses were abolished, some new securities were often demanded. In short, as family interests were not opposed to national interests, there was found, in every age, some prince-abbot, some prince-bishop, who did not feel that instinctive hatred of liberty so common among the powerful; who consented to illustrate his reign by some useful institution, destined to last for ever, whilst he was himself only a sojourner on earth. If he feared a contest with his contemporaries, he did not, on that account, refuse to lay the foundations of rights for generations to come. Thus misers are often generous in their wills, at the expense of their heirs.

Ecclesiastical principalities had existed, as an appendage to the feudal system, in other places besides Germany; and in other places also, the right of electing the prince, however ill exercised, had been a beginning of liberty. The residence of more than one prince-bishop had become a republic. The first enfranchised municipalities in France, those of Rheims, of Laon, of Mons, were held under an ecclesiastical lord. The prince-bishops of Lausanne, of Geneva, of Basle, the prince-abbot of St. Gall, allowed Swiss liberty to spring up among them; the archbishops of Lyons and Arles, the bishops of Avignon and Marseilles, who, in the ancient kingdom of Arles, were in the twelfth and thirteenth centuries elective sovereigns, allowed under their eyes the republican independence of these four cities to become established. The republics of Bologna, of Perugia, of Ancona, were seen to flourish under the government of the Pope: even now if the pontifical government does not sufficiently provide for social order, it does not at least adopt the system of oppression of an hereditary despotism.

The state of servitude to which Europe was reduced before the establishment of the feudal system, could alone permit the institution of sacerdotal government; we cannot believe that such circumstances will occur again; and especially that nations, who can choose their government, will seek for models in those pious foundations of the middle ages. It was worth while, however, to remark what have been the effects of elective principalities, in states where some kind of right of election was the only popular liberty.

Europe, also, has tried elective royalty in some large and civilized states, and until a period not very distant from our times. Venice, with the title of republic, was an elective constitutional monarchy, where the power of the Doge was limited by that of the aristocracy alone: Venice, for a time at least, took rank among the most powerful states of Europe; and the succession of about a hundred and twenty elective monarchs caused neither troubles, nor civil wars, nor any of those inconveniences which are said to be necessarily attached to this form of government.

The defence of Christendom against Turks and Pagans was entrusted during the best half of the middle ages to the two elective monarchies of Hungary and Poland. In both these countries the people were slaves; but the king divided the sovereignty with a numerous equestrian order, warlike, and idolizing their liberty. The electoral right raised to the throne, in both these kingdoms, some of the greatest princes who have ever governed any nation; and perhaps Europe owes even her existence to this constitution, now so decried, which gave a defender to the west in John Sobieski. Elective royalty cannot however be appreciated, either in Hungary, where the hereditary attachment to certain families raised to the throne minors and females; or in Poland, where the most anarchical of all institutions, the *liberum veto,* annihilated all possibility of government, and delivered up the republic by turns to every local usurpation, and every foreign influence.

But the first, in rank and in extent, of the monarchies of Europe, has also been elective by right, till our times, and in fact till the sixteenth century. We might be astonished that whilst Germany, Italy, and part of France were subject to an elective crown, no one has ventured to show the advantages of this government, in opposition to that of hereditary government, if we did not know that the emperor, always desirous of transmitting his crown to his children, and habitually in a state of conspiracy against the constitution in the name of which he reigned, would have looked with much dislike on any apology for the government of his country; and that all the German princes, wishing to preserve to themselves the right of electing their chief, never thought of granting to their subjects the right of electing their lords.

The silence of those who ought to have defended elective royalty, and the noisy vindications of the champions of hereditary monarchy, have established as a principle, generally admitted by all publicists, that a nation cannot reserve to itself the election of its kings without exposing itself on every interregnum to the intrigues of its neighbours, the quarrels of the different parties, to prolonged troubles, and to civil wars. To appreciate this opinion, it will not be unseasonable to compare royalty in France and Germany. The two monarchies sprung from the division of the empire of Charlemagne; their organization was then nearly the same; their power was almost equal; but the Germanic Carlovingian race being extinct, and afterwards the house of Saxony by the death of Otho the Third in 1002, the crown became purely elective in Germany; whilst Hugh Capet, having caused himself to be elected in France, transmitted to his son Robert, by right of inheritance in 996, a crown which from that time remained hereditary. From the year 1000 to the year 1520, when the Germanic empire—thanks to the preponderance of Charles the Fifth—appeared to have devolved on the house of Austria, the two great states of Europe may justly be regarded as having experienced, in nearly equal circumstances, the two opposite systems.

The empire had during this space of time twenty-five chiefs, among whom twelve or thirteen are incontestably ranked among great men. This period of time was marked by a constant progress in Germany and Italy towards liberty, public prosperity, and intelligence: at the end of this period, the monarchy was more united, and more vigorous, than it was at its commencement; but during this time it had several times appeared to be on the point of being dissolved. However, the almost continual contest of the church against the empire was a source of troubles, independent of the elective or hereditary form of government. Of the twenty-five elections which gave heads to the empire, eleven were contested, and were followed by civil wars The church, eager to limit the imperial power, had been a party in all these wars. It was almost always the popes who excited discord among the electors, or called upon the people to take up arms. These wars, though frequent, were short; their duration added together, filled only a period of forty-three years: it must be remarked also, that we reckon as a time of war all that in which one of the two rivals, after his defeat, having retired into his hereditary states, continued to take a title which he could not get acknowledged except in his own country. We have not on the other side comprised in it the long interregnum from 1257 to 1273, because the two rivals, Richard of Cornwall, and Alphonso of Castile, fixing their abode in England, and in Spain, did not occasion bloodshed on the soil of the empire on account of their double election.

During the same space of time France had twenty-three kings; her progress during these reigns is very inferior to that of Germany; none of her cities equalled in commerce and industry, in riches and population, the imperial and Hanseatic cities of Germany, still less the Italian republics; the people in the country were more enslaved and poor; and whilst the lower class in Germany, the landsknechts, had gained a high military reputation, those of France were unarmed, and her kings were obliged to call in foreign infantry for their armies.

The right of the kings of France to their crown was contested by Edward the Third and his grandson Richard the Second, kings of England, who pretended to be called to the throne of France by the laws of inheritance; and again by Henry the Fifth and by Henry the Sixth. If these pretensions were sometimes abandoned by other English kings, it was not because the order of succession was cleared up, but domestic disturbances or minorities prevented their supporting what they called their rights. Adding up the wars with the English for the succession to the crown of France, independently of those excited by other motives, we find that during this period they lasted sixty-three years. In fact, wars for succession are more rare than those for election, but they are much more bloody, much longer, and more ruinous.

We may strictly also reckon as a consequence of the hereditary system, the wars in which the kingdom was engaged to support the succession to other crowns claimed by the kings of France. Twenty-six years of this period were filled by the wars for the successions of Naples and Milan, which began in 1494, and were prolonged far beyond the epoch at which we stop. The wars for the successions to the duchies and lordships of France, reannexed to the crown, alone filled centuries.

Whilst election almost always raises to the throne a man gifted with some talents, or at least of an age to conduct himself, hereditary monarchies must submit to the chances of humanity. We will refrain from examining what was the character of the French sovereigns during this period; we will only remark that the chances of inheritance placed on the throne Charles the Sixth, who was mad for thirty years (1392—1421) and whose madness had the most fatal consequences for the nations subject to him.

Madness is a rare accident; minority is a necessary consequence of the system of inheritance to the crown. During these same 520 years, which form the object of our comparison, France was governed ninety-two years by sovereigns who were under the age of twenty-five, the legal age in this country, and at this epoch, for individuals to take the administration of their own affairs. She was governed fifty-six years by sovereigns who had not attained the age of twenty-one.

Now, the regency of a monarchy, during a minority, is perhaps the worst possible form of government. It is a republic, for the sovereign power is divided between councils and individuals who are intended to balance one another; but it is a republic without republican habits, where the duties are not entrusted either to popularity, or celebrity, or virtue; where foreign females and often enemies are admitted to a command from which the law excludes princesses of the national blood. Among the regents of this period have been placed very high, Blanche of Castile, very low, Isabella of Bavaria, perhaps with as little reason for one as the other.

It is not, then, the wars caused by the elections which must be regarded as establishing the disadvantage of elective royalty, compared to hereditary royalty, since the succession wars have in general lasted still longer, and minorities are more to be feared for nations than interregnums. The example which we have chosen, is not the most favourable to the elective system. We shall scarcely find thirteen years of wars caused by the elections, in all the history of Poland, and ten years in all that of Hungary, though in neither of these countries did the constitution seem suited to avoid these disturbances. As to Germany, when the imperial election was entrusted to seven powerful princes, it seemed from the armies which each of them always kept ready, as if they wished beforehand to organize civil war. It might be expected that in modern times, since rights have been better defined, and genealogies better known, successions to the crown would be more rarely contested; it is not so; questions of succession have arisen on all sides, many perhaps are still dormant, waiting for future wars; for it is the essence of the law of royal succession to be unchangeable and imprescriptible; therefore, whenever it has been misunderstood or altered by legislative authority, or violated by adoptions, legitimation, testamentary dispositions, and renunciations, all those who have been despoiled think they preserve to the end of time the right to reclaim it. In fact, the doubtful cases, which must be governed by the law of royalty, only present themselves at long intervals of time; the reigning prince is then always interested in changing the law, and getting this change sanctioned by popular consent. If his right to do so were acknowledged, the law would only last till it had nothing to regulate. France would no longer know the Salic law, if kings, united with states-general, had been able to change it, as they attempted to do in 1420, in order to expel Charles the Seventh, and in 1588, to exclude Henry the Fourth. Females were not less expressly excluded from the succession in Hungary, Bohemia, and Austria; and the succession of the house of Lorraine to that of Hapsburgh remains an usurpation in the eyes of the partisans of legitimacy, notwithstanding the cry of the diet of Hungary,

Moriamur pro rege nostro Maria Theresa! In Spain, Philip the Fifth had no more the right to introduce the Salic law, than any of his successors had to abolish it. Isabella the Second reigns in virtue of the ancient law of the country, which Don Carlos wished to annihilate. In Portugal the fundamental law excludes all foreigners. Don Miguel made a strange application of it to the sovereign of a detached portion of the empire; but this sophism sufficed to produce a civil war. Even in France, the Duchess d'Angoulême ought to have succeeded to the crown of Navarre, where females are admitted; and this crown would have been detached from that of France, as it was in a similar case in 1328, to pass to the daughter of Louis the Tenth. In Piedmont, at the accession of the present king, Sardinia and Montferrat, which are feminine fiefs, ought to have gone to the daughter of his predecessor, and to have been detached from Savoy and Piedmont, which are masculine fiefs. The duchy of Modena, a masculine fief, should have gone to an agnate of the house Guelfo-Estense, either to the Duke of Brunswick, or to the King of England, rather than to the actual sovereign, who has succeeded in the name of a female. There would be no end of enumerating all the quarrels about succession, which might in our time cause an appeal to arms. A mode of election which would exclude foreign intrigues and domestic factions, would probably not be more difficult to invent for elective royalty than for the presidentships of the different states of America.

At all events, we must confess that it is only a rude kind of constitution which entrusts so much power to the head of a government, and identifies his interests so little with those of the state. The name of king excites, and will always excite, the desire for royalty in the elected chiefs. They will take the measure of their prerogatives from those of the most powerful and most absolute monarchies; they will always look upon every limit to the accomplishment of their will as an injustice, and they will be in a state of habitual conspiracy against the constitution of the kingdom, in order to make a dignity hereditary which has only been entrusted to them for their lives. They will even have for the subversion of the laws, an advantage which hereditary monarchs have not; that is to say, greater activity, a greater personal reputation, and a more immediate participation in affairs.

In hereditary monarchies, with an infinitely small number of exceptions, the king is only a great national elector, who names his ministers and his council, and who afterwards lays on them the whole burden of administration. In constitutional monarchies, this limitation of the personal activity of the king not only exists, but is of right; it is established by the law. It is understood that even the speeches of the king are composed by his ministers; that all acts done in the name of the king are suggested by these same ministers, who make themselves responsible for them: and that in England they obstinately resist the least suggestion, the least recommendation, that comes from the person of the king. In absolute monarchies, the kings do not any more reign themselves. All the power of the state is always in the hands of a council, of a cabinet, which renews itself by intrigues little known, divides all the functions, and commands him whom it appears to obey. All the sovereignty is always lodged in a strict oligarchy, only these oligarchies are not appointed either for their birth, or for their wealth, or for their celebrity, but by the intrigues of courtiers, if not even by corruption and vice. Some absolute monarchs neglect the business of the state for their pleasures; others regularly meet the councils, but are too timid to endeavour to make their opinion prevail over that of men whom they think better informed; others, in short, fancy they govern because they give many orders, which their favourites, their mistresses, or their confessors, have secretly suggested. The power belongs sometimes to public counsellors, sometimes to hidden ones; but except Frederick the Great, and perhaps the czar Peter, there is scarcely to be found one example of an hereditary sovereign, who was himself the soul of his government.

It is quite otherwise in elective monarchies, or under the founders of hereditary monarchies, who are themselves only elective kings. They must have given proof of aptitude in business, of activity of talent, of bravery, to arrive at the rank which they occupy. It is the man himself that has been chosen, not the family; it is the man who is formed to be the general, the administrator, the president of diets, the orator of the government. We have seen what Napoleon was in France; no mode of election, it is true, would easily find his equal. Without doubt, the greater part of the kings of Poland, most of the emperors of Germany, scarcely resembled him; but they had this relation to him, like him they were the soul of the government; their ministers were only their secretaries, and it was the kings alone who gave the impulse instead of receiving it. Those who prefer monarchical government, because they like better to obey a man than a council, or according to a popular expression, they would rather have one king than a hundred, ought to be satisfied only with an elective monarchy, for it is there alone that the individual reigns.

But how much more power will a king, who has himself exercised all the functions with which the law entrusts him, have to overthrow the constitution, than a king of England! He has not only chosen his ministers, he has appointed also, from his own personal knowledge, all the different agents of power, even to those nearest the people; it has always been his piercing eye which has distinguished merit, which has advanced it, but at the same time has enchained it to himself. He has prepared in his cabinet the laws submitted to the legislature; he conceives of them as a whole, and he sees at one glance all the measures which will only be presented in a detached form, to those who are to decide on them. He knows his own projects, and he compares the future, of which he is the sole master, with the present, beyond which his counsellors see nothing. The army is his, for he has commanded it in war, saved it in danger, made it illustrious by victory; still more, because he has formed it, by appointing all its officers, not by the often degrading favour of courts; not after the immoveable rules of age, which often place the most incapable in the first ranks, but from that merit which he has himself distinguished on the field of battle. Among the best citizens there are a great number who would rather trust to him than to national councils. Nor are these councils exempt from deceptive passions; representing the national mind, they can scarcely raise themselves above mediocrity, whilst genius is found in the great man whom the nation has chosen. Whenever his projects have been brought into opposition with common men, experience has taught them that his *coup d'œil* was more prompt and more just; his views more profound, and that he acted as if he already foresaw that future which others only recognise when long years are passed. But how great is their error, if this confidence given to genius leads them to second the projects of the chosen of the people, against the constitution of his country. It is because they look upon him as the only man, that they obey him, and the result of their obedience will be, that his like will never again be at the head of the state. It is because they love heroes, that they give up the power of choosing them, and condemn themselves to have only children of a great man, and children whom a proverb has declared degenerate and incapable of governing.

In fact, it is the singular consequence of elective monarchy, that the better have been its results, the nearer it has been to its ruin. Whenever a great man has been raised to the throne of the Empire, of Poland, of Hungary, he has taken advantage of a brilliant reign, of the lustre with which he has encompassed the nation, of the prosperity which he has been the cause of its enjoying, to change the constitution, to fix the crown in his own family, to leave the inheritance of a hero to an unworthy son. When, on the contrary, his talent was less brilliant, his popularity less seductive, the elective monarch has always taken advantage of his power to enrich and aggrandize his family at the expense of the crown, thus to change in a different way the constitution of the state. In the empire, monarchs have given to their sons the great fiefs which fall to the crown. Rodolph of Hapsburg disposed thus of Austria; Henry the Seventh, of Bohemia: in Hungary, the palatinates, in Poland, the starosties, which ought to have supported the lustre of the crown, were usurped by the children of the kings. The celibacy of ecclesiastical sovereigns has not secured their elective monarchies from this abuse; and the *nepotism* of Rome seems to be an evil inherent in this form of government.

Must we then renounce the signal advantages which seem attached to the concentration of executive power in the hands of one person; the vigour, the compactness, the instinctive knowledge of men, the presence of the head of the government under its banners? Must the country be deprived of those gigantic developments which genius obtains for her, when it is at the head of the state? We propose to examine in another article, the first of those expedients to which recourse has been had to reconcile the power of the favourite of the nation with the institutions and rights, whose duration it is the great object to preserve: it is temporary monarchy, or presidentship. We shall afterwards examine the expediency of the opposite system, that of fixed power, made so much the more uniform, as all extraordinary men are excluded from it: it is hereditary monarchy in all its different modifications.

ON

THE PRINCE,

OR,

EXECUTIVE POWER IN FREE COUNTRIES [a]

PART II.

WE thought there would be some advantage in reproducing, without alteration, the first part of this essay, such as it was printed, but not published, twelve years since. We have not, at the same time, the foolish vanity to think that we can learn nothing in politics at a time so fertile in instruction; in which experience has overthrown so many theories, shaken so many principles, and shed so much new light on the character of men, and of institutions. On the contrary, we feel the necessity of going unceasingly to the school of time and of facts, and we have learned to distrust ourselves as much as others. As, however, in a long life, we have already frequently had occasion to place ourselves in opposition to the extreme opinions which have by turns been dominant, it gives us some satisfaction in comparing what we have alleged against opposite systems, to find that we have been consistent with ourselves; and we believe that our readers will have more confidence in us, when they find us the same after ten, twenty, and thirty years of study [b].

[a] Extracted from the *Revue mensuelle d'Economie Politique*, October, 1834.

[b] I developed for the first time the principles which will be found here, in 1799, in my researches on the constitutions of free nations, which are not printed. I reproduced them in the History of the Italian Republics in 1807; in 1815 in the examination of the French constitution (*acte additionnel*), and elsewhere.

Besides, the end which we propose to ourselves now, as always, is not to present a theory, or new experiment on the constitution of power, but to make men feel in every country, that they ought to ameliorate the institutions they find established, instead of overthrowing them, in order to erect others; that the formation of social power is a work of time, which depends very little on legislators; that they ought, therefore, to receive it as a fact, which they can only modify for the common advantage; that by very different ways they may arrive at the same liberty, at the same improvement of social man; that there is in politics no orthodoxy out of which there is no salvation, and that even in admitting the ingenious theories by which every constitution has been explained afterwards, so much faith must not be given to them as to wish to transport them ready made, from one country to another. We can understand that one system may be less likely to be overthrown by experiments than another, and the revolutions, in the midst of which we have lived, have only served to confirm this.

J. J. Rousseau designated by the word Prince, that power, which in a free state, whatever else might be the nature of the government, had the office of directing the power of the community. There seems to us an advantage in preserving this denomination, preferably to that of Executive Power, more generally adopted at this time, but which supposes beforehand a division of functions which does not always exist. The Prince has often, in fact, an important part in the making of the laws, and he is not always exclusively entrusted with their execution.

The Prince, as he is the first in regard to the happiness of all, is in fact the most important of all the social powers; the existence of a community is a state of continual struggle with all its neighbours, with its own members, with nature itself. It must unceasingly defend its rights against the intrigues, the cupidity, the jealousy of other states, either by skilful negotiations, or by open force; the prince who should be the intelligence and the will of this community, who should watch over it and direct its arm, who should give a common impulse to all its efforts, prevent or repress internal disorder, provide against the calamities of the seasons, the fury of the elements, or repair the disasters they have caused; the prince would need to know everything, to foresee everything; the slightest imprudence on his part may expose the citizens to enormous sacrifices, or to their complete ruin, and to that of their country; his arrogance may provoke war, his humility compromise honour; his versatility will cause loss of confidence in him; his prodigality will multiply expenses, or destroy resources; by parsimony in small economies he may abandon great advantages. There is not one quality, not one virtue which adorns the most distinguished character, which a nation ought not to desire in her prince, the absence of which may not be to her the cause of the cruellest suffering. Vigilance, prudence, constancy, valour, mildness, economy, order, and justice, are by turns required to govern men; and there is not a weakness or a fault of the prince which nations must not grievously expiate.

Political science does not teach us how it is possible to obtain so many brilliant qualities in a government; but it can show us at least what are the defects, what are the inconveniences almost always inherent in certain forms; it teaches us also from what elements of society certain qualities may be expected: it is to the classing of these results of theory, still more of experience, that we intend to devote the following pages.

The existence of the prince is rarely the result of the combinations of the legislator, the product of a charter; it is not by the words of a man, or of a law, that authority and obedience can be created. It is very well to acknowledge as a principle that order is necessary to society, that obedience guarantees the safety of each: all obedience occasions some disorder or some sacrifice, and if before resolving to obey, each one was to examine whether it would be useful to himself, obedience would be very rare, and power could only proceed by the force of punishment. This is nearly the state of a nation after a revolution, or some great social convulsion: the habit of resistance is contracted, authority seems to have only the right to persuade; each order is followed by deliberation, by hesitation; and even should the revolution have established the most liberal principles of government, the prince will find it requisite to employ more restraint, more threats, more punishments to procure the execution of much less severe orders, than were before necessary to obtain the greatest sacrifices, when the illusion was complete, and when each of his injunctions seemed to be supported by all the weight of society. In general, power has been formed by a combination of accidents, which have consolidated it in certain hands. When it exists it may be made use of, it may be regulated, but it is never created.

We shall, however, study the origin of power, as if it were the effect of the will of the people, and we shall ask what is the presiding idea in each form of government, the idea which explains it; not that this idea has been really the cause of its origin, but because being satisfactory to the reason of men, it justifies their obedience, and preserves an order which it did not establish.

It is in this way that we shall consider the power of the people, as being the establishment of the first social power, if not according to the order of time, at least in that of our conceptions. No one, said men at the commencement of society, and especially when it regarded small nations still rude, where all felt themselves nearly equal in intelligence, and equally animated by common danger, no one can take a greater interest in us than ourselves; no one can conduct our affairs more diligently, or will be so incapable of being led astray, or bribed; we will bring to a common fund all our knowledge, all our prudence, as well as all our patriotism, and the sum of all will be greater than the portion of it possessed by the most distinguished man could be. We must have, it is true, chiefs to fight, judges to settle our differences, and secretaries to write our orders; but we will choose them ourselves, dismiss them when we please; we will never permit them to be anything but our clerks, the instruments of our will, and in every important circumstance, even in the army, even before a combat, we will vote before we act.

Such was nearly the origin and the constitution of the Grecian democracies, which on the frontiers of the Persian empire organized themselves to resist the Great King; of the small Swiss cantons which made head against the house of Austria; of the Suliotes, the Sphakiotes, the Maniotes, who maintained themselves against the Turks; the immensity of danger only allowed of one thought and one interest throughout the whole population; patriotism was carried to the highest point to which it has ever risen among men, and these small democracies shone forth with a virtue, a courage, and a devotion, which will for ever excite admiration.

But the danger did not continue for ever; equality, the consequence of their poverty, could not be maintained, and when they began to know the difference of rich and poor, they also became acquainted with different interests, as well as with different degrees of information, of experience, and of skill. Instead of being moved by one common will, which might be called unanimous, as in the time of patriotism and of danger, they were divided into majority and minority, still more into leaders and led; many then changed their government; some allowed the social bond to be slowly dissolved, as the Ætolians, and many nations of Greece, remaining without glory, and without cities; or, like the Grisons in our time, democratic liberty is preserved in the villages, but the prince, the social power, is nowhere.

Some republics maintained their democracy even in their highest civilization, and at their head shines Athens. The torch of mind and of philosophy then enlightened that form of government, and showed those qualities of it which had not been divined beforehand. The first result of observation is, that the will of the people, as it manifests itself by votes, is not the sum of the wills and the intelligence of those who compose it, and that, in every deliberative assembly, the vote of each one on every decision which is to be made, is not identical with what would have been that of this same individual, if he had had to decide alone.

For the interests of morality, for the sake of the improvement of man, we must often combat selfishness, we must often require that utility, that a more immediate personal interest should be subordinate to the consideration of what is just and proper; that the individual should not see only his own safety, his own advantage, his own enjoyment, but that he should be accessible to the inspirations of imagination and of sensibility; that he should admire the beautiful for itself, that he should obey the charms of sympathy and benevolence; but continually meeting with selfishness in man, we do not, perhaps, sufficiently comprehend how necessary it is for the preservation of the individual, that self-interest should be an ever-vigilant sentinel at the bottom of his heart, to raise the cry of alarm when there is danger of his being sacrificed. It is a narrow and false philosophy which finds in self-interest the sole motive of our actions, but it would be denying evidence to refuse admitting its constant influence; we shall rather see in it a law of Providence for the preservation of the species, an ever-attentive monitor, like the fear of pain in the physical laws, without which we should not avoid evil in time to preserve our lives. Social bodies, formed by man, have need of this monitor, which God has put into the heart of every individual. There must be a national selfishness, which is not to decide alone, but which must be first heard in every deliberation. The Prince should be the organ of this selfishness: before every other thought he should be always alive to the interest of preservation in this body, under pain of soon seeing it perish.

Now experience has taught, that in democracies this feeling never presents itself the first. When all concur in power, no citizen strips off the individual self, to consider himself as government. Whereas, if the question is as to a decision to be taken for and by himself alone, he would see his own interest in the first place, then secondly, sympathy, sensibility, imagination, perhaps the sentiment of duty. At the moment when the citizen is called upon to vote with his fellow citizens on the conduct of the nation of which he forms a part, he sets completely aside, perhaps without perceiving it himself, the motives which determine his vote; or rather, he finds them in that order in which they relate to himself, and not to the nation. The interest of the nation discovers itself to him only in the third or fourth degree. He listens before everything else to his private interest, when by chance he finds it opposed to the public interest, on which he is going to give his suffrage; but afterwards he is influenced by all his other faculties undiminished, sympathy, generosity, anger, fear, the point of honour, the influence of eloquence or imagination. Every one speaks as loudly on public affairs as on private ones, whilst true public interest, national selfishness, is only felt last, and in proportion to the infinitely small part which the citizen, as a private man, feels in the decision which is to be made. Most frequently in public deliberations the citizen has only the most vague perception either of public interest or of his own private interest. He votes as a form, without calculation, without reflection, without fixing his thoughts, till the moment when his imagination, his sensibility, or his passions are excited; then only it is with his whole soul that he takes a part in the formation of the public will.

This supineness of national self-love, whilst all the other faculties are strongly excited, gives to the management of democracies a very peculiar character. The sovereign people, the nation as Prince, is much more susceptible of generous emotions than any other sovereign; but it also brings to the conducting of affairs much less steadiness and wisdom—it compromises itself, it exposes itself, and it brings upon itself calamities which a more constant remembrance of its own interests would have avoided. Its pity will be profound when the image of suffering is before it; its decisions, on the contrary, will be often cruel, if it is only by reflection, which it never knows, that it can imagine the evil which anger and offended pride, or vengeance, may induce it to commit. If the question is on a declaration of war, it will not calculate either the dangers or the sacrifices, because the individual risk of each citizen is very little, and his responsibility is still less, whilst the satisfaction which is caused by pursuing the dictates of passion is much more lively than if it regarded himself alone, for all passions are excited in a crowd. On the other side, when it becomes necessary to make peace, the sovereign people will perhaps humble itself more than any other sovereign, for it will then take counsel of fear, and fear is always contagious.

A very natural calculation has led to the supposition, that by uniting many heads much intelligence and many virtues are also united; experience alone has taught, that each one comes to the deliberation, from whence the common will must spring, with attention less strong, a will less firm, a less complete appreciation of consequences, than if he had to decide alone. His responsibility as to the event is diminished in proportion to the number of his colleagues; sometimes he attaches so little importance to it, that men have been seen to laugh at the folly they were going to commit. They laughed with Aristophanes at the image of the imbecile old man, Demos, which he presented to them; the most bitter derision flattered them, because they would only see that part of it which fell on others, though like them they contributed their share to making the vote irrational. Sometimes the citizen, through indolence of mind or from indecision, rests on others. Sometimes from a wish to shine he proposes the most hazardous resolution, that which will give the highest idea of his heroism, of his disinterestedness, without caring for the consequences. Sometimes, on the contrary, yielding to baser considerations, he will attach himself to the weakest, the most perfidious, the most cruel side, because, considering it as useful, he calculates that his name will be lost in the crowd, and that he shall escape blame. Sometimes, even, he will do both at a time, if the votes are secret; he will speak on one side for reputation, he will vote on the other for profit. All numerous assemblies which take a share in the government, may to a certain point give an idea of assemblies of the people, and France need only study the votes of the Chamber of Deputies to understand how a numerous body may show less knowledge of what it decides on, less consistency, less prudence and elevation of mind, than each one of the members of which it is composed would have shown if his opinion had been taken apart.

In every thing the sovereign people acts as a man would do who obeyed every motive to human action, except self-love; who should be deprived of this security to personal interest, which Providence has given to all for their preservation, and who consequently would continually risk his existence from generosity, from imprudence, or from passion. But the people as government, the nation as prince, as was the case in Athens, was besides exposed to all the seductions of power, to all the corrupting intrigues which elsewhere crowd and cross one another around kings, to obtain favours from them. The people of Athens elected generals, elected ambassadors, elected all the officers entrusted with the care of public works, with the police, with all the details of administration. Sometimes in choosing for the highest functions it showed great tact in discovering the most skilful; but often also it showed itself accessible to seduction, to flattery, to feasts, to gifts. It preferred an amusing man to a man of genius; it was infatuated with despicable favourites, such as Cleon, made famous by Aristophanes, and allowed itself to be led with as much folly as the most doting despot.

It was particularly as responsible for the safety of the state that the people of Athens exhibited a proof of the defects and dangers of democracy, whether in taking arms without sufficient motives, or in laying them down from panics; whether in ruining its allies by exacting from them exorbitant subsidies, or in dissipating its own finances in feasts and scenic games; whether by wreaking its anger on men scarcely guilty, or hiding with imprudent indulgence the most criminal enterprizes. Thus antiquity, then enlightened by experiments which are wanting in our days, stamped with unanimous reprobation democratic government, or the system which puts the executive power in absolute dependence on the people. It condemns the nation as prince, possessing the executive power, as being the most imprudent, the most inconstant, the most presumptuous in success, the soonest cast down by reverses, the most obstinate in refusing all taxation, at the same time the most prodigal in expense of any prince to whom men can be subject.

Contemporary observation, when it is applied to the small Swiss cantons, has not certainly such excesses to bring forward; but it is equally impossible to praise the prudence of democracies, whilst they can be reproached with that necessity in which all persons elected by the people find themselves, of flattering the passions of the multitude and yielding to their caprices; the difficulty of causing the laws and the magistrates to be respected by men, who after having made them think they have a right to unmake them; that want of discipline, which in the wars of the sixteenth century so often subjected the Swiss captains to the impetuous decisions of the Landsgemeinde assembled among their own soldiers; in short, that disposition to infatuation and to favouritism which, if it did not give tyrants to the cantons, as it did to the Greek democracies, subjected them, however, almost always to the dominion of some leader.

Whether the people have in themselves a feeling of their own incapacity to govern, of their sufferings under their own government, whether their disposition to infatuation has made them deposit all their prerogatives in the hands of a favourite, or a powerful man has raised himself by violence or cunning, in spite of the popular will, the government of one has always been founded on a principle diametrically opposite to that of government by all. Experience showed that each one did his part very ill in the affairs of all; they wished to try if one, more skilful, would not manage better the affairs of all when they became his own. If the head of the people came to regard the honour of the citizens, their power, their riches, as being his own, perhaps, like the good father of a family, he would only think of increasing them; at least he could no longer think of placing his own person and advantages in opposition to the persons and advantages of his subjects. Why, said they, to the man whom they entrusted with the care of their destinies, why do you wish to increase your treasures? Your wealth is ours; the more freedom you leave us the more will we labour for you, in a profitable manner. Why would you reserve your strength to bend our will? Our will is yours; all that you have decided is law to us. Why do you think of aggrandizing your children at our expense? Your children are ours; as you have been our master, they will be our masters in their turn. We abandon to you all our interests, that between you and us there may never be occasion to say *mine and thine*. Whether language may or may not have expressed these thoughts, whether the contract may or may not have been put into form, is of little consequence, it is the rational idea of despotism, it is the ground on which it is at this time defended, when its partisans or its servants endeavour to explain it.

There must always be a truth at the foundation of a system to which great masses of men attach themselves; and so large a part of the human race have lived, and still live under despotism, angrily resisting every attempt to make their escape from it, that a true idea, perhaps even without their knowledge, must be the anchor to which it is attached. In fact, the necessity of blending personal interest with the interest of the state in the minds and feelings of its governors, is a true idea. Every one's business is no one's business. As long as each depository of power will weigh public good against private good, it may be possible, by awakening his virtue, his honour, to make him acknowledge the duty of preferring the first; but all his interests, all his natural appetites, will make him lean towards the second. If he yields to them, which most often happens, there will be corruptive waste of the public possessions; if he resists them weakly, which is more frequent still, there will be want of care, even if he triumphs over them; the double impulse will always make itself felt, and he will not give himself heart and soul to the public weal, as he would have done to his own.

But though an idea may be true, it is not therefore necessary that the system which rests on it should be true also. It does not suffice for a despot to say, *l'état, c'est moi* (*the state, it is I*), or even always to act upon this idea, in order for the state to find that it is as much cared for as his own person. There are, in this *I*, noble passions and base passions, elevated sentiments and gross appetites. Now our experience teaches us, that a certain restraint is necessary to habituate man to prefer the first to the last, so that he who is habitually placed beyond and above all restraint, will most habitually make the contrary choice. *I am the state*, says the despot, but I prefer the pleasures of to-day to the hopes of to-morrow, and all the security which his subjects expected to derive from his foresight, are lost to them by this one choice; virtue gives place to licence, and one man is seen to consume in a day what might have sufficed all for years. *I am the state*, but I am tired of seeing that nothing resists me; I require stronger emotions, I require to conquer wills opposed to mine, which do not present themselves at home; I want the great game of war, it is so much the more seductive to me, the more its chances are hazardous, and after all, that suffering which I run the risk of my provinces experiencing, does not disturb my sleep. *I am the state*, but there are beyond this *I*, wills which resist me and which offend me so much the more, because I am accustomed to have every thing yield to me. I would give my blood, as I give that of my subjects, for revenge. And despots, in fact, have shown themselves luxurious, prodigal, greedy of war, vindictive, cruel, not like men in general, but infinitely more so, because they have infinitely more excitement for their passions, infinitely less restraint to form their virtue or their understandings. The blending of the state with their person, can only increase the suffering of the first when they are stupid or vicious.

The same wearings of popular convulsions, the same impatience of reverses, brought on by faults continually repeated, which have led many nations to trust themselves in the power of one, decided others to have recourse to the direction of a small number of wise men, to commit, according to the etymology of the word, force, empire, κράτος, to the best, to the most esteemed, Αριστοι; thus arose aristocracy, Ἀριστοκράτεια. The government of the people having constantly sinned, by its nature, against the principle of making the interests of the governed be cared for by the governors as their own, there was an endeavour to introduce even into the most democratic constitutions of which we have any knowledge, bodies made almost independent of the people, councils destined to temper their authority, and to limit their sovereignty. It was thought desirable also to give representatives and guardians to the spirit of conservatism, to introduce some fixedness, some memories of the past, some foresight of the future, amidst democratic fluctuations; above all, it was wished to devote to the worship of prudence, of constancy, of economy, some old men less accessible to enthusiasm, less influenced by eloquence, less greedy of the emotions of the imagination, than assemblies where all being admitted, the young necessarily formed the great majority.

If, even now that the chances of life have been so much increased by the progress of science in preserving health and of medicine, half the individuals who are born do not arrive at the age of thirty, old men must have been infinitely more rare in the origin of nations when the probabilities of life were so much lower. Old men cast into the middle of an assembly where all the votes were equal, formed an imperceptible minority without any political influence; the assembly must, in spite of them, retain in its decisions all the impetuosity of youth. Happily that respect for grey hairs, which we seldom find now, was in the origin of society a corrective to this legal oppression of old age. Almost all nations, even those the most jealous of their liberty, felt that the advantages of the prudence and experience of old men would be lost, if their votes were only counted with those of the crowd, and if they were always thrown into the minority. Amongst almost all nations, the name of the first social distinctions points out that they were bestowed on old age. The names of gerontes, of senators, of patricians, of seigneurs, of aldermen, all present the same idea. By making a separate body of old men, and calling upon it to give its approbation before or after the vote of all the rest, it was only putting them on a footing of equality with the generation which would soon follow; but the certainty of hearing their opinion was secured, since experience had taught that the qualities and defects of advanced age, are in general in contrast to those of the majorities where the young rule.

However, nowhere, perhaps, was age the only distinction required in order to admit old men into those senates, into those aristocratic bodies which were intended to balance the power of the people. The progress of age, which ripens and purifies elevated minds, weakens, on the contrary, and renders inert, those of ordinary qualities; it was not desirable to make dotage a support to the republic; a choice was necessary; always and everywhere the object was to find in what way to distinguish the wisest and most virtuous, that to them alone might be intrusted that moderating power the want of which was acknowledged. Above all, it was desirable that they should not be nominated by the people, for it was felt, that barriers which the people raised, changed, and overthrew at their pleasure, would be no security against their caprice. If the senators were elected by the people, at least it was desirable that it should be for life, to make them thenceforward independent of their electors; or that to the senate should be left the right of renewing itself; or at least that it should present candidates to the people, or choose from candidates named by the people. It was important to inspire those elected by such means with a sense of the value of their body, which might give them energy enough to say to the popular assembly, So far shalt thou go, and no farther.

We have said that there is not one of the democracies whose spirit we have endeavoured to explain, in the midst of which has not been seen to arise some aristocratic body, some senate commissioned to assist and direct the magistrates in whom we recognize the more immediate deputies of the people. The inconsistency, the caprice, and the improvidence of popular assemblies were so notorious, that no democracy thought it could dispense with these preservers of national prudence; but the jealousy excited by every distinction, the impatience which withstood any resistance, most frequently did not permit the senates to use their prerogatives: they were immediately attacked by the demagogues in the name of the sovereignty of the people, and the flood soon overturned the dike which they had made efforts to raise; thus the greater part of the Greek cities, of Athens, and the small Swiss cantons, remained democracies in spite of the weak aristocratic institutions which they had introduced into their constitutions.

But it was not long before there were nations who said to the aristocracies as others had said to the despots, "Look upon us as your property, take care of us as if we were your inheritance; do not put your interest in opposition to ours, for we desire that our wealth should always be at your disposal, that our valour should extend your empire, that our glory should be yours, and that you should always be the organ of our will." Nations in consternation at some calamity which they had drawn upon themselves, ashamed at the results of their deliberations, irritated by the vices and deceptions of their deputies, pass, sometimes with extreme rapidity, from one excess to another. After having felt the most violent jealousy of all inequality, of all distinction, they are all at once disgusted with themselves, they despond under reverses, they see in their own counsels only error and incapacity, and they throw themselves, blinded and without conditions, into the hands of those they think more skilful; but when they have once abandoned themselves to an aristocracy, it is no longer in their own power to get rid of it themselves.

Before going farther, it is necessary to protest against an abuse of language which the passions of our own times have introduced, and which makes it impossible to arrive at any clear idea on constitutive policy. We have seen not only what was the sense of the word aristocracy, the *power of the best*, but also what was its origin, what was the end designed for this power, *distinction in old age*. There exists, however, especially in modern society, a class whose origin is quite different, whose spirit is still more different; it is nobility, which almost all the world agrees to call also aristocracy. The nobility of monarchies has a double origin: part of it is feudal; it was not created for any social object, but has created itself. Amidst the convulsions of a society, which was falling into dissolution, chiefs of soldiers, and masters of slaves, seized on land sufficient to maintain the troop of men eager to obey them; they built strong castles, where they could brave every foreign attack; they persuaded those among whom they divided their lands, that it was they who fed them, and they founded their dominion on interest, force, and fear: feudalism was a federation of small despots; the good or the evil which it has done has no resemblance to the republican origin of aristocracy. On this feudalism has been engrafted, for the last four centuries, a more recent nobility, produced by the favour or service [a] of courts, and by servility in employments given or sold by the monarch. This courtier nobility and this law nobility has also no relation to the aristocracy of republics; their qualities and their defects have quite opposite characters, and the results of experience as applied to aristocracy cannot be applied to nobility without sanctioning the most false ideas. We must submit, however, to this perversion of language, the result of political passions, which has made aristocrat and gentleman into two words almost

[a] *Valetage*, "flunkeyism."—*Carlyle.*

synonymous, since we have no other to designate those peculiar creations of a totally different system, the aristocracies of Greece, and Rome, of Venice and of Berne, which present results so worthy of being studied among the elements of government.

Republican aristocracy, that is to say, the concentration of power in the hands of a body of old men, chosen as being the most able, has always, both in its virtues and its defects, presented a character diametrically opposite to that of democracy. In fact, whilst the simple citizen comes to the popular assembly with a vague desire to do what is best for his country, a desire modified, however, by his personal interest, always present to his mind; whilst scarcely interrupting his daily occupations, he preserves in regard to public affairs only an uncertain recollection of the past, has no fixed system for the present, and feels the vanity of thinking for the future; the senator, on the contrary, has made these public functions the passion of his life, and has prepared himself for them in his youth, as for the highest distinction which he can obtain in his country, the reward of all his efforts: the interest of the body to which he belongs, or the interest of the public weal which he regards as the interest of that body, surpass personal interest in his mind. That national self-love which is absolutely wanting in democracies, which is found in monarchies, but blind and corrupted, is the soul of aristocracies; it is the sole object of every mind, and of minds exercised by collision, by the study of tradition, and by emulation. It must not be expected from the senates of aristocracies, that they should listen either to generosity or gratitude, or pity, in preference to public utility; sympathy scarcely acts on them; eloquence, far from influencing them, excites their distrust; the private conscience of each senator is reduced to silence by that name of country or public good, which with all presents the idea of their first interest and their first duty. The only virtue of aristocracies is their love of this country, such as they have made it; but their qualifications are numerous, and such as are found in no other government. The most able men in the nation applying their thoughts unceasingly to calculate the results of every circumstance, the republic acquires a treasure of skill and experience, and transmits it as a tradition uninterruptedly to posterity; it embraces with its observing glance all the past, and all the future. The conduct and the spirit of monarchies are seen to change with every reign, or even to be modified from year to year, as the prince advances in age; popular assemblies are seen to run from one extreme to another, according as they yield to the impressions of the imagination, of sensibility or of passion; but the senate of an aristocracy rests immoveable in the same idea; the successive renewal of its members does not change its spirit, which the dying transmit, with their experience, to their successors, as a sacred inheritance; their prudence, their moderation in success, their constancy in reverses, make part of this immoveable system; in fact, the average of the wisdom of the wisest of a nation must always be the same.

When the people said to kings that they gave themselves to them for ever, kings believed it, and soon fancied that they had a divine right to their subjects. When the people held the same language to aristocracies, they were never deceived by it, they felt that they held their power on account of their superior ability: seeing the people asleep, they did not forget the force which they might show on awakening; and they guarded particularly against everything which might excite their passions. Distrustful and cruel in regard to affairs of state, they wished to prevent the first attacks on their authority by a system of spies and by the fear of punishment; but when their prerogative did not seem in danger, they maintained equal justice with a vigorous hand; in economy, in the order of their finances, they surpassed all known governments, for they dreaded, above everything, to have to ask money from the people. They wished to impress on the governed fear and respect for the governors; at the same time they endeavoured to efface the idea of individuals, and to present to the mind only the abstract idea of the republic or of her image, the lion of St. Mark, the bear of Berne; no name is brought forwards; the object of all usages is an endeavour to maintain equality on two levels, one among those who command, the other among those who obey. With this object aristocracies have invented sumptuary laws, that the senators, their wives, and their children might never excite the jealousy of the people by their dress or their equipages; in almost all the aristocracies of Italy and Switzerland they were allowed to wear in the city only a uniform dress, simple, and of the colour of black; the Venetians added to this the custom of never appearing in public without a mask, that a rich or powerful man might not have the same wish to shine, since he must not be known.

Even in republics might be distinguished the aristocracy of bodies and that of races; in some, the power and the life of the state might be found concentrated in elective bodies; in others they were preserved in hereditary races. Under whatever form the government of a small number presents itself, its great aim always was, even in spite of the laws, to restrict its distinctions to some families only. But aristocracy is not powerful, is not able, is not enriched by virtues peculiar to itself, unless election alone, distinguishing merit, opens the door of councils. It becomes corrupt, on the contrary; it tends already towards ruin when it becomes an aristocracy of race, when to be born of a patrician family is enough to be secure of arriving at power. Aristocracy is the most durable of all governments; but as all human things decay, aristocracies also fall when they seek to be confounded with the nobility of monarchies; they fall when yielding entirely to the inclination to shut themselves up in the restricted circle of some families, they admit the inheritance of power without election, and lose the stamp of age which election had impressed on them. In wonderful Venice, eldest daughter of the Roman empire, who long maintained herself on an equal footing with the most powerful monarchies, after twelve centuries of wisdom, the spirit of family distinction was seen to acquire the ascendancy over the spirit of civic bodies: then private cupidity divided the riches of the state; then young Venetian gentlemen, who were required only to prove their birth and their age of twenty-five, in order to admit them to the councils, displayed their vices and their insolence before the eyes of a people whom they had accustomed themselves to despise; and the old senators, no longer daring to depend on the virtue of former times, themselves favoured the public license, that no one might have a right to reproach the aristocracy with the corruption of manners.

Even at the period when aristocracies are in possession of all their virtue, they do not answer the end which a nation ought to propose to itself in its government. No doubt when men are forgotten, that the state only may be thought of, no form of government can be found which secures it more vitality; it scarcely ever experiences any changes; it knows no internal disturbance of any kind; it provides for the safety, the prosperity, even for the splendour of the state, at less expense than any other; it takes care of the physical interests of the nation; it protects and develops its commerce and agriculture; it maintains it in peace and abundance, with honour and without sacrifices; but it opposes an almost insurmountable obstacle to that moral improvement which is also one of the great objects of association. The views of the citizens are continually circumscribed and brought down to the earth; all mental activity, all distinction excites the jealousy of power, all glory is a beginning of danger; and as soon as a citizen leaves the path which is traced out for him beforehand, he feels himself watched, persecuted, oppressed by an invisible but all powerful enmity; there no longer exists for him liberty, justice, or safety, by his domestic hearth; he is not secured by any of the common laws of humanity; the state requires, in order to be great, that all men should be small.

Till our time at least, it has been a truth long acknowledged, that none of the three simple forms of government were suited to secure to a nation what it always ought to propose to itself, the union of happiness and improvement. It was a truth acknowledged by the philosophers of antiquity, as well as by all the publicists of the last century, that a really wise, free, and protecting constitution could only be formed by borrowing what was best from each of these three forms. Thus, in reviewing them, we have not so much proposed to ourselves to confirm this often repeated truth as to seek in each form its prominent virtue, to observe the qualities and advantages which it is desirable to borrow from each, in order to arrive at a wisely balanced constitution. However, a new system seems to prevail at this time under the name of Sovereignty of the People; it again questions all those truths so long established by experience. The violent revolution which has withdrawn the French nation from the yoke, and still more from the insolence of a feudal and courtier nobility, has left wounds in all hearts; both parties, yielding to their hatred of one another, do not understand how they can concur in the same government. It is often repeated, that the nobility is as nothing in the customs and manners of this age, that it is dead, that its influence is extinguished for ever. Nevertheless, judging by the jealousy with which it is continually watched, by the hatred which bursts forth whenever it gains some distinction, it must be acknowledged that it still acts strongly on popular feeling; but what is strange is, that since it was attacked with that war-cry, *à l'aristocratie*, no other aristocracy has been acknowledged. In vain it takes for its characteristic the hierarchy of rank and of inequality; in vain it thinks to shine only by elegance, bravery, frivolity, obedience; it calls itself faithful, it calls itself young and brilliant. It is from such an aristocracy that those aristocracies are judged of, whose characteristics are the morose prudence of old age, the pride which acknowledges no superior, the suppression of all splendour and of all pomp, the practice of economy and silence; it is almost established as a principle, that no aristocracy of any kind can be admitted into a free government. The monarchical element, it is true, is called upon to form a part of it conjointly with the popular element, but at the same time to the king must be left neither independence nor the right to have a will; he is only required to name the ministers which are pointed out to him by opinion, on the condition that he shall dismiss them when they have lost the favour of a purely popular assembly. The foundation is laid in the sovereignty of the people, but a confusion of ideas is thus produced which would soon deprive the people of their liberty. Without doubt the constitutional organization of a nation, the legitimacy of all the powers she contains in her bosom, and which ought to concur in guarding and securing her happiness, exist in the name of the national will expressed or understood; for the sole end of their creation has been the greatest good of all, their only right to existence is still this greatest good. This sovereign will, also manifests itself sometimes in the midst of revolutions, a terrible remedy for extreme evils, for it then overturns long before it reconstructs. But this sovereignty, which has established the very bases of society, must not be confounded with that popular action which is exercised by forms predetermined by the constitution; then democracy is not the whole nation, the sovereign nation, it is only one of the voices which concur in the expression of the national will. It must be independent, but it must also allow their independence to the monarchical element, to the aristocratic element; if it governs them, if it pretends to exercise sovereignty over them, there is no longer any balance, there is no longer any constitution, there is no longer the possibility of government.

Thus it seems to us that the party which, calling itself republican, inscribes on its banners *equality*, makes a republic impossible. "Government," we heard the Emperor Napoleon say during the hundred days, "government is like navigation, there must be two elements to be able to navigate; there must be two also to direct the vessel of the state, so that one may be a counterpoise to the other. Balloons can never be directed, because floating on only one element there is no fulcrum to resist the tempests which agitate this element. In the same way there is no *point d'appui*, no possibility of direction in pure democracy; but by combining it with aristocracy, one is opposed to the other, and the vessel is directed by contrary passions." Let us resume these divers elements which it is necessary to unite in the constitution of the state, and let us see under what relation each of them is fitted to concur in the common object, the happiness and the improvement of all.

The interest of all demands one share of the government for the monarchical element, or, that in a certain number of circumstances power should be assigned to the will of one, rather than to the will either of a council or of a body. We have already seen how far the result of a common deliberation is from presenting the sum of the prudence or virtue of all those who took part in it, how far each voter is from preparing his vote by an attention as intense, an appreciation as complete, of all the points of view of the question, as profound a feeling of his responsibility, as if the decision rested on him alone. To these motives to refer the command to one only, (it is the proper and etymological sense of the word monarchy,) is joined the necessity of prompt decision, of entire secrecy, the necessity of calling to the assistance of the state, that devotion, that enthusiasm with which one man only, by his personal qualities, can inspire other men; the need to profit by that penetrating glance with which a man discovers the talents, the virtues and defects of others, which cannot be rendered into language, and which cannot be appreciated by a council; the necessity of placing on the theatre of action a judge and appreciator of merit, who will know how to reward it.

In war, that most important and most critical function of government, when the existence of a state depends perhaps on the quick penetration of the prince, on the promptitude and secrecy of his decisions, the necessity of recurring to monarchical power has been universally felt. It is in war that all the energy of a nation is called into action, when all the citizens are called upon to make the greatest sacrifices, when they must stake, without hesitating, their fortunes, their liberties, their lives; all the advantages which social order is required to secure are then abandoned to the discretion of government, and the consequences of its faults would be terrible. It is the moment, however, when the freest nations have felt the necessity of laying aside their mistrusts, of abandoning themselves without reserve to the power of one, and of redoubling the severity of discipline that the habit of discussion and disobedience may not pass from public assemblies to the camp.

In the origin of society, judicial power was also habitually confided to the prince. Let us choose a king to judge us, is the cry which history ascribes to more than one nation. In fact, judicial decisions require that unity of appreciation, and that undivided responsibility, which can only be found in an individual and not in bodies. At the conclusion of our long series of experiments, Bentham, who had made tribunals his principal study, and whose opinions are more democratic than those of any other philosopher, requires as a security for the knowledge, attention and conscientiousness of the judge, that he should be always alone in his tribunal. Society appeared to him to require, both the complete independence of the judge as regards the sovereign people, as well as of every other sovereign, and an unreserved confidence in his individual conscience, that his judgments may be guaranteed by his character, by his convictions, and by his moral responsibility. This appeal which nations have thought it best to make to the knowledge and conscience of the individual, to the monarchical element, in giving judgment, is found even in the institution which seems most to deviate from it, and whose singularity must be explained by this principle. The English have formed their jury of twelve persons, but they are required to decide unanimously; it is because they have no confidence in deliberations, or in the majority of an assembly; they appeal to the conscience of one man only; they wish each citizen to decide by his own understanding, and without regarding the opinion of another; but they require that this individual judgment should be twelve times repeated, because the question being on the evidence of a fact, they supposed that these twelve individual judgments ought to be all alike.

In all prompt decisions, on all occasions regarding public safety, the monarchical power is also called upon to act independently, in order to procure for a great nation all the advantages of the quick and comprehensive view, the promptitude and energy of one single man: in all negotiations with foreign nations, the necessity is equally felt of perfect secrecy, of prompt decision, of bringing under one point of view, and regarding in the same spirit, all the questions and all the interests which are in suspense.

If the individual to whom the command has been decreed cannot alone fulfil all the functions which the community requires from one man, the same motives seem to exact that at least he should nominate the other individuals who are to stand in his place: such are all those who will be called on to act alone, to exercise personal authority; all those who in any way represent him, and are vice monarchs, all officers of the army and navy, all judges, all defenders of public order, all ambassadors, agents, and those employed in negotiations with foreign countries.

It is impossible not to be alarmed at this enumeration merely of the monarchical functions. The nation is called upon to place in the hands of her chief, all her means of defence or power, whether in her interior, or in her armies, or in her relations with foreign nations, but there is not one which may not occasionally become a means of attack against her and against her liberties; there is not one of them which does not, by the enjoyment which it is the means of procuring, excite in him with whom it is deposited, a longing to increase it, and to appropriate it to himself; there is not one which does not, by the contests in which it engages him, accustom his mind to the desire of suppressing all resistance. Though liberty may also perish by the usurpation, or by the faults of the two other powers, yet it is against the enterprizes of the monarchical power that the nation should habitually be on her guard.

The limitations attached to monarchical power are of several kinds; the most important is that which relates to its duration; since on that is founded the distinction between republics and monarchies. In many free states, the royal power has thus been divided between two equal chiefs; in many, a senate is associated to the chief, so that the latter exercises only those functions in which all consultation would be impossible, whilst with respect to others the authority of the head is watched and limited by the aristocracy of bodies in republics, by the aristocracy of race in monarchies; in short it has often been made impossible for monarchs to exercise those functions which seemed created only for a single person.

I repeat it; among these different systems I do not pretend to decide which is best. I believe that in every nation a system has almost always been founded on antecedent ones; that facts govern it, that powers existed before a nation was called upon to give laws to herself, and that the great skill of the legislator consists in respecting these facts, in profiting by these powers, and in placing the future in harmony with the past. But I am a republican as regards Switzerland, and Geneva, my country; I am one as regards America and all new countries; I am one as to all countries so entirely overthrown by revolutions that the vestiges of the past have disappeared; I am one by all those recollections of love, duty, and gratitude, which connect those of my family with the republics of Pisa and Geneva. I think liberty equally possible in a constitutional monarchy as in a republic; I think this road to perfection the most sure for many nations; but if it was attempted to introduce it into my country, I hope there is not a Swiss who would not be ready to sacrifice fortune and life rather than submit to the establishment of a king.

We have seen that what constitutes the monarchical element is unity of will, and not duration. This unity may be found not only in a president chosen for four or eight years, as in the United States, but in two consuls nominated for a year, as at Rome. The consuls in fact did not deliberate together, did not act by a common will; each was king over his own part and in that province assigned to him; each was king, and exercised all the royal functions according to his own ideas, by his own will; each one was supreme chief of the army, supreme head of justice, and till the time of the institution of prætors, supreme head of the administration to ward off any injury which might threaten the republic; alone called on to name all subordinates in the army, all agents in foreign negotiations. The equality between the consuls and their independence of one another was considered as a guarantee against the usurpation of either of them; and in fact, though always at the head of armies, though often intoxicated with victory, during four hundred and twenty-two years they were never seen to attempt to make themselves absolute, or to perpetuate their power; the bosom of their country was never torn by civil war. No other government in the world has been so long secured against all temptations to usurpation: when the securities no longer sufficed, it was because Rome, corrupted by the dominion of the universe, was no longer susceptible of any good government.

Without doubt, one of the principal causes of the long duration of Roman liberty, and of the impossibility of attacking it, which was felt by all those with whom the monarchical power was deposited, even when this power was united in the hands of a dictator, was the strong constitution of the aristocratic element in the hands of the senate. In fact, the constitution of Rome was so admirably balanced, that the consuls exercised the whole of the powers, which for the good of all are better placed in the hands of one than of many, and the senate exercised all those in which aristocratic bodies display their peculiar virtues, and show their superiority over the power of one person, or that of the people. The consuls gave to the republic great military talents, unity of views, promptitude of decision, secrecy, tact to choose men and to decree rewards; the senate gave to Rome immoveable constancy to one system, the treasure of ancient traditions, a great school of political talent, constant vigilance mingled with some jealousy, order, economy, and modesty in manners. The people finally, by their direct participation in the sovereignty through the elections and through legislation, gave to Rome a security for the liberty of all, formed a barrier against every usurpation, and impressed each citizen with the sentiment of the high dignity of his character.

Two things are necessary for the constitution of the monarchical element in a free government; first, that the man on whom is conferred the power of one should be well chosen, that he should really have the talents, the virtues, the superiority of soul and mind, to which alone a nation should confide the decision of its gravest interests, and the care of its destinies; afterwards that such as he was when chosen, such he should remain. The attainment of these two objects is sought by the aptitude for power in him who is chosen, and by limiting the duration of his functions.

We have already had occasion to observe, in order to reduce to their just value the pretended advantages of the representative system, that to delegate a power is not the same thing as to keep it, and that because a nation has herself chosen her sovereign, it does not thence follow that she is sovereign. Thus we do not accuse of usurpation those who have obtained for themselves, or who have conferred on others besides the people, the right of electing the prince, if they have been able to succeed in procuring a succession of able and virtuous chiefs. Nevertheless, we believe that it is particularly in choosing the head of the government, that the discernment of the people may be most confidently reckoned on. The qualities required in the prince, in the head of an army, are almost always brilliant; often he must act by that sympathetic power which electrifies the masses, which impels them to great actions. He must have that quick glance, that decision of character, that instantaneous intelligence, that facility of elocution, above all, that valour which the people love in their favourites. A man great in action, makes himself remarked almost immediately in the crowd, whilst a great legislator may remain long unknown. Little intrigues, little rivalships, may decide what men are of note, but glory is independent of strict calculation, and the public voice which proclaims it is impartial. If there is a great man in a nation, a unique man, we think it probable that popular suffrage will point him out.

The only way of calling in the democratic element to a share in the constitution of the Prince, is to give to it the privilege of electing him. We have seen how variable, inconsiderate, passionate, the people show themselves in the exercise of power: they can neither govern themselves, nor watch over the government, without exposing the state to those convulsions which the democracy of Athens experienced in her worst days. They cannot even be associated in it without usurping all, by a false application of the dogma of their sovereignty, without reducing the prince to the functions of a clerk, with the threat of being dismissed for disobedience. Nevertheless, the people have virtues which are natural to them, and which the two other elements of government do not possess. They only by their indirect action, are capable of keeping the prince in the way of justice, of virtue, and of honour; it is the representative of these principles that they will seek in choosing their head. They may be deceived, it is true, in their choice, but that the consequences of this error may not be long, that their rights may not become illusory, in short, that the chosen by the people may not have time to change his character, the functions of prince must not be conferred upon him for too long a time.

The head of a small state should be in office for a shorter time than that of a larger one. The commotion excited in the republic by the entrance into office of the Gonfaloniere and of the Signoria, which was changed every two months at Florence, Lucca, Pisa, Sienna, and almost all the Italian republics, began and ended the same day; it will last, perhaps, a month in the immense extent of the United States, of Columbia, of Rio de la Plata; the president, therefore, is nominated for three years. When the Roman republic was of immeasureable extent, the power of the consuls was extended beyond the year, by constituting them proconsuls. There are, however, limits to this duration, and when the French republic named her consuls for ten years, she might expect with certainty, that before the term of their functions was expired they would demand to be consuls for life.

The same republic had before made as imprudent an experiment of another theory, that of entirely suppressing monarchical power, by the institution of the Directory, and the bad success of this experiment had a great share in disgusting France with a republican government. The constitution of the year 3, repudiated in every case all those advantages which are attached to the command of one. The individual never appeared; the Prince was a body of five members, renewed successively, and by rotation. This renewing, which changed the majority every year without changing the body, must bring on revolutions, and did bring them on; but the organization was bad in every way. We have endeavoured to show the difference in the spirit with which a man decides for himself alone, and that with which he votes in a body of men. When this body is so small as the Directory was, new inconveniences present themselves; then the members make reciprocal concessions, sometimes of opinions, sometimes even of interests; between two extreme opinions they take the mean, although often less rational than the other two: the members assist one another in doing what they call business, escaping under a collective name from every honourable responsibility; then as they have never completely approved the resolutions in which they have concurred, they are the first to blame them when they do not succeed; and if the Directory fell into universal contempt, it must not be forgotten among the causes of this discredit, that it began by despising itself.

An expedient of a quite opposite nature has been much more

frequently practised, that of elective monarchy for life; we have considered this at length in the first part of this essay. It will have been remarked that this government was much more frequently the result of extraordinary circumstances, than of a clearly conceived system to temper monarchical authority by the assistance of the aristocracy and democracy of the country. Most frequently it must be regarded as the corrective of an ancient usurpation. Here the elective king was the chief of a confederation of princes, there the head of a body of priests, elsewhere of a nobility which might be regarded as the army of the country. If, however, we wish to find a philosophical idea in order to explain royalty for life, we must believe that it was proposed to satisfy so amply the ambition and the passions of the elective chief, that there would be no necessity for any struggle against him. The constant efforts of elective monarchs, sometimes to enrich and aggrandize their families, sometimes to ensure their succession to the crown, show that this calculation was deceptive; whilst the nation, nevertheless, submitted to see those functions which require most vigour and activity, performed by the imbecility of sickness or old age.

There is little probability that an elective monarchy for life will ever be proposed in our times; but we have seen during a short space of time a great number of monarchs elected for the purpose of founding new dynasties: several have fallen without transmitting their crown to their heirs; but several others, in France, in Belgium, in Sweden, in Greece, still reign, and it will not be uninteresting to fix our attention on their double character of elective and hereditary kings.

Election, when it is not imposed by foreign force, always gives an able monarch, often a great man: it fulfils, therefore, completely the object proposed by calling to the head of the state the talents and decision of a single man; it gives to the monarchical principle all its vigour, at least as long as the chosen of the nation preserves the faculties for which he was chosen. Hereditary succession, on the contrary, may augment the lustre of the monarchical principle, but it destroys its efficacy; all that can be expected from the chances of hereditary succession is, that the man, born for the throne, shall be equal to any man drawn by chance from the crowd. Without doubt he will have in his favour the education of royal preceptors, who will give him the polished manners and the superficial knowledge of a gentleman; but against him the education of the courtiers and ladies of the court, who have no surer road to their own advancement than by flattering his vices; he will have against him the intoxication of power, universal flattery, the habit of seeing all yield to his will. An enumeration of the mad or imbecile monarchs which Europe has seen during the last hundred years, would only too well prove that the chances of hereditary succession are more unfavourable to royalty than if drawn by lot from the crowd.

From this truth, never proclaimed, though known by all the world, must flow this inevitable consequence, that in hereditary monarchies, even the most absolute, the king reigns, but he does not govern. According to the degree of respect for public opinion which is maintained in the palace, the royal power is delegated, either to ministers more or less enlightened, to favourites, or to mistresses, to freedmen, or to eunuchs. From the absolute but liberal monarchy of Prussia, to the harems of Constantinople or of Ispahan, we must not flatter ourselves that we shall find the monarchical element; all the advantages of entrusting the destinies of the state to one firm, enlightened will, disappear at the moment when the monarch resigns his power, whether he assists in council or not, whether he signs the orders of his ministers, or is ignorant of them. In the only monarchy which has given to Europe the model of what is now called constitutional government, this humiliating result of hereditary incapacity has been changed into a rule, into a maxim of liberty. A king of England contents himself with ordering a minister to form a cabinet under his responsibility, and thenceforth the minister no longer allows his master to meddle with any of the details of government. This minister becomes the elective king, he takes upon himself the whole plan of government, he puts it in action, and he must not permit any of his colleagues to dispute his will, without running the risk of anarchy. It is a temporary royalty, like that of the consuls at Rome; only the duration of power is sometimes shorter, and its term is uncertain. When in 1814 France saw an hereditary dynasty reascend her throne, she wished to adopt the rule of that monarchy which served her as a model; a rule which seemed, besides, suitable to the age and indolence of the new kings; but whether it was that these would not divest themselves absolutely of power, or that they did not understand the advantage of delegating it, that it might not be divided, or that the vanity of the ministers would not yield an entire obedience to their chief, it became impossible to give to the cabinet that unity which is only found in individual power. It was a body like the Directory which governed, and the monarchical element was really excluded from the government of France. The executive power, losing personal unity, had no longer that powerful conservative interest which it comprehended in the *I myself*, no longer the prompt will, no longer any secret thought, secure from being revealed by discussion, no longer the sentiment of duration: a minister may any day be overthrown; the future is unknown, he continually sacrifices it to the present; he lives from day to day, aware that he is not like the consuls, sure even of a year in which to establish his glory.

But an elective monarch is a being of quite another nature; he has always in himself the power of mind and character which has secured his election; and even when he has obtained the promise that his posterity shall reign after him, the ability which has raised him to the situation he is in, is not at all diminished, and his interest in maintaining himself in it is, on the contrary, increased. His great business is to preserve a throne on which he does not feel himself very firmly fixed, and it is absurd to require him not to meddle in its affairs, not to look after them. It is probable that he understands his position much better than any of his ministers, that he will become, consequently, the soul of government, that he will keep to himself the direction of it, and that his ministers must confine themselves to obeying him. This has been seen in William the Third, in Napoleon, in Louis Philippe. It will always be seen, when kings have ascended the steps of the throne by their own energy, instead of being placed on it.

In France, the king reigns and governs; it is a fact which the minister does not deny, but which, however, excites the clamours of all the constitutional school, for it overturns the system of balance which they imagined they had brought from beyond seas. What becomes of the difference between the king and the government, between the respect and silence which is due to one, the liberty of attack and discussion retained against the other? What becomes of the responsibility of ministers who cannot be punished for their obedience to the king without a crying injustice? What becomes of the balance which was thought to be established between the king and the people, when the first is endowed with ability, firmness, and address, which the chances of hereditary succession would not have brought to the throne in a thousand years; and if the balance is to be reformed according to the measure of his ability, what will become of his successor?

Thus, when the system of hereditary monarchy is adopted, the essence of the true monarchical principle, the centralization of will, intelligence, and power in one enlightened individual, is really destroyed; when, on the contrary, the dynasty is changed, when an eminent man is made head of the state, the monarchical principle is made too strong, because there is secured to it at the same time, talent and duration. Far from being able to look upon the introduction of an hereditary king into a free constitution as a masterpiece of policy, I can only see in it, I confess, another difficulty;—it is the organization of a perpetual conspiracy against the very arrangement it was thought desirable to establish; it is to conduct an enemy into the citadel of liberty, and to give him arms to defend himself in it.

We have said, however, and we repeat it; when there is a king, it is better to continue to have one, for every convulsion of social order, which is not absolutely necessary, is a horrible misfortune. Still more, when the foundations of liberty are to be laid, and when at the moment of the contest a king offers you, to enable you to do it, treasure, an arsenal, an army, an organization already established, were it only in a small part of the country which is breaking its chains, it is better to accept him, and to make him great: when after a great revolution there is in the country a royalist party powerful by its wealth, by its talent, by its affections, by its traditions, it is also better to accept it, and to unite it to the new order of things, for without this compliance it would perhaps be necessary to exterminate it. Many circumstances may therefore lead a free nation to give itself an hereditary king; it remains only to be considered how his authority may be contained in just limits.

But it must not be concealed, this labour of opposition to the progress of the power of the prince must be constant, for his efforts to extend his prerogative will be constant also. And the very name and idea of opposition are born of constitutional monarchies; the republics of antiquity, even the freest, knew nothing of systematic opposition; the prerogatives of each of the powers of the state were better defined, and the constitution which governed them all inspired more universal respect. On the contrary, amidst the absolute kings in Europe, the constitutional kings look upon themselves as an exception; they think their glory is interested in becoming absolute also. It seems to them that they suffer an injustice when they meet with an obstacle to their will; they believe conscientiously that they are fulfilling a duty towards all thrones, to their children, even to their subjects, when they labour without cessation at extending their prerogatives.

At the same time, royalty excites among its subjects the ideas of obsequious duties, of extravagant respect, of servility, which all make it more difficult to maintain liberty. It creates a class of men who endeavour to raise themselves by favour, and not by merit; it opposes the fashion and opinion of drawing rooms to public opinion; it makes the address of courtiers honourable; it thoroughly corrupts the spirit of the aristocracy, and this is not among its least inconveniences. As we have seen, an aristocracy has all those qualities which ought to make it a moderating power in the state—prudence, fixed principles, an immoveable will. When it is well organized, when the entrance of the senate is open only to eminent talents and to dignity of character, always enhanced by the dignity of age, its interests are mingled with those of the laws and of the country; it is sufficiently elevated to be above all seductions; it considers itself the guardian of what is, and the power of traditions perpetuated in families, gives it a fixedness of principles and of conduct, which is never found in the popular element, and which can alone form an efficacious and unchangeable barrier against power.

But most frequently where there is a throne there has been seen to arise around it, instead of an aristocracy, a nobility; not only has the spirit of caste been substituted for that of a body, but this caste from whence has been effaced all distinctions but those of birth, or of favour, has been arranged in ranks, one subordinate to another. The qualities which the throne requires in the nobility, and which are celebrated by the *beaux esprits* of courts, are those which are most in contrast with the old spirit of aristocracies. Valour, but united to levity, to frivolity; devotion, but to men, and not to things; to kings, to princes, and not to laws, and to the country; forgetfulness of personal interests, contempt for money, but more through a habit of disorder than from an attachment to more elevated objects; in short, a profound sentiment of the difference between man and man, not on account of merit, but on account of blood; a sovereign contempt for all who raise themselves, *qui parvient*, who are signalized by popular choice instead of owing their distinction to their forefathers.

The feudal nobility was a power which had risen from the abuse of force, but which at least owed its origin to a sentiment of dignity and independence; but a courtier nobility is only a fatal invention to inoculate with the servile manners and ideas of domestic servitude those classes which ought to serve as examples to the nation. The feudal nobility has disappeared, and if certain families please themselves with the remembrance of it, they have abandoned its spirit to conform to that of courts. The courtier nobility, which in our time is almost exclusively called by the name of aristocracy, has caused the hatred which its vices and its impertinence have provoked, to fall on that element of all good government; thus it has redoubled the difficulties which are met with in constituting a state.

However, nobility exists in most of those countries which aspire to liberty, and wherever it exists it is important to endeavour to introduce it into the social order; it must be satisfied, for the habitual discontent of a powerful class is a leaven of hatred and disturbance, which ends by corrupting all the state; it must be satisfied, but by changing its spirit, by opening to it a career which will attach it to the country, which will give it importance for the benefit of all, which will restore to it true dignity.

We have, in our essay on universal suffrage, endeavoured to give an account of the action of the people, and of the constitution of the democratic element in free countries; we have afterwards endeavoured, in this and the preceding article, to give an account of the action of the prince, or of the constitution of the monarchical element; but both would remain incomplete if we did not endeavour to study the aristocratic element in free countries, to discover how in them an aristocracy is formed and maintains itself, what share ought to be assigned to it, what part it ought to take for the good of all, either in legislation or in government. The union of the three social elements in government, a union which at all times the most illustrious legislators and publicists have proposed to themselves, imposes the necessary condition of studying them all before attempting to combine them; it is only thus that we can flatter ourselves with having accomplished our task.

In endeavouring, however, to discover the power and the spirit of the different interests which exist in a nation, and the means of giving them an influence in proportion to their importance, we do not propose to place them in opposition, to arm them one against another, as has often been done in pretending thus to establish a political balance. Equal wills opposed to one another, if active, produce only a combat which wears out national strength without any advantage; if they are restrained, government remains inactive, and the government of a nation should constantly act. It is the union, the agreement of interests, of predispositions, of passions, which the legislator should seek to promote; it is the concurrence of different powers to make one strength; it is borrowing all the wills, all the talents, all the virtues that can be found in society, to amalgamate them in one, so as to represent society as a whole.

When from the monarchical system shall have been borrowed a prompt, firm, able, secret, constant will, to place it at the head of government; from the aristocratical system, economy, prudence, secrecy, regard for public opinion, distrustful and jealous vigilance, and that long experience entrusted to the immoveable spirit of a senate; from the democratic system, virtuous and disinterested impulses, life, youth, and the spirit of progress; it is then only that a nation can boast of having constituted the Prince, and with him all the other parts of the social body.

ON

THE ARISTOCRATIC ELEMENT

IN

FREE COUNTRIES[a].

It is in the nature of the human mind to advance to its object through continual oscillations. It is a weak bark which struggles against the wind and the motion of the waves, and yet yields to the oar; by turns it deviates to the right or to the left, as the squalls increase or diminish, and yet the helmsman keeps his eye always fixed on the same point of the shore to which he is directing it. The mind of nations, as well as of individuals, is always fixed on the happiness to which it aspires. Sometimes it deviates by turns to the right and to the left, sometimes drawn by the unruly impulses of the passions, sometimes struggling against them by an interior spring, and gaining upon them when they yield. It wavers, it continually leaves the straight line, but yet it advances.

Publicists have never yielded more to these contrary oscillations than when, endeavouring by the institution of government to secure the greatest good of all, they have wished to appreciate the utility and importance of an aristocracy. Among the political instructors of free nations, Lycurgus and Solon, Xenophon, Thucydides, Plato, Aristotle, Livy, Tacitus, Machiavel, and Calvin, have manifested a decided leaning to aristocracy. In our time, on the contrary, it is attacked with

[a] Extracted from the *Revue mensuelle d'Economie Politique,* July and August, 1835.

such bitter violence, that by this name is designated all that is esteemed most odious in governments, and what it seems determined shall be extirpated everywhere. This fury is not yet appeased, and perhaps the remains of European aristocracy may yet be exposed to violent attacks. The victories of the aristocratic and democratic systems have alternated since the commencement of human communities, and other changes will yet follow. Thought, however, advances, and now begins to be convinced that aristocracy as well as democracy are two necessary elements in all good government; both pernicious when they are exclusive, or even when they govern; both essential to the happiness of nations when they are skilfully combined, so as to work together.

Aristocracy is the power of those who obtain for themselves the name of the best; we shall only call them the most distinguished in society. It is the power attached to distinction. On the first view distinction seems personal; but aristocracy becomes a body, and is animated with the *esprit de corps*, actuated by the same passion, pride, as those who, not belonging to it, are exasperated against it, and eager to destroy it. Every one thirsts for distinction for himself, every one bears it impatiently in another. The received forms of modesty are opposed to any one exalting himself; but we do not fear saying of ourselves collectively, what each one would blush to say of himself. This vanity, this pride, this self-satisfaction, which are ill at ease under the yoke of the customs of the world, are all at once freed from restraint when a man can praise the body to which he belongs. Thus this body becomes dear to us because it satisfies our self-love, because in proportion to the ardour with which we exalt it we exalt ourselves. Each one seems to take a pleasure in judging all human nature from his own eminence, proclaiming that it is egotistical, inconstant, that we must grant little faith to its promises, that there is little foundation for its virtue, provided he can say: Men like ourselves cannot bear to be confounded with the crowd; we never go back; no suspicion has ever reached us; whatever may happen our honour will always remain intact. When any thing regards *us*, not only do we not hesitate to give openly the testimony which each one would hesitate to give of himself, but we make a virtue of our pride in the body to which we belong; we think we ought to worship it; we feel, in fact, that our egotism is annihilated before this existence, greater than our own, and we find in ourselves devotedness, greatness of mind, heroism, when they are required, for this creature of our vanity,

As the most powerful spring of human society, and in particular the strongest support of the aristocracy, is the *esprit de corps*, there will, perhaps, be some advantage in studying it, in those cases where the distinction which it claims for itself is not acknowledged by the rest of society. All those who have any experience of military life know that even the vulgarest minds may be inflamed with the most noble enthusiasm, may give proofs of the most admirable heroism, when the honour of their corps, the honour of their regiment, is given them to preserve. "Remember, soldiers, you are the 35th," their general will say, when leading them to battle, and this number of their brigade, which in other men excites no recollections, is sufficient to inspire all the soldiers with unconquerable courage, to make them advance to almost certain death, to give a vigour to their limbs almost beyond human nature. Yet a few months, perhaps a few days ago, these same men, employed in working in the fields, had no idea either of the interests of their country, or of war, or of glory. They did not rise above the calculations of their domestic economy, they avoided danger, they were wretched at the thoughts of the conscription, they thought of themselves first, then of their families at most. They have become of more consequence by throwing their egotism out of themselves, by placing it entirely in the corps to which they consider it their glory to belong.

The *esprit de corps* is found at this time not only in the poorer classes, whose manual labours prevent all mental occupation, but even in bodies often degraded by intoxication. Such are the associations, *corporations des garçons de métier*, of the journeymen of trades. Even there the *esprit de corps* elevates the character; it leads the workmen to deprive themselves of some necessaries to give a generous assistance to the most wretched among them; it inspires them with more rigorous probity, for they would rather stifle their own consciences than lessen the honour of their trade; it inspires them with a military ardour not to be expected from them, when they imagine that they have to repel an offence from some rival association. Certainly the moral philosopher, as well as the legislator, would be very culpable, if after acknowledging the virtues, the constancy, the self-devotion, the heroism with which men may be inspired by the *esprit de corps*, they neglected to employ it for the advantage of the whole community; if, especially, they neglected submitting to its influence the highest classes of society, from whom the nation may expect either the greatest good or the greatest evil.

The distinctions which the legislator may recognise as pre-existing in society, and which he may regard as so many natural aristocracies, already full of life before a constitution had assigned to them a rank in the social body, are the aristocracy of birth, that of manners, that of talents, and that of wealth.

Among all nations, and in all times, the antiquity of race has been considered as a distinction. There is in all the enjoyments which man can obtain on earth something so fugitive, his life passes away so fast, his name is so soon forgotten, that he seems to be for ever struggling against the devouring power of time. All which can prolong his existence and the remembrance of him appears to him a victory. He seizes with eagerness every means of connecting himself with past or future ages, he says with pride *we* when speaking of his associates, he says it with more still when speaking of his race. It is a successive and not simultaneous body, composed of all those whom he has succeeded, of all those united by the same blood, the same name, in whom the same bond of honour creates mutual responsibility ; who living in different ages have never seen one another, so that he who is among the living is, as it were, in his turn alone entrusted with the defence of all those who have preceded him. Perhaps the most just definition of heroism would be, the greatest development of the energy of one for a common interest, and such is precisely the appeal which the aristocracy of birth makes in every generation to him who has in charge the honour of his race.

The second source of distinction in society is elegance of manners, the knowledge and observance of all conventional forms. It supposes in men who feel themselves associated by this relation in their minds, delicacy of observation, tact, good taste, a sentiment of respect for others in proportion to what they exact for themselves. But the aristocracy of manners generally recognises its members by more frivolous signs. Not only does it require purity of language, it also often prescribes an affectation of a fashionable style of speaking ; to elegance in modes of life, it also joins a knowledge of dress ; for the politeness which shows respect to all, it sometimes substitutes an impertinence so much the more offensive because it is covered by outside ceremony. This aristocracy of manners is found, with the most exclusive pretensions, among those nations where the law does not admit any distinction of birth, and it is there that whatever offence it has given has been the least pardoned.

The third source of distinction in society is that of talents, and education. It is even education only which forms the bond among those who pretend to make part of the aristocracy of talent. No circumstance can place a greater difference between the relative power of two men, than that one has exercised his intellectual faculties, the other his physical strength ; intelligence alone elevates us above the brutes, corporeal labour assimilates us to them. The inequality of the faculties which we bring into the world at our birth, the inequality of our aptitude in learning or reflecting, the inequality of the influences of education and example, are mysteries to us. But it is a fact, that thought is the great human power; it is a fact that education and study enable us to join to our own experience and reflection the experience and reflection of all the human race. A man remaining uncultivated, and knowing only what he has thought, what he has observed himself, opposed to him who is enriched by the thoughts and experience of ages, is like a poor individual who would contend, with his own weak arm, against the combined power of a multitude. The man also, who by the obligation of manual labour must have condemned his faculties to almost constant idleness, opposed to him who by constant exercise has given to his mind rapidity, certainty, and precision, has not the same means of making the most of his individual power of thought; whilst his adversary knows how to employ for his greatest advantage the treasure of thought of all those who have lived before him.

Aristocracy of mind, however, is never a political power, because there is, in the exercise of the intellectual faculties, something independent, which rejects association; something individual which leads men of talent to come forward alone, rather than as part of the body to which they belong; to establish their own thoughts and discoveries, rather than those of their academy. The need of association is felt in a lively manner only by weakness; minds of a superior order do not fear putting themselves alone in opposition to all the world. Of all existing bodies academies are those in which it has always been most difficult to establish the *esprit de corps*.

The last of social distinctions is wealth. Most frequently the aristocracy of wealth is found united with the three preceding ones. Thus, nobility is often only wealth transmitted from generation to generation. In England the proprietor of estates is seen to leave his widow and daughters in a state of deprivation, in order to transmit his estate and his wealth to a relation of the same name as himself, sometimes to a relation he does not like; his house, his estate are to him only the means of perpetuating his name and his memory, of striking posterity with the image of a long succession of ancestors. Wealth also unites more easily than poverty with the distinction of manners; it facilitates exterior elegance; and if a rich man is ever so little endued with tact, he acquires very soon the polish of mind of those with whom he lives, when it is superficial. The constant mockery which crushes upstarts really reaches only some singular persons whom a particular incapacity has rendered rebellious to the teachings of the world. The distinction of education has almost always, after the second generation, been attainable by the rich; it requires only leisure and fortune, and in our times it is seldom that it is completely wanting, even in those who have become most rapidly rich.

But considered in itself, the distinction of wealth is an extra-constitutional power, a power which becomes every day greater in society. The economical organization which now prevails, has taken from the poor almost all means of labour without putting themselves in absolute dependence on the rich; it has detached them from the land, and broken the lasting rights which they formerly had in it; it allows the proprietor to dismiss the cultivator with his family, at least at the end of his lease, after seven years, but often also every year, every week, every day, as his name of day-labourer indicates. The cultivator to whom work is refused by the proprietors, offers in vain the service of his hands and his activity. No labour is possible for him, he must die of wretchedness. The operatives in towns assembled in large workshops, are, if possible, in a state of greater dependence on the master manufacturers. There also they are engaged by the year, by the piece, or by the week, but if the masters refuse to take them in, all work is impossible to them. Besides, they do not run the risk, like agricultural labourers, only of being dismissed for want of respect, or for bad conduct; they are in danger every day of being victims not only of the reverses, but also of the success of the art in which they are engaged. If the manufactory is falling off, if fashion no longer demands its productions, they are dismissed because their master has no sale; if, on the contrary, the application of science to his employment has taught him how to do their work with much fewer hands, they are dismissed because their master reserves for himself all the profits of what he sells. Never has more absolute power been given to man over man, and never has it been more hardly exercised. It is the life and death of thousands of individuals, men, women, and children, on which the head master of the manufactory decides, sitting in his office, adding figures; and he decides without anger, as without compassion, without being acquainted with his victims, without seeing them, without knowing the number of them. His chief agent brings him a calculation: "Your manufacture of glass," says he, "or your manufacture of porcelain, has no longer any sale; but you may employ your ovens in the preparation of chemical productions; by the advance of a million francs you may supply the consumption of all France."—"What is the consumption of France?"—"So much."—"Who provides it now?"—"Such and such manufactories, in such and such provinces."—"Will they not continue the manufactory?"—"No, you can sell 10 per cent. cheaper than the price they get."—"What will they do?"—"They must sink under it."—"What will their workmen do?"—"And they also."—"Begin the work; you shall have the million."

In times of the greatest feudal oppression, in times of slavery, there have been, no doubt, acts of ferocity which have made humanity shudder; but at least some motive excited their anger or their cruelty; there was some hope in the oppressed that they might avoid provoking their oppressor. Besides, the executioners of a ferocious act might soften the execution of it. The wife, the children, the priest may implore pardon, and sometimes obtain it. But in the cold and abstract oppression of wealth, there is no offence, no anger, no known executioner, no relation between man and man. Often the tyrant and his victim do not know one another by name, do not inhabit the same country, do not speak the same language. The oppressed knows not where to carry his prayers, or his resentment; the oppressor, far from being a hard man, is, perhaps, generous and feeling; he takes no account of the evil he does, he submits himself to a sort of fatality which seems at this time to govern all the manufacturing world. It is this fatality which, in spite of the promises of liberty, of equality, overwhelms with frightful oppression millions of human creatures.

Such are the aristocracies, such are the distinctions which are found throughout society. The jealousy against the exclusives, felt by those who are excluded from the distinguished classes, may be violent, may be passionate; the multitude may be led to alarming excesses against the few; the name of aristocracy and of aristocrat may be a death-cry to those whom it designates; still the same pride which shocks us in another rank, will make us eager to have our own held in respect, as soon as we can pretend to have one. The aristocracy of birth, which is beyond the chances of fortune, which neither the prince nor the people can either give or take away, will subsist in spite of the legal abolition of nobility; it will subsist, not only in the hearts of those who claim the distinction of an ancient family, but in the imagination of all those who are attached to the historical recollections of their country. The aristocracy of manners will be so much the more strongly delineated when political institutions have repudiated all others; only it will be so much the more futile as it will be more isolated. When, after the reign of terror, a new *beau monde* sought pleasure with intoxication, its luxury and its pretension to elegance were insolent in proportion to their frivolity. The aristocracy of mind will always repel ignorance and stupidity, for nothing can suppress the inequality of human faculties, nor the inequality of instruction. The aristocracy of riches will increase by the abasement of all the others, for it comprises them all in itself, and its yoke becomes heavier when the others appear to be broken. Philosophers may dream of a social order in which all distinctions shall be annihilated, in which all men shall remain equal; but they can only apply their theory by imagining a community which will abjure all the advantages on which distinction is founded; a community without memory of the past, without elegance of manners, without instruction, and without wealth; a community where all labouring for a common fund, would lose all the advantages which civilized life has enabled man to acquire; where all losing those motives to emulation which now sustain courage, each one would put his private indolence in opposition to the wants of the community, and would accomplish his task with repugnance under the rule of an authority which would soon become tyrannical and detested.

If inequality necessarily exists in all social order, let us endeavour, at least, to discover what advantages a nation desirous of guaranteeing its liberty and prosperity, by its political institutions, may derive from it.

The most absolute partisans of equality and democracy do not say that a nation should be governed by all the citizens at once. They know very well that in every resolution that is to be taken, there must be at least two parties, two opinions to form; to govern is to make a choice between them. At first they advance the abstract idea that sovereignty belongs to majorities; soon they come down to saying that it belongs to the distinguished men which the majorities will choose. The naked sovereignty of the majority, or in other words the sovereignty of rude strength and of the sword, would be, in effect, a very alarming idea. Every day the larger number would make its will prevail over the smaller one, and every day the opposition between these two wills would be irritated by personal interest, or by passion. The four kinds of distinction which we have pointed out in all society, would each in their turn have to decide on those questions which concern themselves: in each, eminent men are the small number; the decision, therefore, would be made by the majority, the sovereignty would belong to their adversaries. On all questions of ancient rights, the decision would be made by new men; in all those of consideration, manners, and civilization, it would be made by unpolished men; in all those in which study, experience, and the power of reflection are essential, by ignorant men; in all questions of wealth, by the poor. Even should all these four distinctions, these four aristocracies, always vote together, they would form only the small, the very small number; they would always have against them the four classes from which they are separated. Is it, then, to the compact majority of new men, of coarse men, of the ignorant, and of the poor, that we should wish the sovereignty to be deferred, to the exclusion of the highly born, the polished, the informed, and the rich? No: no publicist has had such a strange notion; if he has reduced it to practice, it has been without wishing to do so. If he has wished all the nation to be called to the right of election, it has been with the confidence that it would itself choose only distinguished men, that it would have them eminent for some one of the social qualities, and that it would acknowledge that coarseness, ignorance, poverty, even obscurity, are so many inconveniences which may become sufficiently weighty to exclude them, when the question is the choice of the heads of the state.

In reality, the end which the legislator ought to propose to himself, is to intrust power to those who possess, or who deserve distinction; that is to say, to a constitutional aristocracy, instead of letting it be taken by the natural aristocracies already pre-existing in society. This end is reasonable; distinction is necessary for the exercise of power; each kind of distinction presents advantages of its own, each, nevertheless, if power is given up to it without participation, will cruelly abuse it. It is in combining them with one another, profiting by the advantages of each, guarding by means of one against the inconveniences which another would produce; if one is in opposition to the rest, by strengthening its relations with the great mass of the people, that they may give it their support, that the art of well balancing constitutions consists.

In free countries it is universally acknowledged that the end of government is the welfare of all, that government is only made for the nation. From this principle was soon derived another not less incontestable, that all free government not only comes from the people, but is dependent on the people. There is no nation which has not in its turn been brought to acknowledge that the sufferings of the people, or the excesses of its governors violating their duties, have authorized revolutions, or those violent crises which overthrow acknowledged power to reconstruct the social order on a new basis. The right of all to their own safety cannot be doubted; on this right is founded the only legitimate title of all governments which have ever existed; it is this alone which has sometimes sanctioned the abuse of force for the welfare of all. In many countries this fundamental idea has been abandoned, in order to proclaim expressly the dogma of the sovereignty of the people. But this dogma, partly true, partly false, is always difficult to define; it has been only too often interpreted in a way to place command where there ought to be obedience, or rather to leave obedience out of the question altogether. The sovereignty of the people cannot be practically admitted without putting the represented above the representatives, the electors above the elected, the popular masses, sometimes even insurrections, above governments. The nation is sovereign no doubt, or rather its rights are above all constitutions and all sovereigns, but only as far as it is unanimous. For the object of a constitution is precisely to cause that legal fiction to be acknowledged, by means of which the will of such as it designates shall be received as being the will of all. When the people are unanimous no fiction is necessary, the will of all is declared, no will can be superior to it. But if all are not unanimous, the will of the larger number cannot bind that of the smaller, unless there is between them a previous contract on this subject; that is to say, only so far as the nation has voluntarily and unanimously submitted to a purely democratic constitution. The power of majorities over minorities is not a natural right but a constitutional right. When a mixed constitution admits as a principle that in each council the majority shall decide, and that the agreement of these councils shall be considered as the unanimous voice of the nation, the object of this multiplying of councils is to protect the minority. If it had placed by the side of these guarantees the principle that the majority of the whole nation should bind the minority of the whole nation, it would have destroyed with one hand what it had established with the other; it would have suppressed the guarantee of different councils, of deliberations renewed under different points of view, of majorities with different interests confirming one another; it would, as we have seen, have yielded the sovereignty to new men only, the rude, the ignorant, the poor, to the exclusion of all distinction; it would have annulled itself. As to revolutions, even when most legitimate they produce a state of war and victory; without doubt they have been made by majorities, not by unanimity, and they are only truly legitimate when minorities have voluntarily submitted to them.

When, contrary to these fundamental ideas, it is established as a principle, that all power proceeds from the people, and that by the people is understood the majority of the citizens, when each function of government is only considered as a delegation from the people for their own advantage, and which they may resume whenever they consider it expedient; the first struggle between the momentary, perhaps illusory, interests of the population, or of an assembly of a part of the population and the general interest, may bring on the overthrow or humiliation of the government and the sacrifice of the public good. Who can have forgotten to what a point the passions of the multitude are inflammable? To what a point it may be carried by its imagination or its resentment? How soon what are called great principles, such as religious toleration, freedom of opinion, the equality of the races of men, the right to be judged only by independent tribunals, are forgotten, are trampled under foot by an excited multitude! If memory was effaced in Europe, the recent examples in America would suffice to teach us anew, how ill liberty is secured wherever the people can retake sovereignty into their own hands at the suggestions of caprice. From the time that America has had large towns, the people in public assemblies have thought themselves the sovereign people; insurrections, acts of violence, have been frequent of late years, and each of them has been an outrage on true liberty. At one time the people rise to punish those whose religion or whose humanity made them acknowledge negroes to be men; at another they rise to destroy a Catholic house of education; on a third occasion they drag from the pulpit and would tear in pieces a Protestant preacher because he spoke against the Catholics; again, they break in pieces the printing presses of the conductor of a newspaper who combats some reigning opinion; everywhere and at all times they think they are doing justice to themselves, by withdrawing those whom they accuse from the protection as well as from the jurisdiction of courts of justice.

It is not insurrection alone which causes disorder in the name of the sovereign people. Whenever it acknowledges that all power proceeds from the people by means of elections, those who hold their power more immediately from the people, those whose electors are most numerous, must consider their power as most legitimate. The municipal councillors are really men of the people, their fellow citizens have chosen them, they know them, they have often dictated their opinions to them, and they trust themselves to them. The representatives of the nation, on the contrary, even when chosen by a direct election, are always unknown to the greatest number, strangers, and chosen by a limited number of electors; it is worse still when the election is made by several steps, and it is only by a fiction that they can be called representatives of the people. Thus, whatever functions may by the law be ascribed to either one or the other of these, the first, who ought to obey, consider themselves as real members of sovereignty, and the second, who ought to command them, appear to them only as intruders, which a deception has placed above them.

All those provincial authorities more immediately constituted by the people have most frequently, however, to defend the interests of their constituents against central authorities; their resistance may be virtuous, patriotic, even enlightened, but enlightened by a light shed over parts, not over the whole.

The duty of the governor of a great nation often requires it to call upon the nation to make sacrifices; every day it demands its money by taxation, or the purest of its blood by even forced levies of soldiers or sailors. The provinces ill understand this necessity; and in past ages, deputies assembled in the parliament of England, or the States-general of France, wished for war, and refused their sovereigns the means of making it. They came to these assemblies with the true feelings of the people. It is only in later times that parliaments, become the great councils of the nation, have understood the necessities of government. Local assemblies do not yet understand them. They decide on questions of peace and war by their relation to their own province, to its safety, or the danger to which it will be exposed, to its employments and to the interruption of its commerce, or by neighbouring rivalries or hatreds. They decide on administrative questions by their relation to their district. One objects to the embellishment of a capital which it will never see, another to roads and canals which will be of no use to it, a third to scientific expenses, universities, museums, to which its own population will remain strangers. Each provincial or municipal authority chosen by the people, will resist in the name of the people whose sentiments it partakes. It will resist without caring for constitutional phrases, which limit its functions to the administration of police regulations, of the great roads, of local interests; it will resist because it is strongly connected with the people; whereas national representatives, holding their powers by a much less direct election, will be denounced as being strangers to the people.

The French republic, during its short and anarchical existence, presented nothing but these continual struggles between central and local authority, both emanating from the people. Most frequently right appeared to be on the side of the local authority, reasons of state on the side of central authority. Often force was invoked; then the triumph of the local authority was marked by anarchy, that of the central by tyranny.

Are we not ashamed of our short memories when we see at this time the same theory invoked after having produced such results?

Experience ought to have taught it us: the dogma of the sovereignty of the people becomes false, when to interpret it, all the social powers are supposed to have their origin in elections by the people; when they are all considered as delegations from one will only, which can suspend them when it pleases; when, in short, they are all merged in democracy without the publicists of the day being willing to admit even the name of aristocracy either to temper or resist it. It is, on the contrary, one of the most valuable advantages of an aristocracy, that it may be able to strengthen any one of the social powers; so that, not proceeding from the people, it may not be changed by their caprice or overthrown by their breath.

We look upon the social sciences as having advanced since public opinion has acknowledged that there is no other end in association but the advantage of all, no other source of right in a nation but the rights of all. But it is exactly in the name of this advantage of all, of these rights of all, that we claim the existence in the social body, of a will and a power independent of the caprice of the multitude, of a will and a power taking in at one glance the future and the past; employed in promoting the advantages of all, and subordinating different parties to itself; guaranteeing not the satisfying of the passions of the day, but respect for social principles, prudence, constancy, courage, economy, honour, all those qualities without which no government can make a nation prosper.

Among these qualities each one is found more or less placed under the guarantee of some one of the natural aristocracies, of some one of these sources of distinction. That of birth seeks its claim to respect through past ages, looks upon itself as the daughter of time, powerful from the glory of the past, maintaining itself independent of circumstances which can neither give nor take away the glory of its ancestors, and attached strongly to the delicate point of honour which forms its inheritance. Its first attention is not to allow the honour of that name to be compromised, which it would transmit pure from age to age. Forced to choose, it will prefer danger, privation, suffering, ruin, even reproach, to dishonour. Thus, though it is not enough merely to admit an infusion of chivalric qualities into a government, for they are often deceptive, yet it would be a great evil to exclude them, not to give always to these sentiments a voice by which they may make themselves heard; to abandon power entirely to those who, feeling that their names are unknown, that no one is proud of them, escape the responsibility of renown.

The aristocracy of manners cannot pretend to so much delicacy on the point of honour. Subject to the fashion which has created it, quarrelling with it, taking pleasure in effacing the traces of time, in continually renewing itself, and in contrasting itself with the past, it gives to institutions neither the security of duration nor of elevation of mind. Often a certain degree of dissipation becomes the fashion, and favourites of the opinion of the day do not fear impressing on the government the character of perfidy which may be fashionable. Besides the aristocracy of manners is especially formed in the atmosphere of courts; it is there only that it attains its perfection; and that flexibility of opinions and principles which makes the acquisition of fine manners most easy, as it is the quality which pleases the monarch most, is at the same time that which is least suitable for the nation. It is, however, always fortunate when the aristocracy of manners preserves sufficient influence to introduce a system of respect into public life, when it teaches all those who are depositories of some portion of social power to respect themselves, and to make themselves respected by respecting others. It is only in our own times, that it has been completely forgotten in political discussions, how important it is for the good of the country not to offend, not to mortify adversaries; what bitterness and permanence is added to dislike by treacherous insinuations being admitted into debates, by the bitter sarcasms which are thrown out, the malicious intentions which are attributed by one to another. The daily press, which collects with eagerness these frequently calumnious accusations, which gives to them the publicity not of an assembly but of the whole nation, and the duration not of a passing word but of writing, makes forgiveness and oblivion almost impossible; at the same time it accustoms the public to an habitual distrust of, to an habitual contempt for, what it ought to respect. No disloyalty, no aspersions, no perfidy seem to it improbable in men in power. It has for vouchers of its suspicions the insinuations of those whom it believes most capable of judging them, because they are always engaged in a contest with them. First, it is indignant at the corruption of all public morality which is represented as the character of politics; then it becomes accustomed to it, and the level of the degree of integrity necessary in order not to be dishonoured becomes every day lower. It is with deep regret that in our days we have seen men, who by their social position were called upon to show themselves the guardians of good manners, the chiefs of the aristocracies of courts and drawing-rooms, descend in their turns into this shameful arena, and endeavour to cover their adversaries with dirt. We have seen them attack with the same coarseness, or with an impertinence of *bon ton* as insulting, the representatives of authority when they renounced their prejudices, and the ministers of the king when they considered them as too liberal. Their journals are distinguished amongst those of the Opposition by bitterness, personality, sometimes by treacherous insinuations, by indecency and scandal. Of all their faults, this is the one which least deserves pardon, for they sin against the spirit of their caste, and of their principles; they have delivered up to the enemy the post of honour, with the defence of which they were most specially entrusted.

The aristocracy of talent, that which owes its distinction to education and the extent of knowledge, is eminently that from which power ought continually to endeavour to obtain recruits. The government of men is a work of mind; of all sciences, social science is perhaps at this time the most difficult. It comprehends in itself, as it were, the result and application of all others: it requires besides, a quickness in the perceptions, a clearness in the ideas, and at the same time a decision in the character, without which a man may be a learned man of the first order, but could not be a statesman. Besides, a liberal education is necessary to teach men to act on the minds of others. The greatest power of conception would be useless to a statesman, if it were not joined to the talent of making those who deliberate with him adopt his ideas, or of defending them against their attacks. To introduce illiterate men into the councils of a nation, would be, as if in a combat of gladiators unarmed men were allowed to descend on the arena, whilst their adversaries employed the sharpest arms.

But knowledge, mind, and talent, are not caste; those who possess them, deeply marked with individual character, represent not a system, but the ideas and wills of all. They refuse to be enrolled either in the government, or in the opposition; they discuss everything, and combat everywhere, but they cannot be formed into a phalanx either for attack or resistance. Thus, the aristocracy of talent and education, when it would form a separate body, is only the aristocracy of manners. It is not knowledge which makes its distinction, it is the elegance of the form under which it has been received. Thus, in England, a well educated man is distinguished by his profound knowledge of the classics, by the correctness of his ear or of his memory for Latin and Greek prosody. He is not required to have a mind well furnished, to have thought much, but to prove by the first words he speaks that he has received the expensive education of Oxford or Cambridge.

In proportion as other distinctions become effaced, that of fortune is more obvious. We have seen what immense power the rich exercise over the poor, by the organization of society alone; their political power has been increasing ever since credit became the great arsenal whence governments sought their arms. Since then titles and dignities have fallen on those great capitalists, who open or close loans, and raise or lower the public funds. These, however, citizens of Europe, treating with princes, are less than any other wealthy men attached to a country. Their speculations are sometimes lucrative in proportion to its disasters, and the immensity of the interests which they pursue makes them often forget calamities which are advantageous to them. A crown cannot well choose worse advisers than those who are desirous of having great transactions of business with it.

The character which distinguishes those of the wealthy aristocracy, who are not gamblers, is the desire of stability. As long as this aristocracy is excluded from power, which it sees occupied by the aristocracy of birth, it may give heads to the opposition. These chiefs, to the virtuous motives of sympathy with the wants and wishes of the people, frequently add a perhaps natural jealousy of those superiors, who seem to them scarcely their equals. But as soon as they are themselves seated in the curule chairs, their anxiety to preserve their opulence sharpens what they feel for their new dignities. Their suspicions are always alive, their liberality disappears on the first disturbance. They seem to feel that the accident of fortune alone distinguishes them from their fellow-citizens, that an accident may lower them as it has raised them, and render them undistinguished. As their greatness is only material, so they have recourse to material means to preserve it. No compromise with them, no recourse to moral influences, to persuasion, to sympathy. It is they who have brought into use those phrases which invest fear with a character of ferocity; force rests with the law, force must be employed, insurrections must be annihilated. When power has once fallen into their hands, it acquires a character more stubborn, more contemptuous, more inflexible.

Most of the European states have been at first organized as a monarchy, and liberty, as well as popular power, have been only gradually introduced, as a corrective of existing abuses, not as the base on which the edifice ought to rest. The true difficulties of social organization had not then been felt: power was already founded, and was only too powerful; the object was merely to restrain it. Royalty disposed of the army, of the arsenals, of the treasure, of the police, of posts and telegraphs; it disposed of all salaried employments, and there was scarcely a family in the state who was not interested in courting it. The friends of liberty knew where the danger was, almost the only danger; they had little anxiety about the employment of their strength, or of the use they should make of their victory. It is to create by law a government which does not yet exist, and to create it with such a just regulation of its strength, that it shall have enough to maintain itself, and not enough to oppress, in which consists the true difficulty of the establishment of a constitution. In the middle ages, when the people, as it may be said, were not born, kings had only to contend with the aristocracy of birth, which was at the same time an aristocracy of wealth, for all property was then territorial. In this contest, kings maintained the principle of order and unity, nobles that of liberty. All the real progress of independence of character, of the security of rights, of the limits which discussion sets to the caprices and vices of absolute power, were due to the aristocracy of birth, for it formed the opposition. Kings had, on the contrary, on their side, the aristocracy of manners among the courtiers, that of talents in the parliaments and the clergy, that of personal wealth in the financiers. They have since changed parts, when the people were born and seen to grow more important; some of the new aristocracies turned to this power, which was also a new one. The nobility joined the crown; talents the people; the rich were seen by turns with power, or with the opposition; fashion itself hesitated between them. Nevertheless the contest has always been among the members of these different aristocracies, and still continues to be so in all monarchies, for ministers and public functionaries, peers and deputies, are always taken from one of these four aristocracies. Individuals in fact act on the masses only, because they are become of some importance, because they have acquired some kind of distinction.

It is in a republic, and especially in a newly established republic, that the difficulty of the creation of power is felt, and the necessity of finding a support in the aristocracy, an anchor to cast upon a solid bottom, in the bosom of a stormy sea.

The more free a state is, and the more the wishes, the sentiments of all the citizens appear divergent, the more does each party seem subjected to a centrifugal force, which tends to detach it from the mass, and to make it act by a peculiar and independent impulse. For a nation, as for an individual, liberty is the development of will, and its full and entire action. But who does not know how varied will is in man, how much opinions differ even on the most abstract questions, or rather that two are never found exactly alike. How much more complicated this variety of opinions and of wills must be, when all the interests most dear to man are in agitation, and when a man is called upon to decide on each of them in concert with those who differ from him. The submission of the minority to the majority is a continual sacrifice of the opinion, of the interests, of the will of one portion of the nation to another; it is a sacrifice which must be made at the moment, when each one is by discussion most confirmed in his own opinion, when the passions are most inflamed, when the self love of all is most active, when each one considers the opinion of his party, if not as the public opinion, at least as that of all honest men, and when every one considers it a duty not to yield. Now, on every new question the majority may change; each one, therefore, by turns finds himself opposed to it, each one is obliged to obey contrary to his intimate conviction, each one complains, each one thinks himself oppressed. This is not all: in all free countries, not only does every one express his opinion, but he raises his voice to express it, and finds daily papers, who make a lucrative business of fanning the fire of passion, and of giving to every complaint the most energetic, the most offensive expression. Thus there rises from all parties a concert of complaints, of accusations, of detractions, of calumnies, which would make it be thought that free countries are the worst governed, the most wretched of all countries upon earth. Look at the journals of England, America, France, Switzerland, the Low Countries, Spain and Portugal; in all will be found the expression of universal discontent. This discontent will be so much the more violent, the less real suffering in any country is caused by its government. Then consult public opinion, as far as it can be formed in any country under an absolute government, and it will be seen that, bewildered by these clamours, it takes much more interest in foreign quarrels, than in the sufferings of the country where it is formed. Many good Germans, who have no security that they will not be thrown to-morrow into the dungeon of a fortress, that their fortunes may not be ruined by arbitrary decrees, that they may not be overwhelmed by taxes for expenses contrary to the interest of the public, never think of exclaiming against tyranny and oppression, except on occasion of the decisions of a whig minister in England, or a doctrinaire in France.

To resist this continual storm, there must be a vigour in the government of the nation that cannot be created on the moment. There must be that power, produced by the memory of past times, which causes an illusion as to the little real strength of authority when it demands obedience; there must be that love of past glory, that instructive sentiment which, for example, would be awakened by the name of France, and which would make all look upon the project of dividing the country as a sacrilege; there must also, perhaps, be that indifference and that ignorance in the masses, which attaches them to established order without weighing it, and which upholds all that exists by the force of inertia. But give the same government to a country which has hitherto had, as a nation, no political existence, which has had no past in which to glory, or at least, no past analogous to the organization which it is giving itself, and then try to say to it, as was done in the year 3 [a], "That the primary assemblies, municipal and electoral, cannot employ themselves

[a] Of the French revolution.

about any object foreign to the elections with which they are entrusted, that they cannot send or receive any address, any petition, any deputation, that they cannot correspond among themselves." These assemblies, as soon as the passions are excited, as soon as local or provincial interests are agitated, will be busy about everything, will correspond everywhere, will unite by federations, will declare themselves the immediate deputies of the sovereign people, will proclaim that the central government, by not entering into their views, has betrayed its commission, has betrayed the country; they will depose it, or pronounce it illegal. Even in France, where so many retrospections, so many customs, so many affections, maintained the idea of the great national unity; in France, where the preponderance of Paris accustomed the provinces to receive their ideas ready made from the capital, it required the bloody tyranny of the committee of public safety, the arbitrary violence of the directory, in short, the powerful hand of Napoleon, to hold together the fasces, ever ready to separate, to suppress one after another the primary and electoral assemblies, to force the departments, the districts, the communes, at the expense of their liberty, and in spite of their rights, to submit to the central government.

At this time, rash men are continually talking of uniting Switzerland to make her strong; that is to say, to suppress all those institutions which in that country are imbued with life, all those which long recollections have endeared to the mass of the nation, all those which have power only through the affection of every citizen for his old country. Imprudent innovators do not see that on the contrary it is the division of Switzerland into sovereign cantons which maintains its union, because this division has removed from the diet almost all those questions which might have excited the passions, almost all those which would have roused the local against the central authority. In Switzerland, an assemblage of small nations, who are accustomed, from being separated by mountains, to keep their interests also separate, and who have preserved, in fact, the strangest diversity in their manners, laws, language, and customs, each of these little nations is already only too much disposed to consider itself as absolutely independent, each canton to divide as Basle has done, as Schwitz has been on the point of doing. If the radicals should gain the ascendancy, if they should choose a constituency, and if this constituency should endeavour to produce uniformity in civil, religious, and commercial laws, in taxes, in the organization of the militia, in that of the communes, there will thenceforward be no more Switzerland; nor would there be, if any central power were to make a similar attempt. On every attempt to do this, twenty-one of the twenty-two cantons would be wounded in their habits, in their opinions, in their dearest affections; each one would be jealous, would be offended because the system of his neighbour would have prevailed over his own; each one would take up arms to repel what would be called a tyranny, a foreign yoke. If, in the struggle which would ensue, the central government should triumph, it would be obliged to become, in fact, tyrannical, in order to be able to resist the wills of the different localities; if it fell, it could never be replaced by any other.

It should never be lost sight of, that in free countries there is, there must be a constant disposition to resistance; placed under the guarantee of all, their institutions are secured by this disposition to resistance. All the citizens are continually interested on public affairs, which are almost entirely forgotten in despotic countries. They attach themselves warmly to the opinions which they have embraced; they are always excited by all the organs of public opinion, to make it a point of honour not to yield; they allow themselves to be persuaded by party calumnies that their adversaries are traitors or rascals. Those who have only seen nations subjected to absolute power, bowing the head to the first command, can have no idea of their habitual resistance. Thus, those are very poor publicists who imagine that to conduct a free and ardent people, declarations of principles inserted in a charter are institutions.

Every day must convince us more that the ancients understood liberty, and the conditions of free governments, infinitely better than we do. They, at least, did not fall into similar errors; they gave, to sustain their republics, not phrases, but a spirit of life. They taught all the citizens to make a religion of the love of country, instead of considering their country as only a mercantile partnership, where profit and loss are calculated, and from whence a man endeavours to retire when the balance is not favourable. They encompassed the majesty of the people with veneration, but the people was to them the whole of the nation, with every class of citizens, all its interests, all its recollections, all its hopes, and all its glory. By the side of this great image of what they held most dear, most venerable, they knew well how to appreciate at their real value, the fluctuations of the suffrages of the multitude, so often decided by levity and caprice, for want of reflection and opinion. They knew well the importance of the two elements, monarchical and democratical, and they would not have thought of laying the foundations of a free and durable constitution without assigning to each their share. They knew that they could have no liberty, if the people did not preserve a direct action in the sovereignty; if they did not join to the guarantee of their right the exercise of a power which would be respected; if every part of the social body were not animated with their spirit of life, their instinct of greatness and virtue. They knew that there would be no vigour or celerity in the action of the government, if they did not assign to chiefs acting individually all those functions which require a comprehensive view, prompt decision, and the feeling of undivided responsibility. But they knew also that their republic would be lost, if the people thought they could do everything, and undo everything, by their suffrages. They knew that it would be lost if the prince could pretend to perpetuate his power; they knew how the people are carried away by the favourites they have themselves created, and if they allowed them to designate the temporary heads of the state, they took care to require that there should be at least two consuls, two first magistrates, lest, like the presidents of our new republics, a single chief should aspire to royalty. Above all, they entrusted the sacred worships of their country, the priesthood of liberty, the spirit of life and duration, the guardianship of tradition, of glory, of the public fortune, and the constant foresight of the future, to a senate in which they endeavoured to concentrate all that is good and great in aristocracies, and at the same time to keep out of it everything that is vicious in that element of government.

They wished their senate to be the unchangeable representative of the spirit of conservatism, always the same in republics. They wished it to be in some sort immortal, and they avoided with care all those crises which could change its spirit. Thus, in almost all the republics of antiquity, the senators were irremoveable. Elected for life, they grew old in their employment, and died off successively; in this way they were replaced one by one, at uncertain periods, without any excitement; the renewal was unfelt, and no general election caused a fermentation in the state. The new comer entered a body, whose customs were all sanctioned by time, whose spirit seemed superior to the spirit of each man; he soon became animated with the sentiments of this body; he founded his own opinion on that of the assembly.

The spirit of conservatism, the spirit of duration, belongs to antiquity of race. The patricians, in possession of the past, in imagination seized on the future; they identified themselves with their ancestors, and with their descendants; they were deeply moved at any suspicion cast on their forefathers, by any danger which threatened their most distant posterity. The republics of antiquity seized on this precious feeling, they fixed it on the *eternal city*, as each affectionately called his country; they were eager to adorn their senate with noble and historical distinctions. But they did not wish any citizen to think himself great in himself: he must derive it all from his country. They never admitted hereditary rights to power, hereditary rights to magistracy. A peerage is a monarchical invention; republican senates were elective; though they were renewed from the patrician order, it was still by a free choice; but constituted by the ever-governing idea of perpetuity, they were in general authorized to recruit themselves, sometimes by a scrutiny of all the members, sometimes by the election of some officers taken from their own body, as the censors.

The pride of nobility which each family nourishes, often places it in opposition with the nation. Each race endeavours to isolate itself, by comparing its own sources of distinction with those of all others; those who pretend to be of the best nobility, pour down contempt on those who are ennobled, on those who are not of old families. Royal favour has increased these rivalships among the nobility, by granting to some and not to others, different rights, different *entrées* at court, requiring gentlemen to prove their birth, to verify their sixteen quarters. From thence rivalry, jealousy, and hatred among the nobles of a monarchy. The republics of the middle ages taking for their *seigniors* baronial nobles already powerful from their territory and their vassals, could not avoid these quarrels of the nobility and the factions which they excited; but the republics of antiquity did not allow of such distinctions in the aristocratic body: all the patricians were equally eligible to the senate, all the senators were equal. They never permitted, they never would suffer any family to have the power to become a faction. They lowered these proud heads to the level of an aristocratic equality; they scarcely allowed them, whilst their public functions lasted, any personal dignity; but they made the consul on leaving office re-enter the rank of his equals; they wished his glory only to increase that of the senate. It was thus that they fixed their attention on developing more and more that powerful *esprit de corps,* that spirit which taught each senator to forget himself, to desire credit, power, and glory, only for the body of which he made a part; that spirit which united the wills of all into one sole will, every effort into one effort, and which, devoting this gigantic force to the service of the country, kept united the fasces of the state, in spite of the independence of all the different wills, and their constant efforts to unloose it.

In the ancient republics, the electors of the senate chose in preference among families historically distinguished, those who were required to keep up its numbers, but they were not in general restricted to this circle. The aristocracy of manners seemed to them scarcely less respectable, because in republics the best manners were invested with that grave and severe character which is a security of duration. Whilst in monarchies, those manners which mark the great world are elegant but frivolous, in republics, all that belongs to aristocracy must be dignified, chaste, and regular. Purity of morals, reserve in speech, modesty in dress, the absence of pomp of every kind, was not less taught in the best ages of Rome, by the Roman matrons and the censors, than in the republics of the middle ages, by the laws, the sumptuary tribunals, consistories, and chambers of reform.

The aristocracy of talents, less political than all the others, fills, however, the first rank in republics, because the more men live in public, the more their personal capacity becomes known. There, neither secret intrigues nor mean services are admitted, nor can they open a way to favour. In the senate, as well as in the assemblies of the people, capacity is equally necessary to comprehend, and eloquence to persuade and to influence. Talent, the genius of a general, the knowledge of the civilian, have the people for their judges, not a master deceived by flattery or abandoned to favouritism. The senate is continually careful not to compromise its credit, not to weaken its power of action, by delegating its power to those who would let it be lost in their hands. It may make a bad choice for a bad object, but not from ignorance or carelessness. In vain would the patricians of Rome have made a display of their great names, and of the images of their ancestors; if they were not worthy of them, they did not succeed in arriving at dignities, for in a republic the road to distinction is talent.

Last of all, the aristocracy of wealth is not without influence, for in every country opulence is a power independent of the constitution of the state, but it is exactly for this reason that republics are jealous of it. They do not wish to have in the country any power which does not spring from the country. Liberty, order, the protection of law, contribute to increase the wealth of all: but the spirit of the aristocracy in republics, is to honour poverty, to call Cincinnatus from the plough to the command of armies, to maintain equality between the rich and the poor; to forbid the former, if not the accumulation of treasures, at least their display and the enjoyment of all those pleasures of luxury which dazzle the crowd, as well as those which weaken the mind and enervate the body of opulent men; all those which accustom him to think that his fortune is worth more than honour, or than his country.

We shall stop with these general considerations on the aristocratic element. Doubtless they will appear vague, and not to lead to any conclusions. In fact, it is only by examining successively, as we propose to do, constitutional monarchy, indivisible and federal republics, that we can at last understand the combination of these three elements of government, and establish some principles for the constitutions of free countries.

ON CONSTITUTIONAL MONARCHY[a].

IF we were to endeavour to sum up in one word the spirit of our study of the Social Sciences, or the advice which we venture to give to the friends of liberty and of the dignity of man, it would be an exhortation never to be discouraged. The work of bringing men back to the sentiment of the duty they owe to themselves and to their country, is everywhere long and difficult. Everywhere the study of this subject discovers to us the extreme complication of the springs of society; and the uncertainty of all calculations intended to make us foresee how they will act, as well as the vanity of the rules which blind presumption has given us for principles; but on the other side, whenever we see a community emerging from the corrupting influence of despotism, whenever we see the men who compose it looking above the narrow circle of personal interest, and occupying themselves with the advancement of their fellow-men, we are astonished to see what life there is in it, how vicious institutions may be corrected by the constant effort of each man to ameliorate the social state, how they may be made conducive to the welfare of all, and secure the progress of the human race. If there are doubts as to each particular principle, if the social state may admit of anomalous modifications, it is certain that the co-operation for good, of all men of elevated character, will

[a] Extracted from *Etudes sur les Sciences Sociales,* vol. i. p. 329.

produce the good which they seek. Let the friends of humanity, let liberals, let patriots recollect what ages they have before them, that they must work for their descendants to the latest generation, and that the greatest enemy to their success is their own precipitation; let them study the past, let them consult present experience, rather than hold to an always doubtful deduction from controvertible principles, and they will be convinced that social science is not yet arrived at certainty. Causes yet unknown determine the character of nations, of their prejudices, of their passions; in their turn, this character, these prejudices, these passions, cause the success or the fall of institutions. Thus, no wise man will say beforehand with certainty that an innovation will succeed, or even that a practice crowned with success in one country can be transplanted with the same success into another; but still, by means which seem opposite, a good strongly willed is in the end always effected. Let the friends of the human race then never be discouraged, for this human race everywhere wants their assistance; almost everywhere it appears to us suffering, degraded, oppressed, and everywhere there is an immensity to do for it. Let the friends of the human race on the other side never forget, in their impatience, that they know of no sovereign remedy; let them try, by degrees, with caution, always waiting to see the effects of one innovation before they attempt a new one, always acting, yet observing, doubting; and let them always remember that they do not know all the organs of the social body, for its life may perhaps depend on what appears to them an unsound excrescence which they are desirous of removing.

We are not afraid of repeating that we have no affection for hereditary monarchies, no prejudice in favour of them. That we might here show their advantages, we have asked ourselves, with sincerity, what they were, in comparison with other forms of government, and we have not been able to discover them; but they exist, and this single fact has more weight with us than all theories; they exist; they are then, for the most part, deeply rooted in the heart of nations, and these affections are a right, are a national will, on which no theory can be permitted to infringe. They are supported at the same time by a prejudice which appears generally spread among men, that of expecting a more prompt obedience when the form of command is more simple. The orders of a man are sooner understood than the abstract precept of a law, and leave no hesitation. Lastly, monarchies are founded on an idea of right which has acquired general credit. Through a universal, though no doubt vicious confusion of the idea of a function with that of property, men, forgetting themselves, have accustomed themselves to believe that their monarchs had the rights of property, to apply those laws which regulate inheritance among individuals to the transmission of their dignity, to give them the sanction of time, and not to ask the reason of their power. Thanks to these affections, to these prejudices, to these errors, the monarchies which at this day cover Europe are indued with life; they maintain themselves without being shaken; they have no need to inspire terror in order to defend themselves. It would be the height of imprudence to shake the social body on the faith of controvertible theories, perhaps to deprive it of life; to suppress a power which exists, and to substitute another which we have never seen in action.

We have also no repugnance to the system of a simple republic; we see nothing in this theory which appears to us impracticable. We believe that those nations who are accustomed to form only one single empire, who feel their individuality, who are attached by their economic interests, their historical recollections and ancient glory, to a centralized government, may be easily brought to form themselves into republics, one and indivisible, if ever they engage in war with their old dynasties; but we believe also, that they ought to look upon this event with alarm, and retard it as much as possible, simply because such governments do not exist now, and because we do not possess any sufficient experience to throw light on our speculations. History presents us with very few great empires governed by a republican constitution. After Rome, Carthage, and Venice, the only name which presents itself is that of France, during the revolution. Rome, whose constitution appears to us the nearest to perfection of any in the ancient world, cannot however serve as a model. Sovereign city of a great empire, a city with slaves, she cannot teach us how a great nation can combine liberty and sovereignty. We know Carthage only from the circumstances which rank her in the same category as Rome. Venice, glorious and formidable republic, which long held a rank equal to that of the greatest monarchies, sacrificed her liberties, her subjects, her citizens, even her nobles, to dreams of ambition, to the rigorous maintenance of order, of prudence, of economy, and of an unvarying policy. There remains France in 1794; France, whose example can inspire only terror; France, who has taught us what democratic tyranny can do, and into what a gulf a nation may fall, who destroying order, tradition, social power, respect for customs and recollections, trusts to abstract principles to reconstruct everything. Hitherto we have only studied liberty under republican forms in small states. Some of those which have preserved them in the New World are of vast extent, but in their origin had a very small population, and at the most have only a medium one at this day. As their population increases, their experience will spread fresh light. Perhaps the time may come when a large empire, governed as a republic, may no longer be a brilliant dream of the imagination; but hitherto experience shows us no great nation arrived at liberty under any form but that of constitutional monarchy, or of federation, and we too much distrust a theory which does not rest upon facts, not to reject the trial of another system, unless from incontestable necessity.

Let us cast our eyes on the picture of the population of the different states of Europe. This part of the world is estimated to contain two hundred millions of inhabitants at least, and at most two hundred and twenty-five millions. Of this immense population, we only find Switzerland with its two millions, or at most two millions one hundred thousand inhabitants, which has preserved republican institutions; and it is divided into twenty two sovereign states, of which the largest has not more than a hundred and fifty thousand inhabitants. All other Europeans are subject to monarchs, of whom about half pretend to be absolute, whilst the others reign according to constitutions more or less improved. It is then the progress of this constitutional form which must be considered as the great European interest.

For the rest, monarchy, under whatever form it presents itself in Europe, is already in a state of progress, Turkey alone excepted. We must sometimes follow the travellers who have explored the vast countries of Africa and of Asia, to know despotism in its frightful nakedness. We must see the population bending under blows, stripped of all it possesses, continually obliged to fly into the desert, at the risk of dying there of hunger and thirst, throughout Egypt, throughout Nubia, from one extremity to the other of that valley of the Nile over which the river dispenses in vain such a prodigious fertility; we must see the human race perishing from wretchedness, diminishing from generation to generation, in the magnificent empires of Turkey and Persia, where Providence has collected together for the happiness of man every kind of beauty and abundance. We must interrogate a great legislator and a great philosopher, Sir James Mackintosh, as to what he saw in Independent India, which he crossed in 1808. We find in his journal, royalty without laws, without being limited by opinion, without progress, such as it appeared to him in these countries.

"All India, except the British territories, is at present in one of two conditions. Some part of it is subject to upstart military adventurers, Scindia, Holkar, and others of the same sort, but of inferior note, who act pretty openly as chiefs of freebooters, levying money by force or terror wherever they can find it, without troubling themselves to find pretexts; rambling about in search of booty, visiting their capital not once in ten years, not affecting any forms or exterior of civil authority, and not much more connected with what is called their own territories than with any other district equally well situated for plunder. They live in their camps, and they pursue booty as avowedly as any man in a well-regulated society can do his most honourable occupations.

"The rest is in the hands of more ancient possessors, who have dwindled into mere voluptuaries and pageants. Among them is the Peshwa, the Nizam, the Nabob of Oude, &c., &c. They in reality exercise no functions of government, except that of collecting the revenue. In other respects they throw the reins on the horse's neck. In their dominion there is no police, no administration of justice; sovereignty is to them a perfect sinecure. I observe that the want of capital punishment at Lucknow has been quoted in England, with this observation—*such is their tenderness of blood.* This inference is made in a capital where you cannot ride out in a morning without the risk of trampling on a newly murdered man. The very reverse is the proper inference. Such is their disregard for the lives of their subjects, that they do not think it worth their while to punish a murderer. Such negligence of life, by the title of humanity, is a gross confusion of ideas." [a]

Let not the great despot of the Russias, or the little despot of Modena, boast of having remained stationary. They do not resemble the sovereigns of these unhappy countries, much more favoured by nature than theirs, of these countries inhabited by the earliest civilized and the most industrious of all the races of man. They may profess the principle, that the authority of Scindia, of that of the Nizam, is legitimate like theirs; that resistance either to one or the other is a crime, that every attempt to put bounds to one or the other is monstrous; but they have, however, yielded to the empire of public opinion, to the revolutionary opinions which they combat; they are liberalized in spite of themselves; despotism in their hands is humanized, it has not remained in its primitive and Indian purity; they will never return to it, though it would be the natural consequence

[a] Sir James Mackintosh's Journals, vol. i. pp. 500, 526.

of their principles. On the contrary as they have made some progress, they will still make more, unless their hostility towards themselves, as well as towards their subjects, should end by overthrowing them. Without doubt they have a long way to go, before they arrive only at the point of granting their subjects civil securities equal to what their immediate neighbours have granted; they cannot yet flatter themselves that whatever state of society, and whatever security they maintain, is doing more good than harm. Their neighbours have on their side a great way to go to arrive at the constitutional guarantees which we find in France and England, and these two monarchies, in their turn, are not yet arrived at the end which they ought to propose to themselves. Social science, in the times to which we are advancing, will improve; the securities of the citizens will be increased; the dignity of man, his morality, his independence in every rank of society will be more secure than they are now. The human race is continually going forward; whatever disturbance may be perceived in the ranks of this immense column, a high satisfaction is felt in observing that a common movement directs it, and that even the laggers who appear to stop, who appear to wish to turn back, will soon be drawn forward by the same impulse.

In this progression of all the European race, we must not be surprised at the halting of some battalions, or at their hesitating to follow the march of the others. They must have time to become enlightened by experience, and to surmount the obstacles which they meet with. We must remember that those who wished to press on too fast have often thrown the whole column into disorder, and lost much more time than they hoped to gain. Without doubt we find ourselves at this day in one of those epochs when both nations and their chiefs hesitate, and the incontestable cause of this delay is the precipitation of those who wished to give an example to others. From one end of Europe to the other, the feeling of the dignity of man has germinated in every class. There is no longer any nation which resigns itself to being ill-governed, which does not think that it has a right to demand for itself, light, liberty, and virtue. There is no nation in which thinkers have not entered upon the highest social questions, and where numerous and enthusiastic classes are not earnest to understand their lessons and eager to follow them. There is no nation among whom the great events of our era have not awakened an anxious discussion, an active curiosity to know, not only the crises which their neighbours experience, but their causes. Kings have endeavoured to forbid this discussion, to place writings and journals under censorship in their own country, to keep out those of foreigners, and to be informed of private conversations by means of spies; but the fermentation of mind is too strong to be repressed by all these measures; they would have too much to punish if they wished to reach all those who judge them with severity; they are obliged to let them speak. Let them not deceive themselves: those who speak will act as soon as they see clearly what they ought to do.

But is it strange that nations and kings should at this day alike ask, where is the way, where is the object? Nations applauded with transport the revolution in France of 1830, and now they are persuaded, by the declamations of the press, that from that time France has gone back in the career of liberty. Nations received as a great popular victory the Reform Bill in England, and since that bill passed they have only been told of increasing fermentation, of more violent hatred of the ministry, of imminent revolts in Ireland and Canada. Nations looked upon the Iberian peninsula, oppressed under the double yoke of despotism and superstition, as the shame of Europe; and since that double yoke has been broken, Spain and Portugal alarm them still more, by the fury of the people in civil war, by the atrocity of reprisals, by the destruction of property, by the inefficacy of these two governments.

The example of these last revolutions has made an impression not less profound, and not less fatal, on kings. It has arrested their progress, as it has arrested that of their people. Let it not be thought that these princes have never reflected on the advantages of constitutional rule, that they have not calculated what they might themselves gain by it. The splendour, the power, the opulence of the king of England have struck them; they saw him resist alone the French revolution; they had recourse to him as their support in their necessity; they found in him a banker always ready to open his immense treasures; they had learned by experience that his throne was more solidly established than theirs. Again, they had been astonished to see in France after the restoration, a monarchy exhausted by such long wars, by being twice conquered, and by the contributions which Europe levied upon her, raise herself with so much energy. The powerful heads of absolute monarchies were, no doubt, offended to see, in these two states, princes and their ministers submitting to the criticism of their subjects; but they found, after all, that the condition of the constitutional king of France or England is sufficiently noble to cause them much alarm. Their opinion on the consequences of the concessions which they may have made, has changed, and must have changed during the last six years. They have had before them the examples of the queens of Spain and Portugal, which they could not be tempted to imitate. They imagined that the thrones of the kings of France and England were also on a volcano, on which they did not wish to place their own.

Till 1830, the smaller princes thought they had still stronger reasons for drawing nearer to their people. It is not known to what humiliations, to what dependence, they are obliged to submit to preserve the good graces of the great powers which protect them; it is not known to what a degree they sacrifice their rights of sovereignty, how often they act unwillingly, how often it is they who must exhaust their savings to furnish funds for enterprizes which they dare not avow, or for civil wars which disturb Europe. The small absolute princes know well that a constitutional government with its publicity, would soon break these heavy and shameful chains. They know well that in the present balance of Europe a king with two thousand souls is nothing, but a king with two million souls is something.

Small princes have the feeling, that with the representative system they might arrive at increased importance and power, at a more true independence, perhaps might act a more glorious part. But how could they resolve to make this attempt, when they saw that those among them who had tried to call around them deputies from the people, have found in them, sometimes a sordid economy which shackled all their projects; sometimes a systematic opposition, founded on principles inapplicable to the actual state of their communities; sometimes, in short, a greedy seeking after popularity, which they thought to obtain particularly by revealing all the scandal of courts.

If we do not wish to precipitate ourselves into revolutions, we must advance towards liberty without incensing princes. If we would not disturb nations, and render them incapable of profiting by the advantages which are offered to them, the rights of which they are put in possession must be proportioned to their capacity and to their education; silence must be imposed on those flatterers of the multitude who endeavour to persuade every nation that it is the first of nations, and that everything which another is capable of doing, it will with still more reason be able to do itself.

On the contrary, it must not be forgotten that liberty is a generous wine which disturbs weak heads, and that it is only by long habit and by being gradually accustomed to it, that a strong dose of it can be borne. Do not say to the legislator that he has advanced with the age, but rather that he has stopped with the men he led, or that he has regulated his steps by theirs. Let him not be told that he has made the best possible laws, but the best laws that the men for whom they were intended could bear; and let it be remembered that among these men are the princes who must sanction them, as well as the nations who must obey them.

Between the French and English, we do not pretend to decide which have most capacity, most talent, or most virtue; but we can boldly pronounce that the usages, the opinions, and the customs of the French do not yet render them fit to enjoy a degree of liberty of which the English preserve peaceful possession. A respectable newspaper in England recently advised all the nations of the continent to employ, in order to promote their rights, the system which the Irish orator O'Connell has called *agitation*. The editor did not see that throughout the continent this word would be almost immediately translated into those of tumult, or civil war. The English know how to meet in a public place or in a great county hall, there to discuss all political questions, to excite one another by passionate speeches, and afterwards to separate quietly, after having voted a series of resolutions or declarations of principles. The French would immediately pass from deliberation, from a profession of principles to action, and the funeral procession of General Lamarque was a beginning of civil war. The English have preserved the most entire liberty of meeting, of petitioning, of publishing, and they never employ it except to arrive at their object by legal means; the French never get hold of any public power which they do not first endeavour to turn against the government, in order to overthrow it. The English call upon the people to decide by juries, all questions of public order, of the security of persons, of opinion, of property; but then it should be observed with what respect a citizen seated in the jury box submits to the law, to faith in an oath, to the prudence of the judge. The Frenchman, as soon as he is called on to take a place in the tribunal, puts himself above all authority, repels the word respect almost like an insult, and when he wishes to mark his independence, always displays his hostility. We hope when the institutions of France shall have grown older, that the French will learn to look upon them as their prerogative and their glory, that each citizen will feel himself as interested in defending them as the government itself, and that the first use he makes of the means of action, will not be to destroy everything which surrounds him. But now it cannot be said that everything which is allowable to an Englishman, ought to be allowable to a Frenchman; their position is not the same; for the one sees behind the law the respect of the people, love, and long habits; the other sees behind the law only the ruins which his arm has heaped up in preceding combats.

As far as the English are at this day superior to the French, in being able to bear a very strong dose of liberty without disturbance, so far are the French superior to all the other monarchical nations of the continent, at which we cannot be astonished, since they have been labouring for nearly fifty years to accustom themselves to it. All other nations, on the contrary, during these fifty years, and perhaps from the commencement of their history, have found that with them authority was the enemy of liberty. Consequently, every effort which has been made among them to bring down power, to withdraw from obedience, in short, all anarchical efforts, have been looked upon by them as generous undertakings. This illusion was a necessary consequence of the position in which they found themselves; the friends of liberty had no other possible part to act but to attack a power which had been misused. But by anarchical efforts, what exists may be overthrown, and nothing can be founded: now the design of all truly liberal efforts ought to be to lay a foundation. Far from us be the thought of decrying the generous contests which almost all nations in our times have sustained for liberty, or to be unmindful of their rights; but let us examine their history well; we shall everywhere find that these men ardent for liberty, after having overthrown inimical power, have attacked with almost equal ardour protecting power, the saving power which they had at first themselves raised. They have scoffed at it, disparaged it; they have tied its hands, and then reproached it with weakness; and it is thus that they have, perhaps, been the first cause of the reverses of Poland and Italy, of the ruinous insurrections of Belgium, of the anarchy of Greece, of the failure of the revolutions of Germany, of the reaction in some minds in France, in England, and in Switzerland, and lastly of the lamentable civil wars in Spain and Portugal.

When a nation arrives at liberty without a revolution, when it arrives at it by the concessions which it obtains from its sovereign, it must know how to be content with a slow and gradual advance; it must know how to say to itself that all which it wishes would not be suitable for it, that all which would suit it would not suit him who is still its master. It must, therefore, set bounds to its desires and its demands, if it would not let the occasion slip, and run the risk of losing everything. The double end which it ought to propose to itself is, to inform itself and to initiate itself in the management of its own affairs; the second is to prepare the triumph of public reason by enlightening opinion, by maturing it, and by giving it time to become calm. To whatever point nations which are advancing towards liberty may have been raised, this double end is always the same; but the means of arriving at it, the rights to be entrusted to the people, and the form of deliberation under which opinion will become enlightened, must be proportioned to the progress which this nation has already made in constitutional manners and morals, and attachment to its institutions.

The popular formation of local authorities is the first and surest means of accustoming the people to know their own affairs, to rise to the consideration of the community instead of concentrating their attention on their domestic interests. It is in municipal councils that the deputy of the people should learn how to become acquainted with social affairs, to think of them and to speak of them. Those nations to whom this first political education has been refused, will necessarily abuse the powers entrusted to them, or which they have seized. In general, not even absolute governments oppose this, the formation of the first step in popular power. Municipal officers cost them nothing, and they do their business more conscientiously than the deputies of power. Let municipal officers preserve the advantage of serving gratuitously. If they have the offer of payment, let them refuse it. It is because their functions are gratuitous that they are honourable, that they are independent. If they were paid, the people would no longer put any confidence in them, and the prince would soon give their places to his creatures.

The local authorities ought not and cannot anywhere be sovereigns; the unity of the state would be broken if they were not brought back to depend on the central authority. But there are two ways of limiting their power; their activity may be confined to a small number of subjects on which they may be allowed to decide without appeal, or they may be allowed to meddle with everything without their decisions being final. It is towards this last system that all local authorities ought to tend; they should exert themselves to obtain permission to solicit all local ameliorations, to reveal all abuses, to denounce all malversations, even should their part stop there. Let them remember that it is deliberation, and not decision, which forms the minds of the citizens and raises their character. They will have obtained much if on all public questions they can lay before superior authority their opinion and their wishes. Let them not be uneasy if nothing results from their requests. They will have laboured to form and mature public opinion; the moment will come when this will decide.

The second prerogative which gives political education to the people, which develops in them intelligence and respect for law, is their participation in judicial power. Wherever this prerogative exists, even with semi-barbarous forms, care should be taken not to shake it, under pretence of respect for principles or by the division of power. After having lost it, it will not be easy to regain it. The effort should be to enlighten more and more the popular tribunal of the alcaid, of the waywode, or of the burgomaster. Wherever the people have no share in jurisdiction, let laws and customs prepare them for the future introduction of the *jury* by the complete publicity of proceedings and by oral debate. These two innovations are, to the audience who look on, an initiation into the study of the laws and the administration of justice, and they are a safeguard to those who are brought before the tribunals. But let there not be an idea of giving the trial by jury to the people, till they have shown themselves worthy to be constituted the defenders of order instead of being the allies of crime.

The institution of national guards, or the participation of the people in the public forces, is also a concession which despots themselves have sometimes been brought to make for their own interest. Sometimes they only proposed thus to maintain order in the interior; sometimes the trouble which their neighbours occasioned them, led them to prepare resources to defend themselves. Arming the people appeared to them a means of procuring forces with little expense. Now a people which is armed and organized in such a way as to support the first shock of troops of the line, is a free people. We are far from wishing to propose to them to turn the arms with which they have been entrusted against the government from which they have received them; very far from wishing to transport the deliberations of councils into the guard-room, or to recommend any recourse to force. But when the people are armed and have a military organization, they feel that they have strength, and the prince acknowledges it at the same time. Every inhabitant of a town who carries a musket learns to consider himself as a guardian of order in the first place, but also as a guardian of liberty. From a subject he is become a citizen; already he respects himself, and the government learns to respect him also. It would not dare to command the national guard to do anything violently repugnant to public opinion; it would not dare even to execute such a thing in presence of it.

Some governments have made the guilty attempt to establish a party militia, to put arms only into the hands of a violent and irreconcilable faction, and to indulge it in acts of vengeance against the contrary faction. Let the people not be alarmed; let them endeavour to neutralize this institution such as it has been given to them. Let them press into the ranks of this national guard, however factious it may be. No government can long persist in excluding from it good citizens, and admitting only bad ones. The spirit of faction becomes calm, the regulations of public order regain ascendancy; moderate men become the majority even in those bodies which had been formed to exclude all moderation, and the instrument which had been invented to do violence to opinion will secure its triumph. Let the friends of liberty, in countries that are not free, remember that their part must be that of patience and perseverance. Let them not be disheartened because the service of the national guard involves loss of time and some expense; let them not be discouraged even should this body have manifested a bad spirit, even should it have proclaimed it by a bad choice of officers. Let them persist in coming forward, in performing the service; and let them be assured that they will modify this spirit, that they will replace these officers, and that the time will soon come in which the government, although really hostile to all liberty, will acknowledge the necessity of submitting to reason, perhaps even whilst reproaching itself for having given those arms to the people which have caused it to prevail.

It is in the means of forming this reason, of calling on it to declare itself, and of making the prince resolve according to it, that political liberty especially consists. Public opinion is enlightened and matured by a double deliberation; the spontaneous discussion of the whole public, and the official discussion of constituted bodies. There can be no doubt that the first liberty to obtain is that of thought and of the effusions of friendship; that the tyranny which is still exercised in several countries, and which subjects to *espionage* either the secret opinions of men or their intimate conversations, should be everywhere repelled with horror. But we are considering only that point at which political action begins: it is with spontaneous discussion, for it is that which awakens opinion, redoubles its force, and ends by giving it a leading power. Now this is exercised in three ways: books or printed writings, daily newspapers, and popular assemblies. We name them in the order in which the people may demand and obtain them, in which the prince can grant them, as the people are more or less ripe for liberty.

Let not this be mistaken; true discussion, serious discussion, that which makes light and truth penetrate into every thinking mind, is what is kept up by books. It is that for which authors prepare themselves by profound study, by continued reflection; that to which is attached their moral responsibility, and on which depends their reputation; that which is addressed to the intelligence, and not to the passions of the readers; that which forms their opinion by study, and not by the habit of hearing the same thing repeated. The greatest step which the French have made towards admitting the nation to the direction of its affairs, is owing to the publication of the *Esprit des Lois* (Spirit of Laws), by Montesquieu, to that of *l'Administration des Finances* (The Administration of the Finances), by Necker. The first of these works taught men to judge of governments theoretically, according to the advantages they conferred on nations; the second initiated the French into the knowledge of the burdens of government and of all its resources. The veil which had so long hidden the secrets of state from the public was raised, and the eagerness with which men of letters, and thinkers, thenceforth fell upon the discussion of principles and facts, showed that the nation understood her interests, that she was alive, that she would soon be mistress. There is no greater absurdity on the part of absolute governments than to forbid their people this grave and serious discussion. And yet, how many are there at this day, who not being able to prevent the introduction of futile and often corrupting foreign books, yet prevent the publication at home of all those which would advance and purify social science. Let them remember that the discussion of all questions relating to the interests of the people, and the institution of power, has begun even in their own countries, that the elements of it are everywhere disseminated, that every mind is occupied with them. What then can be the advantage to absolute governments of refusing to the people the knowledge of facts, of permitting the discussion of principles only under the surveillance of a censor of the press? Can they have failed to discover that by this method the most dangerous errors for all, and for the government itself, gain credit, whilst anti-anarchical reasonings are decried, are dishonoured, because they appear under the authority of the censor? The first liberty of political discussion for the people to demand, the first for the prince to grant, is that which is exercised by books. Let authors and booksellers remain responsible for what they have given to the public, but let them not be liable to any previous censorship.

With a nation so animated with political passions as the French are, so ardent, so accustomed to the wars of the journals, it was not possible to enforce that law of the restoration which suppressed the censorship of the press only in regard to writings containing more than twenty printed sheets. There was so much avidity for political discussion, that war would soon have been made by means of prefaces affixed to the most indifferent publications. This is not saying that a similar law would be everywhere else as inefficacious. On the contrary, in countries which are not free, the mass of the public is rarely so much awake with regard to political affairs as to seek with avidity the means of informing itself, or of flattering its passions. Serious works meet with only a small number of readers, the mass of idlers are content with any journal which they find at hand; one or two brilliant pamphlets may have temporary success, but the public is too economical of time and money, to give a sustained attention to pamphlets, and to enable these to supply the place of the daily press, by eluding the censorship.

We believe that every nation in Europe would gain by the abolition of the censorship on books; but that only a small number of them could bear its abolition on newspapers. Men of letters must have been long exercised in all the branches of social science before they have learned how to teach the people, before they can be allowed to make their opinions prevail by repeating them every day in the ears of unreflecting minds. In the great free states where the loftiest interests are undergoing discussion, superior men have been seen to descend lightly armed into that arena, and engage in a daily skirmish which has really matured the public mind. In these same states the companies of proprietors of the celebrated journals are so opulent as to attract superior talent among young men still seeking a profession, and who are equally greedy of applause and of ready money. Thus has been formed in Paris and London a school of daily writers, who join to promptitude in labour all the piquancy of mind and elegance of style of the first masters in the art. It was thought that a country might have this advantage without renouncing that of the higher kinds of literature. Experience seems to show at this time that it is not so. Such high rewards have been given to facility, and to literature not requiring labour, as to discourage studious men, and thin their ranks. The public particularly, spoiled by the daily press, has by degrees abandoned all reading which requires application and patience. The booksellers of the two great nations which give an impulse to the mind of Europe, agree in saying that the public does not want books, and that they find no sale for the books they publish, except in the countries where they are prohibited.

In France and England, at least, the daily press makes us feel that they are masters in the art of fencing whom we see combating before us. But in those countries where few thinkers have employed their minds on any of the higher political questions, where writers as well as other citizens are ignorant of almost all the social sciences, when all at once the career of journals is opened to all those who can hold a pen, we are alarmed at the flood of commonplaces, of false ideas and of low passions, with which the public is inundated. To make any impression on this public by a book, there must be always, at least, a certain accumulation of knowledge, a certain fund of ideas, a certain quantity of talent, otherwise the book falls from the hands of the reader, or remains with the bookseller. But people subscribe to a newspaper without knowing what it will contain, they read it in a spirit of idleness between half asleep and waking, they lay it down without reflection, and without giving much credit to what it says: and yet the repetition, day after day, of the same assertions, the same dogmas, or the same calumnies, leaves a deeper impression on the mind than would perhaps have been produced by an opinion subjected to sober examination and serious study. If we run over those journals which have appeared at the period of the suppression of the censorship in revolutionized countries, we shall be alarmed at the ignorance, the prejudices, the virulent passions which are revealed in every line, we shall be ashamed at the degradation of letters caused by such pretenders; and if we reflect that the most distinguished pamphlets cannot compete with the most miserable newspapers, we shall feel that the influence they are allowed to exercise on the public mind, an influence which stifles true talent, would be destructive of all that progress of mind, of all that enlightened discussion, which springs from true liberty.

If only those nations which have made great progress in the spirit and habits of liberty can bear the daily war of uncensored journals, with still greater reason these nations only can admit of assemblies of the people to debate on politics as means of moral development, and of ripening opinion. Such a prerogative must be reserved particularly for those in which the love of the constitution and respect for the laws are universal, of those who feel that they have no need of violent contests to obtain any thing, of those who have as much fear of a revolution as the government itself could have. All these conditions are found united in England, and for this reason England has been able to allow the entire development of a democratic organ unknown in other monarchies. In England, whenever a great political question agitates the nation, a petition is addressed to the sheriff to call a county meeting, and if he refuses, the meeting generally takes place without his authority, in some public place. All the inhabitants, all men come freely, without any distinction, to this meeting; there have been as many as thirty thousand. A temporary platform is erected on a scaffolding or on a cart; a chairman takes his place, the orators succeed one another, and all the fundamental questions of social order are discussed with the most entire freedom of debate. The popular eloquence of Demosthenes, vehement, passionate, or animated and lively, but always suited to the intelligence of the multitude, is never heard in Europe except on these hustings; then the meeting approves or rejects by a majority, on a show of hands, the resolutions which have been presented, or signs a petition to one or other of the Houses of Parliament, after which it quietly separates. There exist also, particularly at times of political fermentation, debating societies, formed with the sole view of the members accustoming themselves to speak in public. Each one may, on paying a small sum of money, speak there, before an assembly formed by chance, on the most exciting subjects, on those which afford most occasion for the display of eloquence; and the police never interferes, and the authorities allow any thing to be done, provided the public peace is not interrupted. Those who now tell us that England was only an aristocracy, was till the reform in parliament governed by an aristocracy, certainly have not attended to this. Such franchises are the highest proof that can be given of the liberty of the English people; of a people independent of all aristocracies. No other nation could bear such an immediate popular action, which would be so soon changed into exasperation. In France, the clubs were in a state of permanent conspiracy; all public meetings, whenever there was any speaking, even at a tomb, even with the solemnities of grief, were always ready to degenerate into skirmishes. Any government which should have permitted a meeting of several thousand citizens, to deliberate in public and to agitate the most irritating political questions, would have been overthrown in that very hour. The constitutional spirit must make great progress in France, the people must learn to be proud of their constitution and of their laws, to feel that every attempt to overthrow them by violence would be a crime of high treason against themselves, before such free customs as those of the English can take footing.

All other monarchies, which in the career of liberty are much behind France, cannot think of permitting assemblies which even in France would be so dangerous. None of them have given their people the right to be content, to be proud of their constitution; none of them have accustomed them to look upon violence with horror. On the contrary, concessions have been probably wrested from their monarchs by fear; the temptation to demand others in the same way would be too powerful; the habit of thinking that the people and authority are in a state of warfare, is too strongly rooted for the two armies to be ranged in order of battle opposite to one another without imminent danger. But the manners of the free nations of Switzerland are much nearer those of England. There also may be seen societies especially formed for political discussion. In each city are permanent associations, known under the name of *circles,* which almost always represent a certain opinion, and which, in moments of fermentation, have frequently acted on the public. There are meetings of bodies, of militia, of persons inhabiting the same quarter of the town, where sometimes many thousand persons are assembled, to whom are freely addressed speeches on the questions of the day; and these assemblies are like the *landsgemeinde* in which the sovereign people of the small cantons deliberate. But in Switzerland, as in England, the country belongs to each citizen, and he would look upon the attempt to do violence to her as a personal insult.

We may also learn, by the example of Switzerland, that in small states, completely free, it is by popular assemblies that public opinion must be formed, and not by the daily press. When the censorship of the press was abolished in Switzerland, it was thought by the example of large states, that journals would very soon be seen to burst forth, which would rapidly circulate progressive ideas among the people, which would bring within the reach of all the result of the studies of the most profound thinkers, as the *Federalist* had done in America and the *Courrier de Provence* in France, at the beginning of the revolutions of these two countries. No one recollected that the really superior men in Switzerland had means of acting more immediately on their fellow citizens, and that they would prefer speaking to writing; that they, on the contrary, the direction of whose studies, or perhaps the slowness of whose minds, kept them in their closets, would wish, if they wrote, to address a more numerous public than could be addressed by the journal of a canton; that thus, all men who had some reputation, would refuse to write in the newspapers of a small country, or would withdraw from it after a short experiment. All these superior men presented themselves in the popular assemblies, and there, in the midst of their fellow citizens who knew them, who heard them, who esteemed them, they regained the rank which ought to be assigned to them from their knowledge, their intellect, their talents, and their virtues; whilst the journals of the cantons fell into the hands of the lowest of those who are capable of writing. By the shameless extravagance of the greater part of these journals it might be thought that the Swiss nation is fallen into the intoxication of revolutions, whilst its popular assemblies afford a proof that it is wise, serious, and attached to the laws. In fact, the influence of every individual can never be equal; but in popular assemblies the aristocracy of talent is soon seen to distinguish itself amidst the crowd, whilst in the journals of small states, journals which contend with one another only for some subscribers in ale-houses, it is soon seen that the pen is abandoned to the aristocracy of ignorance, invective, and presumption.

Lastly, the most eminent of the privileges claimed by free nations is that of causing the affairs of state to be discussed by their official-representatives, so as to enlighten and mature opinion, and make public reason declare its decisions. All the nations of Europe formerly enjoyed this privilege; thus traces of it may be found in countries which are now crushed beneath despotism; but national representation has lost its importance, sometimes by being lowered to the rank of provincial representation, sometimes by restricting the assembly to too small a number of deputies, sometimes by excluding, through the jealousy of the people, the privileged orders from the representation.

Each of the nations of Europe had, in the middle ages, its chambers, its states, its diets, its cortes, or its parliaments; but great monarchs have united under their sceptre many different nations, and even when they did not suppress their diets, to assemble them separately sufficed to reduce them to the rank of provincial diets. These provincial assemblies have without doubt rendered immense services. Before the revolution, it was easy to discover those provinces of France which had states, such as Languedoc, Provence, Brittany, Dauphiny, by the superiority of their administration; as men born in these provinces were acknowledged to have more public spirit and knowledge of business. The Germans also probably owe the progress they have made in the science of administration to the habits contracted in their provincial states. But such assemblies could not carry their views beyond their province; they dared not even have an opinion on peace, war, or alliances. Nevertheless the prosperity, the existence even of a nation, is connected with its exterior policy. Of what use is it to a nation to guard the interior mechanism of its administration, if its collective force is afterwards employed in the oppression of other nations with which it sympathizes? Monarchs have openly enough contracted an alliance to circumscribe more and more the rights of nations, under pretence of defending their own prerogatives; it would be absurd for free nations to give their strength without examination to the service of such an alliance. The first right, as it is the first interest of a nation, is to cause its opinion to be heard, as to the way in which it is made to act on those without. Let each one then, on every occasion on which it can make itself heard, claim, as necessary to its existence, as a right which it cannot abandon, the convoking of an assembly which represents the whole of a monarchy subject to the same sovereign.

The number of deputies of which an assembly is composed determines its character and its capacity for deliberation. We have seen in our times, authors of constitutions attach themselves to a numerical proportion between the represented and the representatives, without any relation to the intelligence of the former. Such a nation ought to have a representative for every thirty thousand souls, such another one for every fifty thousand. These legislators ought rather to have employed themselves in discovering of what number an assembly should be composed, in order that its deliberations may be sound. They would have seen that whenever an assembly consists of so small a number as to occupy itself about the individuals which compose it, and not about the public; whenever, for example, it consists of less than two hundred members, it is much more accessible to personal intrigues, to the seductions of the court, to the influences of money and vanity; it is much more exposed to the chattering of inferior men, who would be intimidated before the public, but who feel at their ease in a committee; lastly, it has much less feeling of its dignity and of its importance in the state. On the other hand, when an assembly is too numerous, when it exceeds six or eight hundred members, it can only be addressed from a tribunal; then the debate is restricted to those who have a stentorian voice, and an assurance not to be shaken by tumult. These are not always the most to be recommended. Besides, to address a crowd, they require eloquence more than a talent for discussion, and they seek to excite the passions rather than to convince the reason.

In countries where the monarch is almost all-powerful, all orders, if they dared express their will, would alike range themselves in opposition. It was seen in the ancient States General of France; the nobility, even the clergy, were not less liberal than the deputies of the people, often they were more so. So in England the aristocracy remained in possession of great power, because the aristocracy had been at the head of the people in all contests for liberty; in presence of the throne the small have need to be supported by the great; without them they would be too easily intimidated or seduced, and all national representation which voluntarily deprives itself of the eminent men who would have directed it, is not long in being reduced to silence. Charles the Fifth knew very well what he was doing, when in 1548, having gained the victory over the *comuneros*, it was not the procurators of the cities whom he removed from the Cortes, but the deputies of the great, and of the prelates, who alone dared to oppose him. Thenceforward, the national assemblies of Spain, divided into provincial ones, reduced in number, in dignity, in energy, have no longer dared to defend any of their liberties.

What nations who are progressively raising themselves to liberty ought to demand from their sovereigns, what they have a right to obtain is, that the national representation should be the great council of the nation; the council which sooner or later must know everything, must express its opinion on everything. Not that the executive power may not need entire independence for the success of its operations either within or without. The minister ought to have the power of refusing to the great council of the nation the knowledge of a transaction not terminated, when he declares that he requires secrecy; but he can in no case declare that a national affair is not among the functions of the representatives of the people, and refuse them the knowledge of it for ever. Nations, after all, cannot reckon upon any other security but this national inspection, this publicity. It has been established as a principle that another power ought to rest with them, serving as defensive arms; that to the deputies of the people should exclusively belong the right to grant and continue imposts. There is no doubt that this right originally belonged to all diets, but it is also the right which sovereigns will least willingly yield to them, and of which they will show themselves most jealous. If it is not possible to induce them to restore it, there is no reason to be immeasurably afflicted at this, for this prerogative is more apparent than real. The deputies feel themselves, in fact, that the refusal of subsidies would overturn the fortune of the state, and precipitate it into a revolution. Thus, since the Parliament of England, and the Chambers of France, have been really associated in the government, they have never made use of such an extreme measure. In preceding ages, the States General, and the Parliament in effect, refused subsidies, but it was often through a sordid economy, through an entire ignorance of the necessities of the state. Now, as the machine must, nevertheless, go on, each of these refusals was followed by the crown raising money in some irregular way, by some concussion which equally endangered public peace and private fortunes.

What secures the finances of constitutional monarchies from dilapidations, is the public and searching discussion of the receipts and expenses of the state; it is the right granted to the deputies of the nation to know everything, to examine everything, and to require an account of everything. No minister would dare to produce to an assembly of national deputies, at least if it is sufficiently numerous to inspire respect, a list of pensions through favour, of treasures lavished on mistresses, of establishments for illegitimate sons, of luxurious buildings raised to satisfy the caprice of the prince. No minister would dare to announce at the same time the laying on of new taxes to cover these prodigalities, even should the Chamber not have the right to refuse these new taxes. In like manner, no minister would dare to lay before the assembly, unjust, violent, atrocious laws, and discuss them with it, and hear the expression of its repugnance, even though the assembly should have no right to suspend them. No minister would dare to communicate to such an assembly an alliance with national enemies, to justify a war against liberty, even if this assembly could not oppose a *veto*. At this very day, even at the gates of France, as well as in Russia, the monarch may be seen overturning the decisions of the tribunals, and from recommendations to favour causing what has been already decided to be rejudged, interrupting prescription[a], or forbidding the prosecution of a debt. This execrable abuse of despotism would become impossible, if the national deputies could always take cognizance of them, even though they had no authority to put an end to them.

Thus, we repeat, the great national liberty, the great means by which the reason of the nation may acquire power, the great step in progress to be demanded from kings and obtained from them, is public discussion on all the interests of the state. It is this public discussion which suffices to awaken opinion, to enlighten and mature it; and when it at last takes the character of reason, it will suffice to make it pronounce decrees of which princes themselves will acknowledge the sovereignty. It is not without reason that monarchs fear publicity, for from sovereigns it makes them descend to the rank of public functionaries. For this very reason the demands which it is hoped to obtain from them must be moderate, must be reduced to what are strictly necessary for the security of liberty, and all those must be renounced, for a time at least, which excites their defiance or their repugnance. Let it be remembered that a numerous assembly is already a great guarantee of publicity; no man would have the assurance to reveal before two hundred persons, turpitudes in the finances, or from favouritism, which, by giving them an interest in so doing, he might make ten or twenty members receive favourably. Even supposing the conscience of the deputies to be equally weak in the great and small assembly, it is, nevertheless, fortified in the former by the public eye, it is seduced in the second by the insinuations of accomplices. The publicity made sure by such an assembly will be rendered still more efficacious, if it is composed of members elected by bodies already constituted, by municipalities which have themselves a political existence, and who are themselves employed in affairs of state.

However, this is not all; the opinions and deliberations of

[a] Prescription, the law which in some countries makes a debt null after a certain period; to interrupt it is arbitrarily to allow the debt still to be prosecuted.

the national deputies must reach the nation, interest it in its own affairs, enlighten it, so that the deputies may be supported by the nation. It is here that it is difficult to conciliate the jealousies of power with the exigencies of liberty. We have supposed a monarch still jealous of liberty, and a nation yet ill prepared for it: we have supposed that it is not yet able to bear being directed by daily journals, free from censorship, and we ought to understand that power will fear the exaggerated flights of a deputy, as much as those of a newspaper editor. It will not have the former speak from the tribune to the people, rather than to his colleagues: it is not the presence of a few inquisitive persons in the galleries which is formidable to power, or which gives any great guarantee to the people. This personal publicity has really no importance, except as giving access to the writers for the press, and subjecting them at the same time to the control of witnesses, who partake it with them. We can understand that a distrustful government will not permit these journalists to give an account of the sittings of the assembly without censorship. On the other hand, it would be deceiving the nation and insulting her rights, to disguise from her the language and the opinions of her representatives. Her interest, her liberty, her dignity, require that she should be informed, not only of the will of the majority, but of the motives of the minority in opposing this will. It is not, however, necessary that she should know the opinion of every individual; thus, perhaps, the Chamber and the Prince would find a security suited to the progressive state which we are supposing, in a prerogative granted not only to the majority, but also to the minority, to publish in the journals a report free from all censorship, provided it were sanctioned and signed by a proportion of the members of the Chamber, which might be fixed at a sixth, a fifth, or a quarter.

To return, then, we demand for every nation which is not free, but which aspires at becoming so, extended municipal rights, complete publicity in the tribunals of justice, the organization of the citizens into a national guard, the abolition of all preliminary censorship on books, and the discussion of all the interests of the state, in a national assembly sufficiently numerous. We believe that every absolute monarch in Europe might, and ought to grant his people these securities, for his own interest, if he would calm increasing fermentation, regain the affections of his subjects, and avoid the chance of revolutions. We believe, also, that every nation, which is entering the career of liberty, ought to be content with these privileges, that she ought to know that it is her interest to pass through the slow and progressive education of constitutional government, and that it is much better for the citizens to gather the fruit of the tree which is flourishing in the midst of them, than to tear it up in the hope of replacing it by one of better quality.

Such an organization will be, however, only the beginning of liberty. The nations which have already advanced, will advance again. France has much progress to make before she really obtains all the development of liberty which another nation under our eyes has attained to, under the monarchical form; this other nation has much progress to make before she attains that ideal of perfection to which she aspires, without changing the form of her constitution. There are reforms, and numerous reforms, to be accomplished in both countries in order that the political action of their citizens may always develop more and more their understanding, their moral character, and their patriotism. But already, at this day, it may be said that in France, as well as in England, whenever progress is really sanctioned by national reason, whenever it is adopted by the calm will of the people, it becomes law, and it is thus that the nation really exercises her sovereignty.

Let us cast a single glance on the anomalies among the English which strike the nations of the continent, and make them think that England is governed by her aristocracy, or on the discussions which at this day agitate England herself, and which announce her future progress. The right of primogeniture is still in England the national law for the transmission of real property; we believe this law to be bad as regards morals and political economy; but we know that it is sanctioned by the reflections and by the affections of the English nation, no more infallible than any other; its maintenance is an act of the national will, and consequently a proof of liberty. So, in our eyes, the organization of the Anglican church is an abuse; her opulence, her political power, the form of promotion which she has adopted, are dangerous for the state, dangerous for the peace of conscience. In our eyes the corporations which governed the towns were corrupt, educational institutions required numerous reforms; England had abused her victories in Ireland, and her government there was unjust and tyrannical; lastly, the economical organizations of England rest upon bases which appear to us continually more threatening. But let us not forget that the whole of England, England, not by counting votes, but by weighing and estimating wills, has willed to be what she is at this day. By establishing it, by maintaining it, she has given a proof of liberty; she will afford an equal proof of it, when after profound conviction she shall have changed what now exists. She will give a proof of it without a revolution, without abolishing her ancient constitution and giving herself a new one; without displacing the sovereignty which now is, and always has been, only the expression of her will At this time England is experiencing a violent fermentation, a symptom of this change, and many passions are irritated at its being resisted. Nevertheless, exactly because the nation is free, whatever exists in her has a right to defend its existence, whatever exists has a right to make itself heard before it yields. The nation has imposed on herself the obligation of reflecting before willing, reflecting even for a long time, and the peerage forces her to fulfil this obligation; but let us trust the English nation, and her long experience; when she wills maturely, when she wills after having weighed every reason, and all rights, whatever she determines on will be the law of England.

EXTRACTS

FROM

THE PRIVATE JOURNAL AND LETTERS

OF

M. DE SISMONDI.

EDINBURGH, AUGUST 7TH, 1826.—We dined with the Horners, and met Macculloch, who has something hard in his countenance and manners, and who for a long time measured me with his eye, as if I was an adversary whom he ought to combat. I led the conversation to political economy: he attacked me on the facts which I gave from the reports of Chaptal, and some others. There was something in his ironical smile which hurt me, so I fought him on his own ground, laying hold on all the errors in facts, which were certainly numerous, as the increase of mendicity in France, the custom in France of borrowing only for life. I think I had constantly the advantage of him, but I fear I was sometimes rude, and that he will retain some resentment against me.

AUGUST 13TH.—Returning from Edinburgh to London I had for a travelling companion a Mr. Graban, a member of the senate of Lubeck, probably a corn merchant, who told me that he could charge 17*s.* or 18*s.* at Lubeck for corn of prime quality, which would be worth here 56*s.* a quarter, so that he could well bear a tax on importation of 15*s.* He was struck, like me, with the absence of peasants, who are rich in his country.

January 2nd, 1826.—I think that the true definition of capital is, the accumulation of the time and the trouble which have created useful things, and immaterial capital is a mortgage on the time and labour which will create them in future.

26th September, 1826.—I had this morning a visit from Say, who said to me that his friendship for M. Ricardo, and his school, has very often cramped him, but that in truth he finds that they have injured the science by the abstractions into which they have thrown it, and that he shall be obliged, in the new edition he is preparing, absolutely to oppose them.

5th September, 1828.—I have had a letter from M. Say, who announces to me a second volume of his book, with some concessions to my principles on the limits of production.

September, 1833.—You have exactly answered my question respecting the peasants of Austria; you have confirmed what I knew already, but you have added facts, both new and well chosen. I call upon your well-ordered mind for still more research into, for more reflection on, political economy. It is a fine science, and a science which is suitable for women, for it is the theory of universal beneficence; but we must not take it from books, we must distrust modern writings, where principles are given as axioms which experience falsifies every day. A noble result of this experience is that which we have gained in regard to the class of cultivating proprietors in Austria, who are in such easy circumstances that they give to their daughters portions which the gentry of England do not give to theirs, who are never displaced by the great proprietors, but who keep up almost always the same number. If all this is contrary to the principles of political economy, those principles are wrong, not because the science is not a valuable one, not that it is not our duty to seek for the greatest good for all, but because we are too eager to reckon an error among the principles in that science, because, in particular, we have for some time imagined that universal competition, that the effort of each one to get every thing for himself, to displace every one else, was the normal state of society; whilst, looking at the past, we often find that the tendency of that legislation which has diffused much happiness was directly opposed to it, that it guaranteed the positions which had been obtained, that it repressed that effervescence of personal interests, that struggle of each against all, which forces all upon the greatest possible efforts with the smallest results. In that old petrified state of society in Austria, which, repelling every change with all the apathy of Germany and all the distrust of the government, has preserved many parts of the organization of the middle ages, there are many things to study, much as to the effects of institutions every where else condemned, and to which people will not believe that any advantages can be attached; this is true even in politics. In that science, also, there are many false maxims which have been elevated into principles during the last half century. If I were to say that to the French, they would think I was abandoning principles to which I have devoted my life. If I were to say it to the Austrians, they would think that I am adopting their system, that these are things which must not be spoken of. Both would deceive themselves; more certainly still they would think me in my dotage if they knew that these reflections were addressed to a young and pretty woman.

19TH SEPTEMBER, 1834.—This morning I had a letter from Fix (Editor of the old *Revue Encyclopédique*), who tells me that my article on the workpeople has made a great impression at Paris, even so far as to have shaken the convictions of Bionqui (an economist who opposed his *Nouveaux Principes*).

I read that article in the *National* of the 12th October, which Mr. ——— had recommended to me. He attacks with violence, and even some *hauteur*, what he calls the English political economy; but I do not see that he has any very clear ideas as to what he would substitute for it; on the contrary, he appears also to lean towards unlimited production.

I read in the *Westminster Review* a striking article on civilization, in which the author points out many of the bad effects of the present system, which hitherto I have been almost the only one to remark. There is much ability in this article, but it inspires one with a melancholy feeling, because the evils are so serious, and one does not see the remedies; the *too much* of every thing is the evil of the day. It may be remarked even in literature,—the impossibility of fixing attention, the certainty that no book will be read a second time, the necessity of making one's-self remarked, making one's-self of consequence; in commerce and in every thing else, the universal idleness and effeminacy, the cessation of all distinction, the growing avidity for money, &c.

NOVEMBER 18TH.—I have a letter from Mr. Tancred, who asks if he may translate my *Etudes Sociales*. I answered him to say how desirous of it I was, and offering him my proofs.

NOVEMBER 27TH.—A letter from Mr. Tancred to say that he had given up the idea of translating the *Etudes*, because a Mr. Taillot, a bookseller at Oxford, had begun to translate them. (The work never has been translated.) I worked this morning at my chapter on Different Conditions, and it interests me, though I have much sadness at the bottom of my heart. I see at the same time the increasing sufferings of society, and the impossibility of persuading any one of it. I do not think my last volume has been read; that which is just going to appear is not likely to be more so, therefore I have little encouragement to publish the third.

4TH MARCH, 1835.—I had a visit to-day from Frederic de Chateauvieux, who came on foot. We had a long conversation on politics and political economy. From his experience, as director of the manufacture of plate glass, no one has yet described to me more strongly the cruel and dependent condition of the manufacturers, the tyranny and hard-heartedness of the masters. He related to me how, at the moment of the revolution of 1830, they had dismissed all their workmen, reducing at the same time all their families to despair, although they made them a small allowance. They made it a condition that they should not engage in the cotton manufactories, because then they would become a degraded population, beasts rather than men. How they had made use of their workshops for the manufacture of a chemical production, ruining at one blow all those in the north of France; from all which he concluded that the social organization, which he called *Mosaic*, and which restricted the number of trades, of families, and of households, was preferable to that of universal competition.

MARCH 14TH, 1835.—I ran over ten chapters of the book of M. de Villemain, a Christian political economist. The principal idea, of mixing charity with political economy, is as beautiful as true. Many developments appeared to me very just, and the work, full of facts, is at the same time curious and interesting; but it is exclusive, confounding religion with Catholicism, and that with the sacerdotal spirit. He would put all public charity into the hands of the priesthood, and at the same time would give them all political power.

EXTRACT FROM A LETTER, JUNE 6TH, 1835.

I have not given up any of my youthful enthusiasm; I feel, perhaps, more strongly than ever the desire for nations to become free, for the reform of governments, for the progress of morality and happiness in human society. I hope that I have gained in theory and in experience, if, on the other hand, I have been disenchanted of what I hoped in almost all the men I have known: but this *disenganno* does not affect the ideas and the sentiments dear to my heart, because my own flag has never been carried into the midst of the conflict. I am a liberal; still more, I am a republican, but never have I been a democrat. I have nothing in common with that party which alarms you by its violence and by its wild theories, any more than with that which is intoxicated with the love of order and furious for tranquillity. My ideal, in respect to government, is union; it is the agreement of the monarchical, aristocratical, and democratical elements; it is the Roman republic, in short, in its best days of virtue and of strength, and not the modern principles, which I do not acknowledge to be principles.

13TH OCTOBER, 1835.—The *Courrier* contains an article on my "Condition of Workpeople," which, though full of fine compliments, is in bad faith and wants comprehension; but as the author has not understood what I have said on the national income, I think it desirable to write a new article on this subject. I shall show, first, the importance of income in domestic economy, and in what it differs from every other form of wealth. I shall then follow out the income of each class in the nation, showing how it arises always mediately or immediately from labour, but from profitable labour; how labour is less profitable the more income diminishes, under its divers forms of wages, profit, interest, rent of fixed capital, and lastly, salaries for services to society or to individuals; whence by a new road I shall arrive at the necessity of labour being in demand in order to be profitable, and that the labour of a great number must be in demand in order for the great number to have income.

I have received two letters from Mad. M., who says she is enchanted with my article on the "Workpeople," and informs me that Didier will make it the subject of an article in the *Revue des deux Mondes;* asks me for the sequel to my article on "The Prince," and to reprint all my articles separately (the first idea of the *Sciences Sociales*). This latter has given me great pleasure, and has a little compensated for my discontent at the article in the *Courrier*.

November 15th, 1835.—At a dinner given to Dr. Bowring by the Syndic Rigaud of Geneva, he says Dr. B. was very animated; he knows an infinitude of things, and is very intelligent. But he hurt me by his tone of radicalism, almost of Jacobinism, for France. Colonel D. hurt me still more; there is in that party a degree of hatred, of defiance, of presumption, which it is extremely disagreeable to me to mention. I did not find it less so to-day in the contrary party at Maurice's. Every one seems to me to require to be converted by my book, but it is exactly the reason why it will have no success. Bowring is here, charged by the English ministry with making researches into the commerce of Switzerland; he appears very much struck with the prosperity of the country.

December 1st, 1835.—Received a letter from Lord Mahon on my last pamphlets, very flattering and very affectionate. It encourages me as to the work at which I am labouring, (*Les Etudes*,) and makes me hope for success.

January 29th, 1836.—I continued the reading of Ropolini's

Egyptian monuments. He inspires me with much respect for his knowledge, for his ingenious inferences, for his modesty. I begin to feel, in fact, how the sacred language of Egypt has been all at once revealed to us, but at the same time the glance which all this enables me to cast upon history afflicts me more and more. I find an affinity between the progress of ancient civilization, which brought on its ruin, and ours, which alarms me for human kind. It is always by the same proceeding, centralizing, uniting states as if they were patrimonies, that it was expected to increase their wealth and power, whilst really they became continually weaker and poorer.

June 2nd, 1836.—I worked at my Introduction to-day. I wrote eight pages, and I take a lively interest in it. Perhaps I deceive myself as to the merit of my last works, but my *Etudes* appear to me to be what I have done best; however, no one in France or England has yet written to me about my politics, and I am afraid when my political economy appears it will be the same. These are subjects on which each one has his opinion settled, and finds it more easy to let his adversary's book fall unnoticed than to answer it.

November 10th.—I worked at my essay on Colonization with great interest. I wrote eight pages to-day, and I have great enjoyment in these summaries, which embrace in one point of view the history of the universe. The particular merit of my political economy is continually to bring together, as relating to one another, history, morality, and chresmatistics. I have succeeded in finding almost all I wanted of Greek history for this article.

EXTRACT FROM A LETTER ABOUT THE YEAR 1836.

But, in fact, the endeavour of my thoughts, the object of my studies, is to ascend to the principles which direct men to see man and not individuals, consequently not to love or hate heroes or the guilty great; they only follow a more general impression which I have endeavoured to elucidate, and hatred, even for the worst men, is a bad passion, which grieves and corrupts the heart. But, in taking from before our eyes the human form, we can indulge all our indignation against what is bad in itself, against what is corrupting; and I feel the interior approbation of conscience when I have contributed to brand a bad tendency, a bad principle, with all the power I possess. I have this kind of satisfaction, in thinking of my pamphlet about Algiers. You will there see that I do not think any more than old Pervad, that our civilization gives us the right to disturb the savage in his liberty and his repose, but it makes it a duty to protect him from tyranny and robbery. The more we improve, the more the artificial barriers of nations will sink before the great principle of humanity and reciprocal assistance. It is not because they are barbarians, it is because they are oppressed, despoiled, ill-treated, that we have the right to fly to their assistance; it is because their tyrants have reduced them so low that they cannot extricate themselves, that we have the right to remain, because conquest is the greatest guarantee of peace, of justice, of knowledge, of moral progress.

1838.—ON THE PUBLICATION OF LES SCIENCES SOCIALES.

It is possible that the self-love of an author may have some share, without my being aware of it, in the earnest thirst I feel to attract the attention of the public; but this thirst seems to me nothing but the feelings of the immense sufferings of humanity—sufferings which we all contribute, without thinking of it, to increase, by a conduct which in its details we figure to ourselves as indifferent. I cry, Take care, you are bruising, you are crushing miserable persons who do not even see from whence comes the evil which they experience, but who remain languishing and mutilated on the road which you have passed over. I cry out and no one hears me: I cry out and the car of Juggernaut continues to roll on, making new victims.

LIST

OF

M. DE SISMONDI'S WORKS.

1796. I began, the year after my arrival in Tuscany, my *Recherches sur les Constitutions des Peuples libres*, inquiries into the constitutions of free nations. This work, which has never been finished nor published, occupied me five years.

In the two first books were contained the exposition of my principles on liberty and government, in the third the analysis of the British constitution, the fourth that of the French republic, fifth on the ancient constitutions of Spain, sixth that of the Italian republics; the four following, on Sweden, Poland, the Hanseatic towns, and the United States of America, were scarcely sketched out.

1798. My inquiries into the constitutions of the Italian republics obliged me to study their history, and from this period are dated my endeavours to become master of it, and my resolution to write it.

1800. At the end of my abode in Tuscany, I wrote my *Tableau de l'Agriculture Toscane*, which I published at Geneva, in 1 vol. 8vo., 1801.

1801. I then undertook my first work on Political Economy, which I published at Geneva, under the title of *Richesse Commerciale*, 3 vols. 8vo., 1803.

1806. I undertook to furnish all the articles on the History of Italy for the *Biographie Universelle*. I had written them all, and sent them to Messrs. Michaud, booksellers at Paris, long before the first volume of this biography appeared in 1811.

1807. I at last succeeded in getting the two first volumes of my History of the Italian Republics, published by Gessner, at Zurich, in French and German.

1808. The following year he published the 3rd and 4th volumes.

1809. Gessner being dead, Nicolle, at Paris, made a new edition of the four first volumes of the Italian Republics, and a first of the four following ones.

1811. I prepared, in 1811, and I gave in the winter of 1811–12, my course of lectures on the Literature of the South of Europe.

1813. I worked at it in Italy, and I published it the following year, with Treuttel and Wurtz, in four volumes 8vo.

1815. I published with Treuttel and Wurtz, the five last volumes, the 12th, 13th, 14th, 15th, and 16th, of my Italian Republics.

I composed for Dr. Brewster the article on Political Economy, for his Edinburgh Encyclopædia. In this I laid down my first sketch of my system of Political Economy, on the abuse of labour, of competition, and on the excess of production.

1819. I published with Delaunay my New Principles of Political Economy, or wealth in its relation to population, 3 vols. 8vo.

In the month of May, 1818, I decided on undertaking the History of the French (*Histoire des Français*) and I had begun to make extracts from books, and to engage in the preparatory studies. In the year,

1821. I published the three first volumes with Treuttel and Wurtz.

1822. I published Julia Severa, or the year four hundred and ninety-two, 3 vols. 12mo.

1822. Published the 4th, 5th, and 6th volumes of *Histoire des Français*.

1826. Published the 7th, 8th, and 9th volumes.

1827. Published a new edition of *Nouveaux Principes d'Economie Politique*, very much increased.

1828. Volumes 10, 11, and 12 of my History.

1831. Volumes 13, 14, 15.

1832. I published in Lardner's Cyclopædia an abridgment of the History of the Italian Republics, under the title of Italian Republics of the Middle Ages, 1 vol. 16mo.; and immediately afterwards the same work in French, under the title of *Histoire de la Renaissance de la Liberté en Italie, et ses Progrès, et sa Décadence, et sa Chute*, 2 vols. 8vo.

1833. I published successively, volumes 16 and 17 of the History.

1834. The 18th.

1835. I published in Lardner's Cyclopædia, in English, and at the same time with Treuttel and Wurtz, in French, the History of the Fall of the Roman Empire, and the decline of civilization, from the year 250 to 1000, 2 vols. 8vo. It was a course of lectures which I had given at Geneva, in 1820–21, on the History of the first half of the Middle Ages. The same year I published, one after another, vols. 19 and 20 of the History.

1836. Volume 21 of the History, and the first volume of *Etudes sur les Constitutions des Peuples Libres. No.* 1, *des Sciences Sociales.*

1837. Volume 2, *des Sciences Sociales. No.* 1, *d'Etudes sur l'Economie Politique.*

1838. Volume 3, *des Sciences Sociales. No.* 2, *d'Etudes sur l'Economie Politique.*

1839. I published the abridgment of the History of the French, 2 vols. 8vo., which I had written at Pescia; and after my return, volume 22 of the History.

1840. Volumes 23 and 24.

1841. Volumes 25 and 26.

1842. Volumes 27, 28, and 29.

G. Woodfall and Son, Printers, Angel Court, Skinner Street, London.